Ethiopian

EXILE

A microcosm of African

DIASPORA

A Journalist's Perspective

NEBIYU EYASSU

First print - July, 2013

Second Edition September, 2014

Revised Edition – October, 2018

Self-Publishing - with an Amazon Company (KDP)

E-mail - Nebeyassu@msn.com

Cover picture – Dawit Anagaw Adamu

BOOKS by the author

1 Africana Ambagenen Meriwechua (Africa and its dictators)

2 Arebochna Esrael (The Arabs and Israel)

3   Yesrael Yesilela Wootet (Israel's espionage)

4 Yehlina Barnet (Mental slavery)

5 Sedet (Exile)

6 Tesfa, Kehedetna Seqoka (Hope, Betrayal & Tragedy)

Dedication

This book is dedicated to those Ethiopians who had no other choice but to risk everything for a better life abroad; to the men and women who survived through astonishing adversity and privation. All people deserve the chance to live up to their God given potential and lead a happy productive life in their own homeland. In this context, a vast majority would prefer to remain and build their lives in their country of birth; Ethiopians are particularly fond of this view, if things were not so different. Leaving one's parents and loved ones is not an easy matter, particularly when that journey entails entering into the unknown.

At present, Ethiopians, like many of their neighboring people of the Horn of Africa, are scattered all over the world, including the most unsuspecting places on earth. Many were driven out as a result of civil war, and a broken economy, with soaring unemployment and social stagnation. Others left for better education to themselves or their children. Some were simply forced out as a result of their political views or background. Despite having to walk arduously across deserts through several countries or having wallowed for years in dire refugee camps, all dream of the day, when they can do more for those they left behind. To those who lost their lives in the process and to the millions of Ethiopians who share the same fate; this book is for them.

Acknowledgements

This book owes its existence to the many Ethiopians who enthusiastically opened their hearts and shared so much insight about their understanding of the situation in Ethiopia and their personal journey to America. In this regard what I experienced is truly a testament to the hunger and desire of Ethiopians to tell their story of exile. My heartfelt appreciation goes to all the people I interviewed in the process. I am indebted to all those professional economists, politicians, sociologists and historians, etc. in providing supporting literature and making their research materials on Africa available to me.

I would like to thank my trusted friend, advisor and marketing wizard Fikru Ewnetu, for his counsel and direction of this book. Without his assistance and encouragement this book would not have been possible. This work began thanks to his unrelenting positivity and the material support which he provided, without even bothering me to find out what I am writing. If it wasn't for his contribution in way of providing current sources from Ethiopia this book would not have begun, much less completed.

Even though only my name appears on the cover of the book, my son Daniel N. Eyassu (Meraf) has been a source of inspiration for many parts of this book. He deserves a lot of credit for his contribution about the root causes of Ethiopian exile. He was instrumental in carrying out the project, including in revising and in depth analysis on some of the topics. He also helped in editing most of the first drafts, rewriting some of it; if you like this book I owe it to him, if not, it is my weakness. However, the views expressed in this book are my own, and any errors and misstatements are my sole responsibility. My appreciation also goes to my former colleague and friend Melese Aweke, for his effort to get this book published in Ethiopia.

Special thanks to all my friends and colleagues, especially Ato Daniel Baharue, who assisted me in finding potential interviewees. I would like to appreciate my colleague Akale Wube Kedu (Akuna), the computer guru who was always at my disposal to fix my problems. I am forever grateful to my longtime friend Fikremariam Boghossian who helped me out during the most troublesome time of my life. I am indebted to my lifelong friend Muluken Mehari and his wife Yewebdar Admassu for welcoming me as a new immigrant in the United States. It is because of their support in those initial days that I am here to write this book today. It is my sincere hope that all the people whom I came across during my own exile and journey to the United States have been in some way or another embraced by this book. I owe a debt of gratitude that hardly can be repaid to many people who assisted me in the making of this book.

My lovely wife Meseret Kebede who helped me in my previous six books has also leant her unending love and support during the research and writing of this book. She has been the backbone of this family in many ways. Throughout our over thirty five years of marriage she has been a key motivator and catalyst of many of my works. My appreciation also goes to my daughter Rebecca Eyassu (Tina), whose e-mails and phone calls have been a constant source of encouragement throughout this work, while she was away attending college. Sometimes a nudge here and there from your loved ones is necessary to accomplish one's goal.

<u>CONTENTS</u>

Chapter Two

Ethiopian Dispersion 47

Chapter Three

Military Derg and TPLF/EPRDF....161

Chapter Four

Government Controlled Media -.222

Chapter Five

Centralized Economy 278

Chapter Eight

Migrant's Long and Arduous Journey in their own words...382

Running away from Red Terror

(Eight years in Sudan Refugee Camps)

Crossing 15 Countries to Live the American Dream

For Better Opportunities

(Seven and half years in Kenya Refugee Camps)

Bibliography 444

INTRODUCTION

During the last four decades Ethiopians have dispersed around the world like never before. From the well-educated to the rural peasantry, Ethiopia continues to hemorrhage people in search of better life abroad, yet not always finding it. The forces that drove them away and still do so today are convoluted, yet the common thread underpinning them is tyranny; and tyranny survives primarily on the ashes of free expression.

I have been a journalist for more than four decades serving the Ethiopian people. My journalistic experience has taught me to cherish the values of free speech. Indeed this is indispensable for the existence of all other human freedoms and activities. In this regard an independent and responsible press plays a pivotal role in society. Yet throughout my lifetime, successive Ethiopian regimes have crushed free expression and independent thought, never allowing it to burgeon out of its constantly infantile state. Whatever little opening presented itself almost certainly occurred between regimes, in that gap following a revolution or an ouster of the former leader, only to dissipate as quickly as it appeared when the new group consolidated its power. Today, the capacity of the Ethiopian free press to check on government power has withered once more. It's not the first premature death of Ethiopian Journalism; still these are somber times for those in my profession. More than one hundred sixty Ethiopian journalists including myself were exiled in the last twenty years.

Millions of Ethiopians have migrated to very many countries in all continents, running away from tyranny, civil war and poverty. Ethiopia lost most of its elite force during the last forty years because the governments have not been truly participatory, consensual and communicative in their approach; they simply impose their will on the people. Brain drain,

1

international transfer of human capital from developing to developed countries has continued unabated. On the one hand tyrant leaders are pushing the elites out of the country because they express their views criticizing government policies; on the other hand developed countries need these highly educated professionals and attract them with good wages and human freedom. The flight of Ethiopia's limited human capital has serious socio-economic ramifications. These skilled citizens could have helped to educate the youth and decrease starvation by developing the staggering economy. The study by UNDP in 2007 reported that fifty percent of all medical doctors trained in Africa leave the continent. Africa loses twenty thousand professionals annually, and at present forty thousand of its PHD holders are living in other continents; this figure is worrisome.

Neighboring countries like Sudan, Kenya, Djibouti and Yemen have continued to see an influx of refugees from Ethiopia, due to civil war, deteriorating human rights and economic situations. These migrants usually use these countries as a stepping stone to North America, Europe, and Australia, where they hope to get better opportunities. In recent years this wave of migration has greatly increased to the Middle East, with the main route being via Yemen. The majority of Ethiopians enter Yemen illegally by small boats crossing from Somalia or Djibouti. Many have lost their lives in the Shark infested sea when their overloaded boat capsized or were attacked by military vessels in the middle of the Gulf of Eden.

These refugees undergo harsh treatment while en route to Yemen and also after they arrive. Criminal gangs manipulate and abuse them to get money. Some smugglers rape the girls and beat the men after taking their money. Even those who succeed in getting to one of the Middle East countries and get a job as a house maid are severely abused by their masters from long hours of work and slavery-like conditions; often beaten and even killed. Out of desperation some throw themselves from their employer's multi-story apartment. Many died in the deserts; others found themselves in the under worlds of the Red Sea, Gulf of Eden, the Mediterranean Sea and the Nile River.

Our sisters and daughters are suffering as house maid in the Middle East by the thousands. The unimaginable horrors and numerous heart breaking stories of our sisters should be addressed and told loud and clear. A limited number of these migrants get better jobs and even send some money back home; the news of which encourage others to migrate. But, most are suffering, stranded as servants, with their passport confiscated by their masters or the traffickers. Among those who manage to escape or return home, most are incapacitated both physically and psychologically. I respect the Arabs, their religion and culture, and believe in the free movement of people. I appreciate most of them for assisting our sisters to have a better life; but, the incredible cruelty of some against Ethiopian women should be condemned.

Despite Ethiopia's vast natural resources, its people remain stuck in the deadly grip of poverty and destitution while pounded by environmental degradation and brutal tyranny. The military Derg and EPRDF made the country a laboratory of foreign ideology; took the wrong approach with their politics of exclusion, class struggle, "Red Terror", "economic apartheid", and ethnic politics. They set the wrong priorities and lack the necessary vision and direction to improve the lives of their people. They refused to learn from their mistakes and take responsibility for the mess they plunged Ethiopia into; instead they preferred to blame others and used force to silence their people. As a result many left the country to save their lives and for better opportunities.

The reasons for the plight of all these Ethiopians, has political, economic, societal, familial and personal dimensions. The root causes of Ethiopian exile being poverty, and mal-governance, the problem is too big to be ignored. The government which should take the primary responsibility to protect its citizens is not even speaking about this gross misery, which greatly compromises the potential and capacity of the country. Ethiopian embassies around the Middle East which should play a crucial role to curb this human tragedy are not even trying. Struggling between life and death at home and abroad, Ethiopians continue to migrate by the thousands; crossing dense forests, steep mountains, deep and wide seas, forbidding sun-seared deserts, dreaming of a better future somewhere beyond the mirage and desert dazzle. It is not just an Ethiopian phenomenon; millions of people from countries in the horn of Africa and many other African countries have been exposed to mass exile because of tyranny.

There is a big work force of new immigrants from Africa in most of the jobs I worked in the US; and we often discuss about our own exile and the chances of Africa for democracy and development. Millions of Africans were kidnapped and dispersed all around the world due to slavery, which lasted for over three hundred years; and Colonialism that lasted for less than one hundred years in most African countries. After independence again, millions left due to bad governance, injustice, ethnic politics and lack of basic freedoms. While the outside world benefited from free labor and brain drain, Africa lost its able hands and productive elite force. These were people who could have changed Africa for the better. Who knows how much the continent could have developed if all her strong and elite force had the freedom to stay home and work. These were the cream of the generations with the capacity to modernize the continent.

Because of tyranny many of the hopes and ambitions of Africans faded away and most became pessimistic about Africa's future. What I learned during my travel to different African countries as a correspondent of the Ethiopian daily newspaper Addis Zemen, and later as head of program division of Ethiopian Television ETV, is the yawning gap between people and their leaders, the economy and the future of their children. They express their deep and complex anxieties by asking the question, "How can we get better leaders?" They want a parental figure who can lead them to prosperity, who can rescue them from poverty, ill health, etc. When they see that they have no answer to these questions, they feel that may be they are asking the wrong questions, and they try to migrate to Europe and America for better opportunities.

This book is an extension of my previous book 'SEDET', meaning Exile, which I wrote and published in 2011 in Amharic language, and 'Tesfana, Kehedetna Seqoka (Hope, Betrayal & Tragedy), which will come out soon. In some ways it is similar to these books, but the structure and content is in many ways different as the readers will be different. Thus the three books are complementary, neither one replaces the other. While writing this book I had in mind young Ethiopians who were born and/or grew up abroad and do not have enough knowledge about Africa and did not learn to read their native language Geez alphabets. I also had in mind the general English reading public all around the world which will certainly be interested to know the truth about the plight of Ethiopians/Africans. It is simply an invitation for discourse, and no doubt that the facts contained in this book will greatly interest academicians.

The content of this book mostly deals with the root causes of Ethiopian Exile and modern day African Diaspora, focusing on the lack of basic human freedoms. When you read this book you might ask yourself why the author is ignoring the positive events that occur daily in Africa and is explaining mostly about brutalities, corruption, human rights abuse, coups, injustice, civil wars, leadership crisis and refugees etc. It is because the book is focused on the root causes of mass dispersion of the African people, and these reasons are not positive. How else can you explain African leaders who bear more allegiance to their bank balances than to their country, the constitution, the flag and their people's future? How do you explain a country where thousands of people have been killed and tens of thousands arrested for no other reason except belonging to the wrong tribe or party? How do you explain a continent whose leaders receive dictators like Idi Amin, Mobutu, Mengistu, Al Beshir, Meles, Issayas, Gaddafi, Bokassa, with applaud and standing ovation when they walk into an African summit, having just massacred and arrested thousands of their own people.

The dispersion of Ethiopians/Africans all around the world cannot be sufficiently told in such a small book. My attempt is to provide a birds-eye-view on the main reasons and the pattern of Diaspora particularly after independence from colonialism. Attention has been drawn to some of the features that were downplayed in understanding the true concept of African Diaspora. The aim of this book is to illuminate the major problems that obliged Africans to leave their motherland. The first chapter will present to the readers the portrait of Ethiopia, its history, people's culture and patriotic struggle to preserve its independence, so that you will have an idea about the country and its people before you proceed to the details. I preferred to quote more from historian comments about Ethiopia so that the readers would not think I am exaggerating. The succeeding chapters elaborate the politics, the economic situation, human rights abuse and dispersion of Ethiopians around the world. One of the chapters exclusively deals with mass media and the lack of freedom of expression and its consequences.

Finding and locating people to interview has been a cornerstone of this project. That way, I would be able to provide a firsthand experience of the victims of tyranny and the migrants themselves. More importantly, I interviewed and distributed questionnaires to scores of Ethiopians in different fields across the social strata in the country, (though many wanted to remain anonymous), and interrogated several new comer migrants to the US about the latest situation. Without these stories this book would have missed its true color. Not all the personal stories made the pages of this book, but, even those that didn't, have profoundly shaped the narrative. The stories of the migrant's journey included in the last chapter of this book show the hardship, the determination, and the difficult choices they had to make risking their life while running away from tyrannical regimes to find better opportunities and enjoy basic freedoms somewhere else. When I interviewed the migrants who took different routes and spent several years in refugee camps in Sudan, Kenya, South Africa and Mexico before they set foot in the United States, I learned a lot and felt like seating in the class room of the teacher I love.

Their daring plight to the unknown to escape tyranny, their arrest at several check points in different countries they crossed, the hardship and danger in the refugee camps, the number of law enforcement officials they had to bribe, the amount of money they had to pay to the traffickers and how they gather information that helped them to cross one country to the other is mesmerizing. When you read their story, it will remind you of what author Eduardo Galeano once said about freedom; *"it's worthwhile to die for things without which it's not worthwhile to live."* Their story is no less than a great adventure motion picture that you see in some Hollywood productions. They are describing their story in their own words (which I translated) through well-chosen details, making it ring through with a sense of place that transports the readers and gives the

7

value and connectedness to the actions; whirling them off a magic ride to faraway places. The resulting experience being the next best thing to being there in person; the only thing lacking is the chance to register as refugees.

This book is about African politics as much as it is about Ethiopian exile. It has facts and opinions, because in politics it's not always easy to separate the two, so I have intertwined the facts and opinions to explain African Diaspora. I am not a politician, a historian, or a sociologist; I am a journalist. I am trying to explain the root causes of Ethiopian exile and how that links back to the lack of freedom of expression. Using the skills I learned as a career journalist and the opportunities I was given to cover and report on the major events in Ethiopia for decades, I am trying to bring you a close-up portrait of the problems of Ethiopia, and more broadly the Horn of Africa and the continent as a whole.

The approaches, examples, analysis and solutions I offer in this book are based on my exposure and experience as a journalist during the last four decades. I have tried to situate current events in a larger historical backdrop by paraphrasing, summarizing, and quoting from historian's excerpts, using description and analysis, part political travelogue, part contemporary history to bring the region to life, and answer one key question; why so many Ethiopians are going in mass exile? Many will be shocked to learn the truth; those who are naïve or have vested interest in the system could be offended; some will reject it out right, but most will agree with me. It takes great courage to take positions on issues and stand up for what you believe in, even if it might be controversial. The most popular entertainer in America, Bill Cosby once said *"the secret of failure is trying to please everybody"*.

Thinking about back home day-in and day-out, what has always impressed me is the unity of the Ethiopian people against all odds; and their courage, compassion and perseverance at the worst of all times. Most of all I admire their humor and art of cracking jokes that comfort them to confront their numerous problems. To this very day Ethiopia remained uneasy blend of hope and tragedy, much discussed by the world about its poverty, indomitable long distance runners, efforts of development, and human rights abuse; but little understood. It cannot dwell forever in the uncertain twilight zone, Ethiopia need to get a fresh start it so desperately needs. Democracy, rule of law, human rights, freedom of expression, political and economic reform, particularly, social justice with equal opportunity for all, where everyone gets a fair shot and play by the same rules must be born in Ethiopia.

The purpose of this book is demonstrating the economic, political, and environmental causes of human migration out of Ethiopia. It tries to look into the many facets of why Ethiopians have been migrating out seemingly in droves over the past half century or so, with particular focus on the past 40 years. I hope this book will explain, engage and encourage all those concerned and have interest in the fate of Ethiopia, to wrestle with the challenges facing the country today. It is an invitation for discourse to find middle ground, and struggle in unity surpassing ethnic, regional and religious differences for a better tomorrow, without being burdened by a troubled past or daunted by a challenging future.

9

A Glimpse of Experience

I would like to share with my readers some of the highlights of my observation and experience in my country of origin and in Diaspora that persuaded me to write about the root causes of exile and the plight of migrants. I thought about it for a long time; I wallowed in it, and procrastinated for years. In the battle of ideas and the struggle to push Ethiopia in a new direction towards democracy and social justice, and the hustle and bustle to make ends meet in the fast pace of American life, certain experiences, however innocent, become memorable and have profound significance in shaping the narrative.

During the later years of Emperor Haile Selassie certain groups and individuals in the different social strata, particularly university students, started evolutionary and revolutionary movements to avert the country's socio-economic stagnation that led to turmoil. When I was a high school senior at Prince Bede Mariam Laboratory School in Addis Ababa, and during my college years at Haile Selassie I University in the 1960's, I was fortunate enough to witness, participate and play a role in the surge of political consciousness among the student population. Concern for the poor landless peasants and famine victims, demand for freedom of expression, and opposition to government corruption were the priorities of the time.

In 1968 while teaching history at Empress Menen Secondary School in Addis Ababa, I noticed how quickly revolutionary ideology had become ubiquitous even among non-university students. During those tumultuous days it was impossible to deny the hunger for radical change. Though not easily accessible and widespread the curriculum and education standard in those days was far from lamentable. The seriousness and scholarship of students was unmatched and it spilled beyond the campuses, much to the embarrassment of the authorities, who

10

were unaccustomed to being challenged by their pupils. Often empty seats greeted a lonesome lecturer, while students demonstrated and debated outside. At Empress Menen High School one leaflet dropped into the compound was enough to ignite a mass protest. Of course, Haile-Selassie I University, as the epicenter, situated right next door made matters all the more interesting.

After two years of teaching I resigned from the Ministry of Education and got a better paying job with a private company, Addis Ababa Bank, where I organized the Addis Ababa Bank Workers Union along with few class conscious colleagues. I was elected as the Secretary General of the first labor union of bank workers in Ethiopia only to be suspended indefinitely by the General Manager, Ato Debebe Habte Yohannes in the middle of a collective bargaining dispute. Regrettably, my branch manager Ato Mekonnen Awoke also lost his job for refusing to suspend me. While pursuing my case with the then Confederation of Ethiopian Labor Unions (CELU) and searching for another job, I was lucky enough to witness the first babe steps of a burgeoning labor in Ethiopia.

It was during the reign of Emperor Haile Selassie I in 1972 that I became a reporter and translator for the state daily vernacular Addis Zemen, which literally translates into the English "New Era". This was the largest daily newspaper then as it is today. The editor-in-chief, my mentor Bealu Girma, was an exceptional journalist and one of the best writers of the time. He would later be killed by the military Derg regime because of his popular historical novel, "Oromay". When I began my career as a reporter and translator, Bealu, who seemed to be impressed by my curiosity and inquisitive nature, taught me the basics of newspaper reporting and sent me on more assignments than other reporters. When asked why, he often replied "*beten matsdat badis metregia now*" (the best way to clean a house is to use a new broom).

Like many of my colleagues I never dreamt of becoming a journalist in Ethiopia. Because the media was always viewed as the personal dairy of the Emperor, its appeal waned, much like the Emperor's popularity. To a large extent, even with a progressive editor in chief, much of the public's views, let alone the views of the radical students, were ignored. I joined the profession to make a living; but in a few months, even with the censorship, I fell in love with journalism. The profession is so exciting and competitive, you encounter men of different careers, and are always involved in reporting different events and phenomenon; interviewing politicians, economists, medical doctors, labor leaders, peasants, teachers, shoe shine boys etc., learning from the population and informing millions at the same time. This is a profession I know of where one can never get bored. The only problem with journalism is that, once you are a journalist, you are always a journalist: and you don't want to change your career and can't like any other job. With all the risks involved in working as a journalist, and the life expectancy being the shortest of all professions, you still prefer to stay in this exciting career.

Journalism is the profession that opened my eyes, fashioned my imagination, and shaped my world view; most of all, I learned about fairness. The hectic newsroom, the fast pace to get and tell the news first, the tight deadlines, cross-checking and double checking for accuracy, that cannot be replicated elsewhere, taught me time management, responsibility and discipline. I was fortunate to work under the supervision of highly educated and experienced career journalists and to get repeated journalistic training in both print and electronic media in Europe, Africa and the United States. As a journalist I travelled extensively to all the provinces of Ethiopia, to many countries of Africa and Europe, and talked to people of different professions. My experience was often related to agro-industrial production, labor unions, peasant associations, civil wars, border conflicts, trade fairs, television film festivals, symposiums, revolutionary movements and upheavals. I was embedded with the Ethiopian army and travelled to the front lines on many occasions during the war with Somalia, and the civil war in northern Ethiopia.

I travelled to many African and European countries (east & west) as a correspondent, a trainee, a student or a seminar participant. These occasions gave me a chance to meet and discuss with experienced politicians and fellow journalists from different countries, about the challenge of the new century. I have covered most of the major events in Ethiopia for decades; and was given a chance to report on some historical occasions in other African countries. I interviewed ministers, university professors, guerrilla fighters, military generals, trade union leaders, students, merchants, religious leaders, and peasants etc. I talked to hundreds of Ethiopians about their lives, their dreams, and their leaders. I talked with several diplomats of East and West, about the chances of Ethiopia, in private and in public over glasses of whiskey at embassy cocktails on their independence day's celebrations. I spent frightening months in the front lines of civil wars and border wars. I spent some fearsome days in Ethiopian jails accused of "inciting" the public in my journalistic work. I also spent many wonderful days visiting Ethiopia's untapped resources with peasant associations and state farm workers, where the quietness and the beauty of the harvest seem eternal. I had the opportunity to visit Ethiopia's unusual wildlife, intriguing historical and religious sites, and breathtaking scenery that fascinate even the most seasoned traveler. I have written numerous news reports, reportages, travelogues, articles, profiles and editorials for print and electronic media. I produced television programs and hosted interviews on many subjects; presented research papers in symposiums at home and abroad, and wrote six books. If there is someone out there who says that he/she understands and that I have reached him/her and affected his/her life in a positive way in what I have written, that is the biggest prize for me as a writer. Any professional can claim his career to be a success only if he/she can look back and say "I made a difference"; unfortunately most of us are not there yet.

While traveling in Ethiopia on journalistic assignments, through the years I witnessed progressive deforestation, dwindling wild life, disappearing wetlands, diminishing rivers, and the south bound push of desertification accompanied with growing poverty. When I worked as the editor-in-chief of a private independent news magazine "Africa Qend" (Horn of Africa), and as an independent author, I explored deeper perspectives on modern African leaders and the root causes of contemporary African Diaspora. But, because Africa is huge, diverse and complex, no matter how much you read and do research, it is not easy to come to grips with the continent. Africa is full of contradictions that seem to defy modern logic and conventional wisdom. That may be partly why the continent has been misunderstood, misreported and mistreated. Along the way I have met many people who assisted me in discerning the secrets of our continent.

I came to the US in June 1994 for a journalistic training sponsored by United States Information Agency (USIA) for private independent newspaper journalists. During the last twenty years of my stay in the United States, besides the formal training I got in Investigative Reporting in the US, I learned about the life and death of American journalism. Journalism in the United States is under corporate control and there is a big tension between advertising-supported profit-making media and democracy-sustaining journalism. Commercial media is affecting

14

independent journalism in the US. The long simmering tension between journalism and commerce has created a crisis not easy to solve. The marriage of journalism and commerce (for-profit-media) in the previous century though at times rocky, generated sufficient resources to sustain freedom of expression by allowing innovation and helping dissident voices to be heard. But, later it promoted monopoly, supported the rich and privileged and put profits ahead of the public interest; thus, commercial pressures gaining ever more leverage over journalistic values.

The track record of commercial media shows clearly that profits come first and journalism finishes a distant second. There is a long-standing tension between editorial integrity of the newsroom and the desire of media owners to maximize profits, and support politicians who will help them secure the policies and subsidies they desire to be successful. The editorial integrity of the newsroom is compromised, it is not independent and freestanding; what events are covered and how they should be framed and presented is decided by media owners. Large corporations that own and control major media outlets also own Congress and regulatory agencies by spending hundreds of millions of dollars in lobbying, to get their politicians elected and making the media mindless amplifier of corporate politics.

"I am concerned that if the direction of the news is all blogosphere, all opinions, with no fact-checking, no serious attempts to put stories in context, that what you will end up getting is people shouting at each other across the void but not a lot of mutual understanding". (President Barack Obama, September 2009 - response to a question)

The United States of America has played a critical and decisive role in the creation and nurturing to strength the most vibrant media system on earth, thanks to the founding fathers (particularly Thomas Jefferson and James Madison) commitment to freedom of expression. At this critical juncture today we need to renew that understanding and act with the same sense of purpose to make the media free and independent and strengthen journalism that sustains democracy in the 21st century. We cannot take for granted that the market is always ready and prepared to generate genuine journalism as long as the government got out of the way.

To take advantage of my stay in the US, which now seems to be my home for good, I attended computer schools and acquired A+ Certification in hardware maintenance and software configuration skills. I also obtained Microsoft Certified Systems Engineer (MCSE) certification in 1999, which got me a job with a web hosting company, Exodus Communications, as an Internet Systems Engineer. Being responsible for monitoring, recording, notifying, troubleshooting, escalating and maintaining customer connections to the internet and respond to their needs and requests, I learnt how to play a key role in customer satisfaction. Monitoring any changes in the flow of traffic between customer's servers and the Internet in a mission-critical Internet operations and offering front-line assistance in resolving incidents that might otherwise bring network connectivity to a halt, I came to understand the ingredients of the information age.

While I was driving shuttle buses and coaches for the Metropolitan Washington Airports Authority (MWAA), transporting passengers between airports and hotels in the Washington DC area, and between parking lots and the Terminal, I noticed the racial mix and the changing demography of this great country of immigrants, which some people like to call 'the melting pot'. Dulles Airport alone reels more than 23 million passengers annually, 25 percent of which travelling on international flights. As 80 percent of the employees of MWAA are foreign-born and have come from very many different countries, each one has a story to tell; a story of social injustice, political exclusion, religious intolerance, and human rights abuse in their countries of origin. Here I learnt about our similarities and differences, and how to work in a multi-cultural global environment. One major challenge for me after I was promoted to be a supervisor, operations coordinator and later assistant manager of Shuttle Bus Operation service, was how to coordinate the much needed team work and create a good working atmosphere with so many people of different culture, background, belief and world outlook involved. One can hear co-workers speaking very many different languages which prove that the United States of America is the only country that speaks almost all the languages of the world. It is by the same token the graveyard of world languages; as the third generation of most migrant children totally switch to English and stop using their native languages.

In the struggle to start from scratch and to make ends meet in the new world, I worked on any job I could find; parking attendant, bus driver, hotel employee, taxi driver, internet systems engineer, program producer, etc. At times I was pleased and humbled to receive certificates of appreciation and recognition including best employee of the year award. I received informal training of heart and mind towards the good- involving rules and percepts- the dos and don'ts of life. During all these years I tried to cope up with the fast pace of American life and continued to do the job I love most: contributing to the different media back home and in the Diaspora, and working on my books. When I was producing programs for Ethiopian Satellite Television, I came to observe our peoples thirst for truthful information and the hunger for a truly independent primary or at least alternate media whereby all sides can discuss the key issues and find solutions.

Working on different jobs for different companies in different fields, being member of a management team at times,

17

and member of labor union at other times, I learnt the fullest and uncontrolled expression of American capitalism which triumphed in a straight-out contest with organized and unorganized labor; assisted by compliant legislature protective of private property, and a political process whereby economic power is translated into government policy. I also learnt about the rise and fall of the American labor movement mainly because of deregulation of industries, and lack of public and political support; the erosion of organized labor's legal rights and the curtailment of fringe benefits forcing unions to engage in concession bargaining or "give backs". According to an official report by US department of Labor, union membership for public-sector workers in 2012 was only 6.6 percent of the total wage earners.

Even though it is said that labor creates all wealth, the capitalists have all the wealth; it is a parasitic relationship. It is morally wrong to see almost all wealth created by workers (wage earners) is taken by the capitalists. The power equation in the work place has gone out of balance; the effective tool to build a voice for working people is getting weaker, exposing workers for abuse by the bosses and corporate greed. Members of lower management are encouraged to wag to the big bosses and bark at workers. I personally have encountered a few good managers who are humane, rational and understanding; and many bad managers who are shrewd, uncaring, intrusive, controlling, picky and incompetent; who revisit past transgressions, play favorites, contradict themselves and even lie. Most of them are in that position 'not because of what they know, but because of who they know'. Their main concern is to get more profit to the companies by squeezing the workers, thereby securing their job and increasing their bonus pay. I have noticed an exodus of talent from the different fields I worked because of bad management. Labor is seen as a commodity, not as a special part of the human experience; workers don't have a say in the conditions under which they labor. Even though they know better how the production or service could be improved, workers are not represented in the decision making process. To bring meaningful social change in America and to enlarge the middle class we should strengthen local unions that are the essential component and embodiment of democracy.

The world economy is fragile; the needs of the world's poor workers are as pressing as ever. As many experts believe all intellectuals who work or study in the field of development and labor relations must find out what is working, and what is not working, and what can work better in this turbulent society. Intellectuals of all fields of study and actors in development, economists, scientists, politicians, investors, workers, governments, donors, lenders and civil society have a responsibility and interconnected roles to engage in unending self-examination to make a useful and essential contribution and revitalize approaches to law, equality and social justice to fight poverty. One of The World Bank Group experts on labor relations, Chantal Thomas suggests in one of his research articles that there is an urgent need for new innovative thinking, to empower the working poor to defend themselves with a deliberate attempt to place the law into their hands, to give them a vital tool with which to resist poverty.

The challenges for rule of law and related good governance reforms in many countries, particularly in Africa have often failed to address social inequities. Under the circumstances, social turmoil, mass exile and the problem of refugees have become a never ending phenomenon. You are cordially invited to share the personal stories, experience and wisdom of many people referred in this book and grapple with the challenges facing society today.

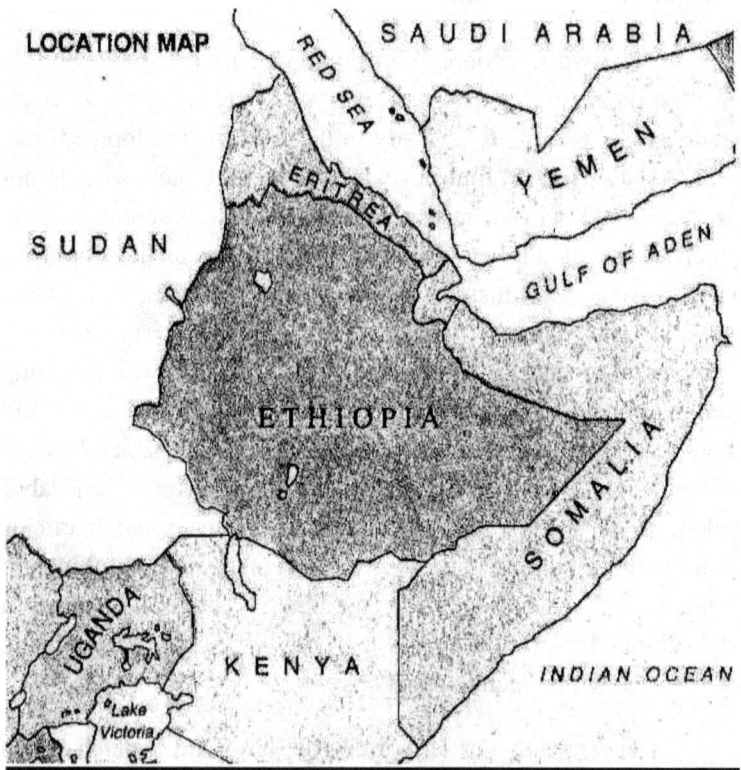

LOCATION MAP

RED SEA

SAUDI ARABIA

YEMEN

ERITREA

SUDAN

GULF OF ADEN

ETHIOPIA

SOMALIA

UGANDA

KENYA

INDIAN OCEAN

Lake Victoria

Chapter One

Portrait of Ethiopia

"Ethiopia is brilliant and beautiful, secretive, mysterious and extraordinary. It is a country of great antiquity, with a culture and traditions stretching back more than 3000 years. The traveler in Ethiopia makes a journey through time, transported by beautiful monuments and ruins of edifices built many centuries ago."

(Professor Richard Pankhurst)

'The man who wants a garden fair,
Or small or very big,
With flowers growing here and there,
Must bend his back and dig.
The things are mighty few on Earth
That wishes can attain.
Whatever we want of any worth
We have got to work to gain'.
(Edgar Guest)

Cradle of Humanity

About one hundred fifty years ago in 1871 Charles Darwin suggested in his book "The Descent of Man" that Africa is probably the origin of human kind. As his book came out it provoked anger and controversy in Europe for two basic reasons. The first was religious, because Darwin challenged the biblical teachings that God created all living creatures in one week. The second reason is that Europeans did not want to accept that their own ancient ancestors originally came from Africa. It was an insult and a slap in the face of their belief in racial superiority.

However, in the twentieth century scientific research has provided sufficient evidence to confirm Darwin's theory. There is no doubt now that Africa is the birthplace of humankind.

In this great continent, mankind originated; the evolution of man from his apelike ancestors took place in East Africa (Ethiopia) many millions years ago. Scientists have discovered the skeleton of the first human, Lucy, (Denknesh) in her native name, meaning (you are wonderful), whose fossil is 3.2 million years old. Scientists have also discovered simple tools, razor-sharp cutters and rock choppers that the first humans used 2.5 million years back.

In the eastern part of Ethiopia and other parts of Africa scientists and archeologists did repeated recovery and examination of fossils, bones, stone tools etc. and provided sufficient evidence to prove Darwin's proposition. Besides, Africa is the only continent where such evidence has been found. From the evidence of these fossils, scientists believe somewhere between ten million and five million years back the earliest form of hominid evolved away from the main family of African great apes, like gorillas and chimpanzees. They moved out of the forests to the grasslands of east Africa and learned to stand on their two feet and look out for predators for survival and walk away.

"The most important evidence for the belief that the Ethiopian rift valley was the first home of humanity was a spectacular discovery, which took place in Hadar, in the Afar region of the middle awash valley in 1974. This was the finding by the American-French team led by Donald Johnson of Chicago University, of the remains of the oldest known Hominid, i.e. erect walking human ancestor." (Richard Pankhurst, The Ethiopians, p-1)

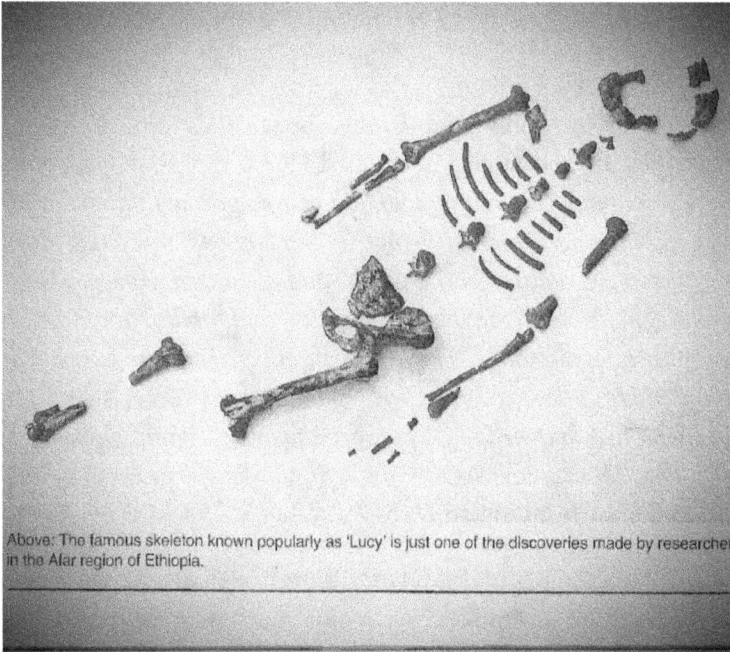

Above: The famous skeleton known popularly as 'Lucy' is just one of the discoveries made by researchers in the Afar region of Ethiopia.

The other advantage of standing on two feet is being able to have their hands free for using tools and carry food. Later with their hands free they learned not only to make tools but also to use them. Even though what made a difference is the capacity of his brain, all the ideas mankind came up with would have been a long to-do list without using his hands. Developing this ability helped them to produce their own food, making tools and using them for hunting made all the difference between homo line and animals. With their brain power getting bigger and standing erect (Homo erectus) they used the tools they made for hunting, fishing and gathering food. Later the human race learned farming, crop cultivation and domestication of animals. Humans learned how to stand upright, to walk and talk, make tools, and use them to produce. Thus society evolved in Africa and started to migrate to the other continents. Shillington suggested that between 5000 and 4000 BCE permanent settlements of full time farmers were established in the Nile valley, and in time these communities grew up into states and kingdoms.

Kevin Shillington in his book "History of Africa" describes the appearance of the first Homo sapiens. *"Sometimes between about 120,000 and 90,000 years ago the final evolution into fully modern human beings, homo sapiens, occurred in the savannah woodlands of eastern and southern Africa. These people had the same brain capacity and ability to think as modern human beings. They were in effect the same as us. The only thing they lacked was our learned experience and accumulated knowledge. They were thus the original pioneers of the development of human thought, philosophy, religion and technology."* (Shillington, P- 5)

According to Professor Richard Pankhurst, the bones believed to be 3.2 million years old constitute a little over half the skeleton, of a fully grown woman; now generally known as Denknesh or Berknesh in Ethiopia or Lucy internationally. Paleoanthropologists call her Australopithecus afarensis. Ethiopia is thus the birth place of mankind. Here mankind learned to stand upright, to walk, talk, love, hate, and make tools to hunt animals and cultivate the land.

Africa/Ethiopia is a land of ancient communal people who mastered the art of surviving in the rain forest for thousands of years, fighting with wild animals and deadly insects, and of caravans who cross vast deserts for centuries with their camels. Most people think of Africa/Ethiopia as a land of wildlife, forests and primitive communal people. There is more to Africa/Ethiopia than wild life, breathtaking landscapes and communal tribes. Humanity was born here millions of years ago, all people of the world belong to Africa. The savannah plain of Africa is the place that engineered mankind; that is the place where we learned to be human, to comprehend and become

24

conscience developing the ability to discern right from wrong; and took the talents that Africa taught us to every corner of the world.

Land of contrasts

Ethiopia with vast central highlands, semi-arid adjacent lowlands, wide tropical jungles, and mighty rivers flowing into neighboring countries and a huge savannah in the east and south, it is a land of unparalleled diversity, that exhibits breathtaking spectacular landscapes, an extraordinary wealth of wild life, and a remarkable range of peoples and cultures.

Ethiopia is a land of extremes; wild and wonderful with some of the highest and most rugged inaccessible places in the continent. The Semen Mountains and the Nile River Gorge offer landscapes similar to the American Grand Canyon. Danakil depression is the lowest place on earth, below sea level, extremely hot, forbidding but fascinating. The highland plateau reaches to the horizon, the big skies and broad landscapes gives you a breathtaking expansive view.

Being a land of contrasts, it has a well-watered mountain plateau and outlying arid lowlands. There are hot, dry and barren semi-desert places, as well as fertile highlands, savannah and rugged mountainous regions. In the high mountains there is frost and even snow. There are many big and small rivers, gorges, canyons, rift valley lakes and beautiful waterfalls. It is a country of breathtaking scenery, a microcosm of an entire continent.

Ethiopia is described accurately by geographers as the roof and reservoir of Africa. Several river basins and its rugged highlands bless Ethiopia with the continent's second largest water resources and plentiful hydropower. Its rivers and drainages flow from the central highlands to the neighboring countries to the west, east and south. The Blue Nile and its tributaries (Beles, Dabus, Baro, Anger/Didesa), which supply 85 percent of the Nile water flow towards the Sudan and Egypt. Lake Tana, the biggest lake in Ethiopia is the source of the Blue Nile. The Wabi Shebele and the Genale rivers, flow to the east to Somalia and finally to the Indian Ocean. The Omo River flows south to Lake Turkana at the Kenyan boarder. The Awash River flows east to the desert in Djibouti.

Many foreigners visualize Ethiopia as a land of draught, famine, civil war, poverty and hunger. Even though poverty and hunger are still serious problems in Ethiopia, the picture is far from complete. Author Ann Heinrichs in her book "Ethiopia' explains the other side of the country.

"The sheer beauty of Ethiopia would surprise anyone who has never seen it. Much of the land is lush and green, with tropical forests, fertile valleys, terraced hill sides, and grassy plains. Rugged mountain peaks overlook sparkling lakes and spectacular gorges. ...Alongside these natural beauty is a rich and vibrant culture that hardships can't crush." (Heinrichs, P-10)

The rift valley has many lakes like Zewai, Langano, Shalla, Abaya, Abiyata, Awassa and Chamo which is an important migration route for birds from Europe to southern Africa. Ethiopia is one of the best places in the continent for bird watching. There are over 860 known species of birds of which 16 are endemic to Ethiopia. These include the Black-winged Love bird (Agapornis taranta) and the thick billed raven (corvus crassirostris). Ethiopia is also home to 263 mammal species of which 30 are endemics, like The Abyssinian Wolf (canis simensis), the Gelada baboon, the mountain Nyala, the Walya Ibex etc.

Ethiopia has many plants in its flora and fauna that are endemic. More than seven thousands of plant species exist in Ethiopia, of which about 12 percent are endemic. As the original home of coffee this plant originated in southern Ethiopia in a place known as Keffa, and the country is known for the best quality Arabica and Geisha coffee. Yemen traders took coffee beans to Arabia and then to Europe. Ethiopia's indigenous coffee Arabica and Geisha are the best quality in taste and aroma. Coffee lovers all round the world and the best coffee brewers like Starbucks swear that Ethiopia's coffee is the best. The other type of coffee, Robusta which is sour is found all over the world. The new quality variety of coffee known as Geisha was discovered in Ethiopia recently and the seeds from that tree found its way to a farm in Panama. This variety which has a unique and wonderful taste quickly became *"a rock star in the coffee world"* says Peter Giuiliano from the Specialty Coffee Association of America.

Coffee is more than a drink, woven into the fabric of every day, connecting us to people all around the globe. Ethiopia not only has given the world its favorite beverage, coffee is very important in the way of life of Ethiopians. The beverage is honored with its own special ceremony and performed with gentle grace and charm in every home after a delicious Ethiopian meal. No visit to Ethiopia is complete without participating in the elaborate coffee ceremony.

Coffee ceremony is Ethiopia's long-established traditional form of hospitality usually conducted by a beautiful young girl in traditional Ethiopian costume. The ceremonial apparatus is arranged upon a carpet of long fresh cut grasses. The green beans are roasted in a pan over a charcoal brazier and the rich aroma of coffee mingling with the smell of incense that is always burned during the ceremony creates a delightful feeling. The beans are then pounded with a pestle and mortar, and the ground coffee is brewed in a black clay pot with a narrow spout. The coffee is drunk with small handless cups accompanied by popcorn or barley roast (*kollo*); welcome to Ethiopia!

Some Archeologists and authors have argued that grass seeds like sorghum and the cereal Teff are native to Ethiopia. The banana-like plant *(Ensete)*, narcotic chat, oily-noog, its finger millet with its cultivation dating back thousands of years are also first domesticated in Ethiopia. Thus Ethiopia is one of the few ancient countries that enjoy the development of cereal cultivation. The charm of Ethiopia in every way is so great that everyone who spends time absorbing the feel of the country and its multi-ethnic peoples will always want to return.

<u>Ancient Nation</u>

Ethiopia being one of the oldest nations on earth is a land of timeless appeal, custodian to some of the world's oldest civilizations. This is the land of ancient kingdoms of Axum and Abyssinia where mighty kings and queens who claimed to have roots from biblical times ruled lands beyond the nations present day borders from their mountain fortresses.

According to historians, south of Egypt was Nubia and the kingdom of Cush which was strong enough even to rule Egypt for a century around 750 BC. These Cushitic kings are shown in Egyptian temples and tombs as black Pharaohs. The Cushitic had distinct art and architecture; they also trained and tamed elephants for war and impressive display.

The Cushitic with their capital city at Meroe were later defeated and governed by their south eastern neighbor Axum around 350 AD. Meroe became part of the Axumite Empire which covered what is now north east Sudan, Eritrea and northern Ethiopia. The king of Axum, Ezana accepted

Christianity around 330 A.D. and made it the religion of the land. After 700 AD the spread of Islam from North Africa southwards across the Sahara brought Arabs with a large caravan of camels to trade their goods and spread their faith. Later, The Congo Empire and the kingdom of Ghana and Mali, the Shaka kingdom, and the Great Zimbabwe kingdom also developed in the different regions of the continent.

The Axumite Empire included Cush and southern Arabia across the Red Sea, Eritrea and northern Ethiopia. In the book "Ancient Africa" authors Susan Altman and Susan Lechner wrote: *"Its Red Sea docks and harbors brought merchants to its shores. They came to buy Rhinoceros horn, Ivory, Gems and more. ...The Axum people minted coins, raised goats and heard cattle."* (Susan, P-12)

Ethiopia, in the old days known as Axum or Abyssinia, is ancient beyond imagination. Its culture and traditions date back over 3000 years with a central administration based in Axum, Lalibela, Gondar, Debre Tabor and Ankober successively. *"By the first century A.D. Axum was the commercial and administrative center of an empire whose influence extended across the Red Sea to southern Arabia. Its rulers maintained close ties with the eastern Roman Empire, and in the third century achieved international prominence by issuing their own coinage, in gold, silver and bronze. Persian leaders of the day described Axum as one of the world's four most important kingdoms, (the other three were Persia, Rome, and Siloes – possibly meaning China)"*. (John Reader, P-143)

Ethiopia's geographical position being by the Red Sea, it has enjoyed close economic, cultural and religious contacts with many parts of the world and significantly with the Mediterranean region and the Middle East countries. Relations with ancient Israel, Palestine, and ties with Armenia were significant. Ties with Armenia were so close many Armenians came to Ethiopia where several of them gained prominence and worked as envoys to the Ethiopian Kings or as independent merchants and craftsmen. The legendary account of Ethiopia's Queen of Sheba's visit to King Solomon, and after Ethiopia accepted Christianity, establishing several monasteries in Jerusalem and Judaic influences in Ethiopian Christianity is also significant, particularly having a tabot (replica of the Ark of the Covenant) in every church. Professor Teshale Tibebu of Temple University in Philadelphia explains this cultural link in his book "The Making of Modern Ethiopia 1896 - 1974".

"The cultural uniqueness of the Ge'ez civilization resides in its tabot Christianity, a Christianity to be found nowhere in the world of Christendom save Ethiopia. From the monasteries of Alexandria and Ireland to the liberal polygamy of the Mormons, one finds no culture resembling Ethiopia's tabot Christianity. ... The cultural universe of Ethiopia's tabot Christianity is one of indissoluble linkage between Judaism and Christianity in which a church is identified more by the tabot inside it than by the cross sign on the roof top of its building". (Teshale, The Making of Modern Ethiopia 1896 – 1974, P- 7)

The famous early fourth century Obelisks in Axum, The 12th century rock hewn churches of Lalibala and the 16th century palaces of Gondar are few of the many historical relics of Ethiopia. The largest Stele or Obelisk at Axum which is carved from a single stone is believed to be, in the words of Professor Pankhurst, *"the largest block of stone fashioned by humanity anywhere in the world."* The biggest three Steles have a height of 33, 25 and 24 meters and measure three by two meters at the base. They are a remarkably impressive piece of workmanship representing several story's palace with a ground floor door and above it a row after row of windows.

The first foreign historian who visited the Obelisks time and again, the English man Henry Salt wrote: "*My attention was for a long time riveted on this beautiful and extraordinary monument. ...on seeing it again after five years, it made nearly as forcible an impression upon my mind as at the first moment I beheld it. Having by then inspected many Egyptian, Greek and Roman antiquities, comparison with them seems to justify that it is the most admirable and perfect monument of its kind.*" (Henry Salt)

The remarkable rock-hewn churches of Lalibala, deserve the same appreciation as it is officially the eighth wonder of the medieval world. These eleven rock hewn monolithic churches, all cut out of red volcanic rock in which they stand, were excavated in the late 12th century during the time of King Lalibala and his sons. Each building is architecturally unique, beautifully carved, and most of them decorated with fascinating paintings. The first foreign traveler who saw these churches, the 16th century Portuguese explorer Alvares wrote his impression.

"*I weary of writing more about these buildings, because it seems to me that I shall not be believed if I write more, and because regarding what I have already written they may blame me for untruth, therefore I swear by God, in whose power I am that all that is written is the truth, and there is much more than that I have written, and I have left it that they may not tax me with its being falsehood.*" (Alvares)

Gonder, a city founded by Emperor Fasiledes as his capital in 1636 is the site of numerous castle-like palaces. In this historic city and its surroundings Orthodox Christians, Catholics, Muslims, Felashas or Judaic Ethiopians also known as Bete Israel lived together in harmony for centuries.

31

From left to right: one of the fourth-century obelisks in Axum, 12ᵗʰ century rock-hewn churches in Lalibela, and 16ᵗʰ century Castle-like palaces in Gonder.

Ethiopia with its numerous historical monuments, churches, and mosques, its ancient traditions and customs, along with its stunning scenery of mountains, forests, waterfalls and lakes, is uniquely different from its neighbors and long attracted the discriminating seasoned traveler.

Patriotic Resistance

Ethiopian history mostly focuses on the kings and emperors, queens and princes that ruled the country for over two millennia. The country's rich history is woven with fascinating facts and legends that attach it to the biblical times. The ancient history melds with the modern to make Ethiopia the unique and fascinating country it is today. One fascinating fact about Ethiopia is its people's struggle through the centuries to defend its independence from foreign invaders. During the last two hundred years alone Ethiopians had to fight against Italians, the British, Ottoman Turks, Egyptians, Sudan-Dervishes (who collaborated with Mahdists/Ansar) and Somalia. Among these the victory of Adwa against Italian invasion in 1896 stands out as the first decisive victory of a black African country over European power. The victory of Adwa is a symbol of Ethiopia's unity in diversity, because our ancestors from different ethnicity all around the country converged to defend their independence. Ethiopia also became the symbol of independence for the rest of Africans in their struggle against colonialism.

Professor Adu Boahen in his book "African perspective on colonialism" refers to historian Akpan who described the Ethiopian victory as, *"The greatest victory of an African over a European army since the time of Hannibal and the only decisive victory won by an African country throughout the whole period of the partition and occupation – was a very great significance. First it insured the continued sovereignty of Ethiopia; ... secondly, the victory spread the fame of Ethiopia throughout the world. Above all the victory filled the hearts of blacks throughout the world with the racial pride and the name of Ethiopia became their symbol of hope, survival and regeneration."* (Boahen – P-55)

At the beginning of the 19th century Ethiopia was divided for many decades and the different regions were controlled by feudal war lords with no real central authority. During this time which is known as *'zemene mesafint'* (era of princes), Ethiopia was suffering from disunity and civil war. While the country was torn by civil war, the Europeans, where industrial revolution was underway were able to deploy war ships and troops and take advantage to deprive Ethiopia access to the Red Sea. This was a time that Ethiopia was not in a position to defend itself and embark to modernization; and was in actual fact technologically falling backwards. Its national integrity was increasingly threatened by Egyptians, Turks, Italians, British, and French who succeeded to occupy some areas of the Red sea coastal line.

Ethiopians first significant attempt at unification and modernization started in the second half of the nineteenth century by the three kings; Emperor Tewodros of Begemidir, Emperor Yohannes of Tigray, and Emperor Menilik of Shoa, who ruled the country successively. These three monarchs though with very different personalities, were all involved with the re-unification of Ethiopia, the preservation of its independence and the necessity of modernization.

Menilik's territorial expansion in all directions and specially to the south and west is of major political and economic importance which helped create a strong united Ethiopia that would later be able to stand against Italian invasion. The unity and modernization these three emperors started was later strengthened by Emperor Haile Selassie (Ras Teferi), who succeeded in making Ethiopia a member of the League of Nations.

"Tafari's most spectacular achievement came in the field of foreign affairs. On 28 September 1923 he succeeded in gaining Ethiopia's entry into the League of Nations, which had been founded only four years earlier, in 1919. Admission to the international body was a notable step in overcoming the country's age-old isolation, and was potentially important in withstanding pressures from Italy and other neighboring colonial powers." (Pankhurst, "The Ethiopians", p- 210)

In-spite of the military and diplomatic effort by Emperors Yohannes and Menilik, Italian invaders occupied the Red Sea coastal line when Britain and Egypt failed to abide by the tripartite treaty (Hewett Treaty) favoring Italian expansion. The dynamic military leader of Ethiopia at the time, Ras Alula Engeda (Aba Nega), drove out the Egyptians from Massawa and from Ethiopia's northern and western border lands which they had occupied for a while. After the Egyptians were driven out,

Italians occupied the port town of Massawa in February 1885 and the adjacent areas creating a blockade to stop arms supply to Ethiopia. Ras Alula, commander of the Ethiopian army protested against Italian penetration and attacked their garrison at Sa'ati; intercepted and wiped out their troops sent for reinforcement at Dogali; forcing them to evacuate. But, because the Europeans supported Italian occupation and made arms embargo on Ethiopia, due to shortage of supplies, Emperor Yohannes's 80,000 strong army that was dispatched the following year, could not succeed to drive out the Italians.

During the same period the Dervishes from Sudan were fighting and looting Ethiopia's western towns to retaliate for Egyptian loss. After Emperor Yohannes was killed in battle against the Dervishes all the problems of the country was passed to the next Emperor, Menilik II. Italy managed to occupy the northern highlands of Ethiopia and on January 1st 1890 officially changed the name of their colony from Midri Bahri to Eritrea, after the Latin word of the Red Sea, (Erythraeum Mare). In 1895 the Italian invaders continued advancing south towards to occupy the whole of Ethiopia. Emperor Menilik has by the time expanded his country's territory to the south and east and was able to recruit enough militia and import firearms via the Gulf of Aden, from Italy's rivals France and Russia. In March 1896 at the battle of Adwa, the Italian army was virtually annihilated. After the defeat of the Italian army at Adwa, it is said that Emperor Menilik did not have the sufficient man power and logistics to continue northwards and liberate Eritrea. Since his army was starving, with more than 6,000 fighters killed and 8,000 seriously wounded and a drought that killed a lot of people and cattle in the hinterland, Menilik refused Ras Alula's request to advance to the coast and drive the invaders to the sea.

Ethiopians lost their kin in the northern part of the country once called Midri-Bahiri administered by the Emperor's envoy (Bahre Negash), and became landlocked. The Italians kept it under their control for two generations, and after their defeat in World War II, it stayed under British administration for about a decade. Ethiopians fought hard and long militarily and diplomatically to bring back their brothers and sisters. The government of Emperor Haile Selassie played smart politics at the United Nations in bringing back Eritrea in the form of a federation, which the Emperor later wrongly dissolved in favor of a complete union. The dissolution of the federation was used as a pretext by narrow nationalist groups and anti-Ethiopian elements to ignite a war of secession which got the support of the surrounding Arab countries. Soon, Ethiopia was engulfed in a civil war that lasted for thirty years.

In 1993, because of EPLF and TPLF leader's selfish motives, Ethiopians again lost their Eritrean brothers and sisters and access to the sea. They could have easily redressed past injustices by totalitarian governments and addressed legitimate concerns through brotherly dialogue. These two narrow nationalist groups, who conspired with Ethiopia's historical enemies, advocated secession; and have been tarnishing Ethiopia's millennia long history and causing friction among its population on ethnic and religious grounds with a sinister motive of "divide and rule". They divided the widely intermarried and intermingled nationality that has the same language, culture, religion, and share the same history, thus damaging national cohesion. The only ones who benefited from the fragmentation of the country are secessionist leaders, their family members, their political loyalists, extremists, criminal elements and international corporations who exploit the country's natural resources. The masses have become the primary victims of a new dictatorship and of deprivation.

Italian aggression of Ethiopia in 1936 for the second time forty years after it colonized its northern province and named it Eritrea brought basic changes. Italy merged almost all regions of the horn of Africa (Eritrea, Ethiopia, and Somalia under a single administration and called it '*African Orientale Italiana*' (AOI). The territory was divided into six constituent regions mostly based on ethnic lines, 1) the mainly Tigrigna speaking north, 2) Amhara, 3) Oromo and Sidama, 4) Somalia, 5) Addis Ababa and 6) Harrar. Mussolini did this not to create convenience administration but to divide and rule the population on ethnic and religious lines and erase Ethiopia's legal entity. Since he was determined to destroy all symbols of Ethiopia's historic independence, he personally ordered the removal of Emperor Menilik's victory of Adwa statue, and the lion of Judah statue and also shipped one of the great obelisks of Axum, royal crowns and historical paintings to Rome.

Even though Italy defeated Ethiopia's weak army in 1935-6 using airplanes that dropped bombs and poison gas, patriotic resistance continued in most regions throughout the occupation. Guerrilla -warfare and coordinated and uncoordinated attacks on the invaders continued for five years all around the country until liberation. Leaders of the patriotic front like Lej Hailemariam Mamo, Dejazmach Aberra Kassa, Dejazmach Balcha Abanefso, Dejazmach Hailu Kebede, Dejazmach Mengesha Jembere and Belay Zeleke, Ras Abebe Aregay, Lej Zewde Asefa, Shaleka Mesfin Sileshi, Belata Tekalegn Woldehawariat, Shewarega Gedlie, Ras Desta Damtew, Dejazmach Beyene Merid, Dejazmach Nesibu Zamanuel, Dejazmach Afework Weldesemayat, Abraha Deboch, Moges Asgedom Lej Yohannes Iyassu to name a few led the resistance war using the support they got from active underground movements (wust arbegnas) in the towns. Emperor Haile Selassie went to appeal to the League of Nations.

Italy's entry into the European war in support of Nazi Germany changed the equation. Britain which had all through favored Italian expansion in Ethiopia changed sides and started to aid the patriots. Most importantly, the Ethiopian patriots played a major role during the five years of resistance and liberation struggle. They isolated, weakened, and tied down the Italian army around the big towns and finally took the offensive with the assistance of the British air support. On 5th May 1941 the patriots captured Addis Ababa. Emperor Haile Selassie, who was flown to Sudan weeks earlier by the British, entered the capital the same day. Mussolini's once triumphant army was reduced to dust in five years of protracted struggle. The patriots continued mop up operations throughout the country.

The legacy of the Italian occupation is immense, most of the educated Ethiopians had died during the occupation; the division of the country on ethnic lines has created a disintegrative tendency among the population and some vicious politicians are still using the same method to 'divide and rule' and if they can't do so, to disintegrate the country. Eritrea's secession movement was based initially on it being an Italian colony for around five decades. Somalia's claim of the Ogaden region, the current TPLF leader's mode of administration, including their name and their motive, and many other problems that followed has their roots in Italian invasion and occupation. The fragmentation of the Ethiopian elite at the end of the war into three different groups, *arbegna, banda, Sidetegna* (Patriots, Collaborators with the invaders and Returnees from exile) also created a problem.

Since most of the historians who wrote on Ethiopia are foreigners one can easily find fallacy, distortion and unfair comments in their books. Ethiopian historians are therefore obliged to look at them seriously and present constructive criticism. Professor Teshale Tibebu of Temple University in his research paper "Ethiopia the 'Anomaly' and 'Paradox' of Africa", that was published in the Journal of Black Studies

March 1996, vol 26 #4, describes how western historians perceive Ethiopia. Teshale explains that unlike other countries *"Ethiopia maintained its brand of African civilization intact"*. He goes on to point out why some western intellectual historians try to see Ethiopia as an outlandish to Africa and associate her millennia-long independence and culture a result of being geographically inaccessible, and not because of its gallant warriors.

In this well-researched analysis of Ethiopian history as part of African history, Teshale appeals to all concerned that *"a political- economy approach to Ethiopian history can be an alternative paradigm for the study of the Ethiopian history."* He also explains the pan- African image of Ethiopia as follows:

"...Ethiopia became the concentrated expression of Africa. Ethiopia carried the burden and suffering that was Africa. Ethiopia symbolized the hope and pride of Africa. The biblical Ethiopia "stretching its hands unto God" became the real Ethiopia invaded by Mussolini. It was in the historical context of Mussolini's invasion, and earlier the Ethiopian victory at Adwa, that the pan-African construction of the Ethiopian identity was formed. It was the feeling that the pride of Adwa, the pride of Africa was to be erased by the second coming of Italy that galvanized a passionate pan-African defense of Ethiopia. Ethiopia has a unique place in the consciousness of Africans. It has been revered as the symbol of black defiance of white domination. From London to Harlem, from Lagos to Kingston, from Accra to Cairo the Italian Fascist invasion of Ethiopia became a rallying ground of pan-African nationalism." (Teshale, P-426)

Some historians and nationalists, try to accuse Ethiopia as a colonial power taking part in the scramble for Africa along with Europeans. Some historians even wrote that Menilik participated actively in the scramble for Africa and saved Ethiopia from being a colony itself. This kind of statement emanates from mere ignorance of the formation of African countries, or deliberate distortion of history. Professor Teshale articulates in his research paper about such vicious comments.

"Africans throughout the continent were forming states through territorial expansion and political centralization so as to face head on the gathering storm of the "white man's burden". Meniliks expansion was part of the larger African scene. Like the Fulani Empire of Sokoto, the Zulu state of Chaka, Samori Ttoure's fragile empire, the Kabakas of Buganda and so on, Meniliks Empire was expanding and centralizing in the midst of growing European pounding of Africa. ... If indeed, what makes Menilik a black colonialist is the fact that he more than doubled the territory and population under his rule, then, obviously, Shaka should be 50 times more than Menilik, because he expanded the territory and people subject to his rule by a factor of more than one hundred."(Teshale, P-422)

Ethiopia is a country with a long history of independence and nationhood, blessed with diverse nationalities who widely inter-marry, and of inseparable and interwoven interests. However much has been done to divide the people; with the love and dedication Ethiopians have for each other, their national unity and territorial integrity, they are still determined deep at heart to remain united, live in harmony, prosper together and create a strong African union.

Africa's diverse peoples, its long and fascinating history, and Ethiopia's historical past can't be summarized in such a short introduction. I am only trying to give the readers a bird's-eye-view to enable them to grasp the following chapters.

Museum of Nationalities

Ethiopia is a home of very many different nationalities and tribes with different traditions, costumes and cultures. It is a museum of nationalities; with diverse, rich and vibrant culture. Even being different they have a long and common history of struggle together to preserve their freedom from foreigners. They are proud of their common history and different cultures. Each ethnic group proud of its own centuries old traditions and believing in unity in diversity, most live side by side in mutual respect. Their different traditions and common struggle against European and Arab invaders give them dignity and meaning to everyday life. In a world of racial conflict and changing values, Ethiopia speaking 82 languages and 200 dialects, offers lessons to its neighbors and the rest of the world how to live in harmony. Historian Richard Pankhurst describes the religious and linguistic diversity of Ethiopia as follows:

"The mountainous character of much of the region, with its innumerable ravines, rivers and flash-torrents, rendered communications within the country difficult, and during the rainy season, virtually impossible. This resulted in the perpetuation of many different ethnic, linguistic, and religious groups, which, though often significantly interacting, were over the millennia never fully assimilated. These varied peoples, whose precise geographical location in not a few cases changed considerably, as well as expanding or contracting, over the centuries, belong to four main linguistic groups, currently known as Semitic, Cushitic, and outside the focus of this book, the Omotic and Nilo-Saharan." (Pankhurst, P-7)

Many historians say that Ethiopians are secretive society. That might be true because as diverse as we are, when you ask us about yourself we tell you what we think you would like to hear. Most people live in the country side leading a very primitive life. But, life in the big cities is like living in Europe or America. Ethiopians exist simultaneously in different time periods. Author Sarah Howard in her book "Culture smart Ethiopia" explains about the people:

"Set in Africa, but, not wholly African; an isolated nation, yet receptive to the outside world; hierarchical and conservative, yet innovative and desirous of modernity; conformist as a people, and yet fiercely independent as individuals – the Ethiopian identity defies definition. No sooner have you made a generalization, than you realize it does not apply to some other part of the country." (Howard, P-12)

Ethiopians have courtesy, this is because of their consciousness of being part of a multicultural and multilingual people, who have learned to live together with respect for each other in order to achieve their common goals and aspirations and defend their motherland together from foreign invaders.

Religion

Christianity came to Ethiopia from Jerusalem around 330 A.D. during the reign of King Ezana of Axum. Islam also came to Ethiopia from Arabia, during the life time of the Prophet Mohammed around 630 A.D. The two main religions in Ethiopia have coexisted since that time. However, the Orthodox Church has dominated the political, social and cultural life in the country as it has been the official religion of the emperors and the feudal establishment until Haile Selassie was deposed and religion and state separated in 1974.

Ethiopia has long enjoyed the most intimate relations with Islam. Prophet Mohammed is said to have told his followers who were being persecuted by the new Arabian king of the time, to go to Ethiopia where he has arranged with the king of Axum who in his words had tolerance to other religions. Some of the earliest disciples of the Prophet found refuge at Axum, which was then ruled by King Armah, ; making Ethiopia probably one of the first countries if not the first to give asylum. Because of this the Prophet later prayed for the Axumite kingdom and instructed his followers to 'leave the Abyssinians in peace', thus exempting Ethiopia from a 'holy war'. The first muezzin calling the faithful to prayer during the Prophet's time was an Ethiopian named Bilal. Ethiopia has an extensive and very active Muslim population throughout the length and breadth of the country. Ethiopia's most holy and earliest Muslim center is said to be at Nagash, north of Wukro in Tigray, where there is a fine historic mosque. But, perhaps the most important Islamic center since medieval times for religious learning, mosques, shrines and tombs is the walled city of Harar. However, an important center of Muslim pilgrimage in Ethiopia today is the town of Shek Husen in Bale region.

A few years after the death of Prophet Mohammed Islam religion also reached Egypt and from there it started spreading south and west to other African kingdoms by means of the desert caravan merchants crossing the Sahara desert with their camels for trade. Later the conquest of some kingdoms and the coming of Muslim kings made it possible to impose the new religion on the people. Traditional African beliefs and Islam co-existed peacefully side by side for some time, and later more and more people were converted to Islam.

"It must be remembered that Ethiopia was the first country outside the Arabian Peninsula to come into contact with Islam. When the new converts to Islam were being persecuted in their own country, it was Ethiopia that gave them sanctuary. Since then Islam has penetrated Ethiopia peacefully through commerce and marriage and at times through wars". (Professor Mesfin Wolde-Mariam, Ethiopia and the Indian Ocean, P- 208)

Both Christianity and Islam came to Ethiopia in the very early years making both religions indigenous to the country, and people of both religions lived side by side with the greatest religious tolerance ever seen anywhere in the world. The Ethiopian Orthodox Church treasures its ancient heritage, the Geez alphabet and written language and other artifacts. According to tradition, Ethiopian Orthodox Church is believed to have the Ark of the Covenant in one of its ancient churches; and the part of the holy Cross (Gemade Meskel) on which Jesus was crucified in one of its monasteries. In his book "Africa" John Reader describes about the coming of Christianity to Ethiopia.

"Ethiopia embraced Christianity less than four hundred years after the birth of Christ – while Europe was still in the dark ages. The church became the font of influence and authority throughout the country. Kings were accorded divine status – and became so famous that tales of the priest- king Prester John reached distant Europe. The Ark of the Covenant, the chest containing the tablets on which God wrote the Ten Commandments and therefore Christianity's holy of holies, is said to be in Ethiopia, taken from Solomon's Temple by a legendary Ethiopian king. A replica of the Ark, called the Tabot, is kept in each of the country's 20,000 –plus churches." (John Reader, Africa, P-157)

The people of this intriguing land are extremely religious, with tens of thousands of churches surrounded by trees and perched on a hill with a cross on their top. Church ceremonies are a major feature of Ethiopian life; church events are extremely impressive and unique. Priests wearing dazzling brocade robes, carrying ornate, and hand crosses, bearing prayer sticks, and decorated huge umbrellas, and swinging bronze censers from which wisps of incense smoke escape into the air, chant and dance to the accompaniment of solemn drums and the rhythmic clink of strums. Ethiopia's Islamic tradition is also old and strong, since the first Muslims brought the religion during the life time of the Prophet Mohammed. It offers colorful contrasts particularly in eastern and southern Ethiopia.

Music and Dance

African music, art, dance, and food have become popular all over the world. Many art forms in other countries are influenced by African culture. The rock music and jazz which is popular in the world today has many of its roots from African music. The drums were used to make music and announce important news and special meetings of the community. The African different kinds of drums and the beat and sounds are very fascinating. Ethiopia as a respected member of the African family has contributed greatly to the development of African music and dance. Ethiopia's different tribes and nationalities have very diverse style of dance and music which is so attractive to see them swing in their peculiar costumes.

Ethiopians use music and dance for all kinds of occasions. They have different kinds of musical instruments like drums, harps, lutes, thumb pianos, horns, flutes, rattles, clappers, xylophones, scrapers, bells, (worn by dancers around their ankles), string instruments, tambourines etc. In many parts of Ethiopia singers keep history alive by singing stories about great events, great leaders and legendary heroes of the community. Each tribe has its own dress, costume and ornaments and they have their own rhythm of music, body movement and dance that made Ethiopia the enchantment of the world.

Music and dance are integral aspects of everyday life in Ethiopia. There is music and dance for all social and /or religious occasions. The country's music is so diverse and they use it in times of birth, death, marriage, work, worship, funeral, and during heads of state visits and sporting events. Each event has a particular music and a corresponding dance. These traditional Ethiopian music don't have a written score or note, it is passed from generation to generation orally by singers who memorize it. Music in Ethiopia expresses various emotions, values of society, belief systems and rituals of the community. African music was affected by slave trade and colonialism. They were banned during these times; because they were considered threatening to slave trade and colonial governments. Some were incorporated with Christian church ceremonies. But, because Ethiopia was not colonized as such, her nationalities music and dance was not affected much by outsiders.

Ethiopians love music to a great extent that every individual sings while he or she performs various activities. Shepherds or cow boys sing as they watch their cattle graze, women sing as they do their house work, girls who baby-sit or take care of young ones sing to the babies so that they can go to sleep or stop crying. They sing when they are happy, and when they are sad. Music is used to entertain, to inspire, to reflect, and transmit ideas and values in private and public. Music is a language of its own, truly an international one.

Chapter Two

Ethiopian Dispersion

"They were peace men; but, they preferred revolution to peaceful submission to bondage. They were quiet men; but, they did not shrink from agitating against oppression. They showed forbearance; but, that they knew its limits. They believed in order; but, not in the order of tyranny. With them nothing was 'settled' that was not right. With them, justice, liberty, and humanity were 'final'; not slavery and oppression. You may well cherish the memory of such men. They were great in their day and generation. Their solid manhood stands out the more as we contrast it with these degenerate times".

(Fredrick Douglas)

'Not gold, but only man can make
A people great and strong;
Men who, for truth and honor's sake,
Stand fast and suffer long.
Brave men who work while others sleep,
Who dare while others fly-
They build a nation's pillars deep
And lift them to the sky'.
(Ralph Emerson)

The history of mankind is littered with accounts of exile and return. For evidence of this, we need not look any further than our own history as human beings. This history is recorded in our holy books and in our monuments. Most importantly, it is recorded in the hearts and minds of people across the world. It finds expression in our poems, songs and stories. Some nations were in fact built upon this notion; the prospect of others lays in large part in the hands of their exiled populations abroad.

Exile and exodus have been the fabric of human existence since time immemorial. To some extent, it is what makes us humans. People have been in constant movement, whether by choice or force, and, as a result, intermingle and exchange ideas. For millennia this has allowed our communities to connect with our distant relatives. The world as we know it today owes a lot to exile and also to return. Human progress, exile and exodus have been inextricably linked. Yet this seemingly most natural of occurrence is as repulsive as it is necessary for survival. By and large, we tend to want to stay in our place of provenance. Home gives a special feeling and a sense of belongingness. The sentiment of home is so resilient; it can sometimes remain part of us for centuries in exile, making its way in our folklore, culture, and faith.

The exile and consequently enslavement of the ancient Hebrews in the land of the Pharaohs, as depicted in the book of Exodus, has a particularly far reaching implication. Not only is this story by now almost universally publicized, it is also a driving feature of a nation and its people. The modern day state of Israel can't be thoroughly understood without taking into account exile and exodus. It is a powerful and moving testament to the strengths of the yearning for home. Centuries of exile may have elapsed, but people have not forgotten where they come from. The idea ends up creeping its way into the fabric of a society in exile, so deeply; it endures the test of time. Eventually it becomes the paramount goal of its people. Ultimately it finds fruition in the realization of that dream. A physical nation is thus created out of the deeply seated belief and aspiration of a people; nothing could be more powerful.

Harsh as the world is, this dream unfortunately comes at the cost of other people's desires and aspirations; in this case the Palestinians. What to do about this problem is a modern day dilemma or a long running human saga. One would hope a historically battered people will have more compassion for others who share similar circumstances. In this sense Palestinians and Israelis are perfectly fit for each other. But history and reality teach us otherwise. In the real world what matters is power over resources whether it is economic, military or political. Following an age old cycle the exiled has thus become the cause of exile for others. It is just to site an example, but the focus of this book is Ethiopia in particular, Africa in general.

In the 1980's and 90's more than one hundred thousand Ethiopian Jews migrated to Israel with the help of the Israeli government. Their courageous exodus from their native land Ethiopia and their mass immigration to Israel is a unique historical event; even though their wish to feel at home in the promised-land is not yet complete. They are engaged in a long and tough struggle to become fully integrated Israelis. In his book "The Ethiopian Jews of Israel" author Len Lyons explain their relocation as follows: "...*No other culture or ethnic population has relocated virtually at light speed from a rural, non-literate culture surviving on subsistence farming and crafts to an urban, high-tech society where they were welcomed to fulfill their religious destiny. In 1977, there were about one hundred Ethiopian Jews in Israel; by 2007, there were more than 100,000 Ethiopian Israelis*". (Lyons, P-19)

The story of the African Diaspora has many aspects: forced dispersion by tyrant leaders, voluntary settlement abroad, slave trade and the return to Africa etc. It is true that some left the continent voluntarily for better opportunities, but most were forced out because of slave trade conducted by Europeans,

Americans and Arabs, who took enslaved Africans by force to the Middle East, Europe and the Americas. African tribal chiefs themselves were not less guilty than the white man and the Arabs when it comes to slave trade. It was the African kings and chieftains who got the slaves captured from the interior and brought them to the sea ports to exchange them for the essentials and luxury items like spirits, tobacco, firearms etc. they get from the foreigners. After independence millions were forced to leave Africa again afraid of persecution by ruling tyrants and running away from tribal conflicts that pop-up here and there.

Today Africans live in every continent in millions. Their descendants are striving to maintain their own identities by upholding to their culture, art and music. African traditions have influenced art and popular music the world over. African musical styles and rhythms are widely accepted and practiced. The world owes Africa for the beauty of its music like blues, jazz, black gospel, samba in Brazil, reggae in Jamaica, jerk and cha-cha in the Americas, and calypso in the Caribbean.

In ancient times Africans travelled to the Middle East across the Red Sea and to Europe across the Mediterranean Sea and to India across the Indian Ocean as sailors, merchants, soldiers and adventurers. Ethiopians settled in the Arabian Peninsula, before the Romans dominated the area. Around 500 AD, Ethiopia occupied parts of Yemen and later left some of its people there when the area became part of the Roman Empire.

Africans were enslaved and taken as far as China to the east and the Americas to the west. Communities of enslaved and free Africans tried to create an independent state everywhere and mostly failed. So, they simply worked as sailors, dock workers, guards etc. Amid racial subjugation and persecution Africans tried to maintain their identities and to form independent sovereign areas. John Middleton refers to some such instances.

"The life stories of some Africans in Asia are known. One of them Malik Ambar was captured in Ethiopia by Muslim Arab slave traders and sold in Bagdad, Iraq. There he learned Arabic and became a clerk. Later he was sold to Indians who took him to central India. He became a soldier, organized a revolt and seized control of Indian state of Ahmadnagar. He ruled from 1601 to 1626, employing Africans, Arabs, Persians and Indians at his court. During his reign Ambar founded towns, built canals, and roads, and encouraged trade, scholarship and arts. He also joined forces with other Siddis against Indian and European foes". (Middleton, Africa- an encyclopedia for students, P-204)

The global presence of people of African descent and their contributions to the societies of the world is immense. Their dispersion started long before slavery around 400 A.D, when Ethiopian Christians established links with Europe. Around 650 A.D, Arab traders took Africans to China. In 1440, the Portuguese began slave trade, and by 1500 enslaved Africans came to America, and so on it goes to the beginnings of our dispersion.

According to a study "African Migration and the Brain Drain" which was presented by Shinn D. in 2008 at the Institute of African Studies and Slovenia global action meeting: *"The number of people of African descent that lived outside the continent is estimated at almost 140 million, most of them in the western hemisphere. Most of these people have lived in destination countries for many generations, often as slaves and have little if any ties to Africa. But, those Africans who left their countries in recent decades are estimated to be more than forty million. These have been in close contact with their relatives and maintain multi-facetted relationships with their country of origin".*

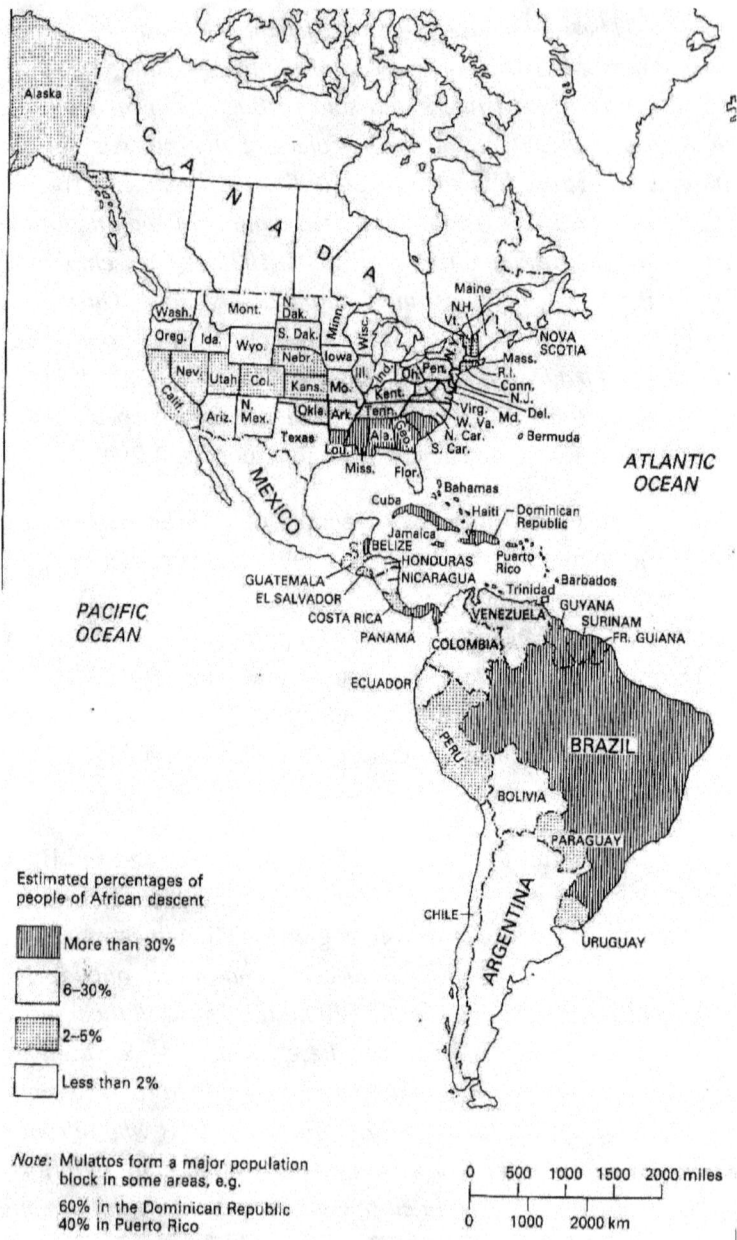

Distribution of people of African descent in the Americas today

The migration of highly educated people from Africa in the last half century has been very critical. The transfer of such human capital is hurting the continent. That is why it is important for African governments to harness the resources of the Diaspora so that it shall contribute to the economic development of their countries of origin beyond the personal remittances they send to their relatives and friends.

Ethiopians have been leaving their localities through the centuries for many reasons. Like all other people, they have been moving from place to place for better life to their families. Besides, it is no secret that the rulers have been abusing their subjects in many ways. During the reign of the emperors, the governors of the provinces, zones and districts (*Enderassie, Meslenie, Chikashum* etc.) used to take bribes often from the area residents they were supposed to serve.

When we look at modern Ethiopia after the Second World War, the reign of Emperor Haile Selassie was relatively peaceful. The country was in the process of modernization during the first half of his rule. He built schools, hospitals, roads, hydroelectric dams, and lately assisted in the struggle of several African countries to win their independence. He strengthened the pan-African movement and became one of the founding fathers and the first chairman of the Organization of African Unity (OAU). But, in his later years the slow pace of economic development and failure to make the necessary reform made violent revolution inevitable.

From Freedom To Despair

Most historians agree that the advances made by most African countries during the first two decades after independence were truly remarkable. School involvement grew faster in black Africa than in any other developing world. Enrolment in elementary schools almost doubled from 36 percent to 63 percent; enrolment in high schools also increased yearly by an average of 8 percent, the number of university graduates increased each year. A World Bank study of 1981 observed: *"the African record is unique; nowhere else has a formal education system been created on so broad a scale in so short a time"*. In the medical field, child mortality rate fell and life expectancy increased due to efficient health care, and the increase of health professionals. New schools, health clinics, roads, rail roads, ports were built at an amazing pace. All these created a sense of optimism about Africa's future; but it was short lived.

In the 1970's, Africa, including Ethiopia, started to experience several calamities. May countries were hit with prolonged drought and famine that killed their cattle and destroyed crops. In the wake of the Arab-Israeli war of 1973, oil prices increased and sent shock waves to the African progress. Then came, the Iraq-Iran war that shot oil prices to the detriment of oil importing African countries; the effect of which put a severe strain on their economies. Civil strife, political instability, and military coups soon followed. In 1974, Emperor Haile Selassie of Ethiopia was deposed. On top of these internal factors like bureaucratic obstructions, desertification, authoritarianism, stringent regulations, inefficiency population explosion and the lack of qualified personnel and a web of corruption, and wrong economic policies quickened the downfall of Africa. African leaders failed to deliver effective solutions; the continent sunk from freedom to despair.

After 50 years of the beginning of independence era in Africa, the future of the continent is bleaker than ever before. It is falling further behind, and its people getting poorer than all other poor regions of the world. Due to dictatorship, illiteracy, lack of skilled and disciplined work force and the necessary infrastructures, it has failed to attract foreign investment and could not benefit enough from globalization.

Africa's potential for economic development and its struggle for democracy have been disrupted by its power-hungry and corrupt leaders, who are not interested to put democracy and pluralism in their agenda. After decades of corruption and mismanagement, they have amassed wealth for themselves and emptied the treasuries of African countries. Because of the selfish and corrupt behavior of most African leaders and their incompetence to face the new challenges, the honeymoon of independence and progress was short lived. Since the boundaries drawn by colonialists are totally artificial and divided the people of the same language and tradition into many different neighboring countries, some countries started war with their neighbors over boundaries. Since nationhood was new to most African countries, the colonial system of 'divide and rule' served to exaggerate the differences between ethnic groups. All these created a serious problem for national unity. As a solution to ethnic rivalry most governments chose the one party system; but, this again curtailed democratic politics.

In the first 20 years of independence there were forty successful coups and many attempted coups. Most coups were bloodless, like all six coups that took place in Dahomey, later renamed Benin. The coup leaders promised to root out corruption, mismanagement, tribalism and restore efficient government, and return to civilian rule. But, they did not do much other than increase the salary of the soldiers. The coup leaders even after some of them returned to civilian government, could not do better than the rulers they replaced. Free elections were rigged, and democracy was in jeopardy as embezzlement, nepotism, fraud and dishonesty reigned over transparency and accountability.

Educated and sincere people disagreed with such governments and rallied their people for change. But as the leaders turn to become totalitarian they forbade public expression. Those who presented new ideas and dissidents were killed, jailed or exiled. The national media become a propaganda tool; private newspapers and magazines were either banned, their distribution curtailed or their editors arrested. They were called unpatriotic, traitors or terrorists.

Many African leaders do not give up power voluntarily; they are either killed or exiled by force. They cannot be impeached or voted out of office. They don't allow free and fair elections and they weaken the opposition parties by creating factions or by killing or arresting the leaders and political activists. Some of these countries' constitutions might sound good, but in practice it is something else. The constitution is to appease the Western nations who support them by giving aid and loan. That is how African leaders become presidents for life.

"The practice of one man one vote became in reality, one man, one vote, for a life time. The president you got at independence was the one you would have until he died or was overthrown. Presidents don't retire to become their country's senior political advisors, because to be an ex- president in Africa is a shame. And the longer they stay in power the more disdainful they _become of their own people, and the greater became their own powers. One of the secrets of their longevity is to share enough of the spoils to create an elite, monied class of loyalists". (David Lamb, The Africans, P-55)

Many Africans lost hope of getting good leaders. In despair, they started to migrate, this time voluntarily. With too much tension, discontent and fear, the educated elites leave their motherland and go to Europe or America. Some of those who stayed languish in jail. Some dissidents betrayed their people and joined the tyrant's camp. Some dropped out of politics and pursue their own self-interest. Others have become disappointed and forfeit the struggle for democracy completely.

Emperor Haile Selassie

Emperor Haile Selassie was respected, honored, and celebrated widely in Africa like no other leader during the years following the end of the Second World War. His defiant stand against Italy's brutal invasion of Ethiopia in 1935, and his historic speech at the League of Nations in Geneva, has won him worldwide fame. In his speech that summer day of 1936, he outlined in detail the crimes committed by the invaders using poison gas and challenged the delegates by asking a forceful question, "what answer am I to take back to my people?" He concluded by saying "God and history will remember your judgment!"

After he was restored to his throne in 1941, he was seen as a symbol of an independent Africa, and was the role model of liberation movement leaders of the continent under colonial rule. Being an emperor of a historic ancient country that traces its origins 3000 years back to biblical times, a national Christian church with a tradition and culture older than many European churches, great historical edifices, and an ancient written language (Geez), and a sacred literature endowed Ethiopia and its emperor with an immense prestige. He was regarded as the eldest statesman in Africa. He helped many African nations win their independence, and was the host, the first chairman and one of the founding fathers of the Organization of African Unity. In Jamaica he was worshipped as a living god (Jah) by the followers of Rasteferianism, an ideology coined in his early title and name Ras Teferi.

Ethiopia's Emperor Haile Selassie aboard a U.S. warship with President Franklin D. Roosevelt, then on his way home from the 1945 conference in the Crimea.

Emperor Haile Selassie was a firm believer and strongly committed to the principles of collective security and world peace which he often uttered in his speech since Ethiopia became a member of The League of Nations in 1923 and later the United Nations. He demonstrated his commitment to collective security in 1951 by sending 3000 Ethiopian troops in support of the UN mission during the Korean War. In 1960 again he demonstrated his unwavering commitment to these principles and to the independence and unity of Africa by sending 3000 Ethiopian troops as part of the UN peace-keeping force to keep Congo united.

Ethiopia and Emperor Haile Selassie in particular played an instrumental role in supporting liberation movements in Africa to ensure freedom, independence stability and unity. The subsequent role Ethiopia assumed in the League of Nations and later in the UN, representing not only itself but also the interest of Africa and the leading role Haile Selassie played served as the impetus towards the establishment of the Organization of African Unity OAU on May 25, 1963. The Emperor made a compelling speech opening the conference, insisting the Casablanca and the Monrovia groups to reconcile their philosophical differences to achieve African Unity. Out of the great admiration and respect they had for him and the gallant history of Ethiopia, the assembled African Heads of States drafted and ratified a single unifying charter enabling the vision of African Unity a reality.

"The conference cannot close without adopting a single charter. We cannot leave here without having created a single African organization possessed of the attributes we have described. If we fail in this, we will have shirked our responsibility to Africa and to the people we lead. If we succeed, then, and only then, will we have justified our presence here". (Haile Selassie, May 1963, first conference of African Heads of States)

Many African politicians considered Emperor Haile Selassie as the "Father of Africa", and Ethiopia as their spiritual homeland. In his autobiography, Nelson Mandela stated: *"Ethiopia always has a special place in my imagination, and the prospect of visiting Ethiopia attracted me more strongly than a trip to France, England or America combined. I felt I would be visiting my own genesis, unearthing the roots of what made me an African".* (Nelson Mandela, Autobiography)

Emperor Haile Selassie has been negotiating in vain with Britain, Italy and France since he came to power in 1930, to get back at least the port of Assab for Ethiopia's outlet to the sea. Fortunately, there came a chance where he played smart politics when he used the opportunity to take advantage of the compromise reached by the United Nations concerning the future of Eritrea. Italy colonized the northern province of Ethiopia by the Red Sea, and changed the name of the territory from Midri-Bahri, administered by the emperor's special appointee, Bahre Negash to Eritrea. The new name was derived after the Latin name of the Red Sea (Mare Erythraeum). When the Italians were defeated at World War II, Eritrea became a British protectorate for a decade administered by the British military. During this period, with the help of the British, the people of Eritrea enjoyed the freedom of establishing political parties, labor unions, and free press which were not allowed in Ethiopia.

Even though the Eritrean population was divided about the idea of being part of Ethiopia, with the Muslim lowlanders favoring independence, and the Christian highlanders tending to support unification, the UN reached a compromise in 1950, linking the two in the form of a federation. The federal status and the constitution drafted by the UN, allowed Eritrea to have its own assembly and elected government, its own flag, and official working languages, (Tigrigna and Arabic). Ethiopia was given control of foreign affairs, defense, finance, commerce, and the sea ports.

Emperor Haile Selassie, who was concerned that other nationalities might request the same kind of federal autonomy, did not want to continue with the federation. Regarding it only as a step towards unification he began to steadily consolidate his control using the Christian Tigrigna speaking politicians. In a few years the various freedoms that the Eritreans enjoyed under the British administration, political parties, trade unions, and free press were banned. The Eritrean assembly in Asmara came under Ethiopian government pressure, and on November 14th 1962 voted for the dissolution of the federation in favor of the territory's complete union with Ethiopia. The Eritrean flag was discarded, and the Eritrean assembly abolished; the region lost its elected government and the working language became Amharic.

This process angered many and became an excuse for narrow nationalist groups who exploited the situation and getting support from some Arab countries, ignited opposition movements. Shortly afterwards, the Eritrean "Liberation" Front (ELF) supported by the Muslim group was organized in Egypt. Later, the Eritrean People "Liberation" Front (EPLF) supported by some Christian highlanders was founded as a militant opposition organization. The Ethiopian people hoped that the movements will focus on democratic change for the whole country; but with the help and pressure from Arab countries, the groups infected with colonial mentality preferred to fight for secession.

Besides, the brutal method the imperial government and particularly the military Derg used to suppress the secessionist movement by burning villages, bombing towns and inflicting reprisals against the civilian population which the insurgents also used as human shield, alienated Eritreans and pushed them to support the war of secession. The emperor, the military Derg and the secessionists blew up one of the greatest political achievements in Africa; the unification of Eritrea, which was exemplary to other countries in the continent. During the thirty years war of secession, millions were forced to leave their home town and migrate to the hinterland or to the neighboring countries; mostly to Sudan which supported the movement and became safe haven to the "liberation" fronts.

Haile Selassie ruled Ethiopia from 1916 up to 1974, first as a regent, then as emperor. He has made enormous undertakings by building schools, hospitals, roads, electricity etc.; to modernize the country. But, besides governing as an autocratic monarch, in his later years he was focused mainly on sustaining his power and failed to make the necessary changes in land tenure and constitutional reform, and answer the requests of the peasantry and the growing educated sector. During his reign, three quarters of peasants, particularly in the south of the country, were tenants who were required to give up to 75 percent of their produce to the land lords. Most of the land was owned by the Orthodox Church and the aristocratic families in the different provinces.

Peasant uprisings in the south and west, the Eritrean "liberation" movement in the north, periodic wars with Somalia in the east and student protests in the heartland needed political and democratic solutions. But, the emperor, instead of using dialogue and compromise, became more and more ruthless in crushing opposition with his army. Even in his late seventies, he was not willing to loosen his grip on power. He alone decided on every state affair of even the small administrative details. When drought and famine claimed the lives of tens of thousands of people and their cattle in Wollo and Tigray provinces, the government tried to downplay it, and made little attempt to alleviate it. I was dispatched to the provinces at the peak of the drought, as a reporter of the daily vernacular Addis Zemen newspaper along with other journalists from other media, to report on the severity of the problem. But, the reports we presented were heavily edited to downplay the seriousness of the famine. This phenomenon created a wave of exasperation among university teachers and students who took to the streets in frequent protests and agitated the masses.

Emperor Haile Selassie held absolute power longer than any other leader in history at the time. He passed the age of eighty and became too old to initiate any meaningful change that the people were looking for. He was not willing to pass over power to the crown prince Asfawesson. The system of government was too bureaucratic and archaic that it did not suit to the needs of the country that was modernizing. The ministers were afraid to ask the emperor for a necessary change, and government kept on drifting away from the interest of the educated class and even the peasantry.

The slow pace of Ethiopian economic development compared with other African countries that gained their independence lately escalated political discontent in the country. In December 1960, the Imperial Bodyguard led by General Mengistu Neway staged a coup. The coup attempt was supported by the students, but not appreciated by the majority of the population; it was crushed by the army and the air force. This incident agitated the country's student body in colleges and high schools. Discontented with the government and its governance, students held peaceful demonstrations every now and then demanding land reform and constitutional reform, and accusing senior officials for corruption.

Relations with Somalia which wanted to take the eastern province, Ogaden from Ethiopia, and Sudan supporting the Eritrean secessionist movements, were tense. The rising prices of food items and gasoline in Ethiopia, following the devastating famine of the early 1970's in Wollo and Tigray, invited wide spread strikes and intensified the opposition. The spontaneous and unstoppable revolution of 1974 erupted. As there was dissatisfaction in the armed forces, they refused to obey the government and crush the uprising. Instead, the creeping coup was strengthened, with the mutiny of army units around the country.

Ethiopia in Turmoil

I was a reporter for the largest daily newspaper, *Addis Zemen*, at the time of the 1974 revolution. I bounced from one protest to another demonstration to report the news; and I remember vividly the many unforgettable events that followed early that year, bringing the collapse of the monarchy. In January 1974, random opposition voices started to be heard from different groups other than the usual student unrest. University student's protest erupted, followed by all high school students. The streets of Addis Ababa were filled with demonstrations. Taxi drivers went on strike in protest of increased fuel price; students demanded the educational reform plan known as 'Sector Review ' be cancelled; labor unions took to the streets over union rights and food price rises; teachers went on strike demanding higher pay.

In January 1974, an army outpost in Negele Borena, in southern Ethiopia, mutinied and arrested their officers. Their demands were better food and replacing the water pump that was broken. The officers who refused to allow the soldiers to use their water well were arrested. Emperor Haile Selassie was informed about the situation as he received a petition from the mutineers. The army general he sent as his personal envoy to investigate the matter was also detained.

The news spread to other military units. On February 10th 1974, the pilots at the airbase in Debre Zeit near Addis Ababa staged a similar mutiny; Haile Selassie promised salary increases to the armed forces, but on February 25, sergeants and corporals took control of the radio station in Asmara and started broadcasting grievances of the army demanding more pay and better conditions of service. In Addis Ababa, rebel officers took eight ministers hostage for corruption charges demanding they should be sacked; Prime Minister Aklilu Habte Wolde's cabinet resigned. Emperor Haile Selassie made more and more concessions and promised to fulfill all their demands; but could not stop the mutiny.

In the following month, the revolution spread all over Ethiopia including small towns and villages. One group after another took to the streets, including priests, Muslims, and women engaged in commercial sex. Ethiopian Muslims took to the streets of Addis Ababa in a massive demonstration requesting for an end to religious discrimination and demanding the separation of church and state. The outburst was in all provinces and towns.

While the emperor was trying to control the unrest with his loyal army units, radical junior officers conspired to take control of the situation. Different units started a series of meetings at fourth army division headquarters in Addis Ababa. They formed a military committee or Derg that had 107 representatives chosen by different units of the armed forces. The Derg issued a statement on July 4th 1974 over the state radio pledging its loyalty to the emperor, and announced a slogan 'Ethiopia Tekdem' meaning, "Ethiopia First." The Derg slowly started to dismantle the whole imperial structure by demanding that all former dignitaries and high government officials to give themselves up or face confiscation of their property including land and houses. At last, Emperor Haile Selassie himself was deposed on September 12th 1974, and all royal family members arrested; the military Derg assumed power.

What followed after the overthrow of Emperor Haile Selassie in 1974 was bitter sweet. The military government, Derg, and the opposition leftist groups fought one another and tried to impose socialist philosophy in a conservative religious society. They ignited more civil war, insurgency, 'white terror' and 'Red terror' that were responsible for the death and dispersion of millions of citizens. With no political compromise possible, the factions continued denouncing and killing each other and the civil war spread all over the country.

Almost all the political groups that came into existence with the spread of the revolution embraced Soviet-style socialism for the solution of the country's problems. Only one group, Ethiopian Democratic Union (EDU), was trying to bring back the monarchy. Even though all other Marxist groups talked about the same ideology, they could not agree on any one thing. They spread hatred about one another and their cadres started killing each other. No one wanted to question whether socialist ideology can go with the culture, history and beliefs of the Ethiopian people. None of them wanted to find a system based on the peoples core values and culture.

The military rulers (Derg) and other Marxist groups continued killing each other in the name of socialism. In the killing spree that was termed as 'white terror' and 'red terror' tens of thousands of young people, most of them students, were killed in cold blood. Every Marxist group claimed to be the genuine socialist ideologue and accused the others as revisionists. Each one claimed their differences as irreconcilable and therefore one has to eliminate the other.

Military Derg and "Red Terror"

After Derg took power on September 12, 1974 it soon changed the bloodless coup to a blood thirsty one. The Derg was led by a radical officer and a key figure, Major Mengistu Haile Mariam. On November 23, 1974 it ordered the execution of sixty high-ranking former officials who were prisoners. General Aman Andom, an Eritrean by birth who was selected to lead the Derg, and two former prime ministers, and the Emperor's grandson, were among the executed officials. This phenomenon sent shock wave in Africa and around the world. After a year, in August 1975, Derg announced over national radio that Haile Selassie died of circulatory failure. According to the royal family, he was suffocated with wet pillow and killed. His body was buried under a lavatory in the grand palace and remained hidden for sixteen years.

Colonel Menngistu and Fidel Castro - 1977

Major Mengistu Haile Mariam, according to his inner circle and associates, was ambitious, shrewd and ruthless. With his oratorical skills he easily connected with and convinced the non-commissioned officers and soldiers who were a majority in the Derg and made them his power base. He also created close links with some Marxist activist groups like *Meison, Wos League, Malreid and Echat,* who demanded revolutionary changes. In December 1974, Derg proclaimed that "Ethiopian Socialism" would be its official ideology. In January 1975, it nationalized all rural land; this move abolished tenancy. In July of the same year, it nationalized all urban land and rented houses and apartments, thus destroying the economic power base of the old regime. All large industrial and commercial companies were also nationalized, including banks and insurance companies.

Derg dispatched fifty thousand students and teachers, from grade eleven up including all college students and faculty members to the countryside, to spread the message of the new direction of the country and to implement the nationalization of land by organizing peasant associations. I have been travelling with three members of the Derg in western Ethiopia who were lecturing to the dispatched students and teachers about the goal of the revolution. The next day after the lecture that did not make sense, the students most of whom sympathized with the opposition groups, particularly EPRP, evacuated the campaign stations. I personally got in a problem with the group leader and Derg member Major Assefa Mekonen, who listening to my daily report of the group activities over the national radio thought I was not reporting in detail. In spite of my explanation that radio is not transmitting the whole report I am sending, he pointed to the trees in the vicinity and said "we can hang you on this". The camera men and other journalists who were there with me used to joke about it for a long time; that was Derg, always in conflict with professionals.

In the process, Ethiopia was engulfed with strife and turmoil. Royalists and landlords organized armed resistance group known as Ethiopian Democratic Union (EDU); ethnic based "liberation" movements like Eritrean, Tigray, Afar, Western Somalia, and Oromo "liberation" fronts were gaining strength. In Addis Ababa, radical opposition groups like Ethiopian People Revolutionary Party (EPRP) that had a huge support among the students, demanded civilian control of the revolution and embarked on a campaign of urban guerrilla attacks. It started terrorizing the Derg and its allies, particularly members of the All Ethiopian Socialist Movement (AESM), better known by its Amharic acronym (MEISON). Scores of officials and supporters of the Derg were killed by EPRP murder squad.

An assassination attempt was made on Mengistu himself, and he was slightly wounded. As a counter measure Mengistu and his Derg comrades organized murder squads and licensed civilian groups, leaders of urban neighborhood associations (Kebeles), and turned ruthlessly against EPRP, embarking Soviet style 'Red Terror'. Mengistu incited his followers to avenge themselves on EPRP in a rally at Addis Ababa Revolution Square, where he smashed three bottles filled with red liquid to resemble blood (representing feudalism, imperialism and bureaucratic capitalism). In his speech at that event he said *"your struggle should be demonstrated by spreading 'red terror' in the camp of reactionaries"*.

Urban warfare, assassination and indiscriminate killing followed and continued for over a year between the Derg, EPRP and MEISON for control of the revolution. The Kebele revolutionary squads and armed cadres (gangs) hunted down students, teachers, intellectuals deemed to be opposition to the Derg and MEISON. Tens of thousands died in the 'Red Terror'; as matters went out of hand, cadres visited past transgressions and killing the man to own his property or take his wife became common; and tens of thousands were imprisoned where they were tortured. Later, Derg turned against its MEISON allies and killed many of them, effectively wiping the young and enthusiastic intellectual activists who had greatly supported the progress of the revolution. A few years before its downfall, Derg assassinated more than a dozen highly educated and experienced generals who have been accused of allegedly participating in a failed coup. These and all the other highly skilled professionals and elites killed in cold blood were the cream of their generation, which the country could not replace in half a century.

There are a number of things we cannot deny which the military Derg has accomplished that were helpful to improve the life of the peasantry. The land reform of 1975 though has some problems, had freed the tenant peasants of the country from debt and the need to give 75 percent of their produce to the land lords. The literacy campaign unleashed in the 1980's was a great success in reducing the percentage of the illiterate population by a big number. I have met and interviewed adults for Addis Zemen newspaper who obtained their high school diploma, having started as a literacy campaign student. Ethiopia was awarded by the United Nations Education, Science and Cultural Organization UNESCO for the result achieved in this endeavor; and it was truly a remarkable achievement.

Among the many measures that the military Derg took that were beneficial to the majority of the Ethiopian people was making the people understand that they were the source of government power, not the monarchy. It preached unity in diversity and equality of all people, as Ethiopians first, no matter to which ethnic group they belonged; emphasizing class differences than ethnicity. Besides, government corruption was the lowest in the history of the country, especially when compared to the present EPRDF government. But, in the later years, peasants were forced to accept low prices for their produce, dictated by officials and forced to deliver grain quotas to the state run Agricultural Marketing Corporation (AMC). Derg wanted to make sure the town people and the army got cheap food at the expense of the peasantry.

In July 1977, Somalia launched a full scale war while Ethiopians were fighting each other in the hinterland. It occupied the Ogaden, and advanced to take over the towns of Harar and Dire Dawa. Ethiopia managed to push back and defeat Somalia decisively. In the meantime Eritrean People "Liberation" Front, EPLF has controlled most of Eritrea; and Tigray People "Liberation" Front (TPLF) was growing in manpower and arms. The youth running away from 'Red Terror' joined the "liberation" movements. Even though the Ethiopian armed forces pushed them back to their base, the momentum dissipated because of Derg's political poverty and its treatment of the military; enemy infiltration, sabotage and breakdown of command and control. All these conflicts forced millions of Ethiopians to migrate to neighboring countries, Europe and America. A mass exile of the Ethiopians started with the 'Red Terror' and continued with the civil war going out of control and covering many provinces. EPLF and TPLF went on controlling more and more areas. After a long civil war, Derg was ousted from power by TPLF and EPLF; Eritrea seceded and Ethiopia became landlocked.

30 Years of Civil War

As we have discussed in this chapter the reasons for Ethiopian exile or African Diaspora are numerous. Slave trade, colonialism, Neo-colonialism, inter-ethnic wars, regional wars, economic apartheid, human rights violations and injustice has all contributed to the plight of our peoples. There have been different kinds of hardship and disaster other than injustice and harassment that forced tens of thousands of people to migrate. Drought, famine, insurgency and counter insurgency measures are other factors for the displacement of millions of Ethiopians. The war with Somalia, insurgency by both EPLF and TPLF who at times used the people as human shield have caused incalculable misery and the plight of hundreds of thousands of refugees. The methods that the Ethiopian army sometimes used under the command of the military Derg in dealing with rebel activity and counter insurgency measures in Ogaden, Eritrea and Tigray have displaced tens of thousands of our citizens. Government forces launched a number of major offensives that lasted for several months in these areas and caused massive disruption.

I was embedded with the Ethiopian army several times, while fighting insurgents in Eritrea and Tigray and the war with Somalia. Even though myself and few other journalists who were at the war front were not allowed to independently report about the war, other than conduct interviews with captured fighters or those who give themselves up, we learned a lot about what was going on by having informal discussions with members of the armed forces and villagers. During informal discussions with high ranking officers over a bottle of beer, I learned about some of the hidden atrocities committed on some officers and the people by both sides.

I met Colonel Wubshet Mamo in Asmara and Keren, who was the commander of one of the four Mountain Divisions (Teraraw Kifle Tor) ready for "Operation Red Star". Since I know him when he was a university student and a roommate of my journalist colleague Girma Seifu, he opened up in his conversation with me and told me his confidence and his division's readiness for the challenge. He expressed his hope that the government will come with a political solution once we get the upper hand militarily. He also hinted his problem with the military bureaucracy where in his opinion there are some Generals who do not want the war to end. In a few weeks, we got news that his division disrupted the insurgents and controlled key strategic areas in a short time in the new war front of Kerkebet, south of Nakfa. Later there came a conflicting story, one saying that he was ordered to retreat from the strategic area; and the other he abandoned his division and they were defeated. In a few days he was accused of treason and killed in front of his army. Since I know this officer's integrity and love for his country, I cannot believe he committed betrayal. Here are a few of the high ranking military commanders I interviewed at the war front during the time of the "Red Star Campaign".

Brigadier General Wubetu Tsegaye

Lieutenant Colonel Eshetu G/Mariam

Lieutenant General Gebreyes W/Hanna

One summer day in 1983 myself and another journalist colleague the late Getachew Haile Mariam were chatting with Brigadier General wubetu Tsegaye the commander of the Nadew war front at his command post in Tiksi, just 15 miles from the EPLF stronghold, Nakfa. During our informal, off the record discussion over a cup of tea after a long interview, we asked him why some soldiers are wearing worn-out uniform and shoes. He seemed to agree that there is shortage in supply and inefficiency in distribution. We understood from his detailed response that moral is down in the army because of several years of fighting without break or change in location, which was not news for us. But, he also told us that the army at times used scorched-earth tactics, burning crops, destroying grain stores, killing livestock, burning pastures and houses, displacing tens of thousands of peasants. These harsh measures along with aerial bombardment, created havoc and drove away the local population to neighboring Sudan creating a recruitment bonanza for secessionists. Hundreds of thousands were forced to flee their country to save their lives; and many had no choice but to join the insurgents.

Reading between the lines from the conversation with General Wubetu and other officers, we felt like there is division, infiltration, sabotage and tag-of-war within the ranks and that there are certain elements bought by outsiders who do not want the war to end in favor of the regime in power. These elements disrupt communication, curtail or delay supplies to the frontline and inform the enemy about the next move and the position of the units, the number and type of weapons they have etc. If a certain Brigade register's victory in successive missions, either the commander is transferred or units are reduced to contain its move. Sometimes they are asked to retreat after they controlled a very strategic position with great sacrifice. Other times when they want to fight the enemy when it is in disarray they are told to stop and wait, giving time to the enemy to consolidate. If the Commander question about the wisdom of such orders, he is reprimanded, transferred, demoted or even arrested and court marshaled. Many of the soldiers seem to know some of these facts; and even though they have full confidence in themselves, were not optimistic about the war. It was heart breaking to hear such stories from the fighters at the war front; and many of us knew what was coming years before the end of the war.

On the other side, EPLF leaders abducted tens of thousands small children from their homes, persuaded families, villages and recruited them for a war of secession as *Keyeh Embaba* (red flowers). The kids who do not know the history of East Africa were brainwashed, persuaded and sucked into the war. I interviewed many of the captives and those who gave themselves up, and was profoundly shocked listening to their appalling story, and clearly saw that these youngsters need counseling. I knew that there were many child soldiers, but, hearing the realities from the child combatants themselves how much they were physically and psychologically ravaged was so hard. Some of these child soldiers suffered terribly from flashbacks, nightmares, about killing and combat (what the Americans call Post Traumatic Syndrome Disorder (PTSD) that they had seen and forced to do. I was stunned that their childhood had been stolen and they will never get it back. Most of all Derg was not willing and able to help get the counseling they need and deserve; in fact it wanted them to fight again for the government against EPLF. There was huge distrust that they might go back to join the secessionists or the insurgents might snatch them again; and they were not even allowed to go back and reunite with their parents to get the support around them and the counseling they desperately need.

Even though most of these teenagers were desperately trying to come to terms with what had happened and to pick up the pieces of their life, it was not easy under the circumstances. I can't forget one of my interviewee, Haile, who was seventeen at the time. Haile told me he was abducted when he was ten. His eyes were deep, very deep that they looked way older than he is. His mannerisms, the considered way he spoke, echoed all that he had been through. He told me that the insurgents came to his house a number of times to ask him and his parents so that he can join the secessionists. He was terrified and his parents had no choice as they had experienced repeatedly an all-consuming and paralyzing fear from the government and the insurgents. At age ten he was taught how to kill, abduct other children and he saw people killed until he managed to escape after seven years when his unit was scattered during a firefight with government forces and gave himself up. Since he was infected with the fear of re-abduction he told me he preferred to go and live with his cousin who is in the capital Addis Ababa. He had a plan to go back to school even if he has to learn with kids much younger than him.

I was touched by Haile, the way he was dealing with his life, his deep desire to go to school and live a peaceful, healthy, productive life. I had no chance to follow up what happened to Haile afterwards, but, I will never forget that draining and emotional day; I left him in silence not knowing what to say. He is one of the dignified young men and women and parents I had the privilege to interview at war fronts, whose stories are very similar.

During the civil war, the military Derg came with a plan to resettle over a million people from the drought-stricken areas of Wollo and Tigray to the more fertile region of south western Ethiopia; which sounded good, but, it was the cause of massive displacement of people. In November of 1985 Mengistu ordered the resettlement of 1.5 million people from the over populated north to the less populated south west. His main motive was not just to help famine victims, but also to depopulate areas of rebel activity and to establish new exemplary collective farms in the south west. He was heard commenting in one of his meeting with officials of the relief and rehabilitation commission and ministry of agriculture, saying that "if we dry the sea the fish will have no place to swim and will die"; thereby referring the rebels as fish. Many of the famine victims volunteered to go to the settlement areas when they were promised by government officials that they will be provided with new homes, electricity, running water, schools and clinics in a fertile land. When news spread soon that the local tribes are fighting the new settlers and the government failed to keep its promise, many declined to go. Things got uglier when Derg ordered forced settlement and thousands were rounded up from shelters and packed in Soviet Antonov airplanes, and trucks to the settlement areas of Gambella and Metekel. In the process families split apart and thousands fled from the relief centers and went to neighboring Sudan. Throughout the years of war and drought millions were displaced most of them ending up in refugee camps in Sudan, creating a fertile ground for EPLF and TPLF to recruit fighters?

It was during this difficult time that Somalia invaded the eastern part of Ethiopia, the Ogaden area with full force. The Ethiopian people suffered such foreign invasion and inter-ethnic wars for many centuries and they were one of the major causes of mass migration in all directions and economic destruction. The governments of the emperor and the military Derg only half-heartedly tried to find diplomatic and political solutions during the long civil war. Even though the government envoys and the "liberation" front leaders at times met with a mediator to discuss a political solution, whoever thinks has a military superiority walks away from the negotiating table. In the middle of all these it is the people who suffered, exposed to starvation and displacement. In the long history of Ethiopia there were major inter-ethnic wars for power and domination. Besides the thirty years of civil war there were other big wars like the rise and fall of war lords like Yodit Gudit and Gragn Mohammed (Mohammed the left handed). There were also a number of foreign invasions, twice by the Italians, the British, Egyptians, Turkish, Sudan Dervishes, and Somalia etc. All these wars have brought turmoil and displacement for hundreds of thousands of Ethiopians.

TPLF (Woyane) and Ethnic politics

The first original *Woyane* rebellion of Tigray started in 1942 in Raya province as a spontaneous reaction to a repressive system at the time of Emperor Haile Selassie. The revolt spread rather quickly to Wejerat and later to Enderta provinces. The imperial government with the help of the British air force bombarded these rebel held areas and caused a wide spread damage. In spite of the bombing the *Woyane* movement was not crushed and was in a strong bargaining position with the government.

In 1943 Dejazmach Gebrehiwot Meshesha along with a few other Adwa residents intervened as mediators and exploited the trust vested on them by killing and arresting some of the leaders of the *Woyane* movement. Ultimately Raya province was divided between Tigray and Wollo provinces, and the originators of the movement either killed or captured, the movement died; while Dejazmach Gebrehiwot and his fellows from Adwa were rewarded by Emperor Haile Selassie.

When Tigray People "Liberation" Front TPLF was founded in 1975, at first it became an Adwa native only club. Because of the legacy of resentment that Dejazmach Gebrehiwot and his Adwa associates left, it had difficulty to get acceptance by Raya, Wejerat and Enderta districts residents. By its inherent act of treachery, the front cosmetically inserted the word *Woyane*, in the Tigrigna version of TPLF. The harsh realities under the Derg regime pushed the Rayans to reluctantly side with TPLF considering it as a lesser evil. But, the Rayans who joined TPLF were seen with suspicion and many of them ended up as canon fodders, while others who raised questions about the movement leadership did not escape *Malelit,* the front's death squad.

The fall of the Derg and the victory of EPLF in Eritrea and TPLF in the rest of Ethiopia ended the thirty years civil war, leaving Ethiopia landlocked. The new leader Meles Zenawi and his TPLF comrades when they took power pledged that they will initiate a democratic government responsive to the needs of the people. The promise was broken before it even started. Being the editor-in-chief of a private independent news magazine "*Africa Qend*", published during the early years of the TPLF-led government, I have personally witnessed and tested the intentions of the leaders, with serious investigative reports, conversations and confrontations.

As soon as EPLF and TPLF came to power strange things started happening in Ethiopia and Eritrea. The de facto government in Eritrea kicked out all people of Ethiopian ethnicity confiscating their property. In Ethiopia some well-known individuals who were outspoken in opposing the secession of Eritrea were kidnapped from their homes and offices and were never seen alive again. Ethiopian radio journalist Sarra Mekonen was kidnapped in broad day light while walking to her home just one hundred meters from the broadcast house. Scores of people have seen her when four men dragged her to their car as she was crying for help and driven away. She was originally from Eritrea and a member of ELF who gave herself up to the Derg regime a few years back condemning the war of secession. Another individual, the outspoken Tesfamariam Georgo, originally from Eritrea, who repeatedly and unequivocally denounced the disintegration of Ethiopia was shot and killed with a silencer by unknown individuals who vanished in their car. Many more such citizens who stood for unity disappeared and the carnage continued for years.

All members of Ethiopian armed forces (war veterans), who fought for the unity and territorial integrity of the country were arrested for months with the pretext of orientation, and laid off without severance pay or pension. To save their lives some went to Kenya refugee camps, while some committed suicide; many became homeless and started begging for in the streets of the capital city Addis Ababa and around churches and Mosques. Some were begging in their worn out military uniforms with their medals on their chest or on the ground where they sit to beg for coins. These were war heroes obeying orders, giving their life for the well-being of the people; decorated for their extraordinary courage to defend the nation against Somalia's aggression and Eritrea's secession. The silent obedience of so many Ethiopians under such despotic circumstances was also puzzling, and needs further examination because it indicates in a tragic way the image of Ethiopia still stumbling in search of itself.

In 1993, the government violently broke up a peaceful demonstration by Addis Ababa University students who were protesting against TPLF and United Nations sponsorship of the referendum on Eritrean independence. During the time, United Nations Secretary General Boutros Boutros Gally was on a visit to Ethiopia and Eritrea concerning the upcoming referendum. One of the ironies of this clash is that the current TPLF leaders themselves participated many years ago in an earlier generation of student protests demanding democracy and the rule of law. When they were in the bushes, they used to condemn Derg in the strongest of terms whenever student protests were crushed by security forces. When they became leaders, it was a different story; they could not tolerate such protests.

I had assigned a reporter and a photographer to observe and record the meeting and discussions of the students that took place at the main campus of Addis Ababa University on the eve of the demonstration, and got action pictures of the protest and clash with police the next day. We published the story and the pictures on our magazine *Africa Qend* after a few days, exposing police using excessive force. This report became one of my charges at court along with fourteen other journalists, and the chairman and founder of the Ethiopian Human Rights Council professor Mesfin Woldemariam, who also reported the story on their periodicals. The charge was dropped by the government after several court appearances because of pressure from the embassies of western countries. According to the government report one student was killed. But several eye witnesses we interviewed that day and the following days told us that 17 to 19 students were killed and dozens, perhaps hundreds, had serious injuries. What was worse was the government told the students to leave the campus within 24 hours and closed the university indefinitely. Following the forced eviction, many poor students who were from the provinces joined the lineup of beggars outside the university campus and at the different places of worship (church and mosque).

This event created more mistrust. It exposed the new government as being no better than its predecessor. In fact, the growing consensus was that the only difference between Derg and TPLF is that this one is clever at concealing its evil deeds. It speaks the right rhetoric of democracy, uses the courts to make the move look legal, but commits the same human rights violations. Besides brutally repressing any opposition, the new leaders were indifferent to the lives of the people.

In 1991, when the TPLF troops took over Addis Ababa, most people's hearts were filled with the hope that tyranny might be over and democracy, compromise and tolerance will prevail in our historic country. But, that jubilation turned into trepidation and people watched in horror when the leaders of the TPLF sponsored the secession of Eritrea through the UN with a wrong wording of a referendum, asking the people to choose either liberty or slavery. They effectively approved and pressured the people to vote for secession and Ethiopia became landlocked. The rest of the country was divided into different administrative regions mainly on ethnic lines, without the chance for the people to discuss the matter. Opposition groups in the country and abroad requested for power sharing and discussion about their agenda and denounced the exclusionary process. But, whoever dissented was detained without court warrant or dispatched through show trials, by planting false evidences, and presenting bribed false witnesses and many others silenced. Again the government squandered a historic opportunity to democratize Ethiopia.

Ethiopia started bleeding again from wounds inflicted by its own brutal, power hungry and disconnected leaders. The hard working great people of this ancient country were grounded into dirt again by its selfish politicians. The western politicians who profess to stand for democracy kept on arming, assisting and financing a government that is killing innocents.

The TPLF/EPRDF leaders dismantled and demobilized the armed forces, the security and police of Ethiopia and replaced it with their own ethnic based militia. They disarmed the whole population and armed only loyalists and people of their ethnicity. The new proclamation forbids former members of the Workers Party of Ethiopia (WPE), members of former armed forces, security forces, and former leaders of urban dwellers and peasant associations to be recruited in the new force.

In effect the new military, the police and the security establishments became subservient to the party rather than to the nation. It is far worse than they were under the Emperor or the Derg regime. The dominance of one minority ethnic group in practically all government institutions and organizations has derailed the promised democratic process and created tension. The armed forces, police and security whose function was supposed to be defending the people and territorial integrity of the country, have been transformed by TPLF leaders to be uniformed groups that kill the very people they are supposed to defend. The repressive apparatus of the security service and police is particularly alarming; with the ethnic based regions unhappy about their leaders, TPLF seems to be planning to take the country down when it ultimately falls. The only hope is that the people of Ethiopia will stand in unity and say no to the possibility of this hidden agenda.

All crucial and decisive positions and major state activities were put effectively under TPLF/EPRDF control. Since the Addis Ababa conference that established the Transitional Government of Ethiopia (TGE) were selected and dominated by the TPLF and its surrogate/puppet groups, as a result their decisions and the 'Charter' they produced created a very unhealthy political climate. The participants of the conference were meticulously hand-picked by TPLF leaders.

The Addis Ababa conference could not provide a forum for airing views from different regions of the country and prominent individuals. The hope that representatives from various administrative regions would be invited to express their views and interests was not fulfilled. Participation was limited to a few ethnic groups and selected political parties; the Ethiopian Democratic Union (EDU), Oromo Liberation Front (OLF), Afar Liberation Front (ALF), Islamic Front for the Liberation of Oromia (IFLO), Omotic peoples party, and EPRDF itself. By the way, TPLF was morphed into the EPRDF by absorbing a number of satellite parties it created mainly from the prisoners of war in its fight to power. Some political parties like Coalition of Ethiopian Democratic Forces (COEDEF) and MEDHIN were excluded or barred because they were labeled as parties that did not renounce violence. However, strangely enough all other parties that were invited to attend have armed wings while the ones excluded have nominal or no armed wing at all.

The conference could be characterized as belonging to the armed Diaspora group not representing the majority of Ethiopians. The level of debate at the conference was very low and uninspiring. It was the usual litany or repetitive recital of oppression, beating dead horse, hindsight rather than foresight. Even though the conference adopted a charter that sounded good, but because of its exclusion of important parties and prominent people from the various administrative regions, its practicality fell in doubt. The hope of Ethiopians for a democratic all inclusive government simply vanished. The general amnesty decided at the London conference earlier with the presence of US representative Under Secretary of African Affairs Herman Cohen was ignored. This also poses a question whether the US was committed to promote democracy in Ethiopia or was just expressing its intent and does not care as long as the regime is obedient to its national interest in the region.

The good wording and attractive phrases that were included in the preamble of the charter, like *"ending all hostilities, the healing of old wounds caused by conflicts....shall make special efforts to dispel ethnic mistrust and to eradicate the ethnic hatred that have been fostered by the previous regime ...rescuing the Ethiopian people from centuries of subjugation and backwardness,...the proclamation of a democratic order is a categorical imperative,... the end of an era of subjugation and oppression,...a new chapter in Ethiopian history in which freedom, equal rights and self-determination of all peoples shall be the governing principle of political, economic and social life... such a government shall be elected and accountable to the people"*; all remained only on paper. Most importantly article one of the chapter adopted the United Nations Universal Declaration of Human Rights resolution 217 that *"individual human rights shall be respected fully, and without any limitation whatsoever"*

In practice the leaders of EPRDF did the opposite, and because of their ethnic politics the situation became worse and continues to worsen to this day. The EPRDF followed dramatically opposed measures that undermined public confidence. The land policy of the Derg is made worse by the new lease hold system which bars any private ownership of land. The principle and the underlying motive of the land lease policy of EPRDF meant to control the economy and the whole population and economically unseat the potential opposition. TPLF leaders are also using urban associations (*kebeles*) to spy and control the people. The nationalized private houses and apartments are not returned to their owners except in Tigray; thus two systems in one country. In effect EPRDF took total control of the whole economy and created a government controlled and dependent work force. Instead of rectifying the economic misdeeds of the Derg EPRDF continues with them as long as they serve its agenda of controlling the population. The Ethiopian Human Rights Council (EHRCO) in its publication of March 1995 on 'Democracy and Rule of Law in Ethiopia' states the following:

"*...In addition it has arbitrarily dismissed hundreds of thousands of workers from various government institutions and organizations, creating a large unprecedented unemployment of skilled and professional manpower. At one time eleven top specialist medical doctors were dismissed from their jobs, in a country which has an acute shortage of such trained manpower. The dismissal of about forty of the well-qualified and well-experienced faculty members of Addis Ababa University, the dismissal of numerous top ranking, trained and experienced managers and various professionals from different government posts and government controlled organizations have the same objective of creating dependency*". (EHRCO, March 1995, p. 19)

I myself was one of the fifty two senior journalists dismissed from the Ministry of Information in just one month after EPRDF took power. I have witnessed firsthand how skilled workers were dismissed and substituted by less qualified and less experienced political loyalists in all key sectors. EPRDF continued to control the national media (radio, television and major newspapers), just like its predecessors. After being laid off from government media, some of us established and started to

86

publish private independent magazines and newspapers as per the charter of the Transitional Government of Ethiopia. Soon after some private periodicals started to see day light, the freedom of expression was stifled and journalists of private/independent periodicals were harassed, arrested, tortured, fined and their publications banned.

These kinds of systematic harassment drove out more than one hundred sixty journalists out of the country. The EPRDF controlled government media promote exclusively one party rule and propagate against all kinds of opposition. The government used all state apparatus to consolidate its own power, not to empower the people. The hope of a possibility for democratic and accountable governance simply evaporated. In every key government organization they have more of their own ethnic group in high ranking positions of real power and influence than the rest. It did not happen by chance; it is not because they could not find capable and talented individuals from other ethnic groups; they did it on purpose. TPLF even interfere in the churches and mosques. Talking about this unfair reality is not ethnic hatred. We talk about such ugly reality because it has to be dealt with before it is too late. We cannot move forward as one people in such a way. The consequences will not be good for anyone. We can't afford to wait and see Ethiopia become another Somalia. That might be the motive of some in EPRDF, but, they have to be stopped. A mind that is focused on narrow ethnicity and village mentality cannot be expected to have magnanimity to govern such a multi-ethnic country. These narrow nationalist leaders cannot be expected to soar like an eagle, but slither like a snake attacking all that cross their path.

Another surprising pattern of EPRDF leaders is the contradictions of their pronouncements with their actions. They do this deliberately, with the pronouncement meant to deceive the international public and donor governments of Europe and America as if they are committed to the democratic process and free market economy. This deliberate policy of deception and acting in an obvious dictatorial manner will have unwanted consequences. Because ethnic policies of the EPRDF has polarized the population and is creating ethnic animosities, warning signs of a possible social turmoil is increasingly becoming apparent in Ethiopia. Its stand not to share power and hold real free and fair elections, suppressing basic freedoms and ignoring the call for national reconciliation and peace is a deadly error leading to violence and another round of civil war. As many historians say 'those who cannot learn from history are condemned to repeat it'. Peace and security rests on freedom and justice for all under the law.

All these dictatorial actions are driving away the professionals in a mass exile to Europe and America. The government does not seem to care about this either. In fact, EPRDF leaders seem to be pushing people out of the country in a very subtle way. Those ex-members of TPLF who know their previous comrades pretty well from the beginning of the struggle are not surprised in what they are doing now; they say it is simply an extension of what they have been doing all through. Two prominent former members of TPLF, Kahsay Berhe and Tesfaye Atsbeha, described their eye witness account of these shrewd leader's actions of murder and sabotage during the last three decades.

"Barbaric acts of murder, vile acts of cheating and lying were used as instruments to destroy   peaceful   opponents. These evil methods, after being rehearsed first within TPLF and then in Tigray are being widely implemented in the whole of Ethiopia at large. The mass murders of 1993 and April 2001 in Addis Ababa, 2002 in Awasa, December 2003 in Gambella, June and   November 2005 in Addis Ababa and many others were

*neither accidents nor unintended   mistakes,   but
continuation of the policies of the reign of terror by Meles
Zenawi, which can   be traced back to the armed struggle".*
(Kahsay & Tesfaye, "33years of TPLF & 32 years of Meles
Zenawi, P- 2)

Elections were held every five years only to confirm the
ruling party and its leaders, a good example being the 2010
elections where opposition parties were told lost all their seats.
To stay in power, the core political party TPLF drained away a
huge proportion of state resources to sustain the security
apparatus and the military that is composed mostly from its
ethnic social base. Leaders of TPLF/EPRDF and their cronies
have accumulated a lot of money by using aid money that come
from foreign donors, like most of African countries mafia leaders
who secure wealth and power through illegal means, amassing
money at the expense of the public.

The highly advocated political liberalization did not
bring economic success to the middle class because of the lack
of honest government, rule of law, democracy and open
economies. Government officials became more and more corrupt
as accountability weakened, public debate discouraged, free
press muzzled, judicial system emasculated and open political
participation restricted or banned. Besides using the state media,
TPLF established a party-run media center.

Most of all TPLF/EPRDF leaders exaggerate or
celebrate ethnic differences in Ethiopia. In the name of the
oppressed nationalities they advocate a kind of revenge instead
of reconciliation. In actual fact there is no genuine autonomy or
self- administration in the chosen federal regions; they are all
under TPLF control. There is also a question of how and why
these regions were formed, their boundaries decided and the
criteria considered all behind doors without the chance for the

Ethiopian people to discuss it. The prominent opposition politician Dr. Berhanu Nega poses a serious question about TPLF leaders ethnic-based federal regions.

"The existence of multiple identities in Ethiopia is obvious. For moderate pan-Ethiopian nationalists the primacy of ethnicity based on language (as opposed to religion or even specific cultural practice for example) is problematic as it will not answer the whole question of identity that prevails in the country. Such definition of identity, when insisted upon as a political basis, say for self- government, then bring a host of questions related to practicability. Why should we have nine ethnic based federal regions, when there are over eighty different language based identities in the country? Why is a Sidama with 3.5% of the population or a Gurage with 4.3% of the population is not a federal region with self-government rights, while the Afar (1.9%), the Benishangul-Gumz (0.9%), the Gambella (0.4%) or the Harari (0.2%) have their own self administrative regions? What should it mean if people want to categorize their identity on the basis of religion than ethnicity, for example? These are thorny practical questions. To raise these issues is in no way to undermine ones ethnicity or to belittle the identification of the group. It is only to raise the complicated nature of the issue we are dealing with and even more to emphasize the need for choice and reasoning to tackle these issues". (Berhanu, "Identity Politics and the Struggle for Liberty and Democracy in Ethiopia" P-15)

Meles Zenawi and his TPLF comrades tolerate neither opposition nor dissent. They are experts in making war, rigging elections, disabling the courts, suffocating the universities, suppressing the press, and making themselves extremely wealthy. Because of its narrow nationalist views, when EPRDF seized power, there was anarchic situation in the country for a short while and many Amharas and Gurages fled from the rural areas to the capital Addis Ababa. As the government formally introduced and began preaching its ethnic based politics by creating the new regions (*Kelel*), people that belong to other ethnic groups especially Amharas fled from small towns and rural areas to the capital for fear of executions by other nationalities. In actual fact with government encouragement some radical Oromos have killed a number of Amharas including priests in Oromia region. Until EPRDF started preaching ethnic politics and propagated a kind of revenge, all Ethiopians were living together in a relative harmony wherever they want without being harassed.

EPRDF's ethnic and economic policy and methods of reform have brought incalculable social and cultural damages in the Ethiopian society. The new wealthy class has developed a behavior that destroys the mentality of the youth by exhibiting abnormal sexual habits; the spread of discotheques, unusual dancing styles, the spread of drugs, shisha and chat, and the spread of dirty video shops, in the big cities. It seems that the government is up to confuse the mentality of the youth.

Ethnic politics and 'divide and rule' has been at the core of TPLF political philosophy to extend its economic and political power by sowing the seeds of hate and fear amongst the Ethiopian population. To get the support of the Tigray people (which was its social base), they spread propaganda saying that if TPLF is overthrown, Tigriyans will be killed by other nationalities. On the other hand, TPLF leaders threaten unity-loving Ethiopians that if they are toppled, Ethiopia will disintegrate like the former Yugoslavia. That seems to have been their aim when they divided the country into ethnic regions and are manipulating self-determination. Many people believe that the formulation of "the right to self-determination including and up to secession" in Article 39 of the constitution is aimed at disintegrating Ethiopia if they lose their grip to power.

To keep the population polarized, TPLF leaders deploy their agents on secret and coded arrangements to instigate conflict between different ethnic groups and followers of different religions. They have been doing this very often since they took power, the sole intent being to create division, fear and suspicion among the Ethiopian population. They instigated the eviction of many innocent Amhara people from different regions by sowing the seeds of hate; and rampant persecution and mass killing of Amharas have been common since the ruling party took government power. Targeting members of the Amhara ethnic group has been the preoccupation of the regime for a long time, because most Amharas strongly disapprove the secession of Eritrea and the disintegration of Ethiopia as a whole. As recently as March 2013, thousands of Amharas were evicted from Benishangul-Gumz region, with all their property confiscated, where they have lived for decades as farmers and businessmen. The barbaric action of targeting and evicting Amharas from other ethnic states is heart-wrenching and a horrific crime against humanity. The victimized Amharas were beaten and violently dragged from their homes and packed in trucks which transported them to the ethnic Amhara border and dump them with no food even for a day. The victims reported over satellite TV that in the process children died of suffocation and at least one lady gave birth in the forest and others were evicted with their newly born babies.

The government media tried to hide this barbaric act because such acts are embedded in the grand vision of TPLF leaders set for Ethiopia. They have been doing this little by little a few victims at a time from different regions since they came to power; but not on this magnitude. When the late Prime Minister Meles Zenawi said in his early days, "what is the Axum stele to the Wolayita and the Gonder Castles to the Oromo", he was trying to create the psychology of inward-looking ethnic nationalism among the people and weaken Ethiopian unity. The creation of ethnic based federal regions was not with the good intention to empower ethnic groups and help them promote their language and culture and do away with ethnic inequality; but to divide and rule. Surprisingly the Amharas who live in other ethnic regions if at all they are not kicked out, they are not allowed to vote, and not allowed to hold even a kebele office; democracy Ethiopian style!!

The forceful eviction of members of the Amhara nationality from Benishangul-Gumz region every year since 2013 is an obvious case of ethnic cleansing. While thousands of men, women and children identified as Amhara were forcefully removed from the region in 2013, 59 of them were killed when their overloaded truck overturned. Thousands of these farmers who were made homeless were living in the woods using self-made temporary shelters in the Amhara region near the town of Fenote Selam for several weeks at which time independent journalists were informed by anonymous authority that the government ordered Ethiopian Red Cross not help the victims. Because this forceful eviction of Amharas sent shockwaves across Ethiopian communities around the globe sparking anger and condemnation, the government ordered their return to their settlement areas back in Benishangul-Gumz. But, since they were afraid to go back and their properties have been confiscated burned and robed by the natives they couldn't resettle again.

The forceful deportation of people because they speak a certain language is a serious crime. This is not genocide; but, an obvious case of ethnic cleansing, which is "the systematic and violent removal of undesired ethnic groups from a given territory". Ethiopian lawyers in the Diaspora are trying to gather tangible evidences to report the case to the UN Security Council so that it could order the International Criminal Court to examine the crimes. Ethiopian authorities could be charged with the crimes of ethnic cleansing at any time. There cannot be any excuse like "resettlement program" or because "they destroyed forests" like the late PM Meles once said of the evicted Amharas from southern Ethiopia. If they commit any crime they shall be prosecuted for that damage; but should not be evicted. Any citizen of a certain country has the right to work and live in any part of his/her country; removing citizens from any part of their country is a criminal offense prosecutable as per national and international humanitarian laws. Ethiopia is a signatory to several conventions, including Universal Declaration of Human Rights, International Convention on Civil and Political Rights, and Africa Human and Peoples Rights Charter.   Besides mass evictions, the TPLF security force is said to have committed ethnic cleansing against Anuak people in Gambella, and mass killings in the Ogaden, Afar, Sidama, Oromia, Amhara, Gumze and other regions.

The ethnic policy initiated by EPLF and TPLF since they came to power and divided the country, has caused untold suffering to millions of Ethiopians in different parts of the country. Thousands of Ethiopians, including Eritreans who were married to Ethiopians, were expelled from Eritrea in May and June 1991. These persons were not allowed to take their property, withdraw their money from the bank, or even to take their best clothes with them. In the same manner, when EPLF and TPLF started their shameful war over Badme, Eritreans who were living in Ethiopia were dragged from their residence in pajamas and expelled immediately.

At the end of 1991, different ethnic groups that have lived in Arba Gugu Awraja of Arssi area were evicted with their homes, grain stores, barns, and churches burnt. Their property was looted and those who could not escape were caught and killed in the most brutal way. It was an ethnic violence with a religious twist directed and orchestrated by the EPRDF members of the area. When the Christians from the neighboring Menze Awraja retaliated violently, government troops intervened effectively. By the time, many persons have lost their lives and thousands have become homeless.

Similar atrocities happened in Metekel Awraja where hundreds of Amharic speaking people killed and thousands displaced and lived in temporary open camps at Menta Wuha and Chagni towns without shelter, clothing and medical facilities for months. In Arssi Negele Woreda non-Oromo residents were attacked, the violence instigated by OLF members that was sharing government power with EPRDF. Scores were brutally murdered, houses and crop fields set on fire, and livestock looted. People from the Gurage ethnic group were subjected to illegal and inhuman treatment and expelled from their homes and businesses in Ellubabor and Keffa regions in thousands. There are so many such stories that I personally learned by talking to eye witnesses and family members of the victims; some of the stories were published in the monthly *Africa Qend* issues.

As recently as 2016 & 2017, more than a million Oromos were displaced from Ogaden by armed Somali ethnic groups. Thousands of Amharas and Oromos were evicted from their home and livelihood in Benishangul-Gumz by the region's ethnic people. After TPLF annexed the northern Amhara provinces of Wolkaet and Kobo to be part of greater Tigray, it displaced thousands of Amharas and settled hundreds of thousands of Tigrayans. Those Amharas who brought up questions of identity and are asking for their children to learn in their ancestors language Amharic, and the provinces to be administered by the Amahara region are being arrested tortured and evicted; some killed in broad daylight.

TPLF's sinister motive and using its armed cadres to start conflict between Christian and Muslim Ethiopians that had been living together peacefully for many centuries had cost the lives of scores of Ethiopians including priests. The pattern of behavior and culture of deceit of TPLF leaders also includes taking cruel measures and accusing the victims for crimes the TPLF cadre perpetrators themselves committed. Its continuous interference in religious affairs is another face of the same coin. The regime is responsible for most of the social unrest in Ethiopia, and it has extended it to neighboring Somalia. The motive behind all these is to create animosity among the people so that they will not be able to unite against the tyrant leaders; when the people fight among themselves and stay divided TPLF will be able to stay in power and embezzle the treasury.

Crack down on all people to terrorize the population and teach them a "collective lesson" has been the blue print of Mele's regime. They have done it time and again before, and they will do it now and in the future, because that is who they are. TPLF leaders marshaled their cadres and security forces to keep on killing whoever they think is a potential opposition to their rule. The TPLF-led regime survives not because the Ethiopian people support the governance, but because of its spy network (which is estimated to be one to five ratio in the population), with multitudes of undercover agents in its payroll. The paid spy agents in the country, in almost every household and in the streets of big cities and in the Diaspora are ordered to inform their bosses everyday whatever information they gather from those they are supposed to spy. The articulate cyber agents are ordered to discredit en masse any article critical of the government to create the illusion that the article is truly opposed by the majority of the Ethiopian people.

The ruling party EPRDF is a front of four ethnic based parties organized by the core party TPLF itself which is the master-mind of ethnic division. The other three affiliates are Oromo People Democratic Organization (OPDO), Amhara National Democratic Movement (ANDM), and Southern Ethiopia Peoples and Nationalities Democratic Front (SEPNDF). TPLF is at the core of the ruling party EPRDF, using the other ethnic based parties to control the society.

TPLF created ethnic based surrogate parties through which it could project the illusion of regional autonomy and multi-ethnic federal state. These puppet parties are simply groups of opportunist individuals who are taking advantage to amass wealth in the name of their ethnic group. The Ethiopian constitution was originally engineered by TPLF leaders to divide, rule and control the population. Most of its chapters appear and sound good on paper, but its general application in practice have been minimal. Its provisions are systematically and routinely ignored or misused, abused or overlooked by the ruling dictators. The constitution and its applications have caused widespread dissatisfaction because it has created more conflict and animosity between different ethnic groups over administrative boundaries, land and resources, and budget allocations. TPLF ethnic policy has failed to resolve the "national question"; instead it has empowered some groups to rule with iron fist; thus ethnic federalism remains artificial.

Theoretically, and at the surface, practicing politics along ethnic lines seem to have no problem, and in fact allow grass root participation, raising political consciousness. But, practically it is difficult to successfully fight for justice, freedom and genuine democracy while being more concerned with one's own ethnicity. Most people have serious reservations about ethnic politics because ethnic parties are thinking within their own boxes of ethnicity, killing strong opposition politics. Ethnic based political parties exclusively focus and are obsessed with their own constituencies; they fail to see the big picture, raise issues about the country's future and its national interest. Ethnic politics sends a false signal as if there is freedom, inclusion and political participation. It does not contribute to peace and cooperation in Ethiopia; in actual fact, it is destructive and a time bomb for future conflict and war among the different nationalities. Ethiopia is much more than the ethnic groups and political parties; we must think and perform out of ethnic boxes and stand on the bigger, common platform – being Ethiopian/African. Ethiopians need to be nationalists with global outlook.

EPRDF's regime obsession with imposing its will illegally on every civic community and professional associations started early on in 1991 as soon as it took government power. The Ethiopian Labor Unions Federation, Ethiopian Teachers Association, The Ethiopian Orthodox Tewahedo Church (EOTC), Ethiopian Free Press Journalists Association, and Ethiopian Human Rights Council etc., were never free from interference by TPLF leaders. The Ethiopian Muslims community is the latest victim where the government tried to impose its will on the election process of its leaders, in its intent to control the faithful.

Using the mighty hand of regime operatives EPRDF has always been interfering and hijacking the process of organizing and selecting the leaders of civic, religious, professional and human rights groups in its aim of controlling the population. In most instances the associations were split in two, one of them always becoming pro-government by the intrigue of government cadres that infiltrate and bribe opportunist individuals in the unions. The pro-government unions are registered while the others are left to float. After we established the first Ethiopian Free Press Journalists Association (EFJA) the government tried several times to interfere and divide the association.

I was the first Secretary General of EFJA and we were forced to call urgent general assembly meetings because of a petition by some bribed and planted journalists who publish periodicals in the name of the free press while receiving under the table financial support from EPRDF. During these meetings the petitioners insist to change the leadership or dissolve it and merge with government media journalists association. Luckily we were able to explain and convince the majority of our members and save EFJA from falling prey to government imposition.

There is no academic freedom in higher-institutions, colleges and universities in Ethiopia today more than ever before. A number of university students who wanted to remain anonymous for fear of retribution explained to me and answered my questionnaires in 2012 explaining their situations as follows. TPLF spy agents create a climate of fear in these institutions and pressure every student to enroll as a party member in one of the four affiliate parties on ethnic lines. Whoever dares to refuse is considered as opposing the ruling party and will be harassed, routinely monitored and reported to the unprofessional notorious security force and could end up in prison. Non-members will have no benefits, no right to scholarships and very likely don't get a job when they graduate, as 90 percent of the economy is controlled or owned by the ruling party and its cronies. TPLF members get the best jobs anywhere in Ethiopia, while members of other affiliate parties are given lower position jobs in their segregated ethnic region (*killil*).

Scholarships for further studies abroad are given to students totally based on party and ethnic lines. TPLF members get the lion's share and the best scholarships to top universities, while the other members are given whatever remains. Scholarships from top universities are mostly not even announced or posted for students to apply. The scholarship committees are run by TPLF cadres or their loyal subordinates.

The racially intoxicated government and cadres have polluted the university atmosphere by dividing the student body as 'developmental' and 'non-developmental' students, the latter being party members. Once in a while these cadres are instructed to play the government's divide and rule game by instigating a fight among student groups on ethnic lines. As a result, students live in fear of the government and each other. They are not allowed to organize on non-ethnic line; those who tried to do so were reprimanded to say the least. One student who asked me not to mention his name, described university campuses as *"fenced lands where wild wolves chase a herd of sheep"*; it is that ugly.

The TPLF led government has been trying to control civil society groups including religious organizations by taking over their leadership. In 1992 it replaced the living patriarch of Ethiopian Orthodox Tewahido Church (EOTC) with its party insider from its own Tigray ethnicity. In 1995 Meles replaced the leader of the Ethiopian Islamic Affairs Supreme Council (*Majlis*) with someone loyal to his party. Most of the followers of the two major religions of the country still resent these acts.

The divide that the government ensued within the EOTC stands out as it is numerically and financially the biggest, the strongest and the most influential organization in the country. Until EPRDF came to power in 1991 EOTC experienced a time of relative tranquility with its sanctity faithfully maintained and the church enjoying a considerable stability and unity of purpose. After 1991 TPLF leaders interfered in the Holy Synod function of the church and managed to kick out the living patriarch Abune Merkorios with a death threat into exile, first to Kenya and later to the US, replacing him with Abune Paulos from their Tigray ethnic group.

In a letter dated October 8, 1992 and numbered 69/298184 the EPRDF regime illegally issued an order to the Patriarch to vacate his office at the patriarchate. Subsequently after two days His Holiness was forced out of his official residence by security forces on October 10, 1992 and remained under house arrest in an undisclosed location in Addis Ababa. Despite His Holiness's plea to the then president Meles Zenawi and the then Prime Minister Tamrat Layne, and the members of the Holy Synod against his forced removal, the regime orchestrated the appointment of Abune Paulos as the fifth Patriarch of Ethiopia in violation of the canon law of the Ethiopian Orthodox Tewahido Church (EOTC).

Patriarch Abune Merkorios was then forced to go into exile to Kenya from where in October 1993 His Holiness announced to all followers of the Orthodox faith around the world via radio and through a press release that he is still the legal Patriarch of the EOTC. All these events were confirmed recently by the then Prime Minister Tamirat Layne and the president, Girma Wolde Giorgis.

Since that time the Holy Synod was divided into two; one at home and the other in exile, till Prime Miniter Abiy helped for their reconciliation in 2018. The opponents of Abune Paulos criticize the pope as a narrow nationalist, for conscripting more new bishops from his ethnic group, and for appointing his loyalists to important positions. He was criticized for not doing much in expanding missionary work in Ethiopia and around the globe, and remained a controversial figure until his death a few days before the death of Prime Minister Meles.

The subsequent installment of the late Abune Paulos while the reigning patriarch Abune Merkorios was still alive was a violation of the church's canon law. The divide that was inflicted to the church in the aftermath, compelling millions of Ethiopian faithful to choose sides by creating two Synods, made it problematic for them to reconcile or forge united front to impact positive change at home and in the Diaspora. Thus the Holy Synod in Addis Ababa remained a political entity and /or an extension of the TPLF dominated government, controlled by some cadres of clergymen who take their orders from political leaders. The government's stubbornness to amend past wrongs even after the patriarch they preferred died, and their treachery to keep the population divided in all spheres of life has disabled the Ethiopian people to unite and use its collective strength to make a difference in all aspects of societal engagements.

Ethiopian Muslims, mostly Sufis, comprise at least one third of the population. During the reign of EPRDF a Muslim sect known as *Wahhabism* was imported from Saudi Arabia and started to pose a danger of extremism. To fight *Wahhabism*, the government imported imams from Lebanon representing Al-*Ahbash* movement within Islam and compelled Ethiopia's imams and educators to embrace and spread their teachings.

In 2011 the government invited a Lebanese Islamic sect known as *"Ahbash"* which was founded in Beirut by an Ethiopian exile to come and preach in Ethiopia. This group preaches obedience to government and opposes politicization of religion. On the pretext that the Islamic community is being radicalized by fundamentalists the government ordered all Ethiopian Imams to go to the meetings organized by the new comers threatening those who refuse with imprisonment. Government officials not only attended these meetings but also were allowed time to lecture to the Imams about "Revolutionary Democracy", the ruling party's rigid political doctrine. Since most of Ethiopian Imams are volunteers who worked other jobs to support their families resisted to attend these meetings and refused to preach the *Ahbash* version of Islam.

The government forced the replacement of these Imams by salaried adherents of this version. The Imams and their supporters organized peaceful demonstrations that spread across the country. The government responded by portraying the protesters as jihadists over government media, raided mosques with its security forces, dispersed demonstrators, killing eight people, arresting 29 Muslim leaders and charging them with trying to use violent means to create an Islamic state. From time to time government cadres have been infiltrating the peaceful demonstrators and provoke violence to prove its case by discrediting the movement, which has not worked. Christians and secular human rights defenders joined the protests in support of the Muslims and the demonstrations were growing from day to day.

Thus, the Ethiopian government which always wants to control civic society went to the extent of changing how religion is practiced in the country, by depriving both Christians and Muslims a recognized independent voice, in contradiction of the Constitution Article 27 that guarantees the separation of state and religion. There are extremist elements in all religions anywhere in the world today. We are not naïve to say that the same is not true in Ethiopia. But, the way the EPRDF government is handing the matter by curbing freedoms and harassing the majority of the believers is bottling-up ethnic and religious tensions; it is not the right way to fight extremism.

Ethnic and religious politics engineered by TPLF has poisoned the Ethiopian society so much that we need a lot of effort to get rid of this cancer that destroys the very fabrics that binds us together.

Tribalism

Tribalism is a very difficult concept to grasp; and even more difficult to find out why it has been messing up countries all around the world. To understand Africa fully well, it is important to know about tribalism and how it works in the context of Africa. It is sad that most African leaders use tribalism to govern by "divide and rule", and they act more like a tribal chief than a national leader. They condemn the practice in their propaganda and rhetoric, but in real fact they use it for power struggle and in day to day ruling of their people. Their national armed forces, police and intelligence agencies command and control are 90 percent from the ruling ethnic group, in fear of over throw.

Most African leaders are surrounded by their kinsmen and tribesmen in their cabinet, palaces, and even in their kitchens. Choosing their closest advisers and body guards from their own tribe or from the most primitive tribe that cannot speak the national working language and can't mix with the great majority of the population, they believe insures security. That is why instead of trying to educate their people that nationhood or African identity is much better and superior to tribalism, they preach tribalism so that their authority will not be challenged. The clan and the tribe are the most essential elements of African society for comfort and security. The leaders use this for the continuity of their rule and never try to consider power sharing. That is why central authority is weak and illegitimate. Kenya's former president Daniel Arap Moi though tribal himself, calls tribalism in Africa as *"a cancer that threatens to eat out the very fabric of our nation"* that binds us together.

Ethnic diversity in Africa brings with it several hundred languages, which make Africa linguistically complex. In black Africa, even though few countries like Somalia, Swaziland and

Lesoto are blessed with ethnic homogeneity, one religion, and language, they have what they call clan differences; which has become the cause of never ending civil war in Somalia. In most other countries there are very many tribes speaking different languages. In Ethiopia there are about 82 ethnic groups who speak different languages, in Nigeria more than 100, in Kenya 42, in Zaire (Congo) there are about 200 tribes, who speak 75 different languages and dialects. Africa has more than a thousand different languages and/ or dialects. Amharic, and *Oromiffa* in Ethiopia, Swahili in East Africa, and Hausa in West Africa are spoken by more than 30,000,000 people. Some African countries use European languages like English, French, Portuguese, etc. as a national working language. Being linguistically complex is one of the biggest hurdles preventing Africa to develop a true sense of national unity.

What happened in Rwanda and Burundi in the 1990's is a good example to understand how bad tribalism could be in the continent. In these two East African countries tribalism took the most extreme and disgusting form after colonialism. The two small countries have three major tribes, the majority Hutus in Burundi make 84 percent of the population. The Tutsis, tall, light skin with long narrow face, are 14 percent of the population, and Twa (pygmies) are only one percent of the people in that country. The minority Tutsi ruled the country for generations with the help of Belgian colonialists, subjugating the other as tenants. After independence the minority ruling Tutsis were worried that they might lose their power. In 1972 they came up with a plan to kill all educated Hutus and massacred about 200,000 of them in just a few weeks. The method of massacre stories they used is horrible. They dumped their bodies in mass graves, dug by bulldozers that worked day and night.

The same thing happened in neighboring Rwanda, also a former Belgian colony. When they gained their independence the majority Hutus overthrow the Watusi government and established majority rule. During the overthrow about 100,000 Tutsis were killed, and the systematic massacre continued up to 1964. The whole world knows what happened then; and the ugliest massacre that followed later in the 1990's. Hundreds of thousands of Tutsis and Hutus fled to neighboring countries, and where ever they are, even though much has changed recently, people are still living in fear that history might repeat itself.

The assumption of Rwanda's holocaust was simply an explosion of bigotry between the Hutus and Tutsis who hated each other because of what happened when each tribe took political power since colonial times. That is the way it is in many African countries, there are tensions between certain tribes. But, in 1994 again, it got worse in Rwanda because political leaders (criminals) who wanted to maintain their grip to power urged them to hate and kill each other. The killing was carried out mainly by the presidential guard and the agitation and propaganda call for more blood was done by Radio Mille Collines; it became the ugliest genocide in history.

"In the Rwandan case, the Hutus and the Tutsis are known to widely intermarry. The ordinary people lived at peace with their neighbors in the true African tradition. The problem is with the leaders who seek to create enclaves and territories for themselves; they find the ethnic card easy to play. They use these cards to saw suspicion, hatred, and fear in the hearts of their people, and literally lead them to slaughter their neighbors". (Nnimmo Bassey, To Cook a Continent, P- 72)

While the massacre was happening no African leader said a word about it, let alone condemn. No African leader broke diplomatic relations with Rwanda or Burundi. The Organization of African Unity (OAU), kept silent. No church or mosque in East Africa condemned the massacre. There was also silence in the part of the European missionaries in these countries. African Unity, that vague formula which brought together and passionately attached the men and women of the continent to defeat colonialism disappeared after independence, because the new leaders wanted only power and wealth for themselves using colonialist's method of 'divide and rule'. Thus, African Unity takes off the mask and crumbles into regionalism and tribalism.

The December 2007 Kenya's rigged elections ignited tribal war and thousands died, while hundreds of thousands were displaced. In a matter of two months Kenya has changed beyond recognition. Hundreds of thousands moved to their tribal areas where they felt safer. Government statement published in the newspapers read *"you have the right to reside anywhere in Kenya"*; but, no one believed that now. Had government abolished tribal favoritism and delivered its original promises Kenya could have been saved from the horrors of tribal conflict. Author Michela Wrong pointed out about the disaster in her book "Our Turn to Eat"; *"...under a system which decreed that all advancement was determined by tribe, such hostility entirely rational. Had all Kenyans believed they enjoyed equal access to state resources, there would have been no explosion"*. In 2013 ethnic violence erupted in the newest African country South Sudan. Because of power struggle between President Salva Kiir and vice president Reik Machar their two tribes Dinka and Nuer respectively killed each other in thousands; it is shameful.

Even though ethnic and language diversity has created a barrier that made the continent unable to communicate with itself, it wouldn't have been difficult to pick one of the languages spoken by the majority as a working language and encourage the people to learn it and understand each other. But the leaders are not willing to do so because they are using it to 'divide and rule'. They don't seem to care if the people understand each other or understand their leader, as long as they don't oppose his leadership. One can imagine what would happen if Mexico or South America or the United States had the same problem; Canada has a problem with only two languages.

At present tribal animosity like that of Rwanda and Kenya is brewing in some African countries where leaders use it to 'divide and rule', and it has to be stopped before it gets ugly. Ethiopia's TPLF led government stirred tribal rivalries for the last 22 years to keep itself in power; and the ethnic politics it institutionalized and promotes could tear the country apart. It is not unusual to have tribal feelings, but it causes trouble and is damaging to politicize and institutionalize it and issue tribal ID cards. In Ethiopia under EPRDF, citizens are obliged to fill their ethnicity in all registration forms and to get identity card; and the categorization is puzzling. Those who have parents of different tribes are not allowed to write both or register as Ethiopians; they are ordered to choose only one, their father's or their mother's ethnicity and ignore the other. It is that irrational.

Treating individuals badly not because they have done something wrong, but because they belong to a particular ethnic group is bad and wrong. Politicians should cease to stir up ethnic passions and instead soothe them and stop discrimination against their own citizens on tribal or ethnic grounds. Somalia, a country with people of one religion and language is divided into warring fiefdoms during the last twenty two years. Clans, sub-clans, and sub-sub-clans pursue bloody vendettas against each other, often fighting over grudges that are centuries old. Here all men carry machine-guns, and the men with guns make the rules.

Ethnic conflicts are not new to Africa. Tribes often fought over grazing pasture and water, but the battles were usually brief and local and reconciled later with the help of tribal elders. But nowadays tribal animosity erupts into large-scale bloodshed because it is deliberately inflamed by irresponsible and power hungry leaders. It is natural that many could nurse old grievances and bear grudges for the wrong doing of previous governments. But, we must understand that it is the leaders and not the nationality they claim to represent that inflicted the misery; that is what it was then, and that is what it is today. Julius Nyerere the first president of Tanzania and Nelson Mandela of South Africa are one of the few African leaders in the continent who showed unusual wisdom in tribal matters. Nyerere banned ethnically divisive talk from politics and even imposed a single official language, Ki Swahili, and urged every Tanzanian to learn it so that they could talk to and understand each other. Mandela fought against both white and black domination.

"During my lifetime, I have dedicated myself to the struggle of the African people. I have fought against white domination, and I have fought against black domination. I have cherished the ideal of a democratic and free society in which all persons live together in harmony and with equal opportunities. It is an ideal which I hope to live for and to achieve. But if needs be, it is an ideal for which I am prepared to die." (Nelson Mandela, at his trial in 1964)

Even though there are so many tribal issues in Africa nationhood is achievable, if there is a strong central government devoted for the wellbeing of the whole population. If we can get leaders who care for the people and are willing to share power and establish participatory democracy and a representative government with fair and free elections by putting nationalism ahead of tribalism, both unity and progress are achievable. The multi-ethnic nature of Africa/Ethiopia should be seen as a virtue and we need celebrate diversity.

Some population groups who propose secession and dividing their country into mini states should stop this senseless and risky proposition. Secession will only create new dictators, more destitution, and uncontrollably messy situation. The fundamental causes for desperation and resentment that lead certain sectors of society to secession is lack of justice, human rights, democracy, rule of law, greater autonomy and freedom of expression. The best solution would be to focus on struggling in unison to achieve our goal for human rights and dignity. Africans should stand together to defend their unity from internal and external threats and try to change the irresponsible, and reckless policies and dictatorial behavior of their rulers. If we stand united to address our political grievances, marginalization, deprivation, oppression and maladministration, we shall be able to achieve liberty and prosperity in unity in a short time.

Prime Minister Meles Zenawi

I was one of the journalists who attended Meles Zenawi's first ever press conference at the Republic's convention center in Addis Ababa in June 1991 soon after EPRDF took power. He was asked by one of the journalists that if the rumor that they are going to change the Ethiopian flag is true. His answer was quick and simple, but disrespectful to the flag and what it stands for. Swaying his hand, he said "we don't care about the piece of cloth, it can fly in the air; our concern is what is behind the cloth". Because he referred to the flag which is revered by many as the symbol of African independence and Ethiopian victory over Fascism as a piece of ordinary cloth, there was a lot of criticism haunting him for a long time. Since he came to power fighting alongside EPLF for the secession of Eritrea, and his mother being from that province, his comment suggested that he harbored hatred, and stands for the disintegration of the country and was alien to the psychology of the Ethiopian people.

As far as the power centers of western influence are concerned Prime Minister Meles Zenawi had been a linchpin against terrorism and "instability" in the Horn of Africa. Once viewed as "a new breed of African leaders" to emerge out of decades of African turmoil, a phrase used by Prime Minister Blair and President Clinton alike to describe the likes of Paul Kegame of Rwanda and Yoweri Museveni of Uganda, official western policy towards the late Prime Minister was ostensibly to lament his government's outrageous human rights violations in public while playing nanny behind closed doors. Indeed, the case of Ethiopia is another example of the clash between western values and goals. But, there is no doubt as to the wit displayed by Meles, who successfully proved indispensable to powerful interests concerned with the Horn of Africa. As a former left of left Marxist guerilla the transformation into a technocratic "think tank like" policy guru was seamlessly achieved, surpassing the precondition to be welcomed by those who rule the world.

Part of the benefits of being accepted by the West has been the flow of massive international financial assistance, a crucial factor without which even civil servants won't be paid. It's with this in mind Meles swiftly abandoned his Leninist ideology, though as we will see much of it remained intact. Nevertheless support garnered from a kaleidoscope of aid agencies and organizations has been relatively well utilized in terms of developing the physical infrastructure Ethiopia needs. Of course, paradoxically, this has been to the determent of democracy. Countless well documented research collected by many international organizations including the U.S State Department testifies to that fact. One of the concerns regarding the distribution of international food aid within Ethiopia was the *"conscience and systematic allocation of aid exclusively to supporters of the one-party state"* as reported by Human Rights Watch. In short, foreign funding is being used for the perpetuation of the one party state. For Meles and his long espoused strategy of "Democratic Centralism", in short Leninism, it's not hard to guess where such leanings emanate. A budding democracy is virtually impossible under the circumstances, yet as clearly shown growth has been rolling along, much like China and Vietnam.

Left to right: Meles, leader of TPLF and Issaias of EPLF partitioned Ethiopia

The cunning, technocratic Prime Minister Meles Zenawi is known for imprisoning his political opponents, messing elections, cracking down civil society, and withholding development assistance from non-EPRDF supporters. But, in the Western countries he is praised for his economic record and for being an anti-terror security partner in an unstable and rough region of the Horn of Africa. One cannot deny his wit to attract Western support and international donors whose money has benefitted Ethiopia while at the same time bolstering up his regime. But, Meles Zenawi's rule has been abusive and heavy handed and Ethiopians have suffered from a lack of civic, human and political rights. Meles was in power for more than two decades during which he ruthlessly crushed opposition leaders and journalists and silenced his opponents.

While Meles was praised for implementing a public sector-driven development model, he is criticized for all vital sectors are controlled by the government and most for-profit companies are owned by the ruling party TPLF and its members. International human rights groups have been complaining of Meles's increasingly repressive rule. But, Meles had managed to persuade donors that his authoritarian rule was necessary for the country's stability and development which many opposition groups do not agree with. They argue that no political party including EPRDF should own for-profit companies in violation of the Ethiopian constitution, and there should be a vibrant free market fair for everyone. His opponents argue that giving everybody a fair shot and playing by the same rule, with equal opportunity and shared responsibility for all, should resonate above all other themes; fairness, justice, rule of law, and democracy should be our core values to guide our endeavor for development.

Meles used 'divide and rule' tactics and brute force to crush opposition. He even outwitted longtime comrade in arms guerrilla colleagues and serious contenders in the TPLF and emerged as uncontested supreme leader of the party. He consolidated power by purging potential rivals and promoting those loyal to him. He strengthened the authority of the ruling party by cracking down on opposition parties and using counter-terrorism legislation to jail journalists and dissenters. The critics of Meles government were jailed, killed or chased out of the country. In the last decade more journalists were exiled from Ethiopia than any other country in the planet. The tactics he used was labeling dissents as terrorists; and he was always at war with his own people inflicting gross human suffering. Meles and his ultra-leftist comrades established a mafia like organization called Marxist Leninist League Tigray (MLLT) popularly known in its Amharic acronym (*Malelit*) early on within the TPLF, and eliminated hundreds who reflected different views. Meles not only supported the secession of Eritrea but pushed for it without formal open discussion and decision of even TPLF, let alone the Ethiopian people. Here is what two of the founding members of TPLF Kahsay Berhe and Tesfay Atsebha have written in their memoir of February 2008 under the title "Suppression in the name of Liberation".

"The phase of relative harmony was partially maintained by avoiding discussions on decisive issues like the secession of Tigray and the independence of Eritrea for which a tiny group of Meles Zenawi (who became a deputy member of the TPLF central committee in 1976) and his cohorts could not expect mass support. These two issues, which were never formally discussed in the TPLF and whose protagonists were not challenged at the right time have proved to be the main dangers to Ethiopian sovereignty. On the one hand almost all members of the TPLF did not rule out a voluntary unity of Eritrea with Ethiopia, while they were opposed to the Eritrean problem being resolved by force. On the other hand Meles Zenawi and his group were so obsessed with the aim of separating Eritrea from Ethiopia that their aim looked like a religious doctrine. Therefore Meles Zenawi resorted to imposing his redundant indoctrination in the absence of open discussion." (Kahsay and Tesfay, Suppression in the name of Liberation, P- 1)

The leader of TPLF Meles Zenawi, coming from a minority Tigrigna speaking people who are to be found in Tigray and Eritrean highlands, has ruled more like a tribal chief than a national leader and promoted the interests of Tigray at every opportunity in his early years. Using his power first as president and later Prime Minister, he tried to demolish the patronage networks of the Amharas (whom he seems to hate extremely) and cripple their business interests. That seems one reason why he does not want to return nationalized rented houses and apartments in other parts of the country except Tigray, as most of it belongs to them. Meles has a way of rewarding the faithful; the ruling party made available donor-supplied benefits such as seeds and fertilizers to party supporters while punishing opponents by withholding services. He constructed a business empire for himself, his party and his kinsmen in power and controlled all vital sectors of the economy. TPLF affiliate organizations became extremely rich by getting priority in government contracts, bank loans and bribes as corruption goes deep into the civil service. Meles built a totalitarian state complete with a cult of personality and zero tolerance to dissent. Just like Saddam Hussein of Iraq and Bashir al Assad of Syria he filled the country's top political and economic positions with loyalists mostly from his own Tigray ethnicity; some opportunists from other ethnic groups, and replaced the country's armed forces with TPLF militia.

Meles knew the interest of his western donors and presented himself as a staunch ally in the fight against terrorism by sending his army to intervene in Somalia and Sudan against the country's long term interest in the region. Under Meles it is true that Ethiopia benefited economically from its partnership with Western allies on security issues. Meles was smart at glossing over the party's misdeeds and crimes at home and boasting about its perceived economic successes. He knew how to create alliance with the west and with his leadership converted Ethiopia into a political and economic power house of East Africa. He built a strong party and a strong but partisan army. But, all these were marred by his human right abuses. He arrested or exiled independent Ethiopian journalists, and in spite of all these he received largely glowing reviews in the international media about his economic development efforts. His Western patrons knew of his crimes at home, including that he routinely denied food aid to non-supporters; and yet he was given unprecedented financial and diplomatic support because he was perceived as an indispensable ally in the fight against terrorism in the troubled region of the Horn of Africa.

Sadly, the West chose to look the other way standing for their vital regional interests rather than for human rights. International donors know what is going on in Ethiopia, but the U.S. officials and European counterparts ignored what they did not want to see. They bought the stability of the region that Meles promised. He sent peace keepers and helped negotiate peace in Sudan, deployed troops for counter-terrorism efforts in Somalia. But Somalia's diaspora politicians believe that Meles himself was creating problems in Somalia by using his 'divide and rule' tactics and bribing a few warlords keeping it unstable thereby increasing his importance for the region stability. Immediately after his death more than eighteen members of parliament in Somalia who were close associates of Meles were dismissed from their membership after their relationship and what they did to divide the country was exposed in a parliamentary debate. It was sited that he often sent them airplane to bring them to Addis Ababa where they met with Meles and given directives and money. It is time for the international community to insist on respect for human rights in Ethiopia that it never should have abandoned in the first place.

"For decades, the United States has struggled with valuable allies who were intolerant dictators at home. The Cold War often provided a reason to look the other way; so did the need for oil imports. Over the past decade, the war on terrorism offered a similar pretext. The world is full of trade-offs and tough choices. But the passing of Mr. Meles ought to underscore once again that, no matter the imperative for embracing a tyrant, it is essential and healthy to declare: Democracy and human rights are universal values, not to be forgotten with the next aid check". (The Washington Post – editorial, August 23rd 2012)

Meles had the potential and the historic opportunity to unify the country and the Horn of Africa by putting in place a genuine federal democratic system. Instead he preferred to use underhand tactics to decimate the budding civil society and free press which are so critical to build an accountable, transparent and democratic system. In a desire to protect his reign Meles grew more and more repressive. Under the guise of national security he ordered his parliament to pass a number of legislation to stifle dissent and control the country's vital sector of the economy including rural and urban land which he put on lease. Amnesty International called the anti-terrorism law "*effectively criminalizes freedom of expression*". United States State Department human rights report notes that the government is becoming more repressive every year. Many wonder why he chose that road when he could do much better and had the potential; some even doubt his love for Ethiopia and its people. The second most populous country in Africa is now more ethnically divided than ever before.

"*Meles was shackled by engrained personal hatred for the history of Ethiopia and strong prejudice against those outside of his ethnicity to emerge as a visionary unifying leader for all Ethiopians. His dogged championship of parochial ethnic/tribal dogma in a multiethnic and multi-religious society and intolerance to dissent impeded what he could have accomplished by way of charting a democratic course for Ethiopia and attaining that rare coveted place for himself in the country's history*". (Ferda Molla, August 2012- Ethiomedia)

After the news of his sickness and later his death many Ethiopian intellectuals who wrote about his legacy hoped the possibilities of a compromise and national reconciliation. But the new leadership looked the other way and by dramatizing his death and burial, trying to create an image of a great leader like Stalin of Soviet Union and Kim Il Sung of North Korea, they seem to be tempted to employ even more brutal measures to suppress dissent. The ruling party leaders who benefited from his rule tried to hide his illness and death for several weeks, to buy time to choose a successor with the desire to maintain the status quo and ensure stability. They used the time having meetings of their party at all levels including in the armed forces and the *kebeles* preparing for country-wide mourning. For a country as poor as Ethiopia the parade, the display, the fanfare, and the ceremony was excessive.

There was a fear that it might provoke a lot of trouble with different parties and opposition groups competing to take his place. Having committed so much human rights abuse for decades Meles was lucky to be buried like a national hero. As author Michela Wrong said *"eulogizing late leaders, while glossing over their very obvious faults, is something you see across the world"*. There are those people from the ruling party ethnic group that truly mourned the death of Meles because they have common and vested interest in the survival of the TPLF regime. There are also those opportunists at home and in the Diaspora that were given land and confiscated (stolen) property and are connected to the ruling party who felt sad and disturbed. These are people who are easily coopted or blackmailed into obedience for fear of losing their vested interest. Some others from the silent majority were so naïve and joined the cry fest for a fallen dictator without examining the truth, his record, crime against humanity, war crimes, arresting, killing, his spreading of fear by warning to cut their fingers and making fun of his opponents and how he used his power to suppress democracy. In his watch routine use of torture by police, prison officers, security forces, and the military against peaceful protesters, students, opposition party members, alleged supporters of insurgent groups has been a deep concern for 'UN committee against torture' who gave a lengthy report about it in 2010.

Even though he has fostered a friendlier environment for foreign investment many say he has gone too far giving away land to foreigners, not caring about the environmental consequences and displacing indigenous people. In spite of the economic growth, wealth disparity between the rich and the poor is growing wider, the middle class is disappearing and most of the people are growing poorer. In his watch thousands of peasants and pastoralists have been forced out of their ancestral land into under-serviced villages and the wilderness while the land was given to foreign agro-business investors. The economic agreement he made with Eritrea was rediculez. Here is what Worku Abera (PHD) wrote how Meles failed to protect the interests of the Ethiopian people when he made private trade agreement with Eritrea's leader Issayas Afewerki as they came to power. *"The people of Ethiopia lost their resources, financial assets, and sovereignty. By contrast, the EPLF gained wealth, power, and influence. Lastly, it was a historically unique arrangement in which a foreign government appropriated the wealth of another country with the full collaboration of its national government. Never in history have we witnessed such an exploitative economic arrangement as the one that existed between the EPRDF-ruled Ethiopia and the EPLF-ruled Eritrea during the 1991—1998 period"*. (Worku Aberra) PHD

The bottom line on Ethiopia was also clearly stated by Global Financial Integrity: *"The people of Ethiopia are being bled dry. No matter how hard they try to fight their way out of absolute destitution and poverty, they will be swimming upstream against the current of illicit capital leakage."*

The paradox of Meles legacy is that he has done much to disintegrate Ethiopia and keep it landlocked and to simultaneously help and hurt the Ethiopian people by advocating minority rights in theory and suppressing all.

Meles has undoubtedly shown amazing economic development, even though those who benefited most are his kinsmen and political loyalists. Meles began an ambitious national reconstruction program financed by the West and also China. But, most engineers agree that he marshaled his cadres to sacrifice quality just to achieve some of the benchmarks for the Millennium Development Goals in vital infrastructures like roads, energy, education, health, and poverty alleviation. Most of the colleges and clinics built lack the necessary equipment and professionals to fulfill their objectives.

Thus, the program that was supposed to spur the country's economy created wealth only to the ruling party and loyal supporters while the rest of the population grew poorer; and now 80 percent of Ethiopian families remain mired in extreme poverty. At the same time Meles mercilessly crushed opposition and dissent and resisted democracy. At one point he even challenged the relationship between political freedom and economic dynamism saying that "there is no direct relationship between economic growth and democracy", referring to China's economic growth under tight communist party rule.

"As they say give the devil it's due ... no one in Zenawi's party can match his intelligence, intellectual agility, shrewdness or plain street smarts. Zenawi stayed in power for 21 years by outwitting, outfoxing, outsmarting, outmaneuvering, out politicking, out tricking, out finessing, and outplaying not only every one of his opponents but also rivals in his own party. But he has his own contradictions. He had sharp intellect but lacked insight; he had ideas but lacked vision; he was smart but not judicious; he was shrewd but not perceptive; he was single minded in his goals but pursued them obtusely. He was driven but lacked conscience or compassion. He pursued politics with depraved indifference. He was a man of many vices and few

virtues". (Professor Alemayehu Gebremariam, Ethiomedia –
August 2012)

Meles promised democracy and human rights when he
took power in 1991. But, as the years roll bye he became
increasingly repressive and in the end he became as tyrannical as
the tyrant he replaced. He created a police state with massive
security network of spies (cadres) and surveillance technology
brought from China. He criminalized press freedom and civil
society institutions like labor unions, student unions, teachers
unions, human rights organizations, free press journalists
associations etc., and organized unions loyal to TPLF and spread
fear that penetrated every family in Ethiopia. He was loved and
admired by his supporters, but feared and hated by his
adversaries.

Where did Meles want to take the country? This man
was always rigid, uncooperative, dictating everyone and
unwilling to compromise. He had an economic agenda based on
winner-take-all policy while the rest of the people are by their
own. He made everything available to his cronies and the rest are
left out. Land belongs to the government, the regime is the
number one employer in the country and essential items like
flour, sugar, oil, and others are regulated by the *kebeles*. The
average Ethiopian is a prisoner in his own land. He never desired
to build a country of shared prosperity and shared responsibility
where everyone played by the same rules. His party loyalists
benefited and profited while others were chipped, squeezed and
hammered. He allowed his party owned for-profit companies to
have priority for government contracts making money without a
moral compass.

He did not just disagree with concerned Ethiopian
intellectuals; he hated them, made fun of them over the media he
control, and threw them to jail. Meles and his party claimed to

121

have won 99.6 percent of the seats in parliament in the 2010 elections. Such electoral victory is a mockery of democracy and electoral politics. During the last 21 years unashamed Meles played a "zero sum game" where he won all the time and everyone lost all the time. Professor Gregory Stanton who leads the global alliance to end genocide said *"the legacies of Meles Zenawi were full of atrocities, gross human rights violations, mass displacement and minority rule. His divide and rule system has greatly fractured Ethiopia and at the detriment of national unity"*. He left us a total mess of a polarized society by his 'divide and rule' ethnic politics that we have to clean up.

Many Ethiopian intellectuals believe that Meles had an agenda, and he was a man of mission, but not vision. He was a man of absolute power. He was the policeman, the law, the judge, the jury, and executioner. During his reign independent judiciary, political pluralism, inquisitive journalism and free press, independent advocacy groups or public consultation were not allowed to function. He missed the opportunity of being an exemplary leader. He could have forged a strong and united Ethiopia; but, he preferred ethnic fragmentation and division to divide and rule. He was not forgiving or tolerant, and never admitted his mistakes. He had the impulse like Gaddafi, Mubarak, Assad, Saddam Hussein, Stalin, and Kim Il Sung who believed in building roads, dams, and high rises; waged war here and there to make them great, and at last they all went into the dustbin of history.

Meles's legacy is the disintegration of Ethiopia giving us a landlocked country, and tarnishing our millennia long history. Even though he helped the people to get rid of the brutal and stubborn Derg regime, and being able to attract western donors has shown amazing infrastructure and economic development from which his cronies benefited most, he failed to deliver in all other spheres. Ethnic cleansing, arrest and torture of tens of thousands, assassination/elimination of hundreds of opposition activists by security forces, killing peaceful demonstrators en masse, toiling peasants in serfdom, inter-ethnic hatred, rigged elections, blocked freedom of expression and forbidden academic freedom, demoralized youth addicted to psycho thermal drugs, unemployment and abject poverty, inflation, corrupt practices, embezzlement of the national treasury and diverting donor fund, rampant breach of the constitution, economic apartheid, multi-party rhetoric but in practice one party dictatorship, and party owned for profit companies, a large fertile land seceded to Sudan, leasing virgin lands to foreign investors for the lowest price ever, displacing indigenous tribes, cross border wars, ethnocentric dictatorship and a polarized society, colonial-like divisive grip and ethnic politics (a time bomb for regional instability and further disintegration of Ethiopia/ East Africa), are his legacies.

But, we have to accept the truth that the faults and vices we ascribe to Meles are not his alone; they are ours also, because we did not do enough to stop or change the course. It is said that people get a government they deserve. Instead of struggling together for the common good, democracy and justice we fight among ourselves on ethnic lines following his agenda; shame on us! We only hope that his successors and all of us will learn from these mistakes and strive for love, tolerance and compassion towards one another and build Ethiopia on a solid foundation of democracy. It needs a visionary leader and a persistent struggle by all the people to save Ethiopia and the Horn of Africa from catastrophe.

Prime Minister Hailemariam Desalegne

Ethiopia got a new prime minister several weeks after the death of Meles. The new Prime Minister Hailemariam Desalegne faced extraordinary challenges. The biggest challenge was to come out of Meles's shadows and become his own man. Personally he seems to be a good guy; the question by many politicians was, will he be able to do that with the big power brokers behind the scenes? Being a member of a minority nationality, many people doubted that he might not be able to maintain an independent base of support and might be forced to rely on those TPLF elites who control the military, the police, the security forces and 90 percent of the economy. His appointment seemed to be a trick by the power brokers to console the people and to calm international donors into continuing to give out billions of dollars in aid.

The end of Meles Zenawi's autocratic rule appeared to offer another historic opportunity. But, TPLF was not ready to make a real democratic turn? TPLF has squandered such an opportunity when it took power in 1991 and again in the aftermath of the 2005 elections. It was naïve to expect that they could allow the new Prime Minister Hailemariam, if at all he was willing, to lead the necessary change and reform. They reduced him to bow down to their dominance and ensure the continuation of the status quo?

Hailemariam himself who was coached by Meles might have been thoroughly conditioned into the priorities, ideas, goals and practices of TPLF and many guessed he might prefer to remain in his ex-boss's shadow. What we could learn from the speech the new PM made after he took oath of office is the determination to continue with what he said was Meles's vision of "democracy" and "development". He failed to engage the opposition in a power sharing discussions and continued with the political stalemate of ethnic fragmentation and division.

With the titan gone and the ruling party EPRDF leaders disturbed by the Arab Spring and the death of their supreme leader, they become increasingly repressive and turned the screw to strengthen their grip on power. They seem to be particularly frustrated by the regular protests of the diaspora exposing EPRDF's human rights abuses to their donors. With no hope that future elections can produce change of leadership, there came an increased pressure for an inclusive unity government with wide spread unrest and violent revolt all around Ethiopia. TPLF monopoly of power was shattered; the state of emergency that lasted nearly a year could not break the systematic civil disobedience that paralyzed the capital city and the whole country. The struggle gave way to the liberal progressive members of the front to come up the ladder and sit at the helm of power. With a protracted struggle by the people of Ethiopia at home and the diaspora, Prime Minister Hailemariam resigned after 5 years.

<u>Prime Minister Abiy Ahmed</u>

After a strong inner-party democratic struggle, in 2018 Ethiopia got a new visionary leader Dr. Abiy Ahmed, who started to take the country in a new and promising direction. But, being a member of EPRDF, the same questions linger again in the minds of Ethiopians. Will he help us build a real pluralistic democracy to create an inclusive political system and an effective party system that help to produce socially desirable alternatives? Will he get rid of extractive economic and political institutions and build real democratic ones? Is he trying to save us from polarization and ethnic politics or trying to save EPRDF, or both by following the right path? Is he truly trying to create equality among ethnic groups or replace one ethnic domination by another with the motto of "our turn to eat"? Only time will tell! We only hope that reason will prevail over political opportunism.

He preaches love and forgiveness more like a pastor than a political leader. But, it is okay for people who were looking for an optimistic and unifying visionary leader, as long as he is able to control peace and order and move in the right direction to create a new democratic Ethiopia. When we see some of his appointees for high office, we can't help thinking that, are there not better candidates or is he infatuated to make some kind of history? His concern should be their resume, performance and character, not ethnic, religious or party affiliation; or gender preference. Besides, what about those who embezzled the country's treasury, killed thousands, arrested and tortured tens of thousands, displaced millions from their homes and livelihood, are they going unpunished? Justice should be served!!!

EPRDF is experienced in rigging elections, buying votes, dispensing patronage, and engaging in corruption including government contracts and jobs in exchange for political support. Examining the political history, ideology and practice of the *woyanes* EPRDF, and its control of the economy, many are skeptical of a possible turn of events towards real democracy or giving up its monopoly of power. The only force that will bring about such a change is the increasing and change inducing pressure from the Ethiopian people, both at home and in Diaspora, and the strength and united struggle of the opposition. All concerned should seize the opportunity and work for a transition to a more free, inclusive and just political order.

Human Rights, Rule of Law and Due Process

Human rights are the fundamental rights of individuals, the right to equality of communities and the civil rights of citizens with respect to their governance. These rights are enshrined in the UN International Bill of Human Rights and everyone has these inalienable rights irrespective of race, religion, color, sex, language, national origin, political opinion, wealth or other status. Human rights, rule of law and due process are inseparable. Besides, there are what we call civil rights, political, cultural, economic and social rights; rights given, defined and circumscribed by laws enacted by people's governments. All these rights are based on the fundamental individual rights, and there cannot be rights that are not based on the rights of the individual.

Human rights violations are the breach or infringement of the above rights in actions of commission or of omission by government officials or security forces. Violations should not be perpetrated by government law enforcement agencies that are supposed to ensure respect for those rights. The Ethiopian Human Rights Council (HRCO) has been dealing with different kinds of rights violations by government agencies in Ethiopia since it was founded in 1991. Extrajudicial killings, torture, involuntary disappearance, Arbitrary detention, defiance of court order, violation of property rights, violation of civil service laws, and prisoners of war rights violations by EPRDF security forces have been reported numerous times to HRCO and to free press journalists. HRCO has published a long report on such violations every six months with the dates, names, and addresses of most of the victims including some photos. It has demonstrated with sufficient evidence that the EPRDF rule in the last 27 years has been marked by gross violations of human rights, total disregard to the rule of law and due process. The promised democratic process has been derailed and the pronouncements or the rhetoric of EPRDF leaders have not been matching their deeds.

EPRDF leaders have consistently shown a manner of deception, and that seems deliberate to most Ethiopians. They talk about the virtues of the rule of law and due process, but on the other hand they are acting consistently in an illegal manner. They express the gross violations of human rights by the Derg regime with moral indignation, but they act in a way that is similar to the Derg. They say that they are committed to the democratic process and a free market economy, but act in an obviously a dictatorial manner. Their pronouncements on the one hand and their actions on the other, so contradictory and demonstrates a pattern that seems deliberate. Many intellectuals say that the pronouncements are meant for propaganda to the Europeans and the United States, while their actions are intended to show the Ethiopian people that they have to abide by the EPRDF rules and policies whether they like it or not.

There is absolutely no rule of law and no independent judiciary; and EPRDF leaders have become inflexible and treat others as objects. The ethnic politics they designed serves only their classic policy of 'divide and rule'. The gross violations of human rights and total disregard of the rule of law and due process, is derailing the promised democratic process. EPRDF's pronouncements about democracy are only meant to appease donor countries; and the action at home on the people is contradictory. The rhetoric about multi-party democracy is not supported in action, and no political party is allowed to operate freely in any part of the country. Particularly multi-national parties are discouraged and weakened by infiltration and other means. The EPRDF led government law enforcement agents committed all kinds of violations; genocide, massacre, arbitrary detention, torture, involuntary forced disappearance, violation of property rights, and extrajudicial killings. There are so many such eye witness account stories, written in the back issues of private independent news magazines including Africa Qend, and HRCO's regular and special reports. Western democratic countries and International human rights organizations also repeatedly condemned such abuses in their press releases and official annual reports; but nothing changed.

I myself was arrested three times at the "Federal Police Crime Investigation Center" better known in its Amharic name

(*Maekelawi*), allegedly for 'inciting' the public. I have faced intensive unprofessional interrogations and verbal threats, luckily I was not tortured. During my stay there I talked to many victims of torture. Some have gone through a variety of torture methods which the interrogators used to extract information and confessions from these opposition politicians, their supporters, protest organizers or alleged supporters of ethnic insurgencies. These detainees were repeatedly slapped, punched, kicked, beaten with gun butts and sticks. Some were forced to painful stress positions, being hung upside from the ceiling. Some were locked in one of the torture chambers like the dark room (*Chelema Bet) for solitary confinement*, others in the wooden house (*Tawla Bet*) which is infected with flees, and access to daylight is restricted.

United States Department of State, Bureau of Democracy, Human Rights and Labor have always criticized the Ethiopian government in its annual Country Report on Human Rights practices. In its 2012 report it has pointed out the most significant human rights problems as, *"...restriction on freedom of expression and association through politically motivated trials and convictions of opposition political figures, activists, journalists and bloggers as well as increased restrictions on print media"*. In the 41 pages report of 2012, the department has described in details various ways of human rights abuse committed by government forces, citing dates, places, individuals and groups who are victims of such practices.

"Other human rights problems included arbitrary killings; allegations of torture, beating, abuse, and mistreatment of detainees by security forces; reports of harsh and at times life-threatening prison conditions; arbitrary arrest and detention; detention without charge and lengthy pretrial detention; a weak, overburdened judiciary subject to political influence; infringement on citizens privacy rights, including illegal

searches; allegations of abuses in the implementation of the government's "villagization" program; restrictions on academic freedom; restrictions on freedom of assembly, association and movement; alleged interference in religious affairs; limits on citizens' ability to change their government; police, administrative and judicial corruption; ..." (US Department of State – Bureau of Democracy, Human Rights and Labor, -2012)

EPRDF law enforcement agencies have caused untold suffering of thousands of persons in different parts of the country. Ato Assefa Maru who was the executive committee member of the Ethiopian Teachers Association ETA and a member of EHRCO was killed by government security forces in the capital while he was walking to his office on May 8, 1997 at 8:20 A.M. According to eye witness report to EHRCO and independent newspapers, about a dozen policemen in two vehicles approached and blocked him; and a policeman from the back seat fired a volley of shots with an automatic gun, killing Ato Assefa. At lunch time news, government radio reported that Ato Assefa was the new leader of an anti-peace group which called itself Ethiopian Unity Patriotic Front and was killed while trying to escape. It begs a question; he was unarmed, alone and walking, why didn't they arrest him? The truth is that, Assefa Maru was killed because he was an unrelenting advocate of freedom of association and individual rights. The security forces arrested other executive committee members of ETA, and the next day they broke the door locks of ETA office and took away various documents; but found nothing to prove their claim. Alebachew Goji was beaten and tortured to death while in police custody in July 1994; Mustaffa Idris mysteriously disappeared the same year never to be seen again. This is not the first or the last extrajudicial killings by EPRDF security forces, hundreds if not thousands have been gunned down the same way and no one was brought to justice.

I personally interviewed a number of victims and published the stories of some of them in *Africa Qend* magazine, while some others refrained for fear of reprisal by government security forces. One of my interviewee, an eye witness and a wounded victim of the Gonder massacre who was hit by a bullet on his thigh is Alemu Belete, who is related to my colleague Metshafe Sirak. He came to Addis Ababa four weeks after it happened, and told us the following. "The Gonder massacre took place on September 7th 1993 at Adebabay Eyesus church in the city of Gonder where thousands of people had gathered for prayer. Security forces came to arrest the chief preacher Abba Ameha Eyesus and opened fire on the crowd indiscriminately killing and wounding scores. Many more were arrested and detained in Bahta prison, the palace and police stations for a long time. There were clearly better ways to apprehend the preacher. It looks like they wanted to arrest the preacher who often criticized government ethnic politics and referred to the leaders as communists who do not believe in God, and at the same time they wanted to give "collective punishment" to scare people who loved to listen to him".

Another such massacre was carried on in Areka, Wolaita earlier on July 14th 1992 where a group of ex-soldiers staged a peaceful demonstration demanding payment of their stipends which they had not received for a long time. According to one of the wounded survivors Corporal Demissie Aga whom we interviewed for the magazine it was a clear cut massacre. "EPRDF forces attacked demonstrators with hand grenades and machine guns killing and wounding several unarmed persons". The committee sent by the council of representatives to investigate the matter came up with 81–pages of report and declared that the government forces killed 31 persons and wounded 29 others. The Ethiopian Human Rights Council report revealed that many more persons have been killed at the incident. Peaceful demonstrations being a legal right allowed by the government charter at the time, and the law violated by security forces, those responsible for this criminal act have not been brought to justice.

Without the existence of independent judiciary and democratic conditions of life in Ethiopia one cannot expect to observe rule of law and due process. It is not enough to prescribe a law on paper if it is not implemented and enforced. In the case of Ethiopia, judges are selected and appointed by the authorities and there is a big contradiction between what is written in the constitution and the action of the government. Out of the eight members of the judicial administration in 1997, five were political appointees. What is more the candidates are chosen and presented to the commission by the president of the supreme court, who is directly selected and appointed by the president of the EPRDF-controlled government of Ethiopia. Many people were suspicious when the commission failed to recommend so many highly experienced judges who were not even members of the Derg's Workers Party of Ethiopia (WPE). This includes highly educated and experienced judges like Ato Kirubel Wolde Amlak, Ato Getachew Haile, Ato Tilahun Teshome, Ato Kifle Tadesse, Ato Woldetensai Woldeamlak, Ato Kirubel Hailemariam, etc. Since the commission is not transparent it is still not clear why it failed to choose such judges who are not accused of corruption and has rich legal experience, and instead it preferred the others it selected; of course one can only say the main criteria is political loyalty.

If the judiciary is not free from the interference of government executives and if qualified judges are not selected without discrimination on the basis of political loyalty and ethnic affiliation, merely stating on paper that the judiciary is independent is not enough. Judges should be free from the influence of government or ruling party authorities and should have the freedom to judge on all matters of judicial nature without any interference, and their orders and judgments should be respected and enforced by the government. Unfortunately, we have seen many who were acquitted or won their case being arrested by police as soon as they step out of the court; and the judges who gave the ruling transferred to remote provinces the following days. The judges should also be free to get promotion based on their performance to upheld rule of law and due process without pressure and manipulation from above.

As it stands now judges are not free and not secure of their tenure; many feel they could be dismissed by the federal government or regional councils if they don't follow instructions from executives on judicial matters. In the current political atmosphere most people conceive judges as partisan and their social status has plummeted. With low pay and poor living conditions and fear of dismissal, judges are more concerned about their living conditions than about the respect of the rule of law, due process and justice. What is prevailing in Ethiopia today is not rule of law, but as many say, "rule of men with guns". This is certainly true and it will be naïve to expect the current government led by TPLF to respect rule of law and observe due process.

Ethiopian Human Rights Council (EHRCO) in its report of March 1995 it cites Prime Minister Meles Zenawi's letter of July 7th 1992 (Ref. no. M80-867/3) instructing the courts not to decide on matters related to property that was illegally confiscated by the defunct regime Derg, and also suspended enforcement of their judgments regarding such property. This is how the top executive blatantly interferes in the functions of the courts by rendering articles of the proclamation inapplicable. This makes it clear that courts are forced to function as the instruments of the executive. There are many examples where habeas corpus is suspended and political detainees are denied access even to get their applications for bail to be considered by the judges.

"... all learned and experienced judges are dismissed and replaced by lay judges assuming the chair after three to six weeks of orientation; all the important positions of justice (presidency, chief justice, registrar) are held by political cadres; thousands of persons are languishing in prison for years without trial; the society is being reorganized on ethnic lines; the driving force is hatred and vengeance against one ethnic group; political kidnapping, disappearances and executions have become everyday phenomenon; people are discriminated against because of their political opinion and ethnic background; there is no political as well as administrative accountability; and all these are described as the "golden era of justice" by the minister of justice." (EHRCO, P- 108, 1995)

The Human Rights Council (HRCO), formerly known as the Ethiopian Human Rights Council (EHRCO), is Ethiopia's first non-profit, non-governmental human rights organization. Since its establishment on October 10, 1991, HRCO has maintained an ambitious and variegated mission to monitor, promote and defend human rights, rule of law, due process and democracy to assist the Ethiopian people in their struggle to establish a system of justice and democracy. To achieve this mission HRCO employs holistic and multifaceted approach to address human rights violations and bring it to the awareness of the government so that it shall create a mechanism to prevent the occurrence. Among the core program activities of HRCO are the provision of legal aid, rights related research, human rights education and human rights monitoring, investigation and reporting.

To date HRCO has published over 40 regular reports and over 121 special reports. The reports provide a comprehensive

134

look at the contemporary human rights situation in Ethiopia, including the wide range of abuses like forced disappearance, denial of justice, excessive use of force by police, illegal detention, forced eviction, arbitrary arrest, torture, extra-judicial killings, rape, denial of habeas corpus rights, destruction of property, threat and harassment, cruel and inhuman treatment etc. The method that HRCO use to document human rights violations is by dispatching experienced investigators to conduct field interviews, and in-office complaint handling with victims and witnesses. The interviews are conducted with a diverse stratum of Ethiopian society, including political party members, journalists, farmers, labor union leaders, teachers, students, and civilian community representatives. It also interviews pertinent government officials (*kebele* to regional) related to the matter. It verifies all complaints and claims with robust evidence including witnesses and victim testimony and uses primary documents like medical and judicial records and photographic evidences. Victims and witnesses routinely decline to be interviewed for fear of government retaliation and concern for their safety. With a strong security network of one to four ratio proportions spying on the population, no one wants to talk about politics; you can easily see how frightened everyone is. The people are afraid of each other and their government; in the same way despite its strenuous denials the government is afraid of the people. That is how life is like in Ethiopia today.

HRCO receives thousands of reports on human rights violations every year and it investigated hundreds of them. During the last 27 years HRCO has reported tens of thousands of human rights violations to the government, the international community and to the people of Ethiopia. It has reported that the recent institutionalization of repressive legislation, including Anti-terrorism Proclamation 652/2009 and Charities and Societies ProclamationNo.621/2009 has escalated the violation of human rights. These laws that infringe on the rights of

135

freedom of expression and association need to be amended or repealed. All citizens, national and international organizations and governments that stand for the respect of human rights and the rule of law should exert pressure on the Ethiopian government to promote respect for human rights.

Amnesty International and Human Rights Watch have been accusing the Ethiopian government for human rights abuse in their reports every passing year; but, nothing improved. According to Human Rights Watch World Report of 2011 and 2012 the Ethiopian government authorities continued to severely restrict basic rights of freedom of expression, association and assembly after the 2005 rigged elections. In the run-up of 2010 elections the government closed down space for political dissent and independent criticism by voter harassment, threats and coercion. The government's grassroots surveillance mechanism extends into almost every community in the country, through an elaborate system of *kebeles* (village and neighborhood administrations) through which the government exerts pressure on the people *"Voters were pressured to join or support the ruling party through a combination of incentives-including access to seeds, fertilizers, tools and loans- and discriminatory penalties if they support the opposition, such as denial of access to public sector jobs, educational opportunities, and even food assistance".* (Human Rights Watch 2011 Report)

During the last 27 years of EPRDF rule, intimidation, arbitrary arrest, torture, forced displacement and killing remain routine throughout the country. Recently, Amnesty International and Human Rights Watch have reported in 2013 providing heartbreaking stories, and cases including photographs explaining how human rights crisis worsened in Ethiopia. The political space in Ethiopia is getting worse; and fair and free election cannot be expected under such circumstances. The great majority of the political parties functioning in Ethiopia and abroad had written a list of complaints and suggestions for negotiations to the Election Commission Board and the prime minister. But, the authorities have rejected all as irrelevant and false. The political parties still persist that there should be a room for negotiations, reform and national reconciliation. The state and the ruling party seem to be adamant and not ready to respond to the right full demands. Instead the parties who tried to appeal to the authorities and communicate with the public by publishing and distributing their demands about free and fair elections, high taxation, forced recruitment of public servants, and maladministration, are being harassed and their senior members and activists arrested. We hope things will change after 2018.

The opposition party in Tigray known as Arena, got in a problem years back with the ruling party for publishing and distributing its complaints to the public. Several of its senior members like Ato Ayalew Beyene, and Ato Tekalegn in Shiraro, Ato Yohannes Kahsai and Ato Ato Sultan Hishe in Samrie, and Ato Tsegaye Hiluf in Abergele were arrested while peacefully distributing the papers from December 12 to 18th 2012, prior to the local election season. Soon after the opening of the Arena office in the town of Adebay near Humera in December 2012, the flag mast was dismantled and taken away by the administration officials. A few days later the building of the office was destroyed, on the pretext that they are going to construct a road across it and materials in the office were confiscated. On December 28th 2012, the authorities used the same pretext and intimidated a member of Arena party who was in charge of the office, Ato Gebreabezgi Nayu by destroying his house and making his five children and his wife homeless. All this was done without prior warning and compensations, in gross violation of human rights perpetrated on all peace loving and democratic minded people of Tigray. It is the same in other parts of the country.

(On February 12, 2012 members of the Somalia Region special police allegedly opened fire on a local assembly in the Ogaden area of the Somali Region, killing 20 persons. The villagers reportedly were gathered to discuss the murder of a village elder the previous day. Many others were detained during the same incident". (Country Reports on Human Rights Practices for 2012, United States Department of State. Bureau of Democracy, Human Rights and Labor)

The EPRDF government wants to continue with its one party system and sham elections. The lack of guarantee to free and fair elections and rule of law has become a recurring concern. The laws that the government promulgated to silence the opposition, in contradiction to the constitution, is inherently unfair. It denies due process, fair trial and has deficient enforcement mechanisms. The legal and judicial systems in Ethiopia have been made partisan and lack legal certainty, clarity, predictability and fairness in the implementation of law.

The legal system is constructed in such a way that it combines the Stalinist theories with Ethiopian characteristics. The constitution is a combination of a system influenced by western legality, traditional legal reasoning as well as modern court practices, to make it sound good; but, it is often violated by the government itself. During the last four decades, a Soviet style criminal justice system has been implemented which created a rigorous and anarchical charismatic rule by Mengistu and Meles respectively. Even though Meles came up, at least in theory, with modern constitution which seems a legitimate instrument of public action, the rhetoric of the rule of law is often confined to a formula of pure theory or legal positivism. Both failed to establish a more rational legal authority.

EPRDF abolished the military Derg policy of class struggle and Marxist concept of law as being an instrument of

138

proletarian dictatorship; but again the party uses legal instruments to its advantage by clearly controlling the legal system. There are clear flaws in the trial, such as bought witnesses, tempered evidences and errors, set ups, insufficient legal representation, and political instructions to the courts. The objective being to establish a one party rule by law (and not rule of law), without offending donor countries, it came up with symbolically good constitution to appease the West; and later promulgated laws that contradict the constitution. What EPRDF wanted is to make sure that the fundamental economic and political system it constructed endures with the structure and power of the political regime. In the same way it established ethnic federation and propagates the principles of autonomy, freedom and equality of nationalities and regions; but, in practice EPRDF is dictating every way of life and administration in all the regions, from local to national level. Professions and academic disciplines have no life and structure of their own, nothing matters beyond politically desirable results; however it is achieved. More and more professions and areas of our culture particularly the life of the intellect became politicized. Anything that stands in the way of EPRDF "correct" political outcome does not count; not logic, not objectivity, not even intellectual honesty.

The power of EPRDF leaders be it at national or regional level is unlimited; the so-called administrative law system it claims to have to control regional autonomy is ineffectual and symbolic. The relationship between the state and citizens in public administration is problematic. People at every level, national, regional or local could not protest or present petition of grievances without fear of retaliation by the authorities. Citizens cannot file law suit against authorities or government for any wrong doing like violation of individual or property rights, inadequate compensation for land or property appropriation, illegal land seizures, expropriation or house demolition, unlawful bribes for performance of duty, etc. Even though compensation is given to some individuals, the judiciary is not sure which one is free from intervention by authorities so as to give consistent and transparent judgments or efficient enforcement.

EPRDF leaders should correct all these mistakes and strengthen the professionalism of the judiciary by addressing judicial corruption and building public confidence. It needs to come up with code of ethics for judges which can be fairly, uniformly and effectively enforced. Lack of confidence and credibility regarding the court system is among the most pressing issues that need to be addressed. People are afraid of retribution to ask openly; but, there is an increasing demand from the silent majority that Ethiopia's civil justice need to be overhauled, with a broad range of reforms covering legal, institutional, as well as procedural aspects to ensure fair justice with greater efficiency. The supremacy of a certain tribe or party over the people and constitution must stop. Ethiopian judges should be free and be given real power to do their job properly in accordance with the constitution. Lawyers need to be free from interference and control by the legislature and executive branches. Media interference and public outreach to court proceedings and scrutiny of the judge's rationale should be allowed. The government must stop the continuing regression of the rule of law year after year, under the guise of anti-terror campaign and preserving peace and stability.

Missed opportunities

It is important to look back and discuss the mistakes we made and the opportunities we failed to use in our long history of struggle for independence, justice, and democracy; it might at least give a lesson to our children not to repeat the same mistakes. It is also important to confess that we Ethiopians made many mistakes that led us to poverty and oppression. We failed to use the many opportunities that arise to build a democratic and prosperous society.

Being an ancient nation with unbroken history of independence and a deep sense of nationhood we could have done much better to have a decent life for our people. Endowed with rich natural resources and hardworking cultured people who have a strong faith in one true God, we should have done much better. But the fickle conduct of our leaders who claim to be a messiah turned into a human monster and took us to the ditch. We struggled hard to come out of the ditch and did repeatedly only to be thrown back by the falls messiah again and again; because we failed to work together to establish a strong democratic order. Instead of struggling together for justice and democracy we fight each other for petty things based on ethnicity.

Among the many opportunities we missed there are three that stand out, other than the failed coup of General Mengistu Neway of the Imperial Body Guard division and his civilian brother Girmame Neway of the 1960's, and that of General Demissie Bulto and a dozen other generals in 1989, (though we cannot expect much from a military coup), which might have changed things for the better in time. One missed opportunity is the 1974 popular revolution that shook not only Ethiopia but also the whole continent of Africa and raised eye brows around the world.

There are so many facts and data and analysis of significant events and the role the military Derg in squandering this historic opportunity. The brave citizens of Ethiopia dared to exercise their fundamental rights to establish a representative people's government, but with despotic intentions and a socialist elimination mentality, Derg quashed all independent political activity with brutality. The military dictators started a war against their own people, with the Soviet Block assisting a government that is killing its innocent people. Ethiopia started bleeding again not from wounds inflicted by external forces like fascist Mussolini, but, from the brutality of ignorant, disconnected, vindictive and power hungry officers. Derg failed to play smart politics and change itself along with Russian politicians to save Ethiopia and its people from disintegration and ethnic division.

The other opportunity was 1991 when EPRDF given the benefit of the doubt by the great majority of the population defeated the much hated Derg and took power. But with divisive ethnic politics and an act of vengeance it repeated the atrocities under different circumstances with gross violation of human rights. It again established a one-party system in the holy name of multi-party democracy aggravating racial hatred and encouraging the disintegration of Ethiopia. The hard working great people of Ethiopia who kept their independence by fighting against invaders through centuries of sacrifices were once again grounded into dirt by their own leaders.

The Ethiopian people have sought for justice, freedom and equality throughout their history. They have faith, they are believers of one true God and they trusted their government in vain. With confidence in themselves and unshakable faith in God to provide them with a good government that would create the conditions to enable them live their God given potential; they go to churches and mosques like no other people. But, what they got was a succession of tyrants each one worse than its predecessor. The Ethiopian people fought hard against the previous regime only to pave the way for a worse brutal regime. For those people who have lived in all these three governments the past that is not so glorious appear so much better and the future so much gloomier than the present. Yet, their trust in God is unshakable, that is why now many people think that God is punishing them because their sins are so much to deserve anything better.

The third opportunity was the 2005 election that was rigged by EPRDF leaders. In the preceding month there was a democratic debate between the ruling officials and the opposition party elites and the people were encouraged to go to the polls to vote for individuals of their choice. May 15, 2005 is unforgettable; millions of Ethiopians started to flood to the polls with the feeling that an era of ethnic division and oppression will be over and a new era of hope, reconciliation and nation building will start. Millions of Amharas, Oromos, Tigrayans, Gurages, Wolaitas etc made their way to the polling stations sharing a common feeling and determined to make the election a success. Many walked miles to reach the polling stations of their district, some came with crutches, some in wheel chairs. Long lines formed outside polling stations circling around city blocks and winding along fields and dirt roads in the countryside. Many had to stand for several hours tired and hungry, yet they remained patient to achieve their dreams of a free and fair election. In rural areas many had to vote until late evening by candle light.

Having stood there all day long to cast their vote no one seemed disappointed. Because they are exercising their right that they have been denied for so long and that their vote is going to be counted right. After long hours at the polls when they returned to their homes everyone seemed to have a profound sense of liberation and fulfillment from participating in what they thought a truly free and fair election of a new unity government. They felt that at last their dignity had been restored. On the polling day and on the days and weeks prior to that Ethiopia was more peaceful than ever. Members of rival parties joined the same queues in cities and rural villages exchanging opinions about the opportunity that opened for them all.

The feeling of relief that the curse of ethnic politics will finally disappear was as strong even among the majority of EPRDF cadres, some Tigrayans and the ethnic based military who has imposed it as among the Amharas and Oromos who suffered under it. Most of all the importance of the occasion was even greater because it had seemed that a peaceful alternative to the ethnic politics that polarized the society was beyond reach and that the most likely scenario that would follow would be another round of civil war.

As polls closed at the end of the day government media started announcing the results in accordance to the agreement reached by all contending parties prior to the election. Opposition parties won at all polling stations in the capital Addis Ababa, and won the majority seats in all other major cities around the country. In Amhara, Oromia, Afar, southern Ethiopia etc. it was disclosed by government media that opposition parties are victorious in the urban areas and the ruling party lost most of the seats. At this moment Prime Minister Meles Zenawi after convening with the executive committee of TPLF ordered that vote counting and broadcasting the results as they get it from the polling stations be halted. He declared a state of emergency and later declared that his party has won the election by securing 70 percent of parliament seats. However he admitted that the opposition has won 207 seats and all the seats for the capital Addis Ababa.

The Ethiopian people were angry that once again their votes were not counted, and came out in hundreds of thousands for a peaceful protest. The EPRDF leaders ordered the killing of peaceful protestors and nearly two hundred were killed in one day and fifty thousand arrested. In the following days many more were killed and arrested and tortured. People live under a regime in which gross violations of human rights are increasingly becoming normal. The blood of those killed in various parts of Ethiopia is crying for justice. The maimed bodies of tortured young people are crying for justice. The numerous families whose loved ones were forcefully taken and disappeared are crying for justice. The thousands of families whose kin languish in prisons throughout the country without any due process are crying for justice. Those who committed these crimes should be apprehended and made to feel the full weight of justice. For the victims and their families it is not important whether the atrocities were committed by the Derg or EPRDF, in the name of socialism or free market. No lesson has been learnt from the brutalities of the DERG. The atmosphere was again contaminated with racial hatred which is the fuel for genocide and hate crime against each other.

"...Ethiopians are a historical people, but, apparently without a sense of history. It is quite obvious that the Derg never learnt any lesson from the ignominious fall of Haile Selassie's regime. Similarly the EPRDF has not learnt anything from the disgraceful downfall of the Derg regime. Those who seek to bring down the EPRDF regime by force are also not pondering over the consequences of their plans. In this respect, the most recent history of Ethiopia is filled with stressful incompetence: a somewhat half-witted understanding of the past and the blurred vision of the future." (Ethiopian Human Rights Council, P-3 1995)

The problems in Ethiopia are intensifying at an alarming rate. There is no trust what so ever between the oppressors and the oppressed, they are driven further away from each other every passing day. PEN award recipient journalist Sisay Agena, in his book *Yekalitiw Mengist*, 2012, has described the failure of the justice system referring numerous tangible evidences and instances. The leaders are anti-dialogue; they don't want to talk with groups that have different view point. The uncertainties of rural land holding and the land lease policy are depressing the already weakened agricultural production, and millions of peasants are surviving under relief assistance; even to get relief food you have to be a supporter of EPRDF. Unemployment of trained persons and college graduates is at all-time high. Millions of young people can't find even menial jobs. Prices of all essential commodities are soaring; and it will continue to do so under the circumstances.

To get admission to public colleges and to get a job when you graduate you should be a member of the ruling party; because they own most of the private companies and the federal offices, it is no exaggeration. In the name of the Structural Adjustment Program (SAP) and performance evaluation meetings that are orchestrated by their cadres, many workers who do not support EPRDF have been laid off and the private sector is not strong enough to absorb them. EPRDF has monopolized power in all areas, vital resources including land and national media are under its control. It seems to me that there is a loss of a moral sense in our leaders, of knowing the difference between right and wrong and of being governed by it.

Under the circumstances, it is right for the people to protest and speak-up; they should never back down from demanding justice and freedom and create the next opportunity. They must continue to fight for the things they want in life; should develop the courage to try again and again to get back their freedom, and never quit. At this point in history the people of Ethiopia are faced with, right versus wrong choices; not right versus right as some like to put it. But, unfortunately they are not yet united to stand together and address the problems right away. Some want to duck them; others are ready to address them, but not in a way of resolving the problems by energetic self-reflection. They simply want to get it resolved by sheer compromise even if it is not right; while some want to get it right. Some are discussing endlessly about the possible outcomes and paths to pursue. They don't need to take so much time to act; don't need approval from anyone to do the right thing.

Most Ethiopians are tired of unethical ethnic politics. Indigenous tribes are dislocated from their ancestral land and means of production and made refugees in neighboring countries. Opposition activists are thrown to jail or fired from government jobs and made to become bystanders on the dusty neighborhoods and streets of Addis Ababa, while the TPLF led government is boasting about development. Ethiopia has been exploited almost to death by *Woyane* leaders and their loyalists. While her children have no water to wash their hands, the exploiters adorn their fingers with Gold and Diamonds snatched from her lands. The working class is starving, while the exploiters dance on piles of Dollars and Euros. All people should come together and build momentum to bring change in our society towards justice and democracy. We cannot wait for another opportunity to arise, we have to create that opportunity ourselves now. We should be aware, focused, united and connected and rise to throw off the parasites and reclaim our historic motherland by overcoming all obstacles. Let us make sure the reform we started in 2018 with the new Prime minister Dr. Abiy Ahmed will achieve its objectives.

"Because reform is required in so many areas, sequencing is critical. Broadly categorized, the area in which reform must take place may be delineated as institutional, political, intellectual, and economic. Since Africa's political and economic systems are inseparable, most analysts affirm that economic and political reform must go hand in hand. However, they do not address where the institutional and intellectual systems should be placed in the sequence or where to begin. Perhaps by deductive analysis, we can make some headway.

(Africa in Chaos – 1999, George Ayittey)

The West and Soviet Union

African politics changed greatly after the coming of the Portuguese explorers who first set foot in the continent and opened the door for the other Europeans to exploit Africa for their own advantage. The scramble of Africa soon followed changing the face of the continent into colonies with artificial boundaries that ignored ethnic lines. Except Ethiopia and Liberia, the rest of Africa was under European rule or protection. These artificial boundaries and the practice of "divide and rule" brought about the failure of Africa. European colonialists favored one tribe and excluded the others driving Africans to fight one another instead of fighting the colonialists together. By divide and rule the colonialists made sure that the transition of Africa to independence will be a failure.

Both the capitalist west and the communist east did not help Africans to liberate themselves from tyrant leaders. As a matter of fact they protected tyrants who helped them to promote their own national interests. The West and the Soviet Block could have used their leverage to promote democracy in Africa, but they did not care to do so. It was offending to hear United States assistant secretary for Africa Herman Cohen who said during his brief visit to Zaire (Congo), in 1982 that "...*Mobutu is enthusiastic for democracy"* (The Washington Post, April1, 1992- p-A28). But it should be apparent that it is African leaders and the educated elites who have betrayed Africa. Africans should be vigilant to take their continent back, make it work and get rid of dictatorships. We should not be a satellite of the West or the East; we should be the master of our own destiny. We must take the initiative ourselves to solve our problems.

Africans have been brutally traumatized as "sub-humans" for centuries by Europeans and Americans during the time of slavery. Millions of strong and active African men and women have been chained in bondage and taken away from their continent as slaves; which left blacks stigmatized as "inferiors" to this day. After slavery was over there came European colonizers, first with the bible then with the gun. Africa was carved up into colonies with artificially drawn boundaries that had little regard to tribal demographic configurations. It took nearly a century of struggle to end colonialism. After independence, before Africans recovered from the trauma of slavery and colonialism, they were taken over by neo-colonialism and suffered greatly in the hands of their own tyrant leaders. The political repression and economic exploitation continued unchanged, and Africans are poorer today than they were at independence. The Diaspora for better opportunities continued and Africa lost millions of its educated children.

The West and the Soviet Union contributed to the entrenchment of tyranny in Africa in general and in Ethiopia in particular. The two superpowers and rich European countries played a role in supporting African tyrants sometimes indirectly, other times blatantly. They start by giving recognition to the despotic regimes followed by diplomatic and cultural exchanges, economic and military aid, military pact and solidarity with the president or prime minister as the case may be of that African country. After the Second World War, the Cold War policy of the super powers played a role to the advantage of tyrant leaders in Africa. Pro-Soviet Mengistu Haile Mariam of Ethiopia enjoyed the unreserved support of the Soviet Union to massacre hundreds of thousands of his people in "Red Terror" in the name of socialism; while anti-terror ally Meles Zenawi was enjoying the support of the West to disintegrate Ethiopia, torture and kill thousands of his country people in the holy name of democracy. Both the West and Soviet Union competed to spread their sphere of influence across the continent for obvious reasons. The Soviet Union supported the tyrant military Derg in the name of socialism for over 15 years; the United States created and supported a monster regime for the last 22 years. China is also doing the same now by supporting African despots with no regard to human rights; it is frustrating.

The strategic and geopolitical importance, the supply of important raw materials and the potential market for foreign goods attracted both the West and the Soviet Block to have access and influence in Africa. They started and continued their dirty game often by playing one country against the other and promoting proxy wars. African leaders also benefited by playing one superpower against another to get more aid, and both sometimes exchanged political dancing partners overnight, like they did during the war between Ethiopia and Somalia in 1976. In actual fact as Alam Gottlieb put it, *'the disintegration of Ethiopia in large part is an outcome of this Cold War policy'*.

The United States foreign policy during the cold war was based on stopping the spread of communism, and at present on anti-terrorism alliance. It blatantly supported many tyrant leaders across Africa, like Mobutu Sese Sieko often whitewashing the human rights violations and corruptions of despotic regimes and branding dissidents, democratic opponents and critics as communists, criminals, terrorists or extremists. To limit the presence of the Soviet Block in Africa to the minimal the United States has gone to the extent of assisting in the assassination of socialist leaders like Patrice Lumumba of Zaire and replaced him with pro-West Mobutu.

The West usually supported African despots for its national interest by providing them in turn with economic and military aid. Western countries continued to help African tyrants knowing fully well that the leaders they are helping are brutally repressive and blatantly corrupt; and their universities celebrated African despots by giving them honorary degrees. The subsequent overthrow of these tyrants often unleashed a wave of intense anti-American sentiments; but those kinds of policies continue. In the same manner today USA is supporting a number of African dictators on the basis of anti-terrorism alliance including the late Meles Zenawi of Ethiopia despite his hideously repressive and neo-communist regime.

The United States and other western countries share the blame for the disintegration and human misery that accompanies the increasing level of political repression in Ethiopia. They are the ones that brought EPLF and TPLF to power by giving them all kinds of assistance; to get rid of the pro-Soviet Derg. During the cold-war Washington cruelly used Africa in a geo-political chess game with the Soviet Union by supporting the most brutal dictators like Mobutu, as long as they help contain the expansion of socialism. In the same manner, today human rights abuses in countries suspected of supporting terrorism are justly denounced by Washington; while the same kind of brutality practiced by countries judged to be anti-terrorism allies is politely ignored. The guns that US supplies to these tyrant leaders are being used to terrorize and silence civilians and up-root villagers to leave the land. Democracy should be the hallmark in shaping US foreign policy, if it is to avert the next catastrophe.

There was also a misconception by some Westerners that "democracy is alien to Africa" and multi-party systems will lead Africa to civil war, so Africa needs a strong man and not strong institutions. Tyrant leaders of Africa used these misconceptions to silence their people and arrest opposition party leaders. The universality of the yearning for democracy and freedom by all races and peoples can be explained by looking at Nelson Mandela who offered his life by going to prison for 27 years for the achievement of basic human dignity. The lone Chinese student who hold the movement of tanks for some time risking his life for the love of democracy and the Russian youth who faced tanks for one party rule to end are good examples to

151

understand that people anywhere in the world have the same degree of love for freedom and democracy. Ethiopian protestors who were killed while asking their votes to be counted prove the universality of the love for freedom and democracy by all mankind.

The struggle of Africans has always been for freedom, but as the two camps competed to expand their sphere of influence in the continent they supported repressive regimes as long as they found them helpful to their national interest in the geopolitical struggle of the big powers. Pro-West African regimes were as brutally repressive as pro-Soviet Marxist governments. These African leaders were so corrupt and disconnected that the financial aid Western governments gave to Africa ended up in the pockets of gangster leaders; or was used to lavish and unnecessary projects. Western leaders, particularly US presidents expressed their appreciation of leaders like Mobutu in public while they know deep inside that he is a butcher who embezzled his country's treasury. Mobutu's bank balance in Europe could have paid his country's total debt easily; and the United States knew this fact. And yet American presidents invited him to the white house a number of times and spoke kind words about him in public, praising him for killing his people whom they called communists.

"Deprived of the chance to learn the lessons of its own history, Zaire's population was kept in a state of infantilism by a more insidious form of colonialism. Instead of the roller-coaster of war, destruction and eventual rebirth, the intervention of the US, France and Belgium, of the World Bank and IMF, locked the society into one slow-motion economic collapse. Balked of expression, unable to advance, mindsets froze over somewhere in the 1960s, leaving the country's leadership at the turn of the century stuck in an ideological time-wrap". (Michela Wrong, In the Footsteps of Mr. Kurtz, P-215)

The Ethiopian Human Rights Council (EHRCO) is often severely condemned and vilified by EPRDF regime and the state media it controls. This is to be expected from a totalitarian regime. But the strange fact is that the council has repeatedly reported in its press releases that most western diplomats in Addis Ababa are collaborating with the regime to vilify EHRCO.

"The ambassadors of Switzerland, of the United States of America and others have made pronouncements to the effect that EHRCO is politically oriented. In fact, the representatives of the diplomatic community in Addis Ababa made up of Canada, Switzerland, and Norway discussed the matter with representatives of EHRCO twice. Their suggestion was that EHRCO remove the democratic process and the rule of law from its three objectives and concentrate on individual human rights. In the interest of accuracy it must be stated that the Norwegian representative was not sure how the democratic process could be removed from human rights without affecting the over-all concern for human rights. Nevertheless, the Executive Committee of EHRCO seriously and sincerely re-examined its objectives in view of the suggestions of the diplomats. It decided to continue with its original objectives." (EHRCO, September 2012)

Opportunist Intellectuals & Political Parties

While blaming the West and the East and economic giant China for supporting African dictators and ignoring human rights abuse by these leaders, we also have to blame ourselves for providing support to these dictators or by not doing anything to oust them. In actual fact the saddest aspect of Africa's down fall into tyranny is the unconditional support of Africa's so called intellectuals and scholars. These African elites

153

compromised their principles for little benefits and go around the world to offer various arguments to justify one party rule. While seeing that political exclusion and economic mismanagement are dominant most African intellectuals refrain from asking for participatory democracy challenging the dictators. The great majority of these intellectuals and the general public choose to be neutral by keeping quiet; but, not doing anything while citizens are suffering is simply siding with the tyrant.

So many Ethiopian elites during the regime of the Emperor, the military Derg or EPRDF, sold out their people in exchange for an appointment or money. Even some gifted intellectuals who used to be human rights activists and standard bearers of our society betrayed the people for power and personal wealth. Many journalists disregard their professional ethics to please dictators and win favors. Dictators stayed in power most importantly because so many intellectuals and even loyal opposition leaders collaborated and allowed tyranny to become entrenched in Africa. A Sierra Leon writer comments:

"We should not forget the optimism, cowardice, and unprincipled role of a section of the so called intelligentsia in leading us into our present quandary. Lawyers, doctors, professors and a whole host of other "educated" people willingly participated in the general repression and corruption that was characteristic of APC (All Peoples Congress) rule..." (New Africa, May 1992, P-10)

The weakness, the nature and the character of the political parties that are organized to oppose tyranny is another major reason for despotism to dominate in Africa. As we have noticed for so long in Ethiopia, the weaknesses, inadequacies, and fragmentation of opposition groups have helped tyrants to succeed and stay in power. Most of the so called opposition party leaders are themselves dictators not willing to give a chance to the new blood, new generation activists to replace them. They exhibit the same tyrannical tendencies they denounce in public. They don't even allow inner party democracy for fear of being replaced by another member of their own party.

They act half-heartedly and are not serious about forming a common front or merge with other parties that have the same program for fear of losing their seats. They simply call hundreds of meetings and keep on talking with no results. Most opposition politicians are excellent in talking, condemning and cursing the leaders in power and do nothing more; except waiting for the next abuse to do more of their talking and condemnation. It seems that there are many opportunist individuals and infiltrators working for the ruling party among the ranks. Even when they try to act in unity against the oppressor they mostly fail because they lack imagination and their methods are foolish. They are not sophisticated enough and their choice of tactics to oust a tyrant is weak. They hold one big demonstration in a city and sacrifice their supporters instead of stretching the military geographically to many cities and towns.

The opposition political parties end up fighting among themselves creating confusion to their followers. They can't get their acts together and some opposition leaders get bribed and co-opted and abandon the democratic struggle and collaborate with the dictator. Sometimes you see political paralysis and inaction by the Ethiopian opposition parties both at home and in the Diaspora, and you would think they are part time politicians functioning half-heartedly. That is partly why TPLF leaders all the time outwit and outplay them easily making them inconsequential, and making sure that they will never be able to pose any serious challenge to their power. TPLF leaders always treated the opposition as trivial, disciplining them using different methods of punishment to keep them in line. Sometimes they bribe some of them with jobs, cars, money, houses, and use them as agents to divide the opposition at best and/or to keep them silent at least, while arresting those who refuse to accept the offer and keep quiet. Other times they use the so-called "elders" and prominent individuals to mediate just to buy time and at the end force them to sign to quit politics. Most opposition leaders have manifested time and again that they are not seriously struggling for people's power, instead are using politics to get power and money for themselves and are easily infiltrated, and bribed to submission.

Thus the opposition remains amorphous, weak, divided and fragmented, often fighting against each other, engaged in factional struggle among themselves than against the tyrant. It is true that opposition leaders, journalists, human rights advocates and civil society leaders have relatively sacrificed a lot more than any of us. Most of them have suffered years of imprisonment and even after they were released they have been denied any meaningful political space. Even though they paid all these sacrifices for the sake of democracy, most opposition party leaders lack accountability and transparency in their actions and often resisting inner-party democracy within their organizations, promoting a cult of personality not to lose their leadership position at any cost and manifesting dictatorial tendencies. The opposition lost public credibility because of the weaknesses it exhibited after the 2005 elections by not being able to stand together and speak in one voice. It failed to stay united and develop coherent policies and programs that are different and preferable than the ruling party and convince the people; most of all for lack of unity of action.

Opposition parties should focus more on ideas and implications and not on individuals and events. So many golden opportunities have been missed because the opposition was not focused and failed to dissect ideas and act grabbing the chances that arise for evolutionary and revolutionary changes. When

Meles was in his death bed the ruling party leaders were frustrated and showed signs of faction. But, the opposition failed to act and take this once-in-a-lifetime opportunity, still talking about unity, division and skirmishes. Many good thinking intellectuals have been trying to give their suggestions and reflections advising the opposition to no avail. The opposition must create a broad coalition with society and be strong enough to overcome the hurdles that the ruling party puts on its way including infiltration and the harsh political climate in Ethiopia.

Opposition parties should not be safe haven for individuals that are frustrated, retired or fired from EPRDF or other parties. Defectors from the ruling party or other political groups need to explain their political history and make public apology like some of them did, if they truly want to be embraced by the Ethiopian people who once have been their victims. It does not end there; everyone should be held accountable and responsible for all their wrong doings. Politicians and groups in any setting who failed to act in time and as a result weakened the struggle should be asked to make public apology clarifying their mistakes and political past.

The opposition parties should do more than just to oppose the ruling party. They should learn from their mistakes and move forward; there is no going back, it is not an option. They must endeavor to attain stronger unity and come out with a set of policies and ideas that are superior to the ruling party and convince the people to make it their agenda. They should replace the old guard and give a chance to the younger generation which has greater dynamism and enthusiasm to play a vital and historic role by allowing them to come up the ladder of leadership. Training successors and future leaders should be one of the important goals of the parties. Most of all, the opposition should be well organized, united and principled, built on a strong foundation of the values of tolerance, cooperation and compromise. They should be ready to work together full time, bargain, lobby and compromise with others including the ruling party and be inclusive to save our children's future.

Most of the opposition politicians feel like being in a prison cell, "institutionalized" in one form or another, locked away in their fortified separate realities, their parochial loyalties, their intellects withering in their fixed way of seeing themselves and others no better than the leaders they condemn. If we start discussing ideas more than individuals, it can liberate us from prisons we have ourselves built. We need to stop constantly inventing new excuses to defend our failures and instead ask the Ethiopian people for their pardon and take the struggle in a new direction. We shall find a kingdom of thought, rich in insights with a love of sharing and a passion of connecting to liberate our people. We need to develop a common agenda around the core values of individual freedom, rule of law, democracy, human rights, and justice in opposition to the ruling party which is playing the ethnic card of 'divide and rule'. Most importantly we need a tool, an independent media of empowerment with fairness and balance that will be the expression of our collective will.

The ruling party TPLF/EPRDF should also start the difficult and arduous journey of national reconciliation and end the one party system before it is too late. The opposition should also work for a common ground in building a peaceful equitable future for all Ethiopians. Many people blame the opposition parties for lack of unity and a coherent alternative vision. If the opposition wants to restore its shattered credibility within the Ethiopian people they must come with a unity of purpose and alternative ideas and should be flexible enough to work with all forces to create a genuine democratic country. All sides should have the determination to transcend narrow ethnic, religious and regional differences to forge a brighter future for all. All sides should bury the ethnic venom and hatred that has been purposely and irresponsibly spewed for the last 22 years. Ethnic and religious animosity should have no place in Ethiopia for the good of all people, instead let us talk how we can establish unity and equality in diversity, democracy and justice for all and be a symbol of Africa again.

While myself and our generation has miserably failed to liberate Ethiopia from tyranny and have left a horrendous trail of chaos, I have hope in the new breed of Ethiopian intellectuals, capable of clear thinking, whose minds are not polluted with all these narrow ethnicity rhetoric and garbage, who can take the country in a new direction. I have met some in the Diaspora and heard about many young Ethiopian professionals in Africa, who are involved in the political struggle recently; can see things in acute clarity, and are not into the blame game. This new generation of Ethiopians with a remarkable spirit of resilience, are our last hope for reason to prevail over political opportunism. They remind me of the late Senator Ted Kennedy who in his last public speech to the US Democratic National Convention in 2008 said; *"The torch has been passed, the work begins anew, hope rises again and the dream lives on!"*

Most of all, we the people of this historic land should assist genuine democratic politicians and struggle to build a strong and durable foundation for a democratic system in Ethiopia that can endure for generations to come. We should not lose hope because of what happened during the past decades; as the famous American civil rights leader Dr. Martin Luther King once said, *"right temporarily defeated, is stronger than evil triumphant"*. Political leaders will never like to give up their power if we the people don't struggle and pressure them to advance the promised democratic process. We the people of this ancient country, have to break with the obedience-imposing Ethiopian submissiveness and transcend the constraints of culture. We have to overcome the structure-imposed sense of fear and docility and break out in spite of the gruesome dictatorial regime, without being suicidal. We should be peaceful, persistent and formidable in our struggle, but not passive to accept living with structural oppression. We should have the unflinching determination to fight peacefully for the prevalence of justice, freedom and equality.

We the people of this great country must say no to dictatorship and create the change we want to see. Democracy should begin in the hearts and minds of us, the people, not in the plans of leaders. We the ordinary people can accomplish extraordinary things again, if we unite crossing the barriers of ethnicity and religion and act together for a common good; democracy and justice. Remember, we are the off springs of a great generation that ignited Pan-African movement for the liberation, independence and unity of the continent with a world outlook to end oppression and exploitation. We cannot indulge to the village mentality of our narrow nationalist leaders and continue the shameful act of fighting each other based on ethnicity and religion. We shall rise to the challenges before us enduring trial after trial; withstand the onslaught and refuse to yield to bitterness and finish the race stronger than when we first began. We should stand united as Ethiopians/Africans and pressure these tyrant leaders like the Biblical Moses, by demanding "Let my people go!!"

"There may be times when we are powerless to prevent injustice, but, there must never be a time when we fail to protest. ... I swore never to be silent whenever and wherever human beings endure suffering and humiliation. We must always take sides. Neutrality helps the oppressor, never the victim. Silence encourages the tormentor, never the tormented".

(Elie Weisel, Nobel laureate and Holocaust survivor)

Chapter Three

<u>Military Derg and TPLF/EPRDF</u>

"Our lives in this planet are too short, and the work to be done too great to let the violence of hate, despair and indifference dominate the land."

(Robert Kennedy)

"There is nothing so dangerous as to allow power to remain for a long time in one citizen. The people become accustomed to obeying him, and he becomes accustomed to commanding. Hence, it's the origin of tyranny."

(Simon Bolivar)

> *'We shall bring to each lonely life a smile,*
> *But, what have we brought today?*
> *We shall be so kind in the after while,*
> *We shall give to truth a grander birth,*
> *And to steadfast faith a deeper worth,*
> *We shall feed the hungering souls of earth,*
> *But whom have we fed today?'*
> (Nixon Waterman)

For all practical reasons it becomes necessary to understand the internal situation of Ethiopia and the Horn of Africa in general in order to fully grasp the plight of the people. No one becomes a refugee of one's own will. There are forces that play an important role in the making of a refugee. Poverty, famine, war, injustice are so interrelated, and at times their reason can be convoluted driving our thoughts away. This is the case when it comes to modern Ethiopia. In order to truly grasp the story behind the story, it is unavoidable to enter into a somewhat dull political discussion. For the benefit of enjoyment the following has been written with "lighthearted seriousness". In this world of sound bites and quick information it can be a daunting task to look at the *"real issues"*. Most of us avoid such undertakings because it requires effort, which takes time, of which we are in short supply these days. For this reason we just accept the news or the story we get and move on with our lives. We are all too often willing to ignore facts and events that displeasure us. To ignore them is a much more comfortable form of existence. Understanding the fate of refugees however requires us to do the things that make us uncomfortable, such as talking about politics, governance, history and extra. The excess supply of acronyms for political parties itself can be a bit enervating. The writer however does not have the luxury of skipping this in-depth analysis, as that would leave gaps.

Revolution and Authoritarianism

In May of 2010 the ruling Ethiopian People's Revolutionary Democratic Front (EPRDF) of Ethiopia declared a "landslide victory" in Ethiopia, garnering 99.6% of all parliamentary seats. Shortly afterwards, in a visit to Colombia University, the late PM Meles Zenawi was asked by suspicious students, as to how one party could score such overwhelming victory in a vastly diverse state, such as Ethiopia. Prime Minister Meles Zenawi, in his all too familiar evasive way responded: *"In a parliamentary system the winning party takes all the contested votes, if it manages to acquire more than half the possible votes for each district"*. To give the mischievous fairy its due, he should be praised for his cunning response. The calmness and shrewd arrogance is impressive; reminiscent of Africa's many past despots, with an aura of sophistication. This was precisely the kind of leader the West had been looking for all along; able to handle the pressure and alleviate them of the responsibility

162

they bear for the many policies of the EPRDF. This masterful manipulator with whom they could hold a codified packet was exactly the answer for the so called vexing problem of Ethiopia. Not too brazen to embarrass them in public but bold enough to carry out their geopolitical interests in the Horn of Africa, even when these policies are detrimental to both parties in the long run. This myopic aspect of Western policy makers is not new. Many scholars have noted it to be a repetitive occurrence throughout the developing world. Latin America, Africa, The Middle East, Southeast Asia, all have gone through bouts of western supported and financed despots. Suharto in Indonesia, Pinochet in Chile, and Mobutu in the Congo are a few examples from a much larger pool. The intricacies of the western global financial power have played significantly in the propping up and maintaining of dictators. Perhaps the most shocking aspect of present day Congo was how much the international financial aid communities knew of Mobutu's crimes all along during their cozy arrangement. Ethiopia's case might have its own peculiarities but by and large the similarities are too significant to be ignored wholly.

In Ethiopia, the May 2005 and 2010 elections may have subdued any doubts about the authoritarian nature of the government. Nonetheless, western backers will continue to muddy the waters and resume their support. In their view "Real politic" requires this stance. In any case with the rise of China and its willingness to ignore democratic prerequisites to do business in Ethiopia; the west may well be on its way to becoming inconsequential for the EPRDF, a premonition the EPRDF is well cognizant of and looking forward to. In an article titled *"Looking east"* the Economist reports, *"trade between China and Ethiopia was $800 million dollars in 2010. It is expected to rise by 27% the following year"*. With this plausible paradigm shift the West may lose its much espoused despot to the Chinese after all. But for now they hold a substantial leverage of 3.3 billion dollars a year in aid, which according to an HRW publication in October 2010 under the Title of *"Ethiopia: Donor Aid supports Repression"* is being used, partly to refine the repression and increase the Party's grip in Ethiopia. This may be an eye opening discovery for the Western public. Nevertheless this is no news to the Ethiopian public, which has become keenly aware of these issues for four consecutive decades. It is also blatantly obvious to western policy makers, who are all too eager to play dumb for the sake of their narrow regional interests. Here it is important to add a well ignored fact; that of the disregarded opinion of the western public, which when it has the means to receive and discern correct information on such African states, mostly prefers the correct path preferred by third world populations, and the path very rarely followed by western policy formulators. This is perhaps an indication of the inherent defect of public participation for aid policy in general. It is an ironic and perplexing discovery to the untrained observer of international aid and its function. How the policy of aid agencies like the World Bank and IMF are largely hidden from the western public, even though the money is generated form the tax payer is indeed mind boggling.

Absurdities in international aid have been documented by many countless researchers and scholars alike over the past 30 years, and more pronouncedly in recent times. And more ominously for the third world, aid is becoming an encumbrance more than a means for advancement. Turning to the real situation we face, we must begin looking at the history of modern Ethiopia and in general the Horn of Africa and consider what has brought us to this point. History is essential to understanding the difficult situation these people face. It is our Global Positioning System, GPS, without which we are bound to get lost in the wilderness. To fully appreciate our current predicament we, at least in brief terms, view the political and societal developments of the past forty or so years, the defining period for contemporary Ethiopia. This period, if we are willing to analyze it unambiguously, will tell us a lot about our unfortunate fate. If we are willing to sift through the den of information we just might find a more auspicious path to the future as well. Indeed it will instruct us about where we need to focus our attention, and save us from the burden of confusion and apathy. Knowing this recent past is essential for any one bent on improving the lot for his fellow compatriots as well as neighboring nations.

The Students and the Coup of 1974

Viewing this recent history one is confronted conspicuously with the theory of Marxism, specifically its many different Ethiopian outbursts and interpretations, all carrying a heavy load of Eurocentric views. I myself having come out of the radical student movement of the 60s and early 70s, Marxist theory was thought of as a brush stroke solution for many of Ethiopia's ills, never mind sweeping and unrealistic generalization, which the emotionally charged radical student movement, disregarded as a small albatross to be rectified along the way. In retrospect we now know this to be a grave mistake. The radical student movement of Ethiopia was the most radical of its type in the whole of Africa, regarded as such by many scholars alike. In fact by most scales of comparison it lacks competitors globally in its fiery fervor. The overwhelming Eurocentric views it advocated were totally neglectful of its African setting, more precisely described as a peasant society, with very limited formal education, no tangible industry or infrastructure. To top this off, the student movement itself was marred with a shallow understanding of Marxism.

Besides repeating mantra such as "Land to the Tiller" ("*Meret larashu tewagulet ateshishu*"), Fight like Ho Chi Minh and Che Guevera *("Fano Tesemara ende Ho Chi Minh ende Che Guevera"),* the student lead revolution had little substantive

165

awareness of the overall picture. In all honesty the feudal system of land ownership caused the tenant farmer great harm. It needed to be reformed urgently; however, correctly implementing such a revolutionary practice in a mostly backward state was difficult. It was certainly more than what the Marxist student movement bargained for. There was very little articulate understanding of the theory of Marxism and its plausible application to Ethiopia. The overriding characteristics of the revolution were, hyperactive emotional hate projected at the feudal system, lack of clarity in principle and depth, and absence of a future plan. It comprised all the prerequisites necessary for the carnage that was to follow. According to Dr. Teshale Tibebu, a professor of African Studies at Temple University in Philadelphia, *'The superficial nature of Marxism in the student movement of Ethiopia is best exemplified by its adherents to quickly shove it aside when it became inconsequential'*. He goes on to state, *'In Russia, Western Europe, and minimally in America we still see communist or socialist parties, while their more radical Ethiopian cousins have simply dissipated into thin air, indicative of their shallowness'*. This thin understanding of Marxism led to its uncritical wholesale acceptance, and to political opportunism, an ailment that continues to bedevil Ethiopia today. It also left its remnants all over the political scene. Not least of which is the ambiguously defined theory of "Revolutionary Democracy", the guiding principle of the current ruling EPRDF party.

The First Political opportunism in this recent historical time period was the Coup of 1974. The Emperor's lack of expediency to meet the demands of the students and the peasantry was a contributing factor to this development. The monarchy's languid pace in delivering necessary reforms worsened the uproar of the students. In this setting of excessive wants by the students and the lethargic pace of the royalty to catch up with the times the door was left wide open to exploiters and political dealers of the most vicious type. With the apparent power vacuum, junior officers of the military led by Colonel Mengistu Haile Mariam assumed the helm of power. Military coups are not new in Africa and their results are well known. Given this factor, what happened after the fall of the Emperor and the rise of Mengistu's regime is not surprising. In one of their first actions the coup plotters assassinated the King's close confidants and later the Emperor himself. Rules of engagement as stipulated by Machiavellianism dictate this course of action. The radical students, in their blissful exuberance at having gotten rid of the Emperor, were incognizant of what befell them. Their goals had been very narrowly formulated, mostly directed at dislodging the powers that be, with little attention given to the post-revolutionary period. *"During the process of the revolution itself, Ethiopian Marxists' time was consumed by revolutionary action, not elaboration of Marxist theory" (Tibebu)*. With the Emperor gone, with no tangible plan for the future, and a military rule lacking a clear ideological or political awareness, the Radical student movement took the only road available for it to pursue. It turned on each other and began pathetically to see who holds the real errand of Marx, Lenin and Chairman Mao. Its whole world view became me against the world. Though there was very little difference with a vast majority of the programs held by the various leftist parties, the incessant finger pointing competition led to further ignorance. No one had the time to look at the others programs. Everyone was turned inward and considered only their view to be correct. What was important was not how to make ones views better and collaborate with other, so called comrade Marxists. Any serious collaboration and consensus was missing. Evolving the theory and trying the best practice was shoved aside. Perhaps this is best illustrated in the slogan *"Timihirt kedil bewhuala"*, roughly translated as *'education after victory'*. The major beneficiary of the constant bickering that ensued was predictably the one that held all the power, the military Derg regime. Here is a stupendous lesson for contemporary Ethiopian politics.

The subsequent political donnybrook came from all sides and was directed at all sides. The key aspects here were *"mutual defamation, recrimination, and dehumanization of perceived or real opponents"*. This dehumanization of opponents led to some of the worst atrocities in the History of Ethiopia, atrocities that shook the backbone of Ethiopian society. *"One of the key tenants of Ethiopian society to be harmed in this way is the ancient tradition of forgiveness, mercy, and reconciliation"*. These are tenants that had remained constant throughout Ancient Ethiopia, with roots in Judeo-Christian and Islamic philosophy. The brutality of the Red terror is a case in point that cannot be skipped here. As a response to what it labeled as white terror of the Ethiopian People's Revolutionary Party (EPRP) on its members, the Derg and its intellectual allies waged a campaign of terror (Red Terror) on young radical EPRP members and their supporters. The broad day light killings followed by criminalization of public mourning, a key Ethiopian cultural characteristic, had dire consequences on the psyche of the people. The most repulsive of these atrocities involved denying the dead the right to be properly rested or remembered. The Derg lost the most elementary sense of morality when it demanded that families of the deceased sing and dance around the body, that it considered enemies of the revolution, instead of mourn a loved one's death,. *"The DERG did not just kill political opponents it tried to kill cultural traditions held sacred by the people of Ethiopia"*. Though the response to the EPRP by the Derg was over kill to say the least, EPRP onslaught against what it deemed reactionary elements was significant and equally vindictive. Never before has Ethiopian politics been marred in such lust for blood.

168

The effects of this traumatic period can still be seen today. Ethiopians from this point on became afraid to engage in politics openly. Politics was considered a fully charged high voltage electric wire, one that could fray you if you dare to touch it. The fear of overwhelming retribution led to the loss of transparency. Everything had to be kept a secret; politics moved into the more sinister, esoteric underground. Secrecy became a necessary tool of survival. Ethiopians would say, 'polling doesn't work in Ethiopia because the people you are surveying will tell you what you want to hear not necessarily what they believe to be true'; a joke with a heavy dose of reality, and a lesson learned by the EPRDF during the election of May 2005. Eventually EPRDF security forces were compelled to put down protests against the contested poll in 2005. In the process it took the lives of some 200 protesters and imprisoned tens of thousands more. All this goes to show how the government was caught off guard, a testament of politics being driven underground as a result of years of repression. This atmosphere of secrecy however, could entail an ominous more menacing feeling under the surface, unless properly mitigated by all those who want to take the right path in history. It is imperative for people to speak openly and publicly about contentious issues in order to avoid violent outbursts.

One of the assets Ethiopia lost in the Derg reign of terror was her intellectual articulate and optimistic class. In this tumultuous political arena, those who were most able to find the solutions were killed, imprisoned, exiled or silenced by a prevailing sense of fear that swallowed the whole country. In the best case scenario, this group, however small, could have made a big difference in the country's future. The prospects of history are too many in the case of Ethiopia indeed; however the silencing of the intellectual class which started during the Derg period had monumental negative effects in the course of the nation's history. Delving deeper on this subject, it becomes apparent the intellectual capacity of each party, including the Derg was diminished as a result. The shortage of an articulate group that can characterize an opponent party based on fact, gave way to short and meaningless tantrum such as Fascist, Anarcho-Fascist, Anarchist, Revisionist, Bonapartist, Chauvinist, Narrow Ethno-Nationalist, and so on. In this fashion, the different parties throw insults endlessly.

Though these words had political meaning by definition, their application was mostly meaningless in Ethiopia. Sometimes they did not apply to any existing party. 'Fascist, used to describe the Derg widely, most enthusiastically by the EPRP, was one of those wrong characterizations. Surely the brutality and totalitarianism of the Derg was that akin to the fascists of Europe during the early part of the 20th century, but it nevertheless was not fascist'. *"It is impossible for a supposedly fascist government to help translate Marx's Capital into Amharic, abolish land lordship to make land available to the peasantry, ally itself with the socialist camp, train guerrilla fighters for Zimbabwe, open offices for the Palestine Liberation Organization, and introduce literacy campaigns in fifteen languages"*, It would have been more appropriate to call Derg Stalinist, however this categorization would have implicated a majority of the parties at the time. By the same token the feats generated by the Derg Propaganda machinery, supposedly trying to describe the EPRP were absurd to say the least. Anarchist and Anarcho-Fascist are the ones that come to mind here. Both far from the truth, given the fact the EPRP was not fighting to abolish the state. Instead it was fighting to be at the helm of that state power. In brief what we can draw from this history is the shortage of intellect in the different political parties. Inarticulacy was the result of this development, followed by simplification of tantrum, and subsequent violence. Leaders of a party would simply pick out a Marxist-Leninist jargon or phrase and hurl it at their perceived enemy. Lower cadres lacking any capacity to interpret these terms simply followed along, without correcting their leaders. As we would later see this sort of shortage in intellect haunts contemporary Ethiopian politics; both opposition and ruling party (EPRDF). The latter is more significant. Those intellectuals are missing, leaving the door wide open for opportunists. '*All that is needed for the forces of evil to succeed is for enough good and learned folks to remain silent*'.

The purges of the Derg did not only result in endemic fear and the decimation of the intellectuals, and thus encouraging opportunists. In a more positive note however, it culminated in its own loss of credibility and led to its eventual demise. Having been witness to the Red Terror, and countless other cruel atrocities, Ethiopians had grown repulsed by it. In fact, if it had not been for the external and internal threat faced by the nation, the Derg would have crumbled under its own wait. The only vestige of credibility it held was that of protecting the nation's territorial integrity. By its own admission, this had become the overriding reason for its stay in power. In fact it used this as pretext to implement many of its draconian measures. Its propaganda machinery was tuned and ready to put down all would be detractors of this. By portraying itself as a patriot government undaunted and undiminished by the task of protecting the nations territorial integrity, it continued its ruthless suppression of the domestic population. In effect, the "liberation" fronts of the EPLF and the TPLF provided cover for the Derg to extend its hold on power and further militarize itself. Other smaller insurrections could also be sighted here.

During this time the regime focused overwhelmingly on purchasing armaments to fight the various guerilla movements within, as well as external aggression by Somalia. In this way all other prime issues, such as democracy were disregarded. To save the nation from possible dismemberment was its stated goal. We should remind ourselves; this was not the first time war was used as justification for totalitarianism. The Derg is not so different from other war mongers in this sense. Its survival depended on the war, without which it would have been left bankrupt on all fronts. Given this factor any politically settled agreements between it and the "Liberation" fronts would have meant facing up to its real enemy, the overwhelming internal population. The same holds true of the 'Liberation' Fronts who never wanted a real political solution, as that would have meant mediocrity for them. Having failed to mitigate these issues politically, the regime embarked on a ruthless and naïve attempt to resolve the demands of the 'Liberation' Fronts by sheer force. Ultimately the victim of such egotistical policy making was the beleaguered civilian population.

In hindsight many of these problems could have been solved politically, if willing parties were available, with the exception of Somalia's aggression under dictator Said Barre, which was a clear violation of international law and needed military action. On the question of Eritrea, there were obvious but missed opportunities to quell the tension. The first of these was the failure to accept re-integration based upon federalism as during the time of the Emperor. It was a failure that the Derg could not learn from this past mistake and possibly re-ratified this old proposal based upon a new negotiation before things got ugly. Where this became intangible is when one inquires as to how an undemocratic state could accept federalism. Not having accepted real Federalism in mainland Ethiopia and democracy as a whole, how could the Derg accept federalist Eritrea? In large measure this was the reason why the proposal had disintegrated during the reign of Emperor Haile Selassie, with the Emperor opting instead to assume all control. After all, why should a king relinquish sovereignty? The priority of any authoritarian regime is to save its position first. Any federal integration of Eritrea during the monarch period or the Derg period would have necessitated other more pressing issues to be solved; such as

172

federating other nations and nationalities as well as creating democratic and accountable institutions, while simultaneously solving issues of land re-distribution. Unfortunately for the respective regime this path would have resulted in the loss of its power. From the perspective of the various regimes this is precisely the things to be avoided, as stipulated by Machiavellianism. (We will return to this subject in more force later). Again, what is displayed by these developments was the absence of the intellectual's ability to exert its influence on these subjects for a genuine fear of retribution. The atmosphere of fear created by the Derg, as alluded to earlier, made it even worse when the second opportunity arose. The Intellectual was drowned out in equal measure by the "Liberation" fronts, which were becoming more centralized and authoritarian as we would later discover. Predictably fate would have it; a political solution wasn't to be. The consequences were measured in millions of lives lost to war and famine. Millions more were made refugees, while economic and social institutions that showed signs of life at the end of the Emperor's era, such as the public school were turned upside down, to never fully recovery again. Most damaging of all, the sanguine more hopeful psyche present in the population was turned into despair and cynicism. Ethiopians and Eritreans alike would come to terms with this reality more transparently in the future.

Preceding events do not require a fortune teller to discern. The weak political position of the Derg compromised its military activities. Quagmire would be the best description of the war, which mostly consisted of capturing, relinquishing, and recapturing hills and mountains in a merry-go-round for decades running. It was the proverbial insurgency with no possibility for military victory. Not having the prudence to see alternatives and with the increasing politicization of the army, lack of moral and nepotism became widespread. A quintessential representation of the situation was presented by Bealu Girma in his book

"Oromay", written on location, in secret, and with credible validation. Its subversive revelation would later result in the author's disappearance; he was never to be seen again. When Derg launched "Operation Red Star", I was working under the supervision of Ato Bealu in Asmara for seven months reporting for government media about the war, while he was writing this book. Incidentally, I happen to be the journalist that Bealu trusted to give me two copies of his first draft, asking me to deliver to his wife Almaz, which I did the same day when I returned to Addis Ababa leaving him behind.

Silencing the intellectual once again proved disastrous for Ethiopia. Meanwhile the civilian caught up in the middle was to bear the burden of the punishment. The collateral damage caused in pursuit of a seemingly invisible target went from bad to worst. Such frustrations led the army to lose discipline, which led to further degradation and abuse of power, including raping of civilians, which was never properly investigated. The liberation camps were only keen to take advantage of this through their various propaganda activities. This drove the able bodied increasingly into the hands of the 'Liberation' Camps. According to Theodore Vestal's *"Ethiopia a Post-Cold War State"*, the Author states *"in this period of the mid to late 1980s the EPLF was beginning to enjoy broad based public support from the Eritrean public. To add to its highly disciplined and regimented apparatus, it was now receiving increased public support"*. The parallel between the squalor of the Derg as a result of its political bankruptcy and the rise of the Front is telling indeed. One could argue public compliance with the EPLF was mostly a defensive stand against a tyrannical regime and lack of alternatives rather than a historical need for secession. Anger and despondency are feelings that cannot be ignored here.

The 'Liberation' fronts for their part did manage to address some of the peasant's concerns in education, women's rights, and land issues. Although minimal in the scheme of things it did have a positive psychological effect among its supposed constituency. During the conflict, EPLF was able to provide underground hospital care for instance, including performing sophisticated surgical operations. These sorts of non-combat actions were also something the TPLF was well adept at. In Tigray the TPLF introduced much needed change for women, who were beginning to view joining the movement as a way to escape archaic chauvinist way of rural life. John Young, author of *"Peasant Revolution in Ethiopia"* commented *"In addition it (TPLF) was beginning to provide administrational services and schooling in the local language in areas it controlled. Such developments were positively taken by the people and helped win more support"*. Peasants of Tigray remained one of the poorest in Ethiopia; rampant dissatisfaction among them is hardly surprising. It was fertile ground for such an insurgency. These facts were well known to the Derg. Choosing to ignore them it relied on force as its modus operandi. Its rigidity was totally paralyzing. Deserters from its rank and file were widespread, who could blame them, as they saw no light at the end of the tunnel. In typical Derg fashion it tried to blame this on infiltration of its forces by rival underground movements, EPRP being the main suspect. It would have been wiser to look at the real background for the conflict instead. This dependence on force led the Derg to lose the hearts and minds of the people totally. Mengistu Haile-Mariam, in one of his cantankerous speeches, addressing this issue, heatedly spoke of how the peasantry was 'attacking his forces like a swarm of locusts'. Such myopic failures should not have come as a surprise; given the fact that debate on the real issues of the conflict was silenced by a culture of fear and coercion.

One consideration must be added here, namely that of the 'Liberation' Front's character during the war. Though they engaged positively with the population in some instances, as mentioned above, this was not always the case. Misuse of power and coercion through violent means were also a noticeable feature applied by all sides during this conflict. Some of these abuses have recently come to the surface. The reason for their belated revelation is perhaps a testament to the lack of unadulterated information. It is extremely difficult to find out the facts about conflicts in Ethiopia because many of the so called news publications are propaganda pieces of the various organizations. The lack of a genuine independent news media with an extensive coverage of events makes the advent of rumors a reality. However, this is not to say all rumors were false or that propaganda does not have the minutest trace of sincerity. Abuses and coercions perpetrated by the 'Liberation' fronts during their time as a guerilla movement have surfaced more forcefully in recent times. In particular the BBC's recent allegation about the diversion of food aid intended to help victims of the horrible drought in 1984 by the TPLF was scathing to say the least. For many it was a reaffirmation of what we had suspected all along. In later paragraphs these issues will be discussed. It is merely intended to be a warning that unsuspecting parties usually have skeletons hidden somewhere in their closet. More often than not, this is true of armed groups operation in Africa, and the TPLF in Ethiopia is no different, as demonstrated by the food aid abuse of 1984.

Although the regime's military possessed one of the most sophisticated weaponry and training available in Africa at the time, it lacked moral, precisely because of its political bankruptcy. The result was indiscipline and abuse of power, generating more dissatisfaction from the population. Repeatedly, lack of political legitimacy derived from democracy and justice would cost Ethiopia dearly. With its principal ally, the Soviet

Union on the decline, the deck of cards would rapidly begin tumbling down as quickly as it had arisen in 1974. A few rogue generals who were beginning to notice the deteriorating circumstances and willing to publicize them in a manner that undermined the dictatorship were also systematically eliminated. Even in our present day some of these developments are not fully uncloaked. What was becoming more conspicuous was the rift from inside the camp that was becoming more pronounced. Signs of this could be seen in coup plots that never saw fruition but nevertheless lurked in the backdrop. Eventually this internal dispute was ruthlessly strangled.

The relationship between The USSR and the Derg was also becoming strained. Moscow no longer had the means to engage in Africa's longest running civil war. The regime in Ethiopia was unwilling to heed the advice of its patron state as well. Their association was purely an opportunistic one, marred in cold war politics. If the Derg could have received what it required from the United States instead, it would have aligned itself in this manner. In fact it tried to do this in its early days. Ideology was secondary to power, as is the case with the EPRDF in Ethiopia today, another indication of the dormant shallowness of ideology and completeness of opportunisms in Ethiopian politics. Ethiopian regimes only consider utilitarianism in their search for powerful allies. The leftist ideology of the Derg was totally instrumental in this regard. Its orientation towards the leftist camp was espoused as long as it served its short term goal of controlling the country. Having no backbone in theory and no support from the public, the Derg, in a desperate Volte-face tried to rescue itself by declaring "Mixed Economy" and restructuring to fit the western liberal model of market liberalization. In the end it was too little too late.

With the rotting away of all aspects of the Regime's Army, the EPLF was able to score quick and successive military victories from 1989 to 1991. In the end it moved from the periphery to city centers, including the capital, Asmara. The port of Massawa fell soon after. With it, all that the Derg claimed to fight for was gone. In this period EPLF captured invaluable weaponry, which would make it a regional powerhouse soon after the collapse of the Derg, at least militarily. Similarly the TPLF, as the overwhelming dominant force assumed the helm in Addis Ababa. On a rare positive note Mengistu's regime relinquished the capital without a fight, which could have been a bloodbath. In retrospect this was a good decision. No tangible exertion of force was necessary in these last days of the conflict. On the contrary, fields of tanks and ammunition where abandoned, gifts of a dying regime.

Here, would be 'Liberators' of Tigray abandoned their original stated purpose of seceding, for the bigger prize of Ethiopia. In retrospect, a correct decision, given the fact that their supposed constituency, which is genuinely patriotic, would have made seceding of Tigray very difficult. Geopolitical circumstances were also unaccommodating to this path. Nevertheless flirtation with the idea in its early days, as indicated in the 1976 TPLF manifesto, is yet another example of the abundance in poorly formulated opportunism that haunts Ethiopian politics. Such ephemeral stated goals, exemplified by the manifesto, are very indicative about the nature of the politicians that manufacture them. Having no concrete principle, no historical support, and no support from public opinion requires this stance. Stated goals are temporary precisely because many of these organizations lack a thoroughly researched and corroborated ideology, a theme we will revisit about the ambiguously defined *"Revolutionary Democracy"*. When it comes to underdeveloped states, undoubtedly some experimentation is unavoidable or even necessary, yet classifying this sort of wishy-washy business as such would be wrong, since their purpose seems to benefit a small number of elites that invent them. As intended, this confuses people; having to constantly guess at the intention of these politicians keeps people away from real issues. In essence it serves to exclude the public. This state of confusion only serves the opportunists, not genuine devotees of the people. And this, by in large is their main function.

Post Derg Briefly

In 1989, on the eve of its ascent to power, the TPLF joined and created other ethnic insurgencies, forming the Ethiopian People Revolutionary Democratic Front (EPRDF). This united front was to cover most of the country, at least as stated on paper. Contrary to their long held beliefs, the Liberation Front began presenting themselves as aficionados of market liberalization, a shrewdly calculated stance, given the shifting of global power structures. Dr. Theodore Vestal alludes to this; *"At the peace negotiations in London brokered by the United States, the Marxist-Leninist skeletons in the closets of the TPLF and the EPLF were kept firmly under lock"*. With the demise of the Soviet Union it became necessary for the TPLF to wear the mask of the Neo-Liberal west, particularly the United States, which replaced the Soviet Union as the patron state of Ethiopia. Again, not out of genuine appreciation of Liberalism or the plight of Ethiopians, but for the sake of convenience. The same convenience the soviets were willing to forge with the Derg, with evident negative implications for Ethiopia. As is standard across the developing world, the respective public opinion of Ethiopia and soon to be independent Eritrea was shoved aside as a burdensome nuisance. According to Vestal's research, the chief negotiator for the United States, Herman Cohen said *'He had no choice because the EPRDF had won the war and other considerations that might include the wider public was beyond him'* This is hardly a surprising revelation for

Ethiopians, who have grown expectant of such harmful political games. *"during these negotiations Chief mediator Herman Cohen of the United states was played like a well-toned Masinko, a one stringed violin by The TPLF/EPRDF, and EPLF, representatives" (Vestal)*. Important issues concerning the fate of the nation did not figure into these conferences. What to do with the disbanded military of the Derg and how to properly deal with the traumatic events such as the Red Terror were not seriously considered. Unlike South Africa, which had a *"Truth and reconciliation commission"* to heal the nation from its horrific past, Ethiopia was left to sort out past crimes arbitrarily. In typical fashion victors were left to dictate terms to the vanquished. A properly justified closer to the country's horrendous past was not put in place. For this reason there was no standard or model set to guide future activities. Though Ethiopians were content at having gotten rid of the illegitimate brutal Derg regime; in all, it could be said, the country lost a great opportunity to charter a nobler course for the future. It was one of many missed opportunities for the country and the region as a whole.

The other organizations besides the TPLF that formed the EPRDF had very little traction to influence policy. In addiction they had contradicting ideas which made them weaker indeed. The Oromo 'Liberation' Front (OLF) is a good example of this antagonistic atmosphere. Its long standing purpose had been to see to the independence of Oromia. Modern Ethiopian history indicates victimization of the Oromo by Abyssinia, Amhara-Tigray together. This was briefly escalated under the reign of Emperor Menelick II conquest of the area in the late 19th century. Using this and other transgressions as pretext, the OLF sought independence for Oromia from Ethiopia. Joining the supposedly United Front of the EPRDF was thus an anomaly. Unlike the TPLF it did not discard secessionist views, even when it was part of the coalition front. Its consent was purely calculated to benefit itself in the short-term. This marriage of convenience would later fall apart as expected. As in all the Parties of the EPRDF coalition it suffered form an ideological deficit. Analysis deeper into its stated mission reveals gaping holes when viewed in the context of Ethiopian history; which contrary to the claims of the liberators runs longer than a few hundred years.

Many 'liberation' Organizations held the view that Ethiopia was a creation of the last century, approximately. The problem with this view is, it was Eurocentric and disregarded African definitions. The African definition of a loosely held state, which had existed for centuries before the arrival of colonial powers, did not figure into this calculation. Besides each region conquered the other followed by subjugation in a circular trend. This view of the OLF was indeed a Eurocentric hangover from the Ethiopian student movement. History before the arrival of European powers was ignored. In addition, a geographical, and demographical realities ran contrary to its mission. Ethnic boundaries are difficult to draw in Ethiopia, as in everywhere else in Africa. Boundaries tend to be a mirage, clearly defined in certain places and almost invisible in others. Mixed races are also a significant proportion of the population. Cross cultural exchange and significant assimilation makes this sort of clear cut categorization difficult. Extensive research still needs to be done in this regard. As a result such political organizations ran a deficit in public trust. Arguing the Oromo were disenfranchised by the Abyssinians was however correct, with one tantalizing addition. The peasantry of Abyssinia, Amhara and Tigray alike, also suffered measurably under successive Abyssinian Emperors. The present day reformation of the OLF, which is positive, is indicative of efforts to correct its past errors.

The primary beneficiary of this ideological shortage and bickering was the TPLF. Though it was also poor in ideology and public acceptance, it at least made up for this discrepancy through military superiority. In this characteristic it had something in common with Derg. It replaced political legitimacy with military power. The cornucopia of acronyms for political parties can be a bit exasperating in the case of modern Ethiopia. Though these letters have meaning by definition, for the most part they have been sluggish as an organization. Organizations housed under the EPRDF, with the exception of the TPLF fall under this category. For this reason when one speaks of the EPRDF, invariably what is implied is the TPLF. The Amhara National Democratic Movement (ANDM), OLF, which was later replaced by The Oromo People Democratic Organization (OPDO), and The Southern Nations, Nationalities and Peoples (SNNP) had neither military power nor political consent. As a result they failed wayward, with their main function being to provide cover for the TPLF. Other opposition parties were very much excluded from the scene. Any overwhelming, contrary view was systematically excluded by the EPRDF. History repeated itself. Earlier in Ethiopia's history, the Derg, as the most armed group took advantage of the political bickering that ensued immediately after the coup of 1974. This squabbling of the parties, as in the past also arose from their failure to formulate a clearly applicable ideological stance, which led them to be shunned by the public. They were politically defunct. We just viewed one such case in the OLF. If you don't have public acceptance then you'd better have the guns, which the TPLF clearly possessed. And so it was déjà vu once again.

There are countless contradictions that marred developments of Ethiopian politics since the rise of the EPRDF in 1991. Not least of which is the wholesale uncritical acceptance of liberalism by many political groups. These former Marxists were able to shed their leftist view without a flinch when it was deemed no longer advantageous. This trend applies to the overwhelming majority of political parties in Ethiopia.

Political organizations of the 60s 70s and 80s found Marxist theory very instrumental in the political landscape of their day, thus they tried to use it to elevate themselves to positions of power. With the fall of communism, liberalism was the new ladder to the top. As in the past criticism of this view was almost nonexistent. *"Just as Marxism was accepted wholesale and uncritically in the past, it is now rejected and liberalism accepted wholesale and uncritically" (Teshale).* The nonsensical developments of this trend are not only exemplified by the TPLF/EPRDF, which provisionally tossed out its heavy Marxist-Leninist overcoat, but also by the opposition.

Implementation of Article 39 of the Ethiopian constitution concerning the right of nations and nationalities for self-determination, including and up to secession, once the mantra of the student movement, and the bulwark of parties such as the EPRP is now used by them to rebuke the EPRDF. In fact had they taken power they would have been inclined to implement the same policies. Given this factor, it is surprising to see the attacks on the EPRDF based on this provision. Many of the opposition who are vilifying this policy as narrow and ethnocentric had at one point adhered to the same view. Yet again we notice another case in point of the instrumental nature of politics in Ethiopia. Realities on the ground however were not befitting to both models. It is impossible to enclose all 80 nations and nationalities in their own regional map. Simplification is almost inevitable when one thinks of the Southern Nations and other small but significant ethnic groupings who are spread across the country incongruously. As an underdeveloped African state, Ethiopia, and the Horn region in general is difficult to categorize in such a brushstroke. Realization of the glaring truth that Africa needs African solutions, which neither Marxism nor Liberalism can wholly satisfy is missing. Wholesale acceptance of Western political theory had the effect of drowning out indigenous African views and circumstances, which predictably had many of the solutions Ethiopia needed.

On the specific question of Article 39 one would be hard pressed to build a well substantiated opposition to its overall attempt. Having said this, it goes without saying; its efforts are heavily diminished in the undemocratic environment we currently find ourselves in. Federalism without democracy makes no sense whatsoever. Article 39 under authoritarianism doesn't result in federalism based on democracy and justice; it instead acts as a utilitarian tool for the ruling party to maintain its grip on power. The current status quo of nations and nationalities doesn't do justice to many of the sacrifices made by the student movement, however inarticulate they might have been. The sacrifice of people such as Wallelign Mekonen, who died advocating self-administration for ethnic nations and nationalities of Ethiopia, has not yet been made worthwhile. In fact thousands of people from all corners of Ethiopia were brutally murdered, imprisoned, tortured, and exiled for this cause. Shamefully their efforts seem not to have been heeded. The solution rests in amending and strengthening Article 39. This requires a more democratic and transparent form of governance. Efforts towards this goal have been retarded, judging by the authoritarian character of the EPRDF regime.

Continuing on the subject of contradictions and ideological deficit, one is unable to pass without examining the many faults presented with the independence of Eritrea and its process. The TPLF/ EPRDF and the EPLF maintained the view that Eritrea was a colonial issue and as such its fate must be determined. The accuracy of this view however, is not beyond debate. In fact a well-established argument has yet to be presented by any of the political organizations that have endorsed this view. The primary advocates of this stance were all born out of the Marxist student movement and thus had

184

Eurocentric views. EPRP, TPLF, and EPLF are the ones that come to mind here. We could add the now defunct Eritrean Liberation Front (ELF), which was the original adherent of this view. Eritrea's anomaly results from the successive colonial occupation of the territory by far off powers. This period was particularly marked by an approximately 60 year occupation of Eritrea, officially from 1889-1947. Prior to the advent of colonialism however, Eritrea was known as Midri Bahri ruled by Emperors envoy, Bahre-Negash, and its historical ties were deeply intertwined with Ethiopia. Successive Ethiopian emperors considered this territory to be part of Greater Ethiopia/Abyssinia.

Historically, highlander Eritrean Orthodox Christians were particularly fond of their connections to the ancient Ethiopian Empire. The primary language spoken in this region, Tigrigna, is also the primary language immediately south of the Mereb River, used to demarcate the border between Eritrea and Ethiopia by colonial powers. Lowlander Muslim Eritreans, though they were disenfranchised by Christian Ethiopian rulers, were also linked through trade with Ethiopia for centuries prior to the arrival of colonial powers. Afar tribesmen traveled freely across the border to exchange goods and ideas with their kin south of the border into the Denakil depression. The very fact that similar cultures, and languages reside on both side of the border is evidence of common history. These conditions of a loosely held state that lasted for centuries make the advent of colonial Eritrea a small drop in the ocean indeed. The colonial period highlighted by the successive powers that tried to occupy Eritrea pale in comparison to this long common history. However, their aftereffect was not to be underestimated. As in everywhere else in Africa the result of colonialism was to be a constant thorn for posterity. Regrettably the political elites of both countries who inherited these circumstances chose to ignore their African history in exchange for European viewpoints. This self-degradation however, has been detrimental to peace, stability, and development of the region as a whole. Subsequently when the time arrived for colonial Italy to relinquish its colony, Ethiopian ruling elites where not prepared to take the necessary precaution to avoid blunders. They chose to follow due course assigned to them by colonial powers, Great Briton being one such primary power. Ethiopia's political establishment was in no way prepared to accept a federalist Eritrea at the time. The country's heavily rigid monarchy system was paralyzing in this regard. Though it offered opportunities, mainly for Eritrean Orthodox Christians, it undervalued Eritrea's peculiarities in general.

Miraculously this long and commonly held history did not appear on the radar screens of the various Marxist political parties that advocated Eritrea's secession. They took the view of Eritrea being a colonial question, a country that was now according to them under Ethiopian colonialism. For them European colonialism was replaced by an African one. Indeed this was a very radical appreciation of history. As we saw earlier, this view is not entirely true either; according to African vantage points, which with all due respect is a more significant vantage point in this case. For Africans history did not begin with the advent of European colonialism. In the case of Ethiopia/Eritrea the overwhelming historical evidence supports this view. Given this reason it would have been wiser to analyze the whole historical time scale. Had this been the case many countless lives and resources may have been saved. Africa in general might have been a different place today. The struggle could have been against totalitarianism and for social justice instead, ideals that could be achieved in unison. In fact it is becoming increasingly apparent; they could only be achieved in this manner. There is no shortage of such trends either. If one is willing to delve deeper, a small but growing call for regionalism is becoming evident. In a recent conference held in San Jose California, with the stated goal of mending the rifts created by successive regimes between Ethiopians and Eritreans, some of these points were raised. Dr. Mesfin Araya, a native of Eritrea and a professor at New York City University, who spoke at the conference, alludes to this issue. He states *"The Horn of Africa, which has been facing cyclical poverty and conflict, has a potential to unify gradually on conditions that the region is free from destructive and divisive tyrannies"*. He continues by saying, *"For that to occur the intellectual class needs to reflect on its past mistakes and develop the capacity to dream big and beautiful, to reconcile with its tragic past and envision a better future"*. Perhaps the above statement could be the fantastic bit of missing ingredient, if only we could have the vision and wisdom to see its stupendous honesty. Instability, underdevelopment, war, and famine could be avoided if policy and governance is incorporated with such vision in mind.

Observing history in this regard we come across inadequacies and blunders, including the failure of the federalist integration model and the dissolution of the Eritrean parliament. The dissolution was the result of a push by the Unionist Party, Yehager Fikir Mahber and vote by Eritrean Parliament members, subsequently accepted by the Emperor. The unionists who were scared of the growing influence of the Islamist Party in Eritrea lobbied for a complete union. These errors made concerning the re-integration of Eritrea during the Haile Selassie I era were heavily damaging, judging by the conflict that ensued consequently. The gradual takeover of Eritrea by Haile-Selassie I and the decree whereby Amharic was made a compulsory language all culminated out of this initial move to annex the region. In this process however, Eritrea was not colonized by Ethiopia as was claimed by the 'Liberation' fronts and the TPLF and EPRP. This process of forceful assimilation would be correctly labeled annexation instead. Nevertheless no one could possibly justify such a move either. In the end it created a wedge between the two peoples. However, the remedies prescribed by the 'liberation' fronts were extreme to say the least. Blunders that were to follow at the hands of the Derg and the 'Liberation' fronts were more scandalous by this standard. Theirs was an offense committed with full acknowledgment, for their narrow interests. Previous monarchs of Ethiopia believed their power was derived from God, thus their will was absolute. In this way, they might have been deceived, having failed to keep up with the times. It is important to realize the profound cultural and religious views that were held in those days. With the advent of formal education and modernization however, later power brokers had no excuse for their ill judgments on this issue. In fact a closer inspection of the policies of the Derg and the 'Liberation' Fronts present more harmful characteristics to the region. We may regard their decision on this subject to be a result of ill judgment, kindly giving them the benefit of the doubt; however the truth is these organizations had all the prior knowledge necessary to make correct decisions. By purposely ignoring facts they only sought to satisfy their organizational appetite for power. To that end they strove, endlessly toiling to achieve the goal of acquiring power or maintaining it. In this regard the people of the region were the primary losers and the ones who bore the brunt of the negative consequences. We see this displayed not only in the 30 year vicious war of 'liberation', but also in the border war that claimed the lives of tens of thousands of people on both sides in the late 1990s.

Having garnered Independence through a U.N mediated referendum in 1993; the EPLF was able to achieve what it fought for. In those early days, possessing an ally in Addis Ababa willing to bend over backwards to acquiesce to its demands was very instrumental in this regard. If it had not been for the full complicity of the EPRDF the referendum could have been impeded. The power behind the throne of the EPRDF, which is inevitably the TPLF, had long stipulated the question of Eritrea as that of a colonial question requiring full independence as the remedy. In the aftermath of EPLF military victory its political clout in Addis Ababa was also not to be underestimated. After all it was EPLF, TPLF/EPRDF troops that marched into Addis Ababa after the fall of the Derg. From the get go their influence and involvement in the policy making of the EPRDF was not miniscule. As a potential power rival for control over Ethiopia, the TPLF had reason to fear the EPLF. For this reason, in its view, the referendum offered an opportunity to shove aside a potential rival out of the scene in Addis. In retrospect this move was highly favorable for the TPLF/EPRDF; which now enjoys preeminence in Ethiopia. Given this factor the conflict that culminated years later between the TPLF/EPRDF and EPLF is not astounding. One could be inclined to judge it inevitable even.

Here another tantalizing consideration must be acknowledged; that the interests and views of the public are totally disregarded. In this fashion the referendum was designed to portray the interests of the victorious parties. Nevertheless the referendum did receive a tremendous reception by the Eritrean community. Decades of brutal warfare and endemic underdevelopment had gone a long way to convince public opinion towards the need for independence as the only means to progress. Given the prowess displayed by the EPLF during the conflict and its ascent to power, no one doubted the result of the referendum either. As expected it was able to garner an overwhelming majority of the Eritrean public in its favor. In this sense it was an absolute mandate. This is not to say however, there were no discrepancies in the process. The presentation of the referendum and its implementation could be argued. The actual physical arrangement of the referendum at polling stations was akin to voting for Freedom or Slavery, freedom being independence and slavery being unison. The referendum's equivocal presentation could open the door for yet more debate. Relationships between the two peoples were not that of a slave master relationship. Eritrean natives who lived in Ethiopia can testify to this.

Contrary to the views held by the 'Liberation' Fronts, the independence of Eritrea did not result in regional stability and development. Its effects were by in large negative for both groups of people. Those living in the region can testify to the dreadful nature of developments since 'independence'. The primary asset lost to both groups of people was regional steadiness and stability, a paramount underlining for development. As mentioned earlier, the disintegration of the cozy relationship felt by the ruling parities of Asmara and Addis Ababa were not hard to predict. Apparently the Eritrean government heavily depended on Ethiopia's resources for its development. This is no surprise given the two regions were once a unit, linked economically in many ways. For the regime in Asmara, attaining these resources, whether in raw material, technical assistance, or even financial support was not difficult in those days of its infancy. As noted earlier, having a regime in Addis Ababa willing to bend over backwards to meet its demands was facilitating indeed. Perhaps the TPLF/EPRDF deemed this necessary as reimbursement for the support it gained from the EPLF during its guerilla days. It seems to have been a preordained contract. However, this state of affairs was inherently unsustainable. A good illustration is international donor aid money garnered by Ethiopia being allotted for projects in Eritrea. In this fashion while the burden of loan risk was fully associated with TPLF/EPRDF, more explicitly on Ethiopians; the gains were transmitted to a potentially rival state. Another avenue by which the TPLF/EPRDF was able to compensate its former ally in arms was by providing submarket cheap raw materials, mostly cash crops, such as coffee. Consequently the regime in Asmara sold these raw materials at much higher profit margins in international markets. Augmented inaccessibility of seaports to Ethiopian exporters was essential in facilitating these trends. In essence the regime in Asmara tried to monopolize and capitalize on Ethiopian exports. If things continued along this trajectory, imports destined for Ethiopia could have possibly been manipulated in a similar way. It is not hard to see why such trade imbalances can lead to conflict, especially in poor third world states.

Currency used by the Eritrean government was still the Birr, Ethiopia's national currency. When it managed to transition to its own new currency the Nakfa, it was unwilling to make the necessary exchange rate adjustments, another source of the conflict that took place between the two regimes. It is important to mention here the profits being generated rarely benefited the Eritrean public in any meaningful way. For the most part these funds were used by the regime to solidify its power and to satisfy its insatiable appetite for military efficiency and arms; arms that would go a long way in subduing any complaint from the TPLF/EPRDF and its own internal population. Given such circumstances the conflict that took place in the late 1990s is not surprising. The status quo could not continue. Something had to give way eventually. Certainly belligerence and arrogance displayed by the Asmara regime is reminiscent of the Derg. It would only result in creating more enemies for itself in the long term. One can sense history being repeated in typical African fashion. In Addis Ababa, the TPLF/EPRDF was in danger of becoming weakened internally for its cozy relationship with the Asmara regime. Further introspection reveals a growing sense of isolation felt by it as a result of these policies. It was willing to stretch itself by getting rid of technically proficient bureaucrats unwilling to carry out its cozy relationship with the regime in Asmara. This process is called *"Gimgema"*. The equivalent of this word in English would be evaluation resulting in revision or correction. It is still used today for relieving potential stumbling blocks to party policy. Eventually this trend would begin to render it less effective in terms of governance. Seeing that its power was slipping away as a result of its dealings with Asmara, it tried a volte-face reversal in policy, which eventually culminated in full-fledged war.

Both sides claim not to have fired the first shot, a pointless argument given the fact casualties on both sides range in the thousands. According to an international report commissioned in The Hague, *"Eritrea broke international law and triggered the war by invading Ethiopia"*. Obviously this conclusion is disputed by the regime in Eritrea. Though the real reason for the conflict is the trade imbalance discussed above, its official given motive was deceivingly, the border disagreement. Three border areas are implicated here, Badme, Tsorona-Zalambessa, and Bure. All are miniscule and insignificant in the whole scheme of things. To think of the war as a purely border dispute was precisely designed to be deceiving. It helps manufacture support for the war for both sides. Imagine the problem of recruiting and waging a war without the emotional backdrop of the border. To galvanize public support for the war there had to be a tangible reason, which the people of this underdeveloped region could easily understand and rally around. The border dispute served this purpose. There were minor natural issues with the border however. And of course this is largely expected, since the border is historically and demographically artificial. For this reason the border region has not been as clearly defined as black or white. Instead it has always remained a gray zone, therefore a point of contention for those seeking to make it so. Naturally the psyche of the people in this region has been akin to the gray zone image. To them the border conflict is a senseless war, instigated for the benefit of politicians.

Nevertheless the fighting was not driven by the border dispute as claimed by both sides. Eventually the conflict would be heavily costly to both sides. Overall accounts of casualties are not clear. Many experts estimate it to be around 100,000. Massive internal displacement and abuse of refugees was also another outcome of the war. About 77,000 Ethiopians of Eritrean origin would be subject to deportation. Their property was confiscated for the most part. This was a step; even the brutal Derg was unwilling to take in its day. Predictably the EPRDF regime sought to cut off the hand that it thought was feeding the EPLF. Unfortunately even those who were not directly involved became victims of this brush stroke policy. Ethiopians living in Eritrea, about 7500 of them were also permanently interned in camps and subject to many abuses, including rape. No doubt many more thousands have been forced to leave their homes and flee as a result of this conflict. In a region suffering from endemic poverty millions were spent on a conflict that ended up in a stalemate. No doubt the psychological image of both people about their identity has been challenged, with the intended consequence of creating a wedge between them. A seemingly endless cold war was created and continues to plague the region. The currency used to wage the war was blood, that which came from the common people, who through no fault of their own became embroiled in a mess. To make things worse the hurt and pain was transferred to posterity.

The worst consequence of the war is tantalizingly the resultant cold war. The heavily militarized border stayed disputed until 2018; and the Ethiopian troops continued to occupy Badme, contrary to a decision made by the UN commission. Massive amounts of resources are being spent wastefully by two nations with populations living in destitute. According to a scathing report, *"Eritrea A siege State"*, presented by the International Crisis Group in September 2010, *"The militarism and authoritarianism which now define the political culture of the Eritrean government have become worst in recent times, overshadowing all other superseding problems faced by the country"*. The report also indicates the real impediment caused by indefinite conscription, which is draining the life blood of the country's youth. In the event development is possible this demographic happens to be the most useful. Being in a constant state of war helps the regime legitimize itself in the face of possible opposition. War is good cover for bad politics. The cold war with Ethiopia and other hostilities with neighboring states have been accommodating to its goal of controlling the internal enemy, which predictably is the Eritrean public. By portraying itself as a patriotic government committed to Eritrean independence it sustains the status quo, seemingly operating under a constant state of emergency. Just as we saw the Derg attempt to turn war into its political advantage earlier; we notice the same trend here. Unlike the Derg however, dislodging it from power will be much more difficult, as it is an internal and a well- entrenched faction. Indeed things have significantly worsened for the region.

Such maneuverings have also been very instrumental for the EPRDF. Now it can easily label pro-democracy dissent in Ethiopia on instigation caused by the regime in Asmara. In this sense, adventurism by the Asmara clique at propping up so called Ethiopian political opposition has been destructive to genuinely pro-democracy movements in Ethiopia. In all probability such efforts by Eritrea collapse under careful examination. One is left baffled as to how an atrocious regime, such as the one in Asmara can come up with the goods to produce a justified outcome in Ethiopia. As we have seen throughout history however, there is no shortage of political bandits willing to jump on the bandwagon. Fortunately for the public, it has become keenly aware of their turncoat nature. Nonetheless such deceit does not bode well for genuine pro-democracy movements in Ethiopia. In the most recent fraudulent election process that took place in Ethiopia (2010), some incidents have been attributed by the EPRDF, as destabilizing efforts undertaken by Eritrea's government. These include the bombing of a civilian bus in Humera, a grenade attack on a house near Mekelle, and other political killings in and around the region. While EPRDF officials are on record stating these events to be 'attacks orchestrated by Asmara linked groups', opposition parties who participated in the election blame this to be the work of EPRDF cadres seeking to distract and scare their supporters. Given the fact these incidents peak around election time is telling indeed.

A brief glance at the other side of the coin reveals the vice versa nature of this political cat and mouse game. The EPRDF is not shy to prop up Eritrean opposition groups either. Like their Ethiopian counterpart these groups tend not to be devotees of the people. Their de facto function, contrary to what they believe is to create confusion, apathy, and sideline real democratic efforts. These results might be unintended consequences for their part, but they are a truism. In the event they do manage to topple their respective regimes, there is no guarantee as to their form of governance thereafter. Turning back the other way, in the unlikely scenario the Asmara based Ethiopian opposition manages to topple the regime in Addis Ababa, the most likely outcome is the disintegration of the nation, hence the support from the EPLF. One can judge this outcome based on their total non-cohesive and even antagonistic nature. Paradoxically the political environment in the region has become Orwellian since the independence of Eritrea. Contrary to prior beliefs, endemic problems faced by the regions have only become aggravated since. Negatively affected are those civilians, impoverished, stifled, unable to speak, and stuck in this political ping pong. Invariably, beneficiaries have been the respective repressive regimes. Unsurprisingly they have benefited from this convoluted regional mess of the Horn of Africa. Perpetual war guarantees everlasting peace for both regimes. Consequently any real positive democratic change in one or the other regional countries spells bad omen for them. It could have an undesired spreading effect, which could inturn affect the prospect of the regimes. This state of affairs is perhaps best captured by George Orwell in his epic novel *"Nineteen Eighty-Four"*. Orwell writes: *"The consciousness of being at war, and therefore in danger, makes the handing over of all power to a small privileged elite cast seem natural and an unavoidable condition of survival"*. The cold war between the two nations has played this role well enough, to the satisfaction of both regimes. Under these difficult circumstances, alleviating the ills of the region henceforth requires real introspection and chartering a plan based on solidarity, sympathy, and care for others.

On the subject of regional conflicts and their effect, one cannot pass without mentioning the war in Somalia and the involvement of regional countries. Somalia is a real concern for western observers who fear it to be the next staging ground for international terrorism. In particular the United States has designated Al Shabab as a regional threat to international peace. Though this happens to be true, the largely military solution prescribed by Western powers with the aid of regional allies, Ethiopia, in particular has been harmful. In a classic example of Western involvement it has been more destabilizing and has brought unwanted players to the conflict, including International Jihadists. The EPRDF's decision to enter Somalia on behalf of Western powers is purely calculated to benefit its ephemeral objective of deriving more legitimacy and resources in the short term. Governments of poor states figure, being a yes man to powerful players is a sure way to gain legitimacy and support for their illegitimate power, correctly so, judging by history. However, this paradigm has been detrimental to the people of poor nations. People of the Horn region also fall under this category. A case in point is; Ethiopians have not been made more safe or prosperous as a result of the EPRDF's involvement in Somalia. By and large the impact has been negative for Ethiopia's security prospects. Nevertheless the conflict has benefited the regime in Addis Ababa in its effort to pull more western support in the face of internal public opposition.

The situation in Somalia has been worsened, contrary to expectations. Inevitably one outcome was the galvanization of extremist groups such as Al Shabab. Many experts now conclude; during Ethiopia's short occupation of Somalia, Al Shabab was able to recruit more fighters and strengthen its ranks. More than ever it was able to foment support from Somalis, who inexorably began to view it as a patriotic front against foreign aggression. Whatever bond was left between the people of Somalia and Ethiopia was harmed, leaving a heavy burden of mistrust for posterity. Through no fault of their own the people of the region have been made to suffer. It also culminated in the detrimental involvement of the Eritrean regime, which in its drive to counter the regime in Ethiopia was shipping weapons and assistance to Al Shabab, categorized as a terrorist organization. Invariably the International community was forced to slap sanctions on the Eritrean government in 2010. Though the sanctions are specifically targeted against the regime and its ability to wage war, undoubtedly the primary victim will be the Eritrean public, which is totally dependent on the regime for its survival. There is no question the Eritrean government will pull meager resources from the people in order to supplant the effect of the sanction on its military. Somalis on the other hand were left to live in a war zone and in a state of chaos, which is threatening to spill over to regional countries. The Ogaden in Ethiopia is a prime concern here. Militancy and extremism has not been quelled, awkwardly it has been exasperated.

Pessimism is a feeling difficult to suppress after assessing developments in Somalia. It seems each group is destined to destabilize the other. Cyclical retribution and poverty could easily degenerate to cynicism. Indeed, the horn region as a whole has not known respite for over half a century. Little by little the effect has been escalating, yet its people have not been rendered listless. Somalis and other regional populations as a whole are not totally devoid of hope. They have displayed tremendous feats of endurance in the face of overwhelming negative forces. The progress in Somaliland, noted in northern Somalia, should not be underestimated in this regard. In July 2010 the Economist reported *"Not so failing"*. In the report is a more auspicious demonstration of what could be accomplished when relative stability and non-interference reside. According to the article *"Somaliland has been building a democratic state. In 2003 it held a presidential election, then a parliamentary one in 2005. On June 26th the 50th anniversary of the end of the British protectorate, a second presidential poll took place, marked with enthusiasm and little violence"*. The report goes on to mention the high level voter registration and participation that took place. Out of a population of 2.5 million about 1.7 million happen to be registered, a tremendous feat for a failed state. Under these circumstances Somalia is not as bleak as at first glance. Investment into the Somaliland economy should bring about much needed progress in terms of basic necessities. Given Somaliland's small population size, this homegrown experiment could endure. If it does, then the international community should help sustain and propagate it without harming its certain Somali nature. These achievements are breathtaking lessons of what could be achieved under dire circumstances, even by seemingly failed nations, if relative peace and openness are available. Though there are many hurdles awaiting Somaliland, it is a laudable occasion for Somalis to cherish and sustain. Success in Somaliland for the democratic camp is a positive step forward for the whole region. If there is a vestige of hope against despotism, extremism, and grinding poverty it rests in this sort of progress.

Though sporadic and at times almost invisible such positive trends continue to peak their heads only to be extinguished by powerful players. Guarding the safety of such developments is the responsibility of enlightened folks, who frankly want to see positive change and betterment of their fellow men. As the most populous, most diverse, and most influential country in the region, Ethiopia is a significant player towards regional peace, stability, and development. Circumstances in Ethiopia have a noteworthy impact in the Horn of Africa at large. This factor necessitates the merit of focus on Ethiopia. Despite what may seem relative calmness, reinforced by power, there is a lack of real steadiness based on consent. This makes any stability fleeting. Long term peace requires more permanent positive change. As we have noted, the country's past has not been one of positive development, instead it has been marred by negative destabilizing revolution, coupes; counter coups, followed by insurgencies that yielded the TPLF/EPRDF.

This country has been haunted by a deficit of justice and democracy, seemingly since time immemorial. As always such events have only benefited the tyrannical regimes that seem to thrive in this setting; while the population has been left to withstand the repercussion of their murderous greed for power. The aspiration of the people for liberty and equality has not been fulfilled because of this. The cries of the student movements have not been satisfied. A revolution that was to bring about so much progress has been left in limbo. Perhaps this has left a bigger more burdensome load for future generations. Though events on the ground that led to this point are naturally very convoluted, it is important to keep them brief and in perspective to avoid confusion. For this reason description of events and eras has been succinctly placed. Conversely it would be impossible to view circumstances in Ethiopia without acknowledging events in the Horn of Africa at large. As a result we rightly included many events from the wider region as a whole. The intention is to guide, particularly those with the means to 'think big and beautiful', to ponder about the region in general. Undoubtedly this requires us to delve into the past, in order to draw a portrait of the present more accurately and possibly allow us to predict future outcomes, based on the new reform of 2018.

EPRDF and *"Revolutionary Democracy"*

The EPRDF prefers to boast *"Revolutionary Democracy"* as its guiding ideological principle. To fully grasp how this came to be the bulwark of the EPRDF, let us consider the roots of this principle in Marxist /Leninist thought. The theory itself has been around longer than the EPRDF or all other political parties of Ethiopia. Its core tenets are found in the Russian Revolution of 1917 and what Lenin coined as *"Democratic Centralism"*. It was a theory formulated to guarantee the survival and perpetuation of the Bolshevik party in Russia. This theory was taken up by Stalin and Mao Tse-tung and further evolved to fit their immediate political needs, with slight adjustment. Other communist, Bolshevik, or Maoist parties around the world have tried to use various forms of this theory. Its flexibility makes it an instrumental tool indeed. According to Lenin, 'the socialist revolutionaries learned astonishing lesson from their history of failed revolutions throughout Europe in the 19th and early 20th century. The failure of the early French Revolution is also sighted here as a lesson learned. Therefore it became important to create a rigid party apparatus that can withstand and carry the revolution forward in the face of overwhelming antagonistic forces.

One of the primary reasons attributed to the failures of the early socialist camp was its factional and disorganized nature which made it vulnerable to outside pressure from the bourgeoisie. To combat this divisional nature and to form a strong party organization Lenin and his comrades designed what they referred to as *"Democratic Centralism"*. According to Lenin this party system allows for *"diversity in Thought and unity of Action"*, meaning members of the party could contemplate and discuss issues within the party, however, once a decision has been reached by the majority then the decision was final binding and irrefutable. What attracted the Bolsheviks to this theory is apparent. As a party operating illegally in Czarist Russia it becomes highly beneficial to have *"Unity of Action"*. In this highly repressive environment this approach was an essential tool of survival. It was an efficient form of organization. Accepting the theory of *"Democratic Centralism"* meant the creation of a vanguard party that would carry the revolution forward. In essence these were professional revolutionaries at the helm of the party apparatus. This introduced a militant-like hierarchy necessary for the dislodging of Czarist Russia.

Mao Tse-tung of China also referred to this view. Obviously some changes to the equation befitting of China's peculiarities were necessary first. In Mao's words this theory was referred to as *"New Democracy"*. Its core principals and function were very much in line with Lenin's Theory. As in Russia, Chinese revolutionaries also faced tremendous difficulty in creating and reaching consensus. They needed an organizational structure that would sustain their revolution and eradicate any counter-revolutionary voice. In fact Chairman Mao suggested on many occasions, about the need to disrupt any other attempt at persuading the outlook of the people. He viewed this as a deceptive attempt to fool the people. Such attempts could only be effectively purged when one has organizational capacity to withstand factionalism. Given China's large population and its diversity, Mao also suggested a vanguard party that would equally make sure that all class interests are represented without discrimination of the minority by the majority and vice versa. Once reactionary forces have been subdued, the ultimate goal of the party is to permeate all levels of society, not even sparing religious institutions. In this fashion the development of socialism can be hastened. It was thought to be the fastest route of transition from a pre-capitalist feudal society to a socialist society. This approach, with minor adjustments, is true of both Russia under the Bolsheviks as well as Maoist China. The mechanism envisioned by Mao to achieve this in China was that of *"a graduated series of Congress'*. This meant, in essence, all levels of governance, from the local to the national were laid out in a pyramid scheme. The advantage of this was it guaranteed centralization. Power was concentrated at the top of the pyramid. The role of this graduated congress was to reaffirm the supremacy of the vanguard party. It allowed for top down control in a hierarchical fashion. As in Russia this system brought efficiency and discipline to the Maoists in the face of overwhelming opposition. By western standards it was also very militant in its approach. It viewed all would-be detractors of its stance as reactionary enemies to be eliminated.

Though the benefits of efficiency gained from centralism propelled the Bolsheviks as well as the Chinese communist party to positions of power, it had negative impacts on the revolution and the population at large. What it did accomplish was it managed to replace one repressive system with another. It made inequality permanent and marginalized the population from the affairs of the state. Now the party was above all else. Individuals were supposed to be subservient to the party. Unavoidably, in this system the party becomes a godlike guide to the blissful heaven of Socialism, which never comes. In reality however, the party is neither immune nor godlike. It is made up of humans that are fallible and prone to the corrupting trends of power. It was the dictatorship of the party that resulted from this mechanism and not worker control, as originally intended. Unfortunately for the masses this was a harder form of tyranny to overcome. Political power and economic power was now fully vested in the party. There was no longer an individual to blame, as in a king, an emperor, or a military general. Blame could not be directed at an individual. The party itself was made up of human beings who controlled the means of production as well as the means of political thought, but since this power was held in unison, it relieved individuals of the responsibility they bear for the actions of their party. Such undue privileges are easier to perpetuate and justify when they are held in common among a group of individuals in the party. Many of these thoughts were pondered by George Orwell, as he cleverly illustrated this fact in the novel *"Nineteen Eighty-Four"*. *'Individual party members might not own any economic or political power, but together they owned the whole country'*. This was the tricky part. Even though socialism has good elements, in this way inequality and repression were made more permanent than previous tyrannies. Ultimately, more than anything else this was what the Bolsheviks and the Maoists achieved. Indeed, it becomes evident the revolution of the people was hijacked by a few party hacks.

Given this factor it is not hard to predict subsequent atrocities committed by the Bolsheviks and the Maoists. The repressive nature of the Bolsheviks was not something that began when it held state power. Instead this was present in the organization all throughout its ascent to power. Its crimes just became more egregious when it held state power. For instance in 1921 the leadership of the Bolshevik party placed a ban on all factions within the party itself. In effect the "democratic" was taken out of *"Democratic Centralism"*. From here on power would rest exclusively in the Politburo, which is composed of a few elite party leaders. The days of one man rule under Stalin and his murderous campaigns were hatched here. The same scenario applies for China. The Cultural Revolution and many of the purges committed by the Chinese Maoist party since 1948 have to be viewed under these circumstances of purity of thought assigned by *"New Democracy"* and what it stands for in reality.

Its purism and supposed absolute monopoly of knowledge and truth makes this theory like a semi-religion. Its stated goal is to facilitate the party in its mission of guiding society to the heaven of Socialism. With this in mind its adherents are capable of committing the most heinous acts, as these are perfectly justifiable. For Party technocrats and leaders it was a perfect system. It empowered them beyond their actual worth. In some cases it made them more powerful than the autocratic kings. One can think of how contrary to socialist views these so called revolutionaries became cult-like figures to be worshiped. Lenin, Stalin, Mao, and Kim Il sung fall under this category. Yes indeed, thanks to *"Revolutionary Democracy"* old masters were replaced by new ones.

The reforms (Glasnost and Perestroika) that took place later in the 20th century, which effectively culminated in the collapse of the Soviet Union, are indicative of the failure of this Theory. Efforts to rectify the problems caused by this way of thinking can be seen in the days after the fall of Stalin as well. Generally, this system of government ultimately leads to failure. It did not respect individual liberties. For that matter even group rights were secondary, as the only entity with rights was the party apparatus. Production was under the control of the party and increasingly under the politburo. The worker owned nothing and had no tangible right to own his or her labor. Although the Soviet Union and the Chinese Communist party were anti-capitalist in their outward appearance; theirs was a capitalism of the state, where power and capital was more concentrated than their western nemesis. The other form of government where production/economy and political power is controlled by a sole entity is Fascism. It is ironic for a communist party to share this characteristic with a fascist government. However, this is what *"Revolutionary Democracy"* did in these countries. In fact, having seen the flaws of this system, the Chinese like the Soviets decided to move away from this sort of governance in the mid to late 70s. Under the reforms of the Deng Xiaoping era, China was able to enter a more economically open polity that eventually led to the booming China we know today. The lesson in Short is *"Revolutionary Democracy"*, *"Democratic Centralism"*, *"New Democracy"*, or however we choose to name it, has become increasingly shunned by many of its previous adherents for credible reasons. Mostly this change has been positive for the prospects of such states. Given this factor it is surprising to see imitation of this failed system by third world governments today, not least of which is the EPRDF regime in Ethiopia

In Ethiopia today *"Revolutionary Democracy"*, practiced by the EPRDF has an overlapping disposition as the examples mentioned. Again we should remind ourselves, when one speaks of the EPRDF it is invariably to comment on the TPLF, where the real power within the organization lays. In the day of the wilderness as an underground rebel movement, the TPLF needed the same "unity of action". This was a fundamental aspect of survival in harsh times, having to face a superior opposition. And as a professed Marxist guerilla movement, it sought to create this unity along the lines of the Bolsheviks and the Maoists. Since military activities overshadowed its actions in this period, centralization of power was inevitable. If it was to launch a successful campaign in the war front such regimentation was a key aspect. One outcome of this was increased concentration of power in fewer hands at the top. This did not come without a cost to the rank and file though. Alienation of the rank and file was escalating as fast as centralization itself. What it yielded ultimately was a secretive regimented war fighting machine. Unfortunately this didn't leave any room for liberty of thought and expression. Priorities of fighting the enemy created this culture of finality, leading to many purges and even violent exclusion of members thought to be disagreeable by top dogs. It was easier to justify these steps as methods of eliminating inefficiencies, which could cost the organization dearly, under circumstances of war. Having said this, it's important to realize these purges were not always done apolitically. Personal clash or the slightest of suspicion could entail horrible consequences for the overtly out spoken. Unable to accommodate differing ideas, the politburo reverted to exclusion of unwanted ideas through intrigue, including murder. Certainly any notion of opinioned thinking in the western sense was nonexistent. Following mantra in lockstep is the singular highest expectation in this party organ. Ironically many of its characteristics were also shared by its nemesis, the Derg, which was all too keen on using malicious methods to intimidate its members who tended to fall out of line. However the Derg was foolishly a bit more overt about the business of intimidation. Surely if it had the chance to do it all over again, Derg would use the superior methods employed by the EPRDF, which happen to be quieter and more effective. Fortunately for the People of Ethiopia the Derg will not be coming back. However this is not to say the EPRDF is less of an authoritarian force. It just happens to have learned from the Derg and perfected the same craft. Expectedly pupils surpass their teacher if they are good students. Students of tyranny are no different.

During the days of the student revolution we learned of the inflexible nature of many of the Marxist parties. Characteristically the TPLF/EPRDF, as an offshoot of this movement also suffers from a similar ailment. Compromising with other political groups is very much an alien habit to Marxist parties, at least in the case of Ethiopia, unless it's done for immediate benefits. Remembering all the bloodshed of the 70s in this regard should refresh our memory. Failure to compromise is what caused such carnage. This ingrained characteristic remains with us even to this day. It has left its mark on current politics as well. For instance on many occasions the EPRDF is willing to make a deal with other organizations when faced with this dilemma, however even these agreements are made with a vision

206

of total victory for itself in the long run. We see this repeated all throughout the history of the organization. Its past dealing with TLF and EPRP are a good illustration of this. One could also include the EPLF to this category. TPLF/EPRDF was only willing to befriend these short term allies to satisfy an immediately pressing issue. In the end, when their services were exhausted, they were not only discarded but also aggressively hunted down by their former ally. According to Marxist theory this sort of behavior is perfectly tolerable; as the end always justify the means in *"Revolutionary Democracy"*. Remember the end is the blissful socialism that never comes in actuality. The party that is thriving towards this 'noble' goal finds itself vindicated no matter how many times it lies, torments, imprisons, kills, or does nothing. It is weird noticing the religious zealousness in a professedly atheistic theory. Such portrayal is not just true of the TPLF/EPRDF in its guerrilla days; it is also the overbidding background of the organization at present. Other Ethiopian Marxist political parties have also been tainted by *"Revolutionary Democracy"*. Whether they acknowledge it or deny it, the same sense of finality and absolute knowledge is also part of their make-up from deep within. Even as recent converts to "Liberal Democrats" they remain haunted by this ghost of their past.

In *"Revolutionary Democracy"* compromise is seen as a last ditch effort to be considered under dire circumstances. Such political organizations fear such softening will lead to the demise of the organizational dominance, and leave its members prone to retribution, which invariably comes because all political parties also use the same modus operandi. As a results only total victory and demolition of opposition is prescribed. Politics is a zero-sum game. The hostility present may be postponed for a later time, but it always lurks in the background. By Western standards, such an existence is overtly combative and absolute in its character. By design all opposing political entities are viewed as enemies of the party and also of the state, which in many cases, in this system, is intertwined with the dominant party. Another mark of such a system is the ambiguous line demarcating the ruling party and the state. This is true of the Bolsheviks in the Soviet Union; it is also true of the Derg and EPRDF in Ethiopia. Unfortunately for the population, reform is scarce and very unlikely to come from within such a system. As we see throughout history the traffic of power and decision making in such governments always flows towards hierarchy. More and more power is stripped from the people and transferred to the party, and it does not stop there. Power is concentrated in the few hands of the politburo. Briefly looking back at the Bolshevik Revolution, we notice the increasing power vacuum at the top. This trend was increasing the further we moved away from the initial revolution of 1917. In this respect the period under Stalin were inevitably more autocratic than the earlier revolutionary period. The peasantry and proletarian were progressively becoming more alienated from the decision making process since the revolution of 1917. Judging by this standard, contrary to the claims of party hacks, the system itself became incompatible to any kind of egalitarianism. To the contrary it runs a divergent course to all democracy or revolution. Trends in the TPLF/EPRDF predictably follow the same path. In the end the party dictates everything. Worst still, a few hands at the top of the pyramid control the party decision making process. It is no different from the autocracy of a king or an emperor. In fact it is more mechanized, and thus harder to reform.

The upward concentration of power present in the TPLF can be viewed in Marxist Leninist League of Tigray (MLLT). According to TPLF officials, MLLT was to function as the vanguard of the revolutionary party. It was chiefly comprised of top ranking party officials of the TPLF; a sort of nucleus organization within a larger body. This organization is mainly filled with decision makers, the movers and shakers of the Party.

Its creation unavoidably resulted in a vertical power structure, whereby all important decisions are made from the top and transmitted down to the rank and file. This was not always the case, however. Before the formation of this organ the TPLF was more egalitarian for a short period in its infancy. Perhaps the MLLT can be viewed as the vertex of the pyramid. It served this purpose for most of the significant years of the struggle. Although this provided the efficiency of hierarchy in the military arena, it lacked real democratic relationships within. Incongruously rank and file fighters remain highly incognizant of this core organ, which invariably dictates many of their activities. Though many ardent TPLF/EPRDF members and supporters proclaim of the organization's egalitarianism from within the camp, evidence for this claim is hard to obtain. Underneath the surface, the Marxist/Leninist hierarchy is clearly visible and operating very much as before. The purges and violent intimidations committed by the Party since its inception tell this story. Its election history and relationships to those that oppose it also paint a depressing picture for the equal minded among us. As a permanent foundation of the organization there is no indication to suggest this state of affairs will change any time soon. It has only become more pronouncedly exacerbated through the passage of time. The ephemeral expectations, namely that the status quo will change after the fall of the Derg has now been clearly falsified. Two decades after the fall of the much derided Derg, it remains unreformed. Results in the last election cycle of 2010, whereby the party secured, by means of coercion 99.6% of the vote, indicate its consolidation, perhaps not for the final time. Repeatedly the hope of reform and democracy is suspended in front of would-be susceptible. In the end the same old result is true. "You can put lipstick on a pig but it's still a pig".

Penetration of all aspects of life, whether it is social, political, religious or economic is the final destination of the party operating under *"Revolutionary Democracy"*. Under this guise individual liberties and opinions are provisionally toasted out as cumbersome burdens to progress. All members of a society with or without their consent are to follow the party. Given this factor it becomes rather unsurprising to see the EPRDF effectively ban opposition parties from assembling in public. If 84 percent of businesses and production units are associated with the ruling Party/State apparatus, it is nothing we haven't expected already. And if all farm land, where 85% of the population is agriculturalist, happens to be government property, thus making the farmer a modern serf, we should not hold our breath. Interestingly the party claims this to be favorable to the farmer, who according to this policy is too stupid and backward to own the farm, as he or she would not know what to do with such a precious gift. However the results of farm output under this strategy have been dismal over the past 30 years, including under the time of the Derg, which also advocated a similar ideology of government ownership of land. It would be more correct to assume party ownership. When independent media outlets and journalists are constantly under the clout of the state for their efforts at exposing this fallacy, we should not be aghast, as this is exactly the kind of "enemy" the party has to extinguish. Students and government employees being coerced to join the ruling party should not alarm us either; as the ways and means of achieving total dominance involves the state's use of violence and intimidation. This was aptly demonstrated by the government when it opted to kill 191 demonstrators after the contested parliamentary election of May 2005. Tens of thousands were arbitrarily arrested and subjected to abuse as well. Undeniably the room for compromise has tightened ever since the disputed election of 2005. The State/Party apparatus has been hammering hard at nails that stick out. With the passage of many draconian laws the playing field has been considerably constricted.

Thus if one political party professes an adherence to *"Revolutionary Democracy"* it is by default saying it is non-democratic, and that it believes in the qualities of the one party state. Such a party finds support for its views based on the efficiency and reliability of the system. Also it reminds us about the backwardness of the underdeveloped nation, which according to the party is not conducive to "real democracy" and individual liberty. The excuse for this is always the need to go through stages of development before liberalization. The ruling party also claims rapid industrialization is more precious that human rights. It is reminiscent of Stalinism indeed. Like its predecessor the reasons given are shallow and fall apart at the smallest bit of analysis. Without further ado, this sort of government only benefits the ruling party. It allows it to strengthen its power, which increases with the passage of time. Meanwhile the population suffers the consequence of the mostly negative policies undertaken. It is dictatorship and ownership of the means of production by the party, despite of the people it claims to represent.

However, when western donors come knocking on the door, *"Revolutionary Democracy"* is not the right phrase to throw around. It is not nice to talk of the efficiency of the one party state when seeking to procure a loan from the World Bank. For this reason the EPRDF has devised a liberal mask to hide its true face. Its constitution is one, which even European states could envy; included are all the bill of rights so admired by the "civilized world". It even champions the self determination of nations and nationalities, if they so choose. Surely such a government must be a tolerant one. It seems almost flawless at first encounter. It even holds highly orchestrated elections whereby the results are guaranteed from the get go. It allows fairly noisy and easily snuffed independent newspapers to exist in Addis Ababa. This is however a façade intended to give the impression of fairness to western donors, which the government has a heavy dependence on. Digging deeper reveals the opposite to be more accurate. In reality, the EPRDF government overrides its own constitution frequently, more than any other body in Ethiopia. Knowing where the party stops and where the state begins is difficult. It is under this system that we are told nations and nationalists have the right of self-administration or determination. It is simply not true, but it works to keep the west in the comfort zone, whereby they can pretend not to know. It sustains the cozy relationship without calling too much attention to ugly realities. Seemingly it is a system perfectly suited for modern day dictatorships.

Overlapping between the State and the party is where the difficulty in reforming such a system lay. It requires touching upon the state to reform the party. It is not merely limited to the Party. The Party and the State act as a blended unit. This quality is the Holy Grail that makes reform improbable. For instance according to the European Electoral Commission, the EPRDF uses State resources to fund its electoral campaign activities. Included in the report are government owned vehicles used by the EPRDF to take the campaign to communities. Reaching rural communities where a vast majority of Ethiopians reside is very much the key to winning elections. In this regard having state means to transport one's campaign to these regions is highly advantageous. Where this is not enough, food aid coming from donor nations can be used as a tool to coerce potential opposition supporters to reconsider their position. Human Rights Watch (HRW) put out an extensive research on this issue in October of 2010. After studying 53 villages in three regions of Ethiopia, it concludes that food aid, which is controlled by the EPRDF government, is being used to force the rural population to cast its vote for the EPRDF. Ben Rawlins of HRW commenting on this issue states, *"People are being asked to disassociate themselves from opposition political parties - rescind comments they've made and write out letters of regret - in order to obtain food aid in Ethiopia."* Compounding this predicament is the non-functional role of non-governmental organization as a result of draconian measures implemented to limit their activities by the EPRDF regime. Laws prohibiting NGOs from participating directly in aid disbursement have specifically intended goals of keeping these organizations at bay, while giving the EPRDF government the chance to turn foreign aid into a weapon of repression. The mercilessness of this weapon is perhaps demonstrated by the confessions of poor farmers. In one occasion HRW heard testaments from affected individuals, one of whom stated *"His wife had run away with the kids after having grown sick of being hungry because of her husband's political affiliation"*. The reporter from CBC radio of Canada, broadcasting this report that same month was baffled by the cruel circumstances.

Even though western donors and governments continue to turn the blind eye, such reports have been ratcheting up in recent times. Judging by accounts coming from the BBC in mid-2010, sinister uses of donor food aid are an all too common political weapon employed by the EPRDF government from the days of its inception in the mountains of Tigray. Consequently the vital organ of the current regime, TPLF, has been accused of using food aid to procure weapons during its guerilla days in northern Ethiopia. According to BBC reports, food aid coming from western donor organization, particularly from Band-Aid, was diverted for the purposes of buying weapons by the TPLF at the height of the regional famine in 1984. Essentially while millions perished from famine, TPLF leaders where systematically diverting aid money to the war front. The authenticity of this report has been challenged, no doubt by TPLF officials and pop star Bob Geildoff, Band-Aid's public representative at the time. TPLF/EPRDF officials, including the current prime minister of Ethiopia categorically deny this claim as a malicious attempt to tarnish their name. In a parliamentary statement made in the aftermath of this report, Primer minister Zenawi explains in Amharic, 'Food aid was never used to buy arms by his party in 1984, as that would mean weakening the party's base', namely the people of Tigray region. He goes on to say, 'weapons were easily available thanks to Derg forces, who easily abandoned their arsenal after a defeat in battle'. However, such attempts at corroborating their stance by TPLF officials are refuted by compelling individuals that were former members of the Party, including ex-TPLF financial officer Gebremedhin Araya. For him the allegations are a bit more protracted. He presents in great detail, his duties and the role of his superiors in the diversion of aid. As the former financial officer of the TPLF party and a non-participant in current Ethiopian politics, his statements make a compelling point. Ridding the shadow of doubt on this issue certainly becomes more complicated for the TPLF/EPRDF, particularly in the aftermath of the latest report put out by HRW. Indeed the similarity of the current findings by HRW and what most likely happened behind closed doors during the 1984 famine is striking.

Foreign aid abuse has not gone unnoticed by donor nations, but it has been ignored. When World Bank officials admit anonymously to HRW about the use of foreign aid as a political weapon in Ethiopia we should believe them. Such allegations are not just libel. HRW speaking to foreign aid representatives in Addis Ababa encounters this not so flattering fact plainly. *"It is clear that our money is being moved into political brainwashing." – Consultant to a major donor, Addis Ababa.* No doubt the recently decreed stifling civil society law, which has more or less eviscerated domestic human rights groups and NGOs, makes the situation even worst. In another similar statement documented by HRW; indicative of the secrecy that presides, a World Bank official in Addis Ababa states incognito *"Politicization of food aid could only be discovered if one is to go undercover in Ethiopia"*, a correct observation, but it still does not account for the disconnect between foreign aid and the aspirations of Ethiopians. Clearly there is a gap between the official story fronted by aid organizations and what their representatives transmit off the record. One stumbles invariably on the general sense of complicity between aid groups and the repressive EPRDF state. Here in lies the discouraging aspect for those seeking to bring sanity into the equation of aid. Not to mention it is also an albatross for many Ethiopians struggling to achieve democracy and civil liberties. Congo was once similarly a victim of neglectful aid policy under dictator Mobutu. Author Michela Wrong, in her book *"In the Footsteps of Mr. Kurtz"* skillfully presents the corruption and demise of The Congo under the auspice of dictator Mobutu in collaboration with the IMF/World Bank. Evidently there is a continuum throughout geography and time. In a sense what is happening in Ethiopia is nothing new. It's just another extension of an all too common procedure. So then, do circumstances require us to review aid policy? Understandably terminating all aid would have negative consequences on the ground, as many millions depend on this aid for their well-being. However allowing the EPRDF government to sell the poor and hungry for a fat payday from western donors should not be tolerated either. It is bewildering to know why donors fail to assign significantly small portions of their money for the purpose of serious aid monitoring. It seems a genuine system of checks, balances and repercussions is long overdue. Certainly the tax payer, from which these funds are generated, deserves to have such systems in place; even if the opinions of third world peoples has no significant weight in aid circles.

Ballot Box or Battle Plans

The election of 2005 was one of those significant events that shaped Ethiopia in the 21st century; like the ousting of the

Derg in 1991 or the coup of 1974 and the conflict with Eritrea. Though it did not result in the transfer of power, it was the first time, where peaceful transition seemed remotely possible. In this sense it was a milestone achievement. Even though the mechanism of repression had been refined since 1991, things began to loosen a little and the state found itself in a kind of apathy during the days leading up to the election. Partly to blame for this is the all too common arrogance displayed by authoritarian regimes, becoming too comfortable, and out of touch. In the aftermath of the war with the regime in Eritrea, there seemed to be an overdrive of nationalism in the country. To combat the "external enemy" many had galvanized behind the EPRDF from the late 90s to 2001. Having come out of the conflict with its former ally intact, the ruling party most probably breathed a sigh of relief. This is exemplified by the brief open atmosphere that appeared in the capital and in major cities. More than ever independent journalists were relatively unbound by the state. Today such relaxation by the EPRDF government would be comparatively unimaginable. The space that opened up momentarily during that time allowed for opposition parties to rally for a short period. Kinijit coalition party was the strongest amongst them.

Post electoral violence mostly perpetrated by government security forces proved this relative openness to be a bit of window-dressing by the ruling party. Though the government was quick to accuse opposition leaders of inciting violence in the wake of the election, these claims would be hard to validate. It would be more correct to say the stone throwing and tyre burning that ensued was a spontaneous reaction. Opposition leaders had little leverage on the actions of city residents, as they never had the organizational capability to dictate such directions to begin with. It would take a considerably well entrenched and organized faction to incite all sectors of Addis Ababa to protest in such a manner. Such events

216

can only be described as spontaneous reactions of a frustrated population. We can begin to assess why the government began to blame the opposition based on such preliminary factors. For the first time the EPRDF was challenged sufficiently enough, where it resorted to undemocratic means to consolidate its power. When the election began to resemble a loss for the ruling party it declared a state of emergency, halting the counting of the ballot. With the exception of this violent aftermath, it was truly remarkable to see the excitement people displayed, particularly given the fact it took the opposition a short period to organize, another indication of the spontaneous mobilization. Eventually this would prove to be the party's weakness, faced with a highly organized opponent. Despite the shortcomings this time period was a testament to the enthusiasm and civility of the population, which displayed tremendous affection for the peaceful struggle. Amazingly, over a million supporters of the opposition marched in Addis Ababa prior to the vote. The procession was untainted by any disturbances or aggression by the marchers. A correspondent of the BBC said *"People showed great character and patience during the march, which was by and large peaceful"*. This kind of thing is rare in Africa and it should be commended. It was a stupendous lesson for politicians of all affiliations and the international community of what the people of Ethiopia are capable of. However, in the post-election violence that followed, the peaceful struggle turned into yet another case of letdowns and betrayals for the people. President John F. Kennedy once said: *"Those who make peaceful revolution impossible will make violent revolution inevitable"*.

The seemingly endemic apathy that was lifted during the 2005 election was a clear demonstration of the astuteness of the Ethiopian populace. Years of oppression, including under the terrible Derg had not managed to completely subdue it. Underneath the surface lies a giant, feared and loathed by authoritarian governments. It requires the least bit of mobilization to tap into this existing potential, but as political leader were made aware, it also needs trust. If people feel they are credibly being heard, they don't require much else to organize themselves and wage a peaceful battle. The participation and enthusiasm of May 2005 was no coincidence, it is simply the awakening of a dormant giant. However, the same could not be said of leaders. Some were not as forthcoming in the aftermath of the election, and thereafter. The division that arose between different personalities in the opposition leadership camp during the post-election turmoil was truly disheartening for their supporters. Pressure from the ruling EPRDF was easily able to subvert the opposition coalition as a result. This is an indication of the opposition's failure to thoroughly organize itself in the first place. Perhaps they were overwhelmed by the wave of excitement displayed by their constituency, which was ahead of them each step. In the end this was deeply troubling, not least to the people that had put hope in opposition leadership. The ruling party was predictably only keen to exacerbate the situation and portray them as divisive, and thus unfit to lead a large nation. As all politicians can testify, playing into the hands of your opponent in such a manner could be suicide. Unfortunately this is the fate that awaited the opposition when a clash of personality broke out. These things should have been rectified well before the campaign had begun. Then again the leaders were overwhelmed by a ready population that gave them unexpectedly high results, at least initially. Eventually the loose ends would cost the Kinijit dearly. In the face a ruling party willing to use unconstitutional means to stay in power, this was suicide for the opposition.

Politicization of Ethnicity

In the aftermath of the 2005 election, during the post-election turmoil, one of the accusations thrown by the ruling

EPRDF party at the opposition was ethnic antagonism. Here the EPRDF is referring to shouts or calls heard during the demonstration directed towards the Tigrian population. The tantrums translate roughly, "Tigrians towards Mekelle, Property towards kebele". Mekelle is the capital of Tigray region and Kebele is the local urban dwellers association administration center. Obviously such calls are undemocratic and the opposition should have condemned them immediately and unequivocally. Even if such ethnic tensions are fanned by EPRDF itself or fringe elements, their end result was to harm the peaceful struggle. To quote what the American Civil Rights Movement leader Dr.Martin Luther King once said; *"We must learn to live together as brothers, or perish together as fools."* Here in lies another lesson for democratic forces and their role as guardians against ethnic violence, which so far has only benefited those in power. Certainly the issue of ethnic politics is of considerable worry in Ethiopia today. Though it naturally existed long before the rise of EPRDF, it has been substantially fanned in recent times, in most cases unnecessarily for political ends.

The creation of an ethnically based federal system, if it works accordingly should have alleviated the situation. Regrettably the federal system falls short of its professed goals because it functions under authoritarianism, in which case it is merely rendered as a method of centralization. It allows for much easier control of the ruling party. Therefore it has become the preferred method of repression as it offers a chance to play one group against another. It also leaves ruling elites sheltered; that is why they encourage political parties on ethnic lines, and not multi-ethnic parties based on principles and ideology.

The EPRDF regime has not found adequate ways to accommodate genuine dissent, except bribing opposition elements and incorporating them into the dominant party. The 2010 election again only reconfirmed the one-party nature of the regime undercutting hopes for even limited degree of political autonomy. EPRDF's stranglehold on elections and top-down control on national, regional, and local levels gives no autonomy to ethno-federal arrangements from the central government. Political domination and economic 'apartheid' present Ethiopia with a range of major social problems and challenges which could trigger another round of civil war and instability unless increased latitude is given to the opposition for the country to advance in a democratic direction.

Resource Allocation

The economic, political, and environmental causes of human migration out of Ethiopia are interwoven. Over the past 40 or so years Ethiopia has had one of the highest numbers of migrants fleeing their country anywhere in Africa. Although an accurate accounting of this number has never been conducted, it is estimated to range in the millions. Now, when you look at this issue and the sheer number of people affected then you begin to ask the question why. Why this mass exodus, especially of the young and educated classes? When you really begin to poke at this question what you get are three fundamentally intertwined issues, and these are economic, political, and environmental problems. The recent historical record of Ethiopia is littered with political conflict arising mainly out of resource allocation, or lack there-of. It's also very easy for anyone in my generation to testify to the population explosion and rapid degradation of our natural environment, which feeds into and exacerbates all of the tensions arising out of the economic and political spheres. All of these things have converged on Ethiopia over the past 40 or so years, bringing a period of unprecedented conflict and competition, be it political, ethnic, or both. Almost certainly all these clashes bowl down to grabbing scarce resources and allocating them for one's political, religious, or ethnic group. Different manifestations of this have come and gone in the past 40 or 50 years and it still haunts our society today, forcing many to seek other option outside of Ethiopia.

For most Ethiopians the empty promise of Derg's Socialism and TPLF's free market has eroded. While the new ruling elites grew wealthy from embezzlement and investment, most hard working Ethiopians are struggling to survive with inflation and costs that are growing, and too many families are racking up debt just to keep up. The income gap between the politically connected rich and the working masses has been widening during the last 15 years. The ruling elites are using their political muscle to gain wealth and stay in power. The TPLF led government is investing too little in the people and its future. Instead, the growth and prosperity of the last decade is enjoyed by the few who are politically associated with the ruling party. The incomes of most Ethiopians have actually fallen by some 50 percent. This is the kind of inequality – a level we haven't seen in our history, and it hurts us all.

What is at stake is whether the hard working Ethiopians will be able to earn enough to raise a family, own a home and secure a modest saving for their retirement. Ethiopia will succeed only when everyone plays by the same rules, when everyone gets a fair shot, and when everyone does their fair share. Ethiopia should be built in a broad-based prosperity. The kind of inequality we are witnessing now will drag down the entire economy and also distort democracy.

Chapter Four

Government Controlled Media

'*He who conceals his disease can't be cured'*. (An Ethiopian proverb)

"*Yet for much of the post-colonial period, exposing a problem in Africa has almost always been   impossible because of censorship, brutal suppression of dissent, and state ownership or control of the media. Corrupt and incompetent governments denied or concealed their embarrassing   failings   (abuse of power, looting, and atrocities) until the problems blew up in their faces. But, by then it was too late to solve them*".

(George Ayittey, Africa Betrayed)

'*Be steadfast, my boy when you are tempted,*
To do what you know to be right.
Stand firm by the colors of manhood,
And you will overcome in the fight.
"The right" be your battle cry ever,
In waging the warfare of life,
And God, who knows who are the heroes,
Will give you the strength for the strife'.

(Phoebe Cary)

The history of Ethiopian journalism is full of widespread errors, spanning from unintentional mistakes to deliberate deceptions, omissions, hoaxes, mischiefs, cover-ups, downright lies, shamelessly invented facts, and tampered evidences. Some of these false reports and unethical presentations have actively influenced events and shaped the country's history. They

222

distorted people's views and understanding of the past. These journalistic wrongdoings were motivated mostly by power hungry government's self- promotion, greed and arrogance. Since state media has always been owned and controlled by the government, most of the journalists simply wanted to earn a living and did not dare to risk their job and their life to provide a true historical record on which future generations would depend. The private sector was not strong enough for them to find another job somewhere else. The journalists, who tried to engage in investigative reporting to uncover important information, reveal corruption, expose public official wrongdoings, and obstruction of justice were arrested, tortured, exiled or killed.

The state media often presented one-sided views that the ruling class wanted the people to hear. Ethiopia never had a truly free and functional press that investigate the truth and watch the politically and economically powerful with suspicious eye. Every time a government is overthrown journalists start to speak out and private papers appear only to curse the defunct regime, riding a dead horse. But, as soon as the new government consolidates its power, the independent press that may start to criticize the policy of the new government is stifled again, and the people are left with only sophisticated propaganda. As such, true journalism withers and dies before it forms roots and blossom. Our people are disgusted and there is a country-wide outrage to change this national drama.

Journalism is a vital public service. It is the media that brings the events of our community, the nation and the world into our homes each day, that makes us an informed society. Journalists with high ethical standard, fairness, balance and objectivity enable us to form opinions about the events in our community and our country. We have opinions and choices if we are free to express them. A free media constructed and woven into the very fabric of our communities and our nation is muscular enough to develop a country, change the life of the people, to shiver presidents, and begin wars and score victories on poverty. The crisis of freedom of expression is a crisis for democracy, because vibrant journalism and vibrant democracy are inextricably interwoven. Therefore, we should start a serious conversation and debate to preserve and extend the public's right to know. Journalists and editors should forcefully and daringly write the truth and test the boundaries of journalistic integrity. We should recognize our duty as journalists' of enlightening our citizens by informing the truth so that they may be able to govern themselves and not remain governed. We should strive to restore values and mission to our profession.

The prohibition of government censorship in whatever mode is vital and non-negotiable. In fact, the government needs to do more than not imposing censorship in the name of state security; it should play a role in preserving and extending the public's right to know. It should hide nothing in the name of state secret, and it should encourage independent journalism with massive subsidies and enlightened policy. This is the time to reveal our shameful shortcomings and propel our citizens to act to fix them. **The role of mass media is to create an informed and engaged community**.

It is beyond the scope of this book and the ability of this author to list all the mistakes, shortcomings and harms done in Ethiopian journalism. There are no detailed studies available about the history of mass media in Ethiopia. But, based on the few materials I could find, I will try to point out some of the major problems and the facts concerning the beginning and growth of modern mass media in Ethiopia. I will share with you my personal experience in the life and death of Ethiopian journalism.

The Beginning of Modern Media in Ethiopia

The traditional means of disseminating message to the people in Ethiopia has been by *negarit megosem* (drum beating), using *meleketna terumba menfat* (blowing horn), or verbal shouting like other African nations. When we look at the beginning of modern mass media, the situation in Ethiopia is different from many African countries. Since Ethiopia has a written language unlike other sub-Sahara African countries, with Geez alphabets (mostly used by the churchs for many centuries), and since it was not colonized by Western powers, modern mass media is indigenous and started long before colonialism. It is true that we got technological help from foreigners, particularly missionaries who came to Ethiopia. But, still it took us a long time to replace the traditional methods of disseminating messages with modern media (Newspapers, Radio and Television).

According to historian Killen Sandrine the first newsletter was printed in Geez (now a church language) at the port of Masswa in 1513 with the help of the Portuguese. According to historian Professor Richard Pankhurst the first printing press was established in Massawa in 1863 during the reign of Emperor Tewedros with the help of Lutheran missionary Lorenzo Beanchuri. In 1879 these Lutheran missionaries started printing newsletters in Amharic and Tigrigna. Later in 1885, Swedish evangelical missionaries started a small printing press in Massawa which they later moved it to Asmara and started to distribute printed Gospel teachings to the public.

"Most Ethiopians making their way to Rome were attached to the Church of Santo Stefano, later known as Santo Stefano dei Morio, i.e.'Moors', which became a cradle of

225

Ethiopian studies in Europe. It was there that a German typographer, Joannes Potken of Cologne, heard Ethiopians singing their mass, and was inspired to print the first Geez psalter in 1513. Later in 1539, the Holy See purchased a nearby hostel for the Ethiopian community, just behind St. Peter's. It was in Rome too that another scholar, Marianus Victorius, studied with Ethiopian cleric, Tesfa Tseyon and published the first rudimentary Geez grammar in 1548".

(Pankhurst, The Ethiopians, P-80)

Periodicals

Professor Pankhurst states that the first non-religious publication started after 1890 by the Italian military press that occupied Massawa. In 'Area hand book for Ethiopia' written by Kaplan and his friends it is stated that at the end of the 19th century there started a periodical journal "Franco Ethiopia" in Djibouti. About the same year another periodical "Le Simiour de Ethiopia" was printed in Harar in French, and distributed with the help of French citizens. According to Richard Pankhurst the editor of the journal, 'Le Seimiour de Ethiopia' (1905-1911) was priest Bernard.

Around 1900 there was a hand-written and carbon-copied sheet produced and distributed by Belata Ghebreegziabher. This original newspaper of modern Ethiopia was named 'AYMERO' by Emperor Menilik II. It was written by hand for over a year until the new printing press was established in 1911 which facilitated the printing of various decrees and other official documents. Emperor Menilik, who is the founder of modern Ethiopia, established diplomatic relations with European countries and with their help established printing presses in the capital. He also built the first modern school, (Menilik II

School). As the number of people who could read and write went up, printed papers and books also increased.

According to the summary of a research paper by Tadesse Zinaye, Emperor Haile Selassie continued with the establishment of schools and printing press along with the publication of newspapers and educational materials. During World War I, with the help of the allied powers, he established an Amharic newspaper called "Yetor Wore" (war news) to counter the German propaganda. In 1923 a modern printing press and a newspaper in Amharic language "Berhanena Selam" was founded; its circulation was only 500 copies. At the same time, the first monthly magazine consisting of different European languages and a section in Amharic was founded by a German national Mr. Weizinger. The government press also published a number of books of literary, religious, and educational materials, along with periodicals.

In 1932 a French business weekly "Le Ethiopie Commerciale" was established. In 1935 a political weekly newspaper "Atbiya Kokeb" (The Morning Star) was established. During the same period a quarterly "Kesate Berhan" (The Light Giver) newspaper started to appear. They both were short lived because of the Italian invasion. The Italian invaders destroyed most of the printing facilities when they were innaly defeated, and it took a while to put them in order and restart printing after liberation.

A few months after liberation, a number of weeklies, monthlies and other periodicals started to be published in Addis Ababa and Asmara. In 1941, the well-known and most popular daily newspaper "Addis Zemen" (New Era) was launched. It is still the largest newspaper of the government. Another newspaper that was established during the same period was "Sendek Alamachin" (our banner). It was short lived due to financial reasons. In the subsequent years, the daily English newspaper "The Ethiopian Herald" was started along with the weekly Amharic newspaper "Yezareyitu Ethiopia" (Ethiopia Today). Both newspapers have continued to this day. In 1942 an official Negarit Gazeta (proclamation Gazette) was founded.

Radio

The first Radio Station in Ethiopia was inaugurated in 1931 which was later replaced by more powerful installations in 1933, in a contract signed with an Italian company. The establishment of this radio station enabled Emperor Haile Selassie to address the world about Italian invasion of his country in 1935. But the installation was retrieved soon following the Italian invasion of Ethiopia in 1936. In 1941 short wave radio broadcasting resumed and in the following years 'Radio Ethiopia' started broadcasting in six languages from Addis Ababa, Asmara, and Harar. Much later 'Radio Voice of the Gospel' owned and operated by the World Federation of Lutheran Churches started broadcasting religious and entertainment materials. Radio Ethiopia which has both national and external services is now broadcasting its programs in all major languages of Ethiopia and also in English, French and Arabic.

Educational Media Agency owned and operated by the Ministry of Education broadcasts educational programs in more than fifteen languages and in English for high school students now almost over forty years. Recently, ruling party affiliate 'Radio Fana' using short wave, medium wave, and FM programs is broadcasting educational and entertainment programs. After 1991 regional broadcast media were established; these are the Amhara regional radio station located in Baher Dar, Southern Nations, Nationalities and peoples (SNNP) radio station in

Awassa, Dimtse Woyane radio in Mekele and an FM station in Dire Dawa.

Television

Television broadcasting started in Ethiopia in 1963 on the founding of the Organization of African Unity (OAU). It was a closed circuit covering only the City of Addis Ababa. Through the years it was expanded to cover the whole country. An educational TV broadcasting project was initiated in 1965 and by 1971 there were five programs covering a range of topics for students up to grade eight. It gradually expanded into adult education covering the whole country in 1981.

Since 1991 Ethiopian Television (ETV) broadcasts its programs in three major domestic languages (Amharic, Oromiffa, and Tegrigna), and in English for several hours every day. It also has additional channel known as ETV2, transmitting programs prepared by Addis Ababa city Media Agency. The contents of all print, radio and television media controlled by the government has always focused on the activities of government officials and it is excessively political oriented, agitational and propagandistic in nature. People's opinion and participation is not given enough attention. As a result, there is a lack of professionalism and ethics, and a shortage of trained media writers and editors. The coverage or geographical reach of radio is estimated to be 70% and that of television is 50%, and its audience reach is urban focused in Ethiopia.

Agitation and Propaganda

In East Germany (German Democratic Republic) GDR, which became part of the Soviet bloc after the Second World War, they had an interesting definition about propaganda and agitation. In 1976, while I was a student at the Institute of

229

Journalism, Berlin, one of our teachers on 'objectivity and partiality in journalism', Hans Proeus told us, that in short "propaganda treated a few things in depth, while agitation presented many ideas to the masses, but in less depth". He also put it in a joke that "propaganda explains the glorious future of communism, while agitation explains the bumps and potholes along the way".

The term agitation and propaganda is said to have originated in workers' struggle of Russia at the time of Lenin. The central committee of the communist party had a "department for agitation and propaganda", which was later renamed Ideology Department. At the time, the term did not have negative connotation. It simply meant "dissemination of ideas". The term later changed to agitprop which gave rise to Agitprop theatre, a highly politicized leftist theatre in Europe in the 1920's and spread to America. After the October Revolution of 1917 in Russia an agitprop train toured that vast country with artists and actors performing short plays about the revolution for agitation and propaganda purposes.

In Ethiopia propaganda was used to advance political persuasion, and agitation to mobilize the masses to action. Having worked for government and private media during all three governments that ruled Ethiopia after World War II, I have witnessed first-hand how they used the media for agit-prop and forced us journalists to function as their cadres. Emperor Haile Selassie's colorful coronation event of November 2nd, 1930, attended by high-ranking dignitaries from several countries of Europe, the United States, Japan and Egypt was accorded world-wide publicity. The coronation attracted considerable international media coverage, and starting from this event The Emperor used propaganda to inculcate in the minds of the people describing himself as descendant of king Solomon of Israel and Queen Sheba of Ethiopia. His official title included, "Lion of

230

Judah, king of kings, and elect of God." In such propaganda machinations, the emperor was accorded virtually absolute powers. In the 1931 constitution and the revised 1955 constitution, The Emperor was given the rank of divine appointment, and his body was declared 'sacred'. The government also used the media to hide the social ills of capitalism and concealing the real goal of capitalist domination from the people by manipulating their consciousness.

The pro-Soviet Derg used the media in the same manner for agitation and propaganda to educate the workers in socialist patriotism and proletarian internationalism, as well as to build their strong class position in the struggle against the 'enemies' of socialism. Propaganda has been an essential part of the ideological work of the Derg. The Derg encouraged Ethiopians to think, feel and act in a socialist way in order to strengthen socialism and firmly oppose bourgeois ideology. In such propaganda, the government tried to explain the far-reaching political, economic, social, and cultural changes that come with the development of a socialist society. It propagated the historical superiority, values and achievements of socialism around the world. At the same time, it propagated how imperialism, led by the United States, is the constant threat to world peace and the future of humanity. Derg used the media to propagate the problems of a capitalist system by explaining unemployment as the capitalist nature of crisis, their inevitability in modern world, and the necessity for the transformation of Ethiopia into a socialist society. By using the media as a propaganda machine, the government does a systematic scheme or concerted movement to propagate some creed or doctrine. It also used the state media as an instrument of agitation to excite or stir-up action around an issue. The party cadres also use the media to stir-up and arouse discontent and indignation against the old order. Sometimes they used concrete or realistic propaganda to influence the masses, other times they incline to abstract propaganda to raise ideas.

In Ethiopia, the government owned and controlled all the major state media (radio, television and major newspapers). The state media function has been focused mainly on agitation and propaganda. During the reign of all three governments, Haile Selassie, Derg and EPRDF, information was severely restricted. The rigid control exercised over the content and the flow of information emanates from the totalitarian nature of the political system of all three governments. When a government is overthrown, the new leaders yield initially to look democratic and fool the people. During this transition, private journals start to appear only to be harassed, stifled and banned as soon as the new government consolidates power.

The state media journalists are not allowed to expose corruption, human rights violations, economic mismanagement, or abuse of power by the politically and economically powerful. If they do so, they risk their livelihood. Most of the journalists would like to report the truth and expose corruption, but they don't have the freedom to do so. Thus the state media is monopolized and turned into a propaganda organ for the ruling elites. The media becomes the echo-chamber of leader's speeches and official functions.

"Leaders have usurped enormous amounts of political power and reduced popular control over the political system by using the media to generate support, compliance and just plain confusion among the public". (Lance Bennett, The politics of Illusion, P-178)

Government media editors are appointed by the ruling party and are instructed every now and then what events to cover and how to frame it. They are often obliged to do disgusting work like distortion, cover-ups, deception, disinformation, or

232

even to present blatant fabrication and lie. They are instructed to engage in diverting the attention of the people away from what is important to them by presenting sensational matters or simply by fear mongering, telling them that a certain country is going to invade us. Sometimes editors are encouraged or ordered to present opinionated, fabricated or exaggerated information. Remember, *"a bullet kills a man; a lying media kills a nation"*. This has been the function of the official, controlled, censored and partisan media in Ethiopia.

The information media in most of African countries including Ethiopia have always been monopolized by the government, and turned into a propaganda machine for the ruling class. During the reign of Emperor Haile Selassie, the editorial of the daily newspapers was sometimes actually written or dictated from the Grand Palace. Particularly at the wake of the 1974 revolution I have observed a number of days the editor-in-chief of Addis Zemen, Bealu Girma getting calls from the Grand Palace and writing dictation over the phone, or receiving written material to be used for the editorial column of the next day's newspaper. The censorship guidelines and the don't lists were so many that it was difficult for journalists to know the limits. Being a journalist working for government media during the time of the Emperor, and the Derg, we had difficulty to understand where the limit of the censorship was until we cross it. The country's media never had the freedom to operate independently of government control or involvement till this day. The state media has always been an echo chamber of leader's day-to-day rhetoric and a propaganda machine to cover up and distort the truth by selective presentation. If the government media journalist tries to expose government corruption, he will be transferred or dismissed to say the least.

The so called democratic western world also uses propaganda to "manufacture consent" and stir up society to action in the direction the wealthy ruling class elite desires. Even here, where we are told that the means of information are open and free, the people are not really free to participate in managing their own affairs and play a role in politics in some meaningful way. Under the Woodrow Wilson administration, the newly established propaganda commission was established to agitate the people to, participate in World War I against the Germans. The people were not interested to be involved in a European war. The propaganda commission known as "Creel Commission" succeeded in turning a pacifist population into a hysterical, war-mongering one who wanted to destroy everything German in just six months of propaganda work. Thus government propaganda was able to drive the reluctant population into war by terrifying them by mostly fabricated awful atrocities. That was a great success for the then president Woodrow Wilson who believed his country needed to go to war against Germany.

"They thereby assured that the public could not exert any meaningful influence on the decisions that were made. ...Not enabling the public to assert meaningful control over the political process, but rather averting any such danger. In these cases, as in numerous others, the public was managed and mobilized from above by means of the media highly selected messages and evasions." (Noam Chomsky and Edward Herman, Manufacturing Consent, P-303)

In the western world, intellectuals working for the capitalist system used the same propaganda technique to control the thinking of the public and stir-up a hysterical "Red Scare" method to destroy the communist parties and labor unions in Europe and America. Hitler of Germany used the same propaganda technique to control the thinking of the people and get the support of millions during World War II; and it worked. The great majority of the people is thus managed and brought into agreement with the governing elites to do whatever they proposed.

The business community and the collaborating intellectuals use the media for different propaganda methods to control society from getting organized and becoming an active participant in the political system. They make sure that the rest of the population just enjoy watching TV and take the message they get and remain a materialist and consumer society. Professor Noam Chomsky in his book *Media Control*, explains a progressive theory of liberal democratic thought by Lippmann, how the masses of the people should be handled in modern democracy as follows:

"We have to protect ourselves from the 'trampling and roar of a bewildered herd'. Now there are two 'functions' in a democracy: the specialized class, the responsible men, carry out the executive function, which means they do the thinking and planning and understand the common interests. Then, there is the bewildered herd, and they have a function in democracy too. Their function in a democracy, he said is to be "spectators", not participants in action. But they have more of a function than that, because it's a democracy. Occasionally they are allowed to lend their weight to one or another member of the specialized class. ...That is called an election. But once they've lent their weight to one or another member of the specialized class they're supposed to sink back and become spectators of action, but not participants". (Noam Chomsky, Media Control, P- 16)

The public relations industry in the United States does the same to control the way of thinking among the population. It is a huge industry spending billions of dollars a year. The business community uses public relations firms not only to promote the sales of its products, but also to weaken labor movements, and socialist thinking by spreading the "Red Scare".

They used effective means of propaganda to turn the public against labor union strike by presenting strikers as disruptive and harmful to the country and associating them as spies for the Soviet Bloc. Since the business community control the media and have massive resources, they used this formula to alienate the strikers from the people and show them as un-American. That was how they broke the backbone of the labor movement in the United States.

Censorship

The desire of Ethiopians to express their opinions and their freedom to receive information from all sources has been systematically strangled due to censorship by the government. Government ownership and control of the media or intervention in the form of regulation and direct censorship has been common in Ethiopia since the beginning of modern mass media a century ago. All the governments that came to power after the death of Emperor Menilik II had the opportunity and the potential to create, energize and subsidize a strong, pluralistic and independent press system. But none of them took the responsibility to do so. Emperor Haile Selassie and the Derg owned and controlled state media and put in place a department of censorship (*sansour memria*) within the Ministry of Information to check the contents of audio, video and printed materials before they are out to the public. The current ruling party of Ethiopia EPRDF own and control all major media, radio, television and newspapers. It declared the freedom of the press in 1991; but in practice it stifled free press right from the beginning with different legislation.

Having worked as a journalist in Ethiopia during all three governments, Emperor Haile Selassie, the military Derg, and The Ethiopian People's Revolutionary Democratic Front (EPRDF), I experienced the varying degrees and

236

techniques of censorship employed by each regime. In terms of media control, the slight difference between them has always been cosmetic. Whatever ideology they professed to follow, all the three governments had an unmistakable totalitarian approach. They appointed their cadres as chief editors and turned the state media into their propaganda organ. Investigative reporting whereby uncovering significant information ranging from the revelation of corruption and crime to exposing problems, issues and wrong-doings, holding public officials and private corporations accountable for their actions is simply unthinkable. The so-called free press, if ever, is not allowed to criticize government policy; the editor or journalist with critical views is highly likely to be jailed or exiled. In some instances journalists, like my former boss and mentor Bealu Girma, were murdered by government security forces.

It has always been risky and dangerous to be a journalist in Ethiopia, whether you worked for government or private media. There were certain topics we were not allowed to write about unless the pertinent authority gave an official press release on the matter; and in that case the carefully worded press release will be used without any alteration or interpretation. For instance, during the Emperor's reign twenty six topics were officially off limits. Price hikes, mutiny, student unrest, coup, government corruption, famine, religion, prostitution, in addition the royal family was among the unspeakable. Censorship guidelines were mostly ill-defined. A journalist usually has a vague idea about the limits until he or she crosses them; by then it was too late. For fear of arrest or abuse, most journalists toe the ruling party line or engage in a debilitating exercise of self-censorship. The slightest deviation from the official line could end a journalist in jail; thus creativity is lost and initiative stifled.

During the reign of Emperor Haile Selassie, there were no real private independent media. The government owned and controlled the state media and allowed no private or public media. Recently I was discussing with one of the prominent journalists in exile Mulugeta Lule, who worked more years as a journalist under the imperial government and personally knows most of the victims of censorship in Ethiopia. He cited that there were certain newspapers and magazine that were created by the government itself to pause like private media so that whenever there were some comments or accusations by a foreign media, these papers were instructed to refute it before the state media does so. All the editors and journalists who contributed to these papers were hired by the government under the organization known as *Yehager Fikr* (love for the country). These papers were published both in Amharic and English, *Yeethiopia Demtse, Sendeqalamachin, and Menen* (Amharic), Voice of Ethiopia, and Addis reporter (English). At the time all periodicals and books that were published had to go through censorship department and get approval before they go for print. Having approval from the censorship department of the Ministry of Information does not mean nothing will happen to the writer if the government finds the literature offending. To mention a few, during the reign of The Emperor a renowned journalist *Abie Gubegna,* who wrote a historical novel *Aleweledem* (I shall not be born), a narration of a child in his mother's womb, was exiled to a remote place in Illubabor for several years. Another journalist of *Yeethiopia Demtse* newspaper, Negede Gebreab, was also exiled to another remote province, Gomu Gofa because of what he wrote on the periodical.

All books had to go through censorship department before print, but even then if you publish something that criticizes government policy, you will be in trouble. During the reign of the Derg, there were a few opposition party periodicals for the first few years like *Gohe* (dawn), a publication of the Ethiopian People's Revolutionary Party (EPRP) and *Yesefew Hezb Dimtse* (voice of the masses) by *Meison*; which were short

238

lived. The magazine *Tsedey*, wrote about social life and healthy living continued for some more years until it closed for drop in sales. The editor of Gohe, Sarah Cossio, was arrested without court warrant and stayed in prison around six years for publishing articles that criticized the governent. It was during the reign of the Derg that the vice minister of the Ministry of Information, Bealu Germa, who wrote his famous novel *Oromay* and get it published with the permission of the censorship department, was fired from his position. He later became an instructor teaching journalism at Addis Ababa University, where he was a victim of lay off by order from the Derg. After a few weeks, he disappeared; it is widely believed that he was kidnapped by government security forces and murdered. His family was told that his car was found in the town of Debre Zeit, 45 kilometers south of Addis Ababa; his graveyard still unknown. Solomon Kifle, now a prominent journalist of the Voice of America, was fired from the Ethiopian National Television, where he worked as an entertainment program producer for over thirteen years, for broadcasting music and entertainment productions challenging the Derg regime.

I have personally experienced harassment, reprimand, court charges and arrest during the reign of the military Derg and TPLF/EPRDF for criticizing the government policy and action of authorities. I have been repeatedly harassed by the Derg's Workers Party of Ethiopia (WPE) Department of Ideology officials for approving the broadcast of certain television productions. To mention a few, one day in 1987 an official in the Ideology Department in charge of overseeing the television programs, Derbew Temesgen, scolded me over the phone for approving the broadcast of the famous film 'The Miserable' ('Les Miserables'). Apparently the content of the film was unacceptable to the regime in a situation where "the question of bread has not yet been answered". Another day in the same year he called and bitterly condemned me for airing a 30 second video of Michael Jackson doing the moon walk. His complaint was that, "it was an imperialist cultural invasion".

On a different occasion, I was summoned to see the Minister of Information Dr. Colonel Feleke Gedlegiorgis who reprimanded me about an aired television program regarding a family evicted from government housing, by Urban Dwellers Association (*Kebele*) leaders and made homeless, while the house was rented to a kinsman of a government official. The journalist who produced the reportage under my guidance talked to all concerned and cared about fairness, balance and accuracy. We knew what might be coming, but we decided to take the risk because ignoring such a true story would be extremely unethical. The viewers who sow the evicted family crying and living under a tree in the middle of the capital city Addis Ababa made it talk of the town. The next day we learned that the government authorities were shocked and took action immediately by firing the *Kebele* leaders, and giving the family a dwelling place; but in their official press release they blamed the Ethiopian Television for airing such a "false" story as being irresponsible.

The television documentary I produced on the then controversial issue of "villagization" in rural Ethiopia was heavily edited with all the material about grievances of the project deleted by the head of ETV, Wolle Gurmu for domestic broadcast. The heavily edited version was to be translated into English and distributed to Ethiopian Embassies abroad. This was done as mandated by the Ministry of Information. It was this kind of propaganda material lacking fairness and balance that was promoted by official bureau. I was later removed from my position as head of program division of Ethiopian Television, for challenging the system and mainly because of the constructive criticism I articulated in a yearly symposium address to government journalists assessing the programs of Ethiopian Television. Most of the journalists loved my presentation and

240

appreciated my daring analysis, but I knew the officials will not be happy. Since copies of the papers of all four division heads of ETV who presented to the symposium were sent to relevant authorities earlier, Wolle told me that the member of the executive committee of the party and head of the Ideology Department Shimeles Mazengia did not like my presentation at the symposium.

The reign of the TPLF/EPRDF is different from its predecessors only on paper, since it eliminated the Censorship Department, and private periodicals are allowed to print responsibly without having to seek approval from a censorship department. But again, it was no better than the previous periods as the journalists who wrote and published anything that criticized the policy and deeds of EPRDF were arrested, most of them without court warrant, and held in prison with no right of bail. Later the government promulgated a draconian press law with many loopholes that in effect crippled freedom of expression. According to the two laws, "Freedom of Mass Media and Access to Information Proclamation" and "Anti-terrorism" Proclamation, any editor who dared to criticize government policy was considered a terrorist and arrested, sentenced to several years of prison, and ordered to pay heavy fine.

Ethiopia has been under repressive governments all the time. Ethiopians never had freedom of expression except for a few bright intervals during government change, and that was short lived. All three governments that ruled Ethiopia after World War II have not been transparent and accountable to their decisions and policies. Ethiopians have been denied to know the whole truth about their government and country. Government media often exaggerate, falsify, fabricate or overlook the real truths which stand naked before people's eyes.

When we look at the private media there are many courageous journalists with integrity and professional ethics, who have suffered prison terms for writing the truth with fairness and balance. On the other hand, in most of the private independent media we notice the same kind of embarrassing mimic styles of government-owned media culture, being either partisan or presenting opposing views –the other side of the coin. Most private media ignore all commendable achievements of the ruling party, and its development efforts are not talked about; never daring to recognize the accomplishments of the government. The criticism they present is not constructive to persuade the authorities to learn from their mistakes and improve their performance; instead it is criticism with hatred that does not help to learn from one another. Thus, both government and some private media are confusing and frustrating the public by not telling the whole truth; further polarizing our society with their infested chronic political virus. These manifestations of political life should be changed and both sides need to tell the whole truth, entering into discourse with each other to start genuine and healthy reconciliation and compromise for the good of the people.

Throughout the history of modern mass media in Ethiopia, governments have censored writers and their works on political, religious, and social grounds. In this age of the internet and satellite broadcast, new instances of censorship and court decisions on journalists in Ethiopia are continually taking place. After the collapse of communism and the fall of the Berlin wall, and the start of the World Wide Web, which allowed even the smallest voice to be heard, you would think there is unparalleled freedom of information everywhere. This is dangerously naïve. The government led by EPRDF tells us there is no censorship, and the country's constitution reads the same; but, in actual fact, with draconian laws that were enacted in violation of the constitution to muzzle the press, censorship has come in many

242

guises and have become complex. I can tell you from my experience that censorship has no boundaries in Ethiopia. The censors patrol not only politics, but every way of life.

Censorship arises out of a paranoid mentality when a dominant ruling class is afraid of losing power and strangles a writer or an artist. In Ethiopia, we have gone through many painful chapters in the history of political censorship. The censor intrudes on your thinking, always in your mind, even if you refuse to recognize it or reject the validity, but always there. In a short time, the censor becomes a secret and shameful intimate of the writer, and the writer becomes the victim suffering the stifling shadow of the censor every day. Writers operating under censorship conditions are in a state of mental slavery. It was the same in Stalin's Russia, in South Africa's Apartheid, in Mengistu and Meles Ethiopia. In all these cases, the battle with the censor invades the writer's psychic life.

Free Press under Fire

The declaration of the freedom of the press in the Charter of the Transitional Government of Ethiopia (TGE) in 1991 encouraged the publication of so many newspapers and magazines. Because there was a serious hunger for information, and people were suspicious of government media, the public chose to buy private publications and they were selling in large quantities. The rate at which new magazines were introduced was unbelievable, every week a new one starts to publish. The quality of their content was also amazing. The talent that has been stifled for so long has been released, persuasive articles and investigative reporting with engaging and appalling narrative, political cartoons with deep meaning and high art quality developed in a very short time. My own magazine, *Africa Qend* (Horn of Africa), where I worked as its editor-in chief, was one leading example.

During the first few years the free press performed crucial functions in effecting the societal purpose by enabling the Ethiopian people to assert meaningful control over the new political process. As the years roll by, the TPLF-led government increased the pressure of harassment, intimidation, arrest, and torture of journalists. Finally, it came out with a draconian press law with many loopholes to stifle the free press. Play-writes, drama, theatre, music and comedians suffered in many different ways.

There is another way of censorship regarding theatre and music. Certain plays were refused performance in government-owned theatres during the reign of the EPRDF. Deha Adeg by Ayalneh Mulatu, and Petros Yachin Sehat by Laureate Tsegaye Gebre Medhin, and a few other plays were not allowed to be performed in the government run theatres. While Tsegaye Gebremedhin's, "Hahu Weyes Bebu" was staged in the town of Awasa, the actors and actresses were beaten and the performance was stopped by people who were referred to as hooligans, but in actual fact were ruling party cadres. Three singers and one entertainer including Teddy Afro (vocalist) and Tamagne Beyene (entertainer/activist) were arrested and banned from any public performance including any advertisement of their work in government media for months.

I was the editor-in-chief of a private independent news magazine *Africa Qend* for two years starting 1992 only to suffer at court and in jail for the articles I published. Although Prime Minister Meles Zenawi and his government tried to tell us that there is no direct censorship, and journalists are free to publish professionally ethical articles, the exercise of this freedom only led editors to jail. With a draconian press law, and the absence of independent judiciary, I was one of the first casualties of the regulation. EPRDF leaders don't like to see an independent paper of real substance with in-depth analysis of current issues that affect our society. They use all kinds of methods to muzzle editors and to silence journalists.

In the early years of EPRDF regime, I worked as an independent author and a columnist for a popular private newspaper *Tobia* before I became the editor-in-chief of Africa Qend. I also published two of my books "*Africana Ambagenen Meriwochua*" (Africa and its Dictators), and a historical novel on the life of a journalist in a totalitarian state, "*Yehlina Barnet*" (Mental Slavery); both in Amharic. The Ministry of Information's censorship department of the Derg regime had blocked these works previously. Since the subject matter affects the previous regime overthrown by the EPRDF, the new officials were very much enthused by the prospect. Yet, even though EPRDF officially proclaimed freedom of expression in the transitional charter and later in the constitution, it promulgated draconian press laws subsequently. As the editor-in-chief of Africa Qend, in the first three years of EPRDF rule I was arrested five times, each time for few hours and days, and had two charges at the Federal High Court and one at the Federal Supreme Court, on articles I published in the magazine. Given the heavy hand of the state inside the judiciary, I was surely going in for a long prison term.

I experienced the prisons for a few days and they are so dirty, unhygienic and lack appropriate sanitation; smell horrible. Severe overcrowding is common, the authorities provide very little food, water, and health care for prisoners. Many prisoners have to supplement this with daily food deliveries from family members, which is a burden on the nearest kin. Medical care is unreliable in federal prisons and almost nonexistent in regional prisons. On top of that, you are thrown into a room with scores of criminal gangs on purpose, who abuse you and sometimes instigated by government cadres to beat you up. That is why I decided not to return to Ethiopia after I completed my training in the U.S on investigative reporting.

"Information released by the Ministry of Health during the year reportedly stated nearly 62 percent of inmates in various jails across the country suffered from mental health problems as a result of solitary confinement, overcrowding, and lack of adequate healthcare facilities and services". (United States Department of State, Country Reports – 2012)

To defend ourselves we started to organize free press journalists for unity of action. On March 11th 1993, a congress of Ethiopian journalists working for private independent press established the Ethiopian Free Press Journalists Association (EFJA). It was the first professional association of its kind in Ethiopia free of government intervention. The founding congress of journalists thoroughly discussed, reviewed, polished and unanimously adopted the draft by-law constituting the association. It also elected a five-man executive committee; including myself as the Secretary General, to manage and guide the activities of EFJA.

The aims and objectives of EFJA was to create a common forum for working journalists and enable them to coordinate their efforts to develop their professional skills, to maintain a higher degree of professional ethics, to win the respect and trust of the public, to uphold basic freedom of the press, to ensure progress and continuity of the independent press, and to collectively protect the rights of all Ethiopian free press journalists.

Consistent with the relevant legal provisions, the executive committee of EFJA submitted a formal request to the ministry of Internal Affairs to register the association. The president of EFJA, Kefale Mamo, and me the Secretary General, were driving to the government office at Old Airport zone every week to get the license we formally requested on behalf of the association. Every week they turned us down with silly excuses, like the boss is not in or has gone for the day, etc. We kept on going to ask for the license for over a year until I left the country for journalism training in the United States, where I preferred to stay.

Even though we could not get a license for our association, the executive committee proceeded with the regular function of the association. The executive committee involved itself in such activities as to enhance the professional ability and ethical standard of the members, promote peaceful business relations between the private independent press and the government, building a closer tie and cooperation between EFJA and other domestic and international professional organizations.

In spite of our effort to provide greater service to the people by reporting the truth and making the media a market place of ideas where all sides could debate, our endeavors were stifled by the government. By the time I left Ethiopia in June 1994, more than twenty journalists were languishing in prison, many of them without being charged or convicted. They were arrested without court warrant and denied their right to be released on bail. Their cases were similar "inciting the public against the government".

In one year alone, from July 1993 to June 1994, about 84 journalists were arrested, out of which only eight were formally convicted by the courts. During the same period, 63 journalists, including myself, were defending the charges brought against us in federal high courts. In that same year, 55 monthly magazines and 26 weekly newspapers were banned by government order. We have been reporting all these problems to the government that gave us a deaf ear. We asked the International Federation of Journalists (IFJ) and Committee to Protect Journalists (CPJ) for help. Arresting journalists continued unabated, and in the years of 2006 and 2007, the TPLF-led government broke the record: Ethiopia was the number one country in the world with the highest number of journalists incarcerated. By arresting journalists, human rights activists, and opposition political party members, the government made Ethiopia a country with the largest population of political prisoners in Africa.

The climate for press freedom in Ethiopia steadily deteriorated. Members of the private press are almost daily bombarded by the government media, and are subjected to all kinds of harassment, including detention and torture. This gross injustice continued unabated to this very day where journalists are accused of terrorism charges, and some are sentenced to life. The provisions in the law are ill-defined; they can be interpreted to encompass any criticism of the TPLF-led government. Sometimes, journalists are detained for months without trial. I personally was charged with sedation and "inciting the public" in connection with the articles I published in my magazine. Because of such continued harassment, 160 journalists have fled the country during the last twenty years.

The intentions of the free press journalists were clear then and are clear today: to use the freedom of the press for building a strong community that stands for justice and democracy.

"Democracy sustaining journalism has three components:

1) *It must be a rigorous watch dog of those in power and those who wish to be in power.*
2) *It must present a wide range of informed views on the most pressing issues of the day.*
3) *It must be able to expose deception and permit the truth to rise to the top.*

If not; the watch dog becomes a lapdog and huge expanses of power in our society (government, and/or corporate) go unexamined in our journalism."
(Nicols and McChesney, Tragedy and Farce, P-76)

To accomplish this important mission, journalists should be guided by their ethical standards in seeking truth and reporting it. Responsible journalists must test the accuracy of information they gather from all sources to avoid error. They need to stay clean from deliberate distortion. While fulfilling their obligation to uphold the public's right to know, they should be voice to the voiceless and be vigilant and courageous to hold those in power accountable. It is important that journalists avoid all kinds of conflicts of interest and stay free of activities and associations that might compromise integrity. The Society of Professional Journalists clearly defined these responsibilities in its code of ethics.

"Members of the Society of Professional Journalists believe that public enlightenment is the forerunner of justice and the foundation of democracy. The duty of the journalist is to further those ends   by seeking truth and providing a fair and comprehensive account of events and issues. Conscientious journalists from all media specialties strive to serve the public with thoroughness and honesty. Professional integrity is the corner stone of a journalist's credibility. ...Journalists should be honest, fair and courageous in gathering, reporting and interpreting information". (Fergusen and Patten, Opportunities in Journalism Careers, P-21)

Ethiopian journalists do not have the opportunity for in-depth training of their career, and might make mistakes. But again, the solution will be to give them more training and encouragement, and more freedom. Harassing and arresting journalists is not the way to develop their career and strengthen democracy. The first institute of journalism was established in Addis Ababa only recently, and even that is run by government cadres. It teaches journalism of the socialist way of the Stalin era. Courses in journalism were given in Addis Ababa University in 1990's only to senior graduating students who are majoring in language and international relations. Under the circumstances, we can't expect much from these inadequately trained journalists. Besides, every time there is a government change, the experienced journalists are laid off and replaced by new cadres who are less educated and less qualified but loyal; thus the profession lacks continuity.

The TPLF-led government discouraged the press by increasing the cost of paper and printing; it owns and or controls the major printing houses. It also denied the free press the opportunity to advertise their publications on state media. In spite of these shortcomings, Ethiopian Free Press journalists have performed a commendable job to serve the truth and the people. With all these intimidations, the free press journalists continued to fulfill their professional and social obligation by raising key social issues: like Ethiopia's unity, regional autonomy and self-administration, land ownership and lease policy, ethnic politics, multi-party democracy, labor union autonomy, Structural Adjustment Program, currency devaluation, independent judiciary, government corruption and lack of magnanimity, human rights, police brutality, free and fair elections and problems of the free press, etc.

Some of our fellow journalists received international awards and medals for their outstanding contribution in reporting the truth. Dawit Kebede received the International Press Freedom Award from CPJ. Eskinder Nega, who was in prison in Ethiopia, also received the Freedom to Write Award (PEN) in April 2012. President of PEN America Center (Barbara Goldsmith Freedom to Write Award), Peter Godwin once said that "Eskinder understood the risks of continuing to speak out publicly". A former federal judge and opposition party leader in Ethiopia, Birtukan Mideksa, who was a prisoner herself, said in an interview that 'Eskinder Nega has been unwavering even in the face of death threats from security forces of the government'.

The other journalist, Reeyot Alemu, received the Courage in Journalism Award from the International Women Media Foundation. Reeyot also won the UNESCO Guillermo Cano World Press Freedom Prize in 2013 in recognition of her "exceptional courage, resistance and commitment to freedom of expression". She was recommended by an independent International Jury of media professionals. The UNESCO Guillermo Cano World Press Freedom Prize was created in 1997 by UNESCO's Executive Board and is awarded annually during the celebration of World Press Freedom Day on May 3. The prize honors the work of an individual or an organization which has made a notable contribution to the defense and promotion of freedom of expression anywhere in the world, especially if risks have been involved. Another journalist Serkalem Fasil also received award and recognition for excellence in journalism.

In recognition of their effort to promote free expression in Ethiopia four journalists have received the prestigious Hellman/Hammett award of 2012. An independent journalist and blogger Eskinder Nega, An English teacher and columnist of the banned newspaper *Feteh* Reeyot Alemu, the closed *Awramba Times* newspaper editor Woubshet Taye, and editor of *Addis Neger* online Mesfin Negash, are among the 41 writers and journalists from 19 countries who received the award. Among the four Ethiopians who got the award, three were jailed, the fourth, Mesfin Negash fled the country in 2009 and lives in exile.

The Hellman/Hammett award is named after two American writers Lillian Hellman and Dashiell Hammett who were harassed during the 1950's anti-communism investigations.

Hellman suffered professionally and had trouble finding work, while Hammett spent time in prison. The award is administered by Human Rights Watch and is given annually to writers and journalists around the world who have been targets of human rights abuse and political persecution. The Deputy Africa Director at Human Rights Watch Leslie Lefkow said, "*The four jailed and exiled journalists exemplify the courage, and dire situation of independent journalism in Ethiopia today. Their ordeals illustrate the price of speaking freely in a country where free speech is no longer tolerated.*" (Human Rights Watch press release, December 2012)

These award winning journalists represent a much larger group of journalists in Ethiopia suppressed by the Ethiopian government in its effort to restrict free speech and peaceful dissent, clamp down on independent media and limit access to and use of the internet. In 2012 alone eleven Ethiopian and foreign journalists have been charged and sentenced under Ethiopia's anti-terrorism law. The Ethiopian parliament passed a new Telecommunications law in 2012 further controlling internet usage. According to the Committee to Protect Journalists (CPJ), the largest number of journalists forced to flee their countries since 1992 have been from Ethiopia, Somalia and Iran.

The ruling party of Ethiopia EPRDF has been in conflict with foreign countries, based on media coverage and broadcast by a media based in those countries criticizing the government. These include Voice of America (VOA), Deutsche Welle of Germany, Al Jazeera from Qatar, Kenya's NTV and Eritrea Television to name a few. US government funded Voice of America and Germany's Deutsche Welle which broadcast radio programs into Ethiopia in local languages were targeted and jammed several times, their local correspondents arrested and forced to flee the country at different times. Later, VOA used about a dozen different wave length frequencies which the government was not able to jam.

The government raided news rooms and editorial offices, blocked newspapers from publishing, expelled a number of foreign reporters, shutdown newspapers and magazines. Amnesty International researcher Claire Beston was expelled from Ethiopia in 2011 for criticizing the anti-terrorism proclamation. Ethiopian leaders have been sensitive about what is said concerning their governance, panicking, and picking a fight on every little comment about their administration, blaming it as a "covert political agenda".

In 2009 the Ministry of Foreign Affairs of Ethiopia summoned the ambassador of Kenya in Addis Ababa for a series of media coverage entitled "Inside Rebel Territory", by Kenya's NTV about the struggle of an opposition group OLF. NTV is a privately owned broadcaster which is part of the Nation Media Group and its broadcast is beyond the control of the ambassador, and even the government of Kenya to curb its editorial independence. A few years ago the Ethiopian government severed relations with Qatar by cutting diplomatic relations because of what Al Jazeera broadcast out of Doha, which did not please the ruling party. The government also filtered Al Jazeera's website for months, for its coverage of Ethiopian Muslims protest. Qatar and Ethiopia restored diplomatic ties in 2012 may be because Ethiopian authorities found out that they cannot succeed in changing Al Jazeera's coverage by taking such actions.

There are only few private newspapers and magazines in Ethiopia today. They are operating with less and less freedom every day, engaging in self-censorship for fear of arrest. There are also some periodicals that are getting secret support from TPLF leaders and functioning in the name of an independent press. Besides, it is sad that the Ethiopian Teachers Association which is the oldest professional association in the country has not been registered by the government for a long time. The government organized some opportunist teachers at one point, and registered it as the only teachers association. The Committee on Freedom of Association of the United Nations International Labor Organization (ILO), singled out Ethiopia along with four other countries in its report of 2012 after it reviewed cases involving rights to organize, negotiate through collective bargaining and engage in social dialogue. The committee criticized the government for refusing to register the Ethiopian Teachers' Association for so long.

Internet Filtering/Spying

Telephone and internet service is very poor in Ethiopia compared to many African countries. *"Elsewhere in Africa the debate is about Blackberry and IPhone, in Ethiopia it is simply about getting a phone."* (*The Economist*, May, 2010 edition).

According to *The Economist* investigative report, the number of internet users in Ethiopia in 2010 was estimated to be 360,000, which is only 0.4 percent of the population. Besides, a 2010 study by the International Telecommunications Union (ITU) found that "Ethiopia's broadband internet connections were among the most expensive in the world when compared with monthly income, second only to that in the Central African Republic." Prices are set by the state-owned Ethiopian Telecommunications and made artificially high on purpose. The combined cost of a computer, internet connection, and usage charges makes internet access beyond the reach of Ethiopians. The Ethiopian government has been reluctant to liberalize the telecommunications sector which would likely drive prices down.

According to a study by another non-profit organization, Freedom House, although Ethiopia is the second most populous country in Africa, poor infrastructure and government monopoly on telecommunications have significantly hindered the expansion of digital media. As a result, Ethiopia has one of the lowest rates of internet and mobile-phone penetration in the continent and the digital divide is getting bigger every year. To restrict dissidents inside the country and in the Diaspora from using the internet as a platform for political discussion, the government has instituted filtering systems. Besides the increased censorship and surveillance practices, blocking online political and news sites, the government owned Ethiopian Telecommunications in 2009 began Deep Packet Inspection DIP, of all internet traffic in the country. In September 2012 the EPRDF government ratified the new "Telecommunications Service Infringement Law" that criminalizes online speech that may be construed as defamatory or terrorist and holds the website or account owner liable even if the speech is posted as a comment by someone else on the website.

The Ethiopian government is currently using a system for monitoring large scale internet material that spies on all web communications, wiretapping and illegal hacking in the country and on political opponents abroad. The government has established a system of Deep Packet Inspection (DPI), a technology that enables to scan the data travelling over a network and reading the contents without opening the mail. According to Reporters without Boarders report of May 2012 published by French newspaper *Le Monde*, the Ethiopian government is spying on its elites by using this technology. The government also banned the use of Internet phone service, Voice over Internet Protocol (VOIP), citing reasons of national security. Until recently, using a service like Skype was punishable by fifteen years in prison. The government spokesman asked to comment on the matter later announced that the story is not true. Whether they admit it or not, using the country's sole telephone company, Ethio-Telecom, the government has established a system for detailed monitoring and filtering of communications over the internet, using Chinese technology. This has greatly affected freedom of expression.

"The government has responded by instituting one of the few nation-wide filtering systems in Africa, passing laws to restrict free expression, and attempting to manipulate online media. These efforts have coincided with a broader increase in repression against independent print and broadcast media since the 2005 parliamentary elections, in which opposition parties mustered a relatively strong showing. The crackdown gained new momentum ahead of the next elections in May 2010". (Freedom House, July -2011).

China has emerged as a key investor and contractor in Ethiopia's Telecom sector. There are allegations that China has provided technologies that can be used for political repression, such as surveillance cameras and satellite jamming equipment. China may also assist in developing more robust internet and mobile-phone censorship and surveillance capacities in the future. Even Prime Minister Meles Zenawi admitted that the government was jamming The Voice of America VOA Amharic service. The United States State Department of Human Rights report released in February 2009 also accused the Ethiopian government of restricting internet access by blocking politically oriented websites. *"The key government agency allegedly involved in surveillance is the Information Network Security Agency (INSA). It is suspected of engaging in internet filtering and monitoring of email. There have also been reports of the government using technology obtained from the Chinese authorities to monitor phone lines and various types of online communications."* (Freedom House, July -2011).

Although the Ethiopian government denies engaging in online censorship, studies conducted by Open Net Initiative

(ONI) in 2009 indicate that Ethiopia is the only country in Africa to impose nation-wide, politically motivated, internet filtering. The majority of internet users rely on cybercafés to access the web, even though connections are very slow and unreliable. Accessing an online email account and opening one message takes several minutes in a typical Addis Ababa cybercafé even with broadband connections. Whenever I forward some articles to my friends back home, they have a hard time to read the contents or get it printed out in a cybercafé; it's discouraging. In 2002, it so happened that the TPLF-led government shutdown private cybercafés, declaring them illegal. Since then, the Ethiopian Telecommunications Agency (ETA) has been authorized to issue licenses for new cybercafés, which are suspected to be owned by political loyalists.

Ethiopian Telecom has placed restrictions on advanced internet applications like the use of Voice over internet protocol (VOIP), and internet-based fax services. Using these advanced internet applications is prohibited. It could lead to punishment including fine and up to five years in prison. After the 2005 elections, Ethiopian Telecommunications blocked text-messaging via mobile phones for two years for fear of the opposition using the technology to organize anti-government protests. Some political commentators use proxy servers and anonymizing tools to hide their identity. EPRDF leaders do not want to allow greater public access to information and telecommunication technologies for fear of losing their grip on power. In addition to increased repression of journalists, Ethiopian authorities use regime apologists, paid commentators, and pro-government websites to proactively manipulate the online news and information landscapes.

The government approach to internet filtering appears to entail hindering access to specific internet protocol (IP) addresses or domain names around important political events or elections focusing primarily on independent online news media, political blogs and human rights groups. The victims in this sporadic government blockage were international news outlets like US-based Cable News Network (CNN) and non-governmental organizations such as Human Rights Watch, Amnesty International and Reporters without Boarders, all of which have criticized the Ethiopian government's human rights record. Other websites like Ethiomedia, Ethiopian Review, Cyber Ethiopia, Quatero, Ethiopian Media Forum, etc. are also affected by the blockage.

Concerning this fact, Freedom House conducted a survey and found out that in mid- 2010 these websites were blocked, and after the parliamentary elections they were accessible again. Pro-democracy groups commented that the erratic nature of internet filtering is a deliberate tactic of the government aimed at creating confusion and buttressing claims that there is no systematic filtering in the country. The World Wide Web Foundation led by Web inventor Sir Tim Berners-Lee in a new global study of 2012 revealed that Ethiopia ranks fifth from bottom in global web index use to improve people's lives. Ethiopia, the second most populous country in Africa, ranks considerably lower than many African countries in the freedom in economic and social impact of the web, communication infrastructure, and web usage. Sweden topped the index ahead of the United States.

Online freedom has suffered setbacks in Ethiopia. According to the research group Freedom House's recent report released on September 24th 2012, covering the period from January 2011 to May 2012, Ethiopian authorities used newer and more sophisticated controls to quell dissent on the Internet. Project Director at Freedom House and co-author of the report Sanja Kelly said, *"The findings clearly show that threats to*

Internet freedom are becoming more diverse. As authoritarian rulers see that blocked websites and high-profile arrests draw local and international condemnations, they are turning to murkier – but no less dangerous – methods of controlling online conversations." (Freedom House, September 24, 2012 report).

This latest study found that Estonia has the highest level of online freedom, while the United States ranked second. The countries that received the lowest scores were Iran, Cuba and China. Ethiopia is among the ten countries that received a ranking of "not free" along with Saudi Arabia, Belarus, Bahrain, Pakistan, Myanmar, Thailand, Uzbekistan, Vietnam and Syria. Thus, the Ethiopian government has been active to choke off free expression at every corner. In a country where people are hungry for access to truthful news coverage all vital sectors and voices for independent journalism have been shut down.

Rhetoric and Practice

The Ethiopian Constitutional provisions guarantee freedom of expression and media freedom. But the press law that the government adopted in recent years restrict free expression. According to Human Rights Watch, the new "Freedom of Mass Media and Access to Information proclamation" and the "anti-terrorism proclamation" of 2008 and 2009 respectively, introduced crippling fines and licensing restrictions for establishing private media. The 2009 "Anti-terrorism Proclamation" has an overly broad definition of terrorism giving authorities wide discretion to arrest critics. Under this legislation, publication of a statement that is likely to be interpreted by the government as a direct or indirect encouragement of terrorism is punishable by up to 20 years in prison.

The criminal code that was enacted in May 2005 provides; *"special criminal liability of the author, originator or publisher if writings are deemed to be linked to offences such as treason, espionage or incitement, and carry a penalty up to life imprisonment or death"*. The scale and scope of the harshness of the law and its arbitrary interpretation by the government and such practices as surveillance and internet filtering have led several journalists and pro-democracy activists to flee the country in recent years alone.

Besides the draconian press law, in the absence of rule of law and due process which are essential conditions for the prevalence of fundamental rights and democratic conditions, there can't be an independent judiciary. One can't expect the authorities to respect the rule of law in the absence of free and fair elections whereby people can elect and call back their leaders. How can we expect government authorities to respect rule of law and due process while the people are not free to form civil associations, trade unions and political parties without the interference of the government.

While I was defending myself from the charges brought against me at two federal high courts and later the Supreme Court in 1993 and 1994, on the articles and poems I published, I have witnessed government interference in the administration of justice. I was acquitted of the first charge by a panel of three judges at the second *chilot* of the high court: Judge Berhanu Gebreselassie, Judge Belayneh Mamo and Judge Dadimos Haile. When I went back after three days to get my vehicle ownership certificate *(Libre)*, that I have deposited as bail, the court secretary told me that the three judges received a transfer letter to different remote provinces because of their ruling in my case. These were experienced and educated judges with law degree from Addis Ababa University. I was shocked; but, this was not the first time or the last one where government authorities have interfered in the administration of justice.

My attorney who represented me in this case was Haile Kebede who was U.S.-educated and one of the most famous lawyers in the country. As he continued to defend many more journalists and politicians at court, a few years after I left the country, he was gunned down in front of a district court in down town Addis Ababa, in broad day light, while he was walking to his car after a court session. His killer has not been apprehended for many years. His killer, and whoever might be behind the killing of this great man who chose to stand for justice, did not kill only Haile, but justice.

It is not enough to prescribe a law on paper, the most important part is to observe, implement and enforce the prescribed law indiscriminately. While I was pursuing my charges at court and doing investigative reporting, I learned two instances where the registrar of the court refused to even accept the bail application of two prominent politicians, Abera Yemaneab, leader of MEISON, and Colonel Getahun Ijigu and to present it to the judge. There are also many instances where the courts gave orders for the release of defendants on bail; and when the jail or the police station release them as per the court order, a security car awaited them at the gate and took them to another jail. A good example is Seye Abraha, a founding member of TPLF and the first Minister of Defence of the EPRDF government who had to face charges after he fell from power. He was acquitted of the charges brought against him by the all famous Ethiopian judge Bertukan Midekssa who later became a leader of the biggest opposition party UDJ, only to be arrested as soon as he left the court room; and spent over six years in jail along with his brother and other family members. When the court summons the authority and ask why he arrested them, other fabricated reasons are given to the judge. With all these injustice going on, the government is telling us that there is justice in Ethiopia today.

In some instances, the owner/publisher of a periodical is also charged along with the editor-in-chief for an article that was printed. A case in point was the owner of my magazine "Africa Qend", Hamid Kamil Faris, who was charged and acquitted with me. The law makes it clear that in the presence of the editor the publisher will not be held responsible for the contents of the paper. Because Hamid was a foreign relations secretary of the Ethiopian Muslims Supreme Council at the time, the government was looking for a reason to lock him up; sadly, there came an incident at Anwar Mosque in Addis Ababa the following year where one person was killed and he was arrested along with other committee members for several years.

Similar things happened to other publishers. A vivid example is Berhane Mewa who was the secretary general of the Ethiopian Chamber of Commerce and manager of Alef Enterprise, a publishing and advertising private limited company. Through the same tactic, Berhane languished in prison for five months in connection with an article that one of Alef enterprise newspapers *Dewel* has published. The editor-in-chief, Meleshachew Ameha, was also charged with the same offence. In actual fact, prior to this incident, Berhane Mewa had severely criticized the drafting process of the Ethiopian Constitution and the land lease policy of the government in public meetings. In his capacity as the representative of the Ethiopian Chamber of Commerce, his speech was broadcast over the radio and television and published in some newspapers. It was a topic of discussion among the people. Shortly afterwards, they found a reason to arrest him and search and take all his computers at Alef enterprise. There are numerous such instances that have been reported and registered or published on private newspapers. And there are many more that are never reported.

Free press survives in Ethiopia in the balance by the perseverance and dedication of a few journalists. The proclamation issued in 2008 known as "Freedom of mass media and access to information proclamation No. 590/2008" provides preposterous penalties for multiple misdemeanors. Besides, government printing agencies which at present are the only service providers for newspaper publishing have been ordered by the government to use the new form "Standard Contract for Printing", which entitles these publishers to conduct a form of censorship giving them the authority to reject requests for publishing if they deem the contents of the material submitted for publishing contains questionable matters. This pre-publication censorship vividly contradicts relevant provisions enshrined in the Ethiopian Constitution. The government should not have allowed any such practices that may directly or indirectly intend to undermine the supreme law of the land.

On July 20, 2012 a widely read and popular newspaper *Feteh* (justice) has been proscribed by the Ministry of Justice from publishing its weekly issue. The newspaper was actually denied printing service by the government-owned Brehanena Selam Printing Enterprise for a news item they believed contains criminal matters. The injunction order that the ministry wrote to deny the printing is against Article 42 (9) of proclamation 590/2008 that provides "*an impoundment of a periodical or a book shall relate only to copies intended for dissemination*".

During the same month, another newspaper, *Fenote Netsanet*, was denied printing by the same printing agency, this time giving technical reasons. This direct and indirect pressure upon the few remaining free press symbols has become another obstacle for freedom of expression in Ethiopia. Because of such intimidation and harassment that continued undeterred, exercising freedom of expression in Ethiopia is next to zero.

Many prominent journalists have fled the country for fear of imprisonment and persecution. The few journalists who remained in the country and dared to work for serious private independent newspapers are facing many obstacles and legal problems.

In July and August 2012 the two newspapers, *Feteh* and *Fenote Netsanet*, both known for their critical view on government policies and practices and their focus on political matters, have stopped their publication due to the refusal by the printing enterprise. This same enterprise has continued printing other pro-government newspapers, sending a message that the enterprise is being selective and partisan deriding the constitutional principle that holds the press shall entertain diverse opinions and the people have the right of access to information of public interest.

Several hundred journalists have been thrown to jail by EPRDF authorities; some stayed in prison till 2018, accused of "terrorism". In February 2013 government authorities arrested journalist Solomon Kebede and Yusuf Getachew for publishing about the Ethiopian Muslims protest in Addis Ababa in their newsmagazine *Yemuslimoch Guday ("Muslims Affairs")*. The government accused them of incitement of terrorism, for covering demonstrations staged by Muslims and criticizing the government's perceived intrusion in religious affairs. The EPRDF government is often accused of intrusion in religious affairs (Christians and Muslims alike), and for its interference in the country's Orthodox Christians Patriarch election and the Muslims Islamic Council election. In an effort to suppress coverage of the protests authorities have banned all three Muslim-oriented publications including *Yemuslimoch Guday*. The publishing enterprise Horizon Printing Press has also been ordered not to publish these periodicals. The Ethiopian government also arrested two reporters working for U.S. government funded Voice of America. The New York based

Committee to Protect Journalists (CPJ) as usual condemned the government crackdown on journalists to no avail.

A new bimonthly magazine *Addis Times* created by a few intellectuals after the outspoken weekly *Feteh* was banned, was also facing charges and was closed in February 2013 after it was published for four months. The grounds given by the Ethiopian Broadcasting Authority (EBA) for withdrawal of its license was failing to report a change of owner and change of address and a lack of transparency in its funding. No evidence was provided to support these claims and the magazine director-general disputes the allegations and regards the punishment as illegal and unconstitutional. The Ethiopian constitution guarantees freedom of expression and media freedom and the press law provides for a fine of up to 15,000 Birr (800 dollars) for contraventions of this kind but not for closing the publication or withdrawal of its license.

The managing director of *Addis Times* Temesgen Desalegn also faced charges and was imprisoned in connection with his journalistic work while he was the editor of the banned newspaper *Feteh* including "dangerous information" and "inciting unrest" against the constitutional order and the government. The publishing company *Mastewal* also faces charges for allowing them to publish these materials. Under Ethiopian law a printing company is also held accountable for a press offence by publications. Reporters With-out Borders strongly condemned the decision by the Ethiopian government in a press release. *"The way the authorities are persecuting Addis Times and its employees is indicative of the strength of the Ethiopian government's determination to restrict media freedom and silence its critics"*. The Committee to Protect Journalists CPJ also condemned the government's action.

Besides, the cost of printing has gone up tremendously on purpose and artificially by the ruling party, to discourage the journalists and to make sure the public cannot afford to buy private newspapers and books. I myself have witnessed this when I was obliged to pay 88 thousand *Birr* to print only three thousand copies of my latest book *Sedet* (exile) in 2012, while twenty years ago I paid only 10 thousand *Birr* for ten thousand copies of the same size book.

The Ethiopian constitutional provision Article 29 reads: *"Everyone has the right to freedom of expression without any interference. This right shall include freedom to seek, receive, and impart information and ideas of all kinds, regardless of frontiers, either orally, in writing or in print, in the form of art, or through any media of his choice"*. In violation of the Constitution, journalists are arrested, their publication impounded, their distribution limited only to the capital city, and printing service denied.

> *"For any person who has been observing the hurdles thrown against the independent media in   Ethiopia it is easy to confer that the free press exists in an unpredictable environment where its   life hangs on the caprice of government authorities.   ...without the press freedom, it is entirely   impossible to protect pluralism, insure justice, generate accountability, and develop good   governance.   In   our country however, its status of development is in deplorable stage which is   suffering repeated incidents of repressions. It's so much at stake that its overall existence is   attributed to the unwavering struggle of few professionally committed individuals and   organizations   working   in   various   challenging circumstances"*. (HRCO, Press Release – September 2012)

The Universal Declaration of Human Rights Article 9 stipulates *"no one shall be subjected to arbitrary arrest, detention or exile*". A provision enshrined in Article 6 of the African Charter on Human and Peoples Rights highlights likewise that in particular, "*no one may be arbitrarily arrested or detained*". Concerning the right to liberty, Article 17 (2) of the Federal Democratic Republic of Ethiopia (FDRE) Constitution also clearly maintains that "*no person may be subjected to arbitrary arrest, and no person may be detained without a charge or conviction against him*". In breach of all these domestic provisions of laws and international human rights proclamations that uphold common standard of achievement for all people, to which Ethiopia is a party, our people are tortured for expressing their opinion. In complete disregard of the articles in the Ethiopian Constitution and the international human rights declarations which Ethiopia signed, journalists and opposition party members have been subjected to ignominious harassment and unlawful detention for the last two decades.

The EPRDF regime has thus managed to cripple both the traditional and the digital media through jamming and illegal interference, abusing its diplomatic leverage and the country's finance. The US Bureau of Democracy, human rights groups, researchers and writers exposed in detail the gross violations of human rights committed by the EPRDF regime. In spite of all the pressure, it continued to crush practically all independent and private media outlets. This unbearable oppression and tyranny has forced many Ethiopians to flee their beloved country to escape unjust imprisonment and torture.

To our dismay, the United States and Europe continued to provide support to this oppressive regime by giving substantial amounts of aid annually. It is ironic that western countries are supporting a vicious tyranny that has been jamming media outlets including VOA and BBC. It is clear that the EPRDF government is an ally of their anti-terrorism campaign in the Horn of Africa whom they can ask to dispatch its military to Somalia or other areas, contrary to the long term interest of Ethiopia. If they don't use their leverage and change the situation, I am afraid they will lose the friendship of the Ethiopian people and shall be risking another Egypt-like revolution that could destabilize the region badly. We would like to remind them what president Obama said during his visit to Ghana in July 2009, and we insist that he live up to his words; *"Africa does not need strong men, it needs strong institutions;"* tyranny has to give way to democracy. But unfortunately, Africa has vicious tyrants and weak institutions, and the West share the blame for courting so many dictators from Mobutu to Mubarak and Meles for the last 50 years considering them allies in their anti-communism and anti-terrorism struggle respectively.

If Ethiopians are given the freedom to express themselves, and debate their ideas and problems freely, they are quite capable to find solutions and perform economic and political miracles. They will be a dependable and lasting anti-terror ally to shape the region for a lasting peace and cooperation. But unfortunately, both the West and the East allied with totalitarians like the Derg and EPRDF and deny the Ethiopian people a chance to create a prosperous country and enjoy greater freedom and stability. Because of tyranny and excessive fear, a "culture of silence" now grips Ethiopia. The people can't discuss the solutions to their problems; as a result, they remain poor. To gain control and compliance of the population, besides denying of information to our people and keeping them in the dark, EPRDF leaders use different methods of falsehood propaganda barrage to engineer people's way of thinking to turn the country into one big concentration camp.

Inhibition of Freedom

The TPLF-led government has denied the Ethiopian people freedom of expression in many ways than one by inhibiting the freedom of the media. Autonomy of the media from state ownership and influence is crucial to establishing an independent media. The Ethiopian government owns and is in full control of the national television, radio, and all major daily and weekly newspapers. After the 2005 elections, the government has intensified strict control of the media, stifled independent civil society, and restricted political space for the opposition parties.

The government introduced through the years tighter methods of control even to the government- owned media. Even though they have allowed some of their loyalists to use domestic FM broadcasts around the capital Addis Ababa, there is no truly independent radio or television in Ethiopia today. Human Rights Watch (HRW) has commented in its 2012 report 'one hundred ways of putting pressure', *"the independent media has struggled to establish itself in the face of constant government hostility and an inability to access information from the government officials."*

Prime Minister Meles Zenawi ruled Ethiopia with a heavy hand with control, repression and intimidation, in violation of freedom of press and association. In 2008 and 2009, EPRDF passed pieces of legislation for greater repression and political intolerance. This controversial Anti-terrorism "law" was referred by HRW as *"one of the most restrictive of its kind and its provisions will make most independent human rights work impossible."* The counter-terrorism "law" that was introduced at the same time allows the government security forces to persecute non-violent protestors and dissenting persons or dissidents as terrorists. This "law" has been criticized by the international community, including the United Nations Human Rights Council recommending its repeal; but nothing changed.

EPRDF leaders should repeal the so-called "Anti-terrorism Proclamation No. 652/2009". This "law" has been used to round up and jail journalists, opposition party activists, and dissidents as terrorists. The "law" has been condemned by all international human rights organizations. The vaguely drafted "anti-terror" law is not a law as such, but an instrument for EPRDF leaders to smash opponents of the regime. In this "law", making a speech or publishing a statement "likely to be interpreted as encouraging terrorist acts" is a punishable offence. Anyone who provides "moral support or advice", or has any contact with an individual accused of a terrorist act, is presumed to be a terrorist supporter. Under this "law", anyone who writes, edits, prints, publishes, publicizes, disseminates, shows, makes any promotional statements encouraging, supporting or advancing what the government considers "terrorist acts" is deemed a terrorist. Any person who "fails to immediately inform or give information or evidence to the police" on a co-worker, a neighbor or others as a suspect of terrorism could face up to ten years of prison for failing to report. Two or more persons who have contact with a "terror" suspect could be charged with conspiracy to commit "terrorism". The police have the right to arrest without court warrant and engage in random search and seizure of a person he suspects of "terrorism". A police can intercept, install or conduct surveillance on the telephone, fax, radio, internet, etc. of a suspect. Police can order any government or private organization to turn over documents, evidences or information on the suspect. According to this "law" thinking, speaking, writing, printing, peaceful protest, standing up for democracy and human rights is terrorism, demanding for the rule of law is terrorism. Simply it is not a law; it is state terrorism.

There is also another "law", so-called "Charities and Societies Proclamation" No. 621/2009, that has been severely criticized by international human rights organizations. This "law" prohibits foreign non-governmental organizations (NGO's) from engaging in human rights and democratic activities in Ethiopia. A local NGO that receives more than ten percent of its funding from foreign sources is considered foreign and its registration will be revoked immediately. The paradox is that twenty six percent of the Ethiopian government budget is covered by foreign donors. Since most Ethiopian NGO's are not self-sufficient and depend on foreign sources, this "law" has effectively put them out of service. The law is restrictive and confusing making help difficult for world donors advocating civil society, rights to education and clean water etc. This "law" violates many sections of the Ethiopian constitution; as such it is one of the "laws" that should be repealed immediately if Ethiopia has to march into good governance and democracy. Otherwise Ethiopia will continue to slide backwards and deeper into extreme dictatorship, and the consequences could be very ugly.

Amnesty International argued in 2009 that the new law is being used as a political sledgehammer to thwart and crush dissent, which is hostile to freedom of expression and association and is harmful to Ethiopia's fledgling civil society. There is also a law that was promulgated in 2011that put all land (rural and urban) under government lease. According to this "law" it is only the government that can sell a land or a house by putting it in auction and forcing the new owner to pay 20 percent of the cost for the new lease.

Anyone who disagrees with the ruling party or state line continues to be labeled "terrorist" as the definition of terrorism and terrorist remain vague and ambiguous in this law. But, it suits the regime by providing a pretext to manipulate and justify to put any dissent behind bars. The government has arrested and sentenced many journalists like Dawit Kebede, editor-in-chief of *Awramba Times*, and Eskinder Nega, a well-known blogger, and others and banned the remaining last popular newspaper *Feteh* in August 2012 using the anti-terrorism law. The Geneva-based International Press Institute in its 2012 press release said, "*it is a mockery of the universal right to hold opinions without interference and to seek, receive and import information and ideas through any media and regardless of frontiers*". This practice also undermines the fight against real terrorists who use violence and not words to achieve their ends.

In a democratic society, the primary function of the media is to examine the policies and functions of politicians and present constructive criticism to the government and opposition parties and provide a public platform for debate and participation. The press law and anti-terrorism law in Ethiopia deny such interaction and expression of opinions in violation of the constitution of the country. It also violates the UN Declaration of Human Rights and the International Convention on Civil and Political Rights (ICCPR), both of which the Ethiopian government has ratified in 1993.

The laws that deny media freedom and freedom of association and expression must be repealed. To incapacitate the people by keeping them uninformed, uneducated, restricting their freedom of association and expression and keeping them entrapped by intimidation, violence and instilling fear is ugly dictatorship which push the people into mass exile.

The conduct of the Ethiopian government is in conflict with the protocols of the African Union (whose headquarter is in Addis Ababa), the African Union Charter, and the UN Universal Declaration of Human Rights. Journalists should not be arrested for their critical reporting of dictatorship, for reporting on organized crime, political corruption and human rights abuse, for accusing high level political figures and their cronies of being involved in assassination of dissidents and intellectuals. Journalists should not be put in solitary confinement for reporting the truth about injustice, and their defense for democratic freedom should not be harassed or forced to live in exile for criticizing the government. The whole world is calling the Ethiopian government to end the persecution of journalists because media freedom is a basic pillar of any democratic society. In spite of all calls courageous journalists battling government censorship and interference with their truthful reporting and uncompromising journalism are thrown to prison.

Absolute prerequisite

Human beings are endowed with inalienable rights like thinking and expressing their ideas and opinions. They do not need permission from the government to exercise their natural rights. In actual fact the government must respect, protect and encourage the practice of these rights, as it is the corner stone of all other freedoms and an absolute pre-requisite to build a democratic society. No society has become prosperous without freedom, other than a small sector of the ruling class. Freedom should be conceived in cultural, scientific, spiritual, intellectual and material terms. Freedom is essential for releasing the best in a human being, especially freedom of conscience. There is a famous saying of Voltaire, *"I despise what you say, but will defend to the death your right to say it"*. Freedom of speech is worth defending vigorously even if one disagrees with what is being said. It is the same thing with freedom of the press.

The United Nations "Universal Declaration of Human Rights" in 1948 explicitly recognizes the need to protect free expression of ideas and opinions. *"Everyone has the right to freedom of opinion and expression; the right includes freedom to hold opinions without interference and to seek, receive and import information and ideas through any media and regardless of frontiers.*" (Article 19, Universal Declaration of Human Rights, UN- 1948) The first amendment of the constitution of the United States reads, *"Congress shall make no law… abridging the freedom of speech, or of the press or of the people peaceably to assemble, and to petition the government for a redress of grievances.*" Both of these articles indicate the fundamental importance of a free speech and free press. The aim of the US first amendment is to block central government from making incursions into the free press. It is a bulwark to prevent the government from using censorship against criticism of government policy. It is important to deprive the government the temptation of using law to block free speech or press. The moral justification of the freedom of the press is enormous.

People express their opinions in the form of poems, novels, films, videos, photographs, paintings, drawings, cartoons, lyrics, and art. People are interested in being active participants in politics than being passive recipients of government policy. Unconditional protection of free speech and free press is the pillar of a democratic government. The pre-condition of democracy and of genuine participation of the people is free speech and free press. People should be allowed to express their views without fear of retribution. Censorship cannot be tolerated for those who value free speech. We should be vigilant against any attempt to silence opinions. Ronald Dowrkin expressed his strong position on this matter. *"Free speech is a condition of legitimate government. Laws and policies are not legitimate unless they have been adopted through a democratic process, and a process is not democratic if government has prevented any one from expressing his convictions about what those laws and policies should be.*" (Nigel Warburton, Free Speech, P-3)

To communicate their opinions people should be free to use symbolic public acts like burning a flag or tearing constitution document to express their opposition. Every citizen should be free to speak out, to publish a book, a poem, a photograph, a cartoon, broadcast over a radio or television. Writers need freedom of the press to communicate with the public. Many leaders in Africa have thrown many writers to jail accusing them for inciting violence, terrorism or overstepping 'acceptable' limits in their writing. Many great writers have been imprisoned, tortured, or even killed in the hands of tyrant leaders for just expressing their ideas. Solitary confinement is practiced against dissident writers and thinkers all around the world. Yet, many authors are brave enough to publish their views even when it means they will face imprisonment or even death.

"To preserve the freedom of the human mind then & freedom of the press, every spirit should be ready to devote itself to martyrdom; for as long as we may think as we will, & speak as we think, the condition of man will proceed in improvement". (President Thomas Jefferson, 1799)

We should recognize freedom of the press as the center of democracy, and oppose all efforts by the government to restrict and control expression. We need unrestricted freedom of expression for the legitimacy of democracy, otherwise the government and its laws are not legitimate. This is what we want our governments to know. Societies can't advance economically unless they allow greater freedom of expression.

Information is Power

In the 21st century, information is not only knowledge, but also power. In the industrial age information was knowledge that helped to expand and improve the industry product. In the 20th century information was redefined as more than knowledge when scientists created methods to transmit signals (coded, analog or digital) to guide the missile, the fighter jet, the anti-aircraft guns to position and operate their war machine on the enemy. Thus information became a commodity that can be used to amass wealth and win wars, and the age we live in came to be known as information age. To be competitive in the modern world we need to give priority to information.

When the two Americans Bill Gates and Paul Allen launched the Microsoft Corporation in 1975 to create computer machine software that can be available in every household to move data, the information revolution reached a new height. The information superhighway, an ever-expanding network of networks that links all people in the world that have computers, the internet was created. The meaning of information super highway is best described by Bonnie Bracey, a member of the president's National Information Infrastructure Advisory Council (NIIAC) of The United States, as follows.

"It is more than the Internet. It is a series of components, including the collection of private and public high-speed interactive, narrow, and broadband networks that exists today and will emerge tomorrow. . . . Information superhighway is a term that encompasses all of these components and captures the visions of a nationwide, invisible, dynamic web of transmissions, mechanisms, information, appliances, content and people". (Bracey, 1996)

The world is in an ever-expanding information age. But many African heads of state have turned back the clock. They are engaged in censorship, internet filtering and jamming of broadcasts. Hundreds of journalists are languishing in jail for informing the public the truth; hundreds have mysteriously vanished. Hundreds of editors, journalists, writers, poets, scholars, university professors are forced to migrate to Europe and America to save their lives from African tyrants. The others who remained in the continent lay their lives on the line with each word they utter or the sentence they write. Intellectual repression has continued to this day in many African countries.

I am not trying to suggest that African journalists and writers do not make mistakes, but the solution is not to arrest or kill them. We need more educated journalists who can report truthfully, accurately, fairly, and objectively. We can get these only if they are free to do their job. To solve the current crisis and fulfill the promises of the new reform and evolutionary change, we need to unleash a new age of great journalism and enhanced democracy. **Free speech is democracy's last line of defense; we need to demand it, defend it and, most of all use it. Journalists should shine a spotlight on Government authorities and corporations abuse of power. We need a media that covers power, not covers for power**.

"The way to prevent these irregular interpositions of the people is to give them full information of their affairs thro' the channel of the public papers, and to contrive that those papers should penetrate the whole mass of the people. The basis of our governments being the opinion of the people, the very first object should be to keep that right; and were it left to me to decide whether we should have a government without newspapers, or newspapers without a government, I should not hesitate a moment to prefer the latter. But, I should mean that every man should receive those papers and be capable of reading them."

(President Thomas Jefferson - 1787)

Chapter Five

Centralized Economy

"The death-knell of the republic had rung as soon as the active power became lodged in the hands of those who sought, not to do justice to all citizens, rich and poor alike, but to stand for one special class and for its interests as opposed to the interests of others."

(President Theodore Roosevelt – 1903)

'For life is all too short, dear,
And sorrow is all too great,
To suffer our slow compassion
That tarries until too late;
And it isn't the thing you do, dear,
It's the thing you leave undone
Which gives you a bit of a heartache
At the setting of the sun'.
(Margaret Sangster)

Most economists agree that a centralized economic system is structurally rigid and functionally inefficient. Centralized economy also known as planned economy, basically gives the government dictatorship control over the resources of the country. This type of economy alleviates the use of private enterprises and allows the government to determine everything from production to distribution and to pricing. Most economists agree that this kind of planned economy can provide better stability if there is no favoritism on ethnicity or party affiliation; but it also limits the growth and advancement of the country's

278

economy if the government does not allocate resources to the innovative enterprises.

A centralized-economy is a command and control-economy which is actually planned economic system in which decisions regarding production and investment are embodied in a plan formulated by a central authority, usually the government. This is an economy where the government controls all major sectors of the economy and formulates all decisions about the use of resources. Centralized and government controlled economy is in contrast to market economy where production, distribution, pricing and investment decisions are made by autonomous firms based on their individual interests and supply and demand or profit and loss.

Economists also agree on the advantages of a centralized or planned economy, that it enables the government to harness land, labor and capital to serve the economic objectives of the state. The government can start building heavy industry or other big development projects in an underdeveloped economy without waiting years for capital to accumulate through the expansion of light industries and without reliance on foreign finance. That is what happened in the former Soviet Union in the 1930s when it experienced massive growth in heavy industry.

The disadvantages of a centrally controlled planned economy, is that, the planners cannot detect consumer preferences accurately and that it has difficulty identifying shortages and surpluses before it affects the market. According to many economists the only way to determine what society actually wants is by allowing private enterprises to use their resources in competing to meet the needs of consumers rather than to allow the government to direct investment without responding to market signals, which is supply and demand. Economists argue that even if controlled-economies overcome the inherent problems of incentives and innovation it would nevertheless be unable to expand economic democracy and self-management for overall economic freedom. Centrally-planned-economies are always slow to innovate and they would be susceptible to inefficiencies as the managers, planners and workers do not have enough incentives to promote their social economic interest. Central planning is incompatible with economic democracy; it only survives because it is propped up by totalitarian power.

There is also what Economists term as Social Democratic Mixed Economy, which many countries in Western Europe like Britain, France, Sweden, Norway experimented during the 20th century. These countries retained a wage-based economy and private ownership and control of the decisive means of production. These Western European countries tried to restructure their economies away from a purely private capitalist model and towards social democratic welfare states like in Sweden, or mixed economies where a major percentage of production comes from the state sector like in Norway. These countries rank among the highest in quality of life standard of living, and equal opportunity to their citizens. Many countries have experimented state capitalism to a certain extent whereby large commercial state enterprises operate according to the laws of capitalism and pursue profits.

During the last thirty years China has opened its economy to free market-based trade and foreign investment. It has carefully managed the transition from a planned socialist economy to a market economy and has continued to experience strong economic growth. The current Chinese economic system is not as such a centralized economic planning, but rather characterized by state ownership combined with a strong and relatively free private sector where privately owned enterprises generate 70 percent of GDP according to a Business Week article of 2005. Most of the state and private sectors of the economy are governed by free market practices with little or no government interference, with most economic activity left to the management of both state and private firms. Most state institutions have been privatized and according to the magazine report, only around 150 state owned enterprises remain and report directly to the central government. A significant number of privately owned firms exist, especially in the consumer service sector, engaged primarily in commodity production and light industry. The state sector is concentrated in the vital sectors commanding the overall economy and it led the economic recovery process and increased economic growth after the financial crisis of 2009. Chinese socialist economists believe that a socialist planned economy can only be possible after first establishing the necessary comprehensive commodity market economy.

Ethiopia's centralized economy is very different from all of the above, because 90 percent of the economy is not only controlled but owned by the ruling party and its cronies; not everybody play by the same rules. Economic favoritism, segregation and exclusion has distorted the emergence of a vibrant private economy and instead created economic 'apartheid'. The country gets billions of dollars every year in the form of aid and grant from Western donors, which has propped up the ruling party and the economy.

Millennium Development Goal

During the last 27 years Ethiopia did a big stride in building and improving basic infrastructures such as roads, hydroelectric dams, health and education institutions and expanding businesses. It is also good that many low income citizens are being provided with apartment residences at government subsidized low cost. Many schools and colleges have been built around the country and a huge number of students were able to attend higher education. It is right to acknowledge this commendable progress which is said to be the highest expansion of the education sector even by international standard. Ethiopia has now around 30 public universities and over one hundred higher education institutions; and schools are built in almost every village. However, these great efforts need to be supported by quality. With the standard of education being poor, because of lack of teaching materials and sufficiently educated teachers, many graduates do not acquire enough knowledge and skills and appear to be incompetent to solve problems and propel a company that hire them to the top. The government should focus on strengthening the quality of education in existing universities and higher education institutions rather than opening new ones to achieve numerical benchmarks to please donor countries. If the system of education remains weak, all sectors of the economy will be suffocated. A university is more than a building. It requires several logistical, philosophical and contextual grounds to carry out its role as a place of higher learning. The lack of academic freedom and autonomy, the absence of qualified instructors and tutors, scarcity of laboratories, libraries and books, Internet communication tools, and control by TPLF cadres who teach them how to think, instead of what to think, makes it difficult to discharge its responsibilities. In 1993 TPLF fired 42 seasoned academics from Addis Ababa University and replaced them with loyal cadres.

World leaders adopted Millennium Development Goals (MDG) in 2000 which is set to be achieved by 2015. They set numerical benchmarks for tackling extreme poverty and to cut world poverty by half. Ethiopia is one of the countries chosen for accelerated and sustained development to end poverty in ten years. According to The World Bank, IMF, UN, and Ethiopian government report, the progress registered in most economic and social sectors is encouraging. There is reduction in poverty in some rural areas from 44 percent to 29 percent in 2010; but, urban poverty has increased even more and hunger and malnutrition are endemic. Ethiopia has become one of the world's ten fastest growing economies in 2010, and it was expected to achieve more than 7 percent (GDP) growth in 2013 and it did. For a country lacking the natural resources bonanza like oil, gas, or diamond that is driving other high performers, Ethiopia's growth is truly surprising and should be appreciated. In spite of the GDP, the standard of living of the masses did not increase; there is a weakness in agricultural development and as a result shortage of food crops. The government should focus on essential products like food crops and give priority to feed its hungry population. Making sure that the standard of living of the working people is going up every year will guarantee stability and peace.

"As we think about how to strengthen our economy, it is imperative that we not succumb to GDP fetishism. We've seen that GDP is not a good measure of economic performance; it doesn't reflect accurately changes in the standard of living, broadly defined, of most citizens, and it doesn't tell us whether the growth we experience is sustainable."

Joseph Stiglitz (Nobel Prize winner in economics) - The price of inequality pp -335

The Ethiopian government came up with another ten years development agenda known as Growth and Transformation Plan (GTP), (which has no clear link with MDG), with the aim of sustaining faster economic growth. All said, most experts agree that there is growth in Ethiopia, but only little development to reduce extreme poverty of the people. Income disparity is growing wider and with the top down growth formula, wealth is not trickling down to the masses. The middle class is shrinking, government employees are living from hand to mouth, only political loyalists benefit from the economic growth; it is growth for the few and controlled by the few. The economy is in a problem because of inflation, unemployment and macroeconomic instability. Ethiopia is still tied to small scale and subsistence farming dependent on rain-fed agriculture. Periodic drought is still a major threat, because there is not enough structural transformation in agriculture with increased irrigation and water conservation methods. Ethiopia has major challenges with structural food insecurity, as millions of its people are still dependent on aid food.

The country has made impressive gains in building schools, and primary school enrollment has gone up at an alarming rate. But, low quality of education, large class sizes, shortage of quality teachers, and lack of teaching materials is posing a major problem. The same is true of the health sector where the country has made major expansion and strengthened primary health care and preventive services. Ethiopia has made impressive progress in maternal and child health; maternal and child mortality is falling. In appreciation of these specific results Ethiopia got twenty million dollars grant from the Health Results Innovation Trust Fund managed by the World Bank in 2012. In addition, $100 million zero-interest credit was said to be disbursed to Ethiopia over the next four years. Ethiopia has deployed a large national network of more than 35,000 trained health workers and expanded the network of health centers dramatically.

This result is heart-warming and commendable; but, with the shortage of the necessary highly skilled man power and equipment, Ethiopia still has one of the highest maternal and child mortality. The problem is even serious when we see that many skilled teachers and health workers are marginalized and pushed into exile because of their political affiliation or opinion.

The improvement in health care has been most pronounced only in some selected regions and big cities including Tigray. Tigray region happens to be the home of the ethnic group TPLF leaders who are highly repressive and autocratic in their leadership. With low productivity in the agricultural sector, a modern but narrow industrial sector, and environmental degradation and rapid population growth, government corruption and capital flight, with skilled professionals often migrating to the west because of political exclusion, Ethiopia faces serious development challenges. Government-owned national and commercial banks are inclined to serve party-owned and endowed enterprises and loyalists. According to Human Rights report of 2010 on Ethiopia, *"developmental aid is not used fairly; it has been subject to distortion for political purposes. Lack of good governance and absence of fair play ground for all citizens and development partners, the absence of inclusive and multi-party democracy is hampering the countries development efforts"*.

The United Nations Development Program annual report and index of human development that was released on March 15, 2013 ranks Ethiopia 173rd out of the 187 countries. The index measures life expectancy, income and education since 2000 in countries around the world. Even though Ethiopia has registered great economic growth, the human development progress within the country is still low and the country ranks close to the bottom of the index. To improve this situation the government must overcome many challenges, such as life expectancy, high level of inequality, the growing threat of environmental disasters and should continue the social protection programs which are so important in reducing poverty and wealth disparity. According to the UNDP Human Development Report and index, 24 out of the 25 lowest ranked countries are in the African continent.

"Fueled by massive foreign aid, remittances and deficit financing this growth is stimulated by massive investments in

285

social and physical infrastructure: education, health, sanitation, water, roads, bridges, conference halls, villas, condominiums, buildings, hydropower electric generation plants, and the like. However, this growth has not benefited the vast majority of the population. The linkages that would normally stimulate employment, formation of a representative and strong middle class, fundamental changes in the structure of the economy et cetera are not evident. For this reason, it is socially irresponsible and dysfunctional when assessed against the only measurement that counts---People's wellbeing"

Aklog Birara (phd), Dynamics of Conflict...

Economic "Apartheid"

The economic system in most African countries is a mixture of state-owned and private; but, is tinted with favoritism, nepotism, segregation and exclusion. One of the Pillars of a rigid political system is what is termed as economic 'apartheid', whereby vital sectors of the country's economy is controlled and owned by the ruling party and its cronies. This has created institutionalized corruption that distorts the emergence of a vibrant market economy and democracy with the empowerment of the private sector. The growing business empire owned by the ruling party in Ethiopia like most African countries under the disguise of privatization of formerly nationalized economic entities is very disturbing.

After the 1974 Ethiopian revolution the pro-Soviet Derg regime nationalized all rural and urban land and extra rental houses and all major enterprises in the name of Socialism. After TPLF/EPRDF took state power in 1991 it kept much of the nationalized property including rural and urban land, rental houses and apartments and key sectors of the economy like banks and telecommunications etc. Besides, whatever enterprise it privatized later, it made sure that they are owned by the ruling party and its loyalists under clever disguises. By doing so TPLF introduced the phenomenon of party-owned-for-profit companies, which is illegal according to the Ethiopian commercial law. Most of all, EPRDF kept all the Derg apparatus of control, especially land (urban and rural) and the associations of peasants and urban dwellers *(Kebele)* which it uses to control the population.

Berhanu Abegaz, Professor of Economics at the College of William and Mary in Virginia explained the situation in the horn of Africa in a January 2006 research paper prepared for the meeting with The World Bank officials, as follows.

"What has emerged in Ethiopia (and Eritrea) after 1991 is a model of governance that strives to use political power and economic power under the control of a vanguard party:

"1) EPRDF's political strategy known as "Revolutionary Democracy" is anchored in a neo-Stalinist ideology that mixes class and ethnicity. It views political and civic organizations as subservient to a vanguard party which seeks to co-opt them and failing that, to stifle their emergence as independent agents. It lists as its greatest political achievement the enshrining of an ethnocentric political system – a state within a state.

"2) EPRDF's economic strategy is best described as a state-led or governed market economy whereby party-controlled parastatals, and party owned "parastatals" and "endowments" would dominate key sectors of the modern economy, with the private sector playing as a loyal junior partner". (Berhanu, P-5)

Professor Berhanu Abegaz insists that to ensure a successful transition to an open political and economic system, the institution of the country have to be freed from what he called "the web of control of the ruling party". He emphasizes that restoring the long standing tradition of private ownership of rural and urban land will create the emergence of robust growth in the agricultural and small scale industries sector; and dissolving the large business empire of TPLF and its affiliates will eliminate institutionalized corruption and create a vibrant free market economy and democracy. The Professor warns about the consequences of a half-hearted move towards the empowerment of the private sector and the ruling party's determination to stay in power at any cost.

When privatization was introduced in Ethiopia there were not many rich people who could afford to buy the industries and run them efficiently. This created the situation that only the ruling party and its cronies who are related to the party and easily get bank credits (as banks are owned by the state) could partake in the privatization process. The privatization measure was ideologically motivated by the ruling party to control the economy and enrich themselves at public expense, not to create a market economy dynamism that brings prosperity and create jobs and raises workers income. As a result there is too much government intervention in the economy and unfair competition that weaken the private sector and hinders market economy operation. The role of private initiative is restricted and government assistance is limited; only those companies owned by the ruling party import merchandise without paying tax for customs and easily win contractual bids by the government. Scarce resources are allocated only to these companies, and a price distortion and unfair competition is created that leads to disequilibrium in the economy.

Declaring the privatization of all firms that were nationalized by the previous regime, they discovered ways to manipulate the reform process to their advantage. They came to realize that the business of privatization could be used, and with the help of money from the World Bank and the International Monetary Fund (IMF), towards parastatal reform they built their business empire. In the process of privatization of public companies they discovered the golden opportunity to sell off government assets to their political cronies, kinsmen, party loyalists and family members. The sellout of these public companies was made at minimum prices, favorable terms and low interest long term loans. Most of the state owned firms before 1991 now belong to the TPLF business empire and selected businessmen like Saudi billionaire Sheik Mahammed Alamudin. TPLF-affiliated business groups like Tigray Development Association, Tigray Relief Agency, and Endowment Fund for the Rehabilitation of Tigray, better known with their acronym *Telma, Rest and Effort* respectively, monopolize the economy by running many companies involved in finance, construction, mining, transportation, production, distribution, agriculture, health and education. These companies easily win contracts of federal government projects. There is no economic freedom and fair competition in Ethiopia today. The playing field is not level for everyone, not everybody plays by the same rules; some well-connected loyalists get their imports tax free from customs, and so how can others compete? Equitable distribution of wealth and economic freedom is central to social justice if we want to make real progress.

"Ethiopia under performs in many of the ten Economic Freedoms. The business and investment regime is burdensome and opaque. The quality and efficiency of government services are poor and made worse by the weak rule of law and pervasive corruption. State distortion in prices and interest rate undermine monetary stability". (Heritage Foundation, 2010)

The present economic policy of EPRDF has only produced mass poverty and created wealth only for the chosen few. The political and economic policy of EPRDF is like the two sides of the same coin, and it will not enable our country to have real growth based on science and technology which will have a multiplying effect of wealth, and give a strong base to the new economy. If we want to develop a well- functioning capitalist economy based on science and technology which will also have a human face, we have to establish a quality educational system that can produce capable young intellectuals.

The ruling party should get its hands off from companies for profit and dismantle the oppressive structures that hamper development. Only those groups that have party affiliation and money are benefitting from the present government structure in Ethiopia. As long as the people are not allowed to organize freely under democratic principles they could not have the necessary power to control the state organ. The government should advance the interest of the whole society without favoring one party and its loyalists. It is not appropriate for the government to use its power and the state apparatus as an instrument of certain groups to control the entire society systematically. The private sector should be free from government intervention and suppression and favoritism, and party owned corporations must cease to exist; that is the only way we can develop a well-functioning society. *"Social capital by which is meant the invisible glue of relationships that holds business, economy and political life together, is at the core of any country's development. At its most elemental level, this boils down to a matter of trust. ...Soft factors —such as governance, the rule of law, institutional quality- play a critical role in achieving economic prosperity and putting countries on a strong development path. But these things are meaningless in the absence of trust. And while trust is difficult to define or measure, when it is not there the networks upon which development depends, break down or never even form"*.

(Dambisa Bayo, Dead Aid, P-58)

Economic development should be able to raise the standard of living of the whole population by providing positive incentives and expanding choices for the poor. The impoverished masses should be our center of focus when we think about development. If it does not change their livelihood for the better it shall not be called development. EPRDF boast about a double digit GDP, Gross Domestic Product. Many African economists explain GDP as a misleading concept loaded with ideology which does not reflect the realities on the ground. GDP considers only market transactions and not human activities and standard of living of the people, or the ever increasing inequality and wealth disparity, which are destroying the entire social fabric of the country and the environment. The economic growth in Ethiopia only benefited the ruling elites and created rising inequality. Such growth created overcrowded cities, and destroyed cultural, social, ethical and moral values that are the attributes of all human beings. The so-called economic growth is not organic and does not have evolutionary character that lead to economic, social, cultural, and political transformations supported by science, technology, and cultural renaissance crucial for a cumulative development. Innovation and invention are not part and parcel of this kind of economic growth.

During the last 27 years the gap between the rich and the poor has widened in Ethiopia. The economic growth created few very wealthy ruling elites and loyalists, destroyed the middle class and pushed the majority of the people to abject poverty. The economic policy is not planned to fulfill the basic needs of the people, but for the market. EPRDF's half-hearted support to the private sector and civil society will not produce the kind of sound development the country needs. Inflation is high due to lavish government spending; it reached 40% in 2011. As the great majority of the people live on farming, due to population explosion the average family plot has shrunk to one hectare/family which is not enough to support them. It is time to start industrialization and urbanization. The government is slow in encouraging private sector development and industrialization.

Due to centralized draconian controls in banking, finance and telecommunication sectors, there is still a frosty investment climate in Ethiopia. Foreign investment in financial services is prohibited; domestic financial services are concentrated in a few big cities, like for example Commercial Bank of Ethiopia having 40 percent of its branches in Addis Ababa. In Ethiopia mobile penetration in 2012 was lower at 3.05 than the African regional average 3.68; further the mobile and electronic payments infrastructure is weak. Internet connections are slow and unreliable even by African standards; most of all content is censored and filtered, with internet spying in place. The state owned Ethiopian Telecommunications Corporation dominates the landscapes of telephone, mobile and internet services. Ethiopia needs to have a more liberal approach with technological readiness, innovation and financial sophistication. A country with over 100 million people like Ethiopia would benefit from an open approach and with less hostile posture.

"When we look at the most successful electronic payment systems, they are those that are open, completely open, and the government sets standards for how different entities can participate. ...Given its large population, given the potential, Ethiopia would benefit from an open approach to electronic payment systems." (Elithabet Buse, VISA's group – President for the developing world)

Professor Teshale has also articulated about what he calls the three D's in his research paper "Modernity, Euro centrism, and Radical Politics in Ethiopia 1961-1991.

"It is essential that Ethiopians fight for the three D's: Democracy, development and dignity. The point is: as much as we care about the development of democracy, we need to ponder

292

over the democracy of development. That is, Ethiopia needs an environmentally friendly development but with social justice. Development as conquest of nature per se is not a viable option. And a democracy where the rich and the powerful buy their way to power is not the democracy Ethiopia needs. Such democracy is a legalized hypocrisy. Democracy should be a socially conscious democracy, a socially responsible democracy, a democracy that takes its primary goal to be the liberation of the majority of the Ethiopian people from their emersion in the bottomless pit of abject poverty. As Gandhi once said, poverty is the higher form of human rights violation. We need to have both political democracy and social justice together, not one first, the other later. They should come together as two sides of the same coin." (Teshale, P-368)

Besides economic apartheid; centralization, inflation, corruption and illicit flows seriously impede Ethiopia's efforts to development. In a recent study by United Nations Development Program (UNDP) on how poor countries handle aid money, during the last 18 years (1990- 2008) out of the money 48 poor countries received, 197 billion dollars is unaccounted for and considered as illicit flows. Ethiopia being one of the ten top countries who have been accused of illicit flows is said to have squandered around 8.4 billion dollars. In the Fourth International Conference of Poor Countries organized by UNDP, on Global Financial Integrity held in Istanbul, Turkey in 2010, the Director Helen Clark exposed to the commission the problem of development and aid money illicit flows. *"Illicit flows seriously impede the least developed countries efforts to raise resources for social and economic development"*. Donor countries need to follow up what is being done (and to whom) with the money they donate. Otherwise like Michela Wrong cited Paul Collier's comment in her book "Our Turn to Eat", *'if you pump money into a system where there is leakage, you are effectively rewarding leakage and disincentivising those trying to stop it; counteracting their fight for change'.*

According to the report by International Monetary Fund (IMF), in June 2011, the inflation in Ethiopia itself was mainly, caused by the excessive growth of the money supply and the country is not as the government claims, a victim of international food prices. The report states that *"in fact global food prices have a minimal impact on agricultural economies like Ethiopia's. Moreover, imposing price caps to fight inflation without any careful study about the causes of rampant inflation has been a fool's errand; it wouldn't solve the problem other than to distract public anger and potential unrest"*.

There are many studies by different non-profit organizations about a large amount of illicit transfer of resources from Ethiopia through several channels, mainly diplomatic, in a way of "service acquisition" for political elites and their families. Diplomatic representation has become the most common form of resources transfer from Ethiopia favoring family ties and ethnic affiliation as well as political loyalty. Many Ethiopian ambassadors to foreign countries have become millionaires in a short time and some had to pay millions of dollars to their spouses upon divorce. According to dependable sources, it has been reported that the wives of some EPRDF authorities are usually assigned to the New York permanent mission of Ethiopia to help educate their children in private educational institutions. In Geneva Switzerland, out of the ten Ethiopians in the permanent mission to the United Nations in 2012, eight were from one ethnic group. Ethiopian embassies have become the main channels of resources leakage, whereby its diplomats facilitate direct money transfer to foreign banks, facilitating legal services, access to education and health insurance facilities.

The other direct transfer of money is done through farm land lease arrangements as the bulk of the deal is being settled through foreign accounts. These accounts are known only to the political leaders, and the so-called investors through the embassy staff concerned. Indian investors who grabbed fertile land in Gambella Region deal directly with the ambassadors to India, who is said to be a close associate of Meles or his widow former first lady Azeb Mesfin. Walta Information, a pro-government media had an interview with Ambassador Genet in 2012 which clearly indicates her role in the farm land lease and money transfer. Children of most political figures are studying abroad, their families travel for medical reasons; they also pay legal services fees to protect their political and business establishments in North America and Europe. Thus, several legal firms, education institutions and health service providers abroad have become another area of resources leakage from Ethiopia.

Land Policy

Previously we discussed in plain terms about the policy of government land ownership and agriculture in Ethiopia. For continuity sake we had to place this important subject in a slightly different part of this chapter. We bring up this issue here and briefly analyze the positives and negatives of this policy here. The government has monopoly over rural and urban land. Ethiopian peasants are denied their right to own land; they have use right only, and are in effect tenants of the state, lacking pride and security of an owner. The government enjoys monopoly and profits by displacing people at will and leasing the land to developers, usually ruling party owned companies. The whole country is owned by the ruling party and its loyalists; and not even by the Ethiopian government as such. Besides, TPLF/EPRDF so-called developmental state is discriminatory tribal state. The government divided the country into several ethnic territories (Kilil). In each territory people are divided into natives and settlers (so-called Amhara neftegnas). The settlers are barred from possessing use right over land; they cannot participate in the political process and cannot work in the local bureaucracy. Thus, they live as second class citizens in their own country in fear and humiliation.

On the part about farmland ownership, it is surprising to see the EPRDF defend the policy of government ownership as developmental. The common political catch phrase used to defend this policy is "Land belongs to the government and thus the people", never mind the people are not equally represented by their government. In addition this policy is also represented as developmentally sustainable because it prevents the selling of land by desperately poor farmers to wealthy individuals. EPRDF warns of the danger of farm privatization in that it would cause poor farmers to sell their plot and move to urban locations, thus compounding urban population planning. Though it is not the most preferential, it is an appreciable point. Indeed poor and under-educated farmers would find it hard to prosper in cities, which offer considerable difficulty even to the urban educated young. It would thus result in the proliferation of the urban homeless. This is of course a valid point. Consider the following scenario. If land was privatized and at least 25% of all farmers decide to sell their plot, this would mean close to 17 million people would have sold their land and relocated to urban areas. 25% of Ethiopia's approximately 62-65 million farmers is around that number. In an economy that is not yet ready to absorb these people the obvious prediction is that a vast majority of them would become part of the urban poor. This is a legitimate fear. Therefore privatization of land in the western liberal sense would be tantamount to exacerbating the nation's ills. Indeed, leaving such existential issues to the arbitrary will of markets would lead to worst disasters. Having said this we

296

should not ignore the facts about the current status quo, which has been ineffectual at reducing the threat of famine.

Leaving land under the auspice of the government has proven disastrous, judging by the endemic lack of food security and threat of famine. Food security is not significantly better than it was 30 years ago. By some accounts, given the exploding population it can be seen as worse than 30 years ago. The rural population, particularly in Afar, Somali Region, Tigray, and certain parts of Amhara remains under the constant brink of famine. That can be attributed to several factors, including limited technology, but not entirely. Other more fundamental problems associated with the government's policy contain significant impediments. Farmers generally do not feel a psychological sense of ownership and attachment to the land, effectively retarding productivity. There is no guarantee that the farmer is reaping the full benefit of his labor. Imagine toiling away all your life without any significant progress which requires certain independence and risk taking. Virtually it leaves the country ownerless, without a custodian. Arguably it is not just productivity that suffers from this policy, but also a sense of worth by the farmer. Undeniably it becomes difficult to see the difference between this and serfdom, particularly given the fact that contemporary farmers in Ethiopia find themselves heavily indebted to government banks. In many cases these debts are being incurred by forcing the farmer to take up loans against his will. It is highly plausible for the farmer to default on loans, in which case the government takes further manipulative action under the pretentious guise of increasing productivity, such as compelling the farmer to plant a certain kind of seed, which might be destructive to the environment or have lesser market value. Undoubtedly it is a system of forced farming that has rendered the Ethiopian farmer a modern day serf. To make things worse the EPRDF government has total control over the ownership and distribution of fertilizer, without which the farmer is virtually paralyzed.

In an apparent, in your face maneuver, fertile Ethiopian land is being sold cheaply to global agro-businesses that would inevitably export their produce to affluent international markets, where they would garner the best return for their investment. Therefore, it is correct to assume rising food prices in Ethiopia would not be the least bit lessened. Leasing of cheap land is happening while millions of Ethiopian farmers find themselves tilling depleted soils with centuries old technology. When one considers these realities have become the norm of Ethiopian agriculture for the past 44 years, then it is no wonder productivity and efficiency has been so low. It also becomes obvious why modern scientific farming has not taken hold yet. These failures are directly associated with government policy that disregards the farmers.

The solution is in finding a middle ground to be advanced, whereby the farmer regains his independence and finds security in his craft. It is possible to introduce scientifically driven farming from the multi-national agro-business industry, while simultaneously helping to make local farmers competitive. However this requires paying attention to the farmer and giving him assistance and speed up the process of his independence. It is difficult to swallow the actions of the government, namely the giving of virgin lands to foreign investors, while farmers in Ethiopia are continually squeezed. This is especially true in regions that are arid, overpopulated, and inhabited since antiquity. Unfortunately these are steps the government is unwilling to consider. It prefers to be blinded because implementing such policy requires giving the farmer the right to choose, a seemingly unbearable thought to *"Revolutionary Democrats"*.

Another overlooked aspect of land leasing to big agro business is, that the process requires a considerable violation of human rights. Consider traditional minority tribal people being forcefully evicted from lands their ancestors have lived off. Whether it's for grazing or farming these traditional communities have become dependent on the land. These people are now on the move, not by choice but because of government policy. Unfortunately their voices, though in many cases legitimate, are rarely heard by the government or by big agro-business, and the powerful national interests behind them. As expected there have been cases in Ethiopia, poignantly in the south western Gambella Region and Omo valley where this is true. Incidents of violent conduct intended to remove the localized population from these lands is no secret. We should recall this area holds some of the country's most fertile land. The relationship between these violent incidents, mostly perpetrated by militias related to the government is thus hardly a surprising factor. If the indigenous population decides to organize and demand its rights, then what awaits them is usually an overwhelming retribution. This was aptly demonstrated by the massacre of the Anuak tribesmen, orchestrated by government troops in collusion with local militias.

According to Genocide Watch, on December 13, 2003 government troops and local militia members entered Gambella town and killed close to 420 young Anuak men thought to be local activists. The egregious act demonstrates the calculated method of instilling fear in people. Local witnesses attest to the burning of homes and even raping of women during the massacre. More evidence will surely surface, as is usually the case for such things. It is however an isolated incident in a grand plan to tap into the region's rich natural resources. There is no guarantee such outcomes will not be repeated again. EPRDF officials are understandably in denial of events in Gambella city.

This does not bode well for the future of small indigenous populations of Ethiopia that happen to sit on valuable land.

Besides the direct and forceful removal of weak minority populations, there is also the long term disastrous effect on the environment. Surely heavy industrial farming will pollute the local ecosystem. As a result many more indigenous inhabitants will be uprooted from their ancestral homes. Rivers are fast becoming sources of poison in certain place in the region. There are populations who depend totally on fishing for their survival, a practice forced upon them by changing times. Such alternatives to revert to are however becoming fast obsolete. The fertilizer, pesticides and other chemicals used to boost production is killing the fish the natives depended on for centuries.

"We Export Food to Import Food"

In recent years we have witnessed an upsurge of agricultural investment in the third world. Its alleged purpose is to curb the recent global food crisis that has introduced serious volatility in the global food market system, causing significant price hikes on key global foods, such as rice. The price hike in global food trade has prompted certain countries to seek cheap and fertile farm-land beyond their borders, in order to guarantee food security for themselves. To achieve this goal such states are encouraging their domestic agro-businesses, tied to their national interests, to invest in countries like Ethiopia, Sudan, Madagascar, Tanzania, and Argentina to name a few. Capital invested in these far away farms will produce food cheaply, which will then be exported back to the country where the original capital came from. In this way the volatility of the international food market can be avoided and national food security could be achieved.

To accomplish this goal a key step is to convince developing nations to give up their fertile land to foreign investors. One of the baits designed for this purpose of persuasion is the promise of infrastructure and the sharing of information and technology in agricultural science. The other promise made to host nations is of capital gained from food exports, which can then be reinvested in the country. For underdeveloped countries, who face serious food insecurity, and who are often times unable to feed their population, this may sound too good to pass by, particularly if host nation governments are too naive, or are otherwise unconcerned. For instance in Ethiopia we have had hundreds of foreign investors grabbing fertile land at incredibly low cost. The scale of the spree is unprecedented in the country's history. Investors are describing the deal as "green gold". Ethiopia's never before tilled land, located in some of the most fertile parts of the country is now being sold to foreign interests for less than its true worth. Foreign investors are given perks, tax holidays lasting years and essentially they are exempt from any royalties.

The government of Ethiopia promises this process will mitigate the nation's chronic food insecurity and allow domestic farmers to gain knowledge from the expertise of foreign agro-business. It also says dollars gained from exporting food can alleviate the countries own endemic food crises. By this analysis, the premise of the EPRDF government seems to be "we export food to import food". Leaving aside the initial absurdity of the claim, it is necessary to note, the inadequacy of this argument has been amply demonstrated in many developing countries. Although this issue of land-grabbing by foreign interests is new to Ethiopia, it is no stranger to other parts of the developing world. The history of foreign agro-business intrusion in some Latin American and the Caribbean countries is enlightening to say the least. In northeastern Brazil, the region was extensively farmed by foreign agricultural interests for centuries. Unfortunately this region has nothing to show for it now. Today the region is the poorest part of the country with the least food security and one of the highest malnutrition rates in Latin America. Contrary to the promises made by companies that farmed Brazil's fertile soil, the outcome has been very grim. In his famous book "Open Veins of Latin America", Eduardo Galliano, commenting on Brazil's northeast, says *"Naturally fitted to produce food, it became a place of hunger. Where everything had bloomed exuberantly, the destructive and all dominating plantation left sterile rock, washed out soil, and eroded lands"*. Are Ethiopia's own fertile lands headed for the same fate? What makes the current foreign agricultural adventure in Ethiopia any different?

In fact the overwhelming environmental destruction of the land has already begun in this initial phase. Around Gambella Region recently, Karuturi, an Indian company, which owns large swaths of the region, was heavily involved in burning forests and grasslands to make way for potential farm land. It would be unfair to single out and accuse Karuturi alone. Other foreign companies who have settled in the region are no more saintly with the local environment. They are also simultaneously using slash and burn techniques to clear land. There is no doubt the flora and fauna will be lost forever as a result, in this process. Pastureland is fast becoming eviscerated, affecting local herders, who depend on their livestock for survival. This process of pastoral land elimination can have negative consequences for currently inflated meat prices in Ethiopia, which will undoubtedly exasperate existent levels of high malnutrition in the country.

According to the government these lands given to foreign investors were idle lands, ready to be gobbled up into the global food system without much disturbance. However, this view depends on one's definition of "idle land". Pastureland may seem idle, but its usefulness is undeniable. Another key consideration should be about the inevitable damage and cost to

302

future generations. Given the fact Ethiopia is very much a country of the future demographically speaking, this should concern us. Intensive farming by foreign agro-business has a history of ravaging the land and turning fertile soil into depleted soil in a short period of time. Other parts of the globe where this had been practiced testify to the inevitability of environmental destruction, resulting in soil degradation, which eventually leads to more domestic food insecurity. In a land that is potentially the breadbasket of Ethiopia, if not the whole Horn of Africa, such degradation is a real loss for future generations and a moral challenge for us today.

Employment offered by these farms is purported to be a benefit for local communities. Never mind the main reason why locals seek this work is primarily because the agro-businesses have forced them to abandon their old way of life, which had originally consisted of a pastoralist way of life. Take away this sole viable option of survival for local people, and then the people are left with no other choice, but to accept slave wages working on foreign farms. In a way the agri-business creates the labor surplus for itself and manages to keep wages extremely low. The wage paid to workers, on average about $1.50 (25 Birr) for a day's work, is nowhere near enough to survive without additional food aid. According to a recent documentary some farm workers in southern Ethiopia complained they were getting paid 7 birr per day, instead of the 25 birr initially promised. That is about 50 cents a day in dollar terms. By these estimates the lives of these workers were considerably better before the introduction of foreign agri-business. Instead of food security, food insecurity is created, perhaps even serious malnutrition. To add insult to injury none of the produce from these farms will be available to local markets. However, there is talk of selling some of the produce to aid agencies. The World Food Program intends to buy some of this grain in order to assist hungry people. Ironically this group of intended food aid recipients will include those working to produce it in the first place. Ethiopia's government is calling this sustainable development. Shame!

In an effort to rush through this controversial issue unimpeded, the government has sought to bypass all transparency; and with genuine apprehension. It is fully aware that an open discussion on the issue would expose the absurdities of its claim. Deals with foreign investors were approved backhandedly for this reason. The government expects a few scattered utterances here and there by its officials to be accepted as national discussion on the matter. The government also knows it has no chance of convincing people because further evaluation of the agreements reveals gaping holes. The people of Ethiopia are being asked to believe absurdities such as "we export food in order to import food" as a viable economic option to guarantee national food security. However, the most basic comprehension of economics tells us this is nearly impossible. Given Ethiopia's dwindling currency exchange what sense is there in purchasing grain from the international market, while exporting domestic grain? Can exported grain used as a cash-crop generate enough capital to be able to import food affordably and sustainably? Muddying the waters and diverting the issue under the guise of food security is certainly a cruel way of hoodwinking a hungry population. It is not clear what the benefit will be to Ethiopia. In most instances the harm done is much greater than the gain.

When all explanation fails to suffice, the ones left to ponder are much more sinister in nature. Perhaps the EPRDF government views these deals as solidifiers of its international connections, especially with emerging markets. Gifting land can guarantee political support. As a beleaguered party, EPRDF knows its survival depends on bringing some particularly heavy hitters into the fold. What better way to bring them on board than to give them what they most require and what Ethiopia has to offer, namely land and water. It is important to point out that some of these excited shoppers include states with dreadful human rights records. One of these among several is Saudi Arabia. Surely if the going gets tough for Ethiopia's ruling party, the Saudi's can be counted upon to prop up their friend in need, no matter how badly democracy and human rights are trampled. It seems these two are a match made in heaven. Generally, although the loss is great for Ethiopia, the gain has been significant for the ruling party. Is the EPRDF trying to garner vested interest in the country for its own political existence at the cost of the nation?

"The global crisis has triggered land grabs that could not have been imagined before. Nations with cash but not much arable land are buying up chunks of land in Africa, mainly for the purpose of cultivating crops to be used in biofuels production or to grow food crops that get repatriated to the country that bought the land. The logic is that of the market: you have land; I have cash; we are both happy. But, there is far less land left for cultivation of food crops for local consumption and the diversion of labor, water and other inputs from producing food for local communities will have an adverse impact on food production". (Nnimmo Bassey, To cook a Continent – Pp53)

Politics aside, there are other alternatives for agricultural development in Ethiopia. If the government was truly interested, Ethiopia's agricultural output can be developed in a way that is much more sustainable and equitable. For instance, although small, there is a significant amount of capital within the country to boost farming capacity in hitherto unexplored areas of the country. Perhaps a genuinely interested government can enhance and facilitate the efforts of investors within Ethiopia's borders to import technology and to train domestically run agro-business interests. The aim here is not to blow the bank, but to increase investment in a sustainable way. After all, isn't this how major agri-businesses got their startup in their country of birth?

Another option to boost domestic farm output would have been to invite wealthy Ethiopians living abroad, especially those with interest and knowledge to invest in the area. Even though these later approaches were never discussed, for political reasons, there is a strong argument for their viability. Certainly, they are much more likely to produce the intended result than the mostly unaccountable foreign companies ever will. 8

The scale of farming that is based on domestic investment would be smaller, thus friendlier to the local environment and local communities, while simultaneously allowing for a significant increase in domestic farm output. Most importantly this option would have placed domestic interests in control of national food production, a much more viable and positive proposition for Ethiopia's prospects. If Indian, Saudi, and Chinese companies are extending their reach beyond their borders to secure national food security for their domestic economy, why can't Ethiopia do this within her own borders? In terms of food availability, it seems like we are in a much dire situation than they are. Moreover the involvement of global agribusiness in Ethiopia would have been more acceptable; on condition that Ethiopia's own farm industry, however small it maybe, is given priority first. This is not xenophobia; it is how the most food secure nations in the world today came into being. However the guise that local farm industry will develop alongside major foreign agricultural companies does not make economic sense. It is only a matter of time until they are eaten up. A developmental state does not endorse such unfair takeover of key national assets in this way. It is simply not developmental policy. It is a giveaway.

Ethiopia's fertile land is offered at near give-away prices to overseas companies who have no interest in the country, its people and their culture. This incredibly fertile virgin land is cleared violently, indiscriminately, totally, and handed to the companies; with native people displaced, forests burnt, woodland desecrated, villages destroyed and services relocated. The repression of social resistance to land investments is even specified as a condition of an agreement in these contracts that it is the obligation of the Ethiopian government "to deliver and handover the vacant possession of leased land free of impediments and provide free security against any riot, disturbance at any turbulent time". To fulfill contract obligations the government is dealing with dissent brutally in complete disregard of human rights and environmental damage.

Displacing indigenous people, large number of small-scale farmers and concentrating crop production in the hands of multi-nationals is intensifying hunger, not solving it. The driving force behind such destructive land development by poor governance and corporations is obsession for profit. Instead the government should focus in substantive agricultural reform and real development by supporting small scale producers who have generations of local knowledge and love of the land with needed capital and technology and giving them access to markets. This will create an environmentally healthy, ethically sound, and socially sustained agrarian revolution that would secure long term food security and feed the hungry.

The unintended consequence of such myopic development schemes is the genocide of indigenous populations. Confronted with such grim realities, government officials and multinational businesses reiterate the Hobson's choice presented in development. Their claim is very much tantamount to saying the following. The sacrifices of certain populations are an unavoidable consequence of development. This way of thinking is very much familiar to "Revolutionary Democracy" as well, namely the ends justify the means. Essentially saying, the heaven we create tomorrow will compensate for the damage we do today. However, as is always true, there are better alternatives. It is not difficult to find ways of sustainable development. Unfortunately for the government, pursuing these options requires listening to the people, which requires the "anathema democracy".

Land Grab – a Colonial Phenomenon

The scramble for Africa's natural resources have continued to this day in different ways and with varying intensity; be it for precious minerals or fertile farm land. The current scramble manifests itself in the form of land grab. Land Grab is no doubt a colonial phenomenon. Colonialists never cared about indigenous people who lived on the land for centuries when they took the land from them. The same is true now with the land grab in Ethiopia. For power and money, the EPRDF government is giving, selling and leasing away land to foreign companies in abundance in the name of development.

Meles gave a big piece of land to Sudan, 1000 by 50 kilometers (1000 Kilometers long from Eritrea's boarder in the north to Gambela region in the south and 50 kilometers deep towards Gonder). It is not clear as to who signed the deal on behalf of the Amhara Region, along with the regional administrator of Benishangul-Gumz. It has been reported that the chief administrator of the Amhara region at the time, Ayele Gobeze refused to sign, and some other authority agreed to sign in his place. The gift was to show the ruling party's gratitude for Sudan serving as a safe haven for TPLF during the "liberation" war. There was dispute over the need for the re-demarcation of the border with Sudan since colonial times. In 1903 and 1909 the colonial master of Sudan at the time Major Gwynn had proposed border demarcation line to the Ethiopian government. This unilateral decision was rejected both times by the Ethiopian government in power. The distinguished Ethiopian scholar Professor Alemante G. Selassie told the Ethiopian Border Affairs Committee in 2013 that the 1972 exchange of notes between the governments of Sudan and Ethiopia clearly explain this stand and call for the re-demarcation of the boundary. He said EPRDF's acceptance of the Gwynn line is not only a treasonous and shameful act but also a radical departure from the attitude and patriotism of previous Ethiopian governments.

Big corporations from China, India, Pakistan, Europe, America and the Middle East are grabbing millions of hectares of Ethiopian land. The Ethiopian people were not given the chance to discuss the matter, and there was no debate in the almost one party parliament. Millions of people are affected by the land grab, driven from their land by force, sold into destitution by their own government that has distorted notions of development and motivated to amass wealth by working with big companies. EPRDF leaders did not care about the indigenous people, their traditional life styles that are generation old, or the environment when they leased millions of hectares of fertile virgin land to corporations from around the world. Because for dictators, economic and military might is always right. People who have lived on this land for centuries are kicked out overnight because they are poor to hold on to their ancestral land and say no to the dictators or the lease holders. They are too weak to fight back or to protest in demand of justice. They are rounded up and taken to a different place for settlement. Ghaham Peebles in his June 2, 2012 article in Ethiomedia website describes the land grab in Ethiopia.

"Huge industrial agricultural centers are created, off shore farms, production of crops for the investor's home market. Indigenous people, subsistence farmers and pastoralists are forced off the land, the natural environment is leveled, purging

*the land of wild life and destroying small rural communities that
have lived and worked and cared for the land for centuries.*"

The government of Ethiopia is talking about forced
villagization programs like the previous military Derg in the
provinces of Gambella, Ogaden, Afar, Oromia, Benishangul-
Gumz and Omo valley in the south of Ethiopia. Nearly two
million indigenous people are displaced by force from their
fertile land and water and involved in these resettlement
programs in these regions. The government is following Stalin-
style collectivization and Mengistu-style villagization that
increased poverty. This forced relocation to clear land for
investors carried out by beatings, arrest, rape and killing has
displaced millions. Some of these displaced people are now in
Kenyan refugee camps and are explaining the atrocities openly
to human rights organizations, while those in the country are
quiet, afraid of retributions.

The government denies all allegations as usual, but, the
one-party state's use of authoritarian methods, repressive tactics
and restrictions has been confirmed by victims and eye
witnesses. Mengistu's military junta conducted its own form of
villagization during the 1984-85 drought, with the pretext "to
streamline distribution of basic services" like schools, clinics,
pipe water, electricity etc. But, even though it had some merit, it
was also a counter-insurgency tactic which was not performed
the right way, and caused mass suffering. Tens of thousands died
in transit, or in new locations from disease and starvation, the
promised services were not in place, hundreds of families were
separated. Today EPRDF is applying the same type of approach.

The companies who lease the land have no restrictions
on any environmental issues and can divert rivers, build canals
and dams, drilling boreholes, clearing the forest and damaging
the environment by doing so. The human cost and environmental

310

damage was never taken into consideration, simply ignored. This virgin fertile land was given away to big companies at a very low lease rate, with tax holidays and duty-free advantages to the machines they import.

By doing so EPRDF has violated not only people's rights but also the current Ethiopian constitution, Article 40 of the constitution states the following.

1. *"Land is a common property of the nations, nationalities and peoples of Ethiopia and should not be subject to sale or to other means of exchange".*
2. *"Ethiopian peasants have right to obtain land without payment and the protection against eviction from their possessions".*
3. *"Ethiopian pastoralists have the right to free land for grazing and cultivation as well as the right not to be displaced from their own lands".*

In addition to these, the UN declaration of rights of indigenous peoples, which was signed by the Ethiopian government in 2007, states that:

"Indigenous peoples have the right to the lands, territories and resources which they have traditionally owned, occupied or other-wise used or acquired".

The action by EPRDF leaders contravenes the Ethiopian constitution, because the people have not been consulted or included in the discussions to lease their homeland. EPRDF leaders who routinely violate all manners of human rights have again sacrificed the native people, destroyed the environment and prostituted the land for little money. It is a colonial phenomenon!

These regions in the western and southern parts of Ethiopia particularly the Omo Valley, Gambella and Benishangul-Gumz are one of the most remote and culturally diverse areas of the planet. These areas are home to more than a million people with very many unique agro-pastoral communities who have lived there for centuries. Their way of life is linked to the land and the big rivers (Omo, Baro, Beles, Dabus) that run through these areas to the neighboring countries, Sudan and Kenya.

The southern Omo Valley near the border with Kenya was designated by the United Nations Educational, Scientific and Cultural Organization UNESCO as World Heritage site in 1980. This is the area where EPRDF leaders have planned to build a huge dam along the Omo River and a big sugar plantation downstream with irrigation canals. The Omo River valley self-sufficient tribal natives like Mursi, Suri, Kwegu, Bodi and others are being violently evicted from their most valuable agricultural and grazing ancestral land. The food security and livelihoods of some 200, 000 people are jeopardized as the government pursues its huge plantation project in the valley. Security forces have used brutal measures to clear the area for a vast sugar cane, palm oil and cotton plantation alongside the controversial Gibe III dam. Their houses and food stores are destroyed, cattle confiscated and communities ordered to abandon their homes and move to designated resettlement areas.

According to Human Rights Watch report of June 2011 the government has used force to drive the native people away to realize this project. The 35 residents interviewed by HRW asserted that government security forces have been forcing communities to relocate from their traditional lands through violence and intimidation, arrests, detention, beatings and killing the cattle of those who resisted the plan.

The government does not seem to care about the environmental and social impact of these so-called commercial agriculture developments in these areas. The communities property rights are not respected, no consultations were made with the people, and no compensations discussed. Under such situations forced displacement and clearing the land has continued unabated. These pastoralists have been told by government forces that they have to reduce the number of their cattle and resettle in one place of the government choice with no access to the Omo River which they used for centuries.

The Ethiopian government is guilty of atrocities against the indigenous peoples of Gambella and the Omo Valley. These are people who have lived without government or outside help for hundreds of years. With the building of the Gibe III Dam in the Omo valley and the Karuturi farm in Gambella this is changing forever. The Agnwak, the Mursi, the Bodi, the Bongo, the Daasanach etc. tribes who are strongly attached to their way of life and their traditions are forced to relocate and give up their herds and become sedentary cultivators or dependent on government handouts. These are people who have never asked for food aid for centuries and survived with a pastoralist way of life which is disappearing forever. With no chance of redress through the courts and no political power, these tribes have no means to protect themselves.

The resettlements should have been voluntary, and they should have taken place after a feasibility study and discussions with the communities. There should have been prompt and effective compensations paid for losses they suffered. Most of all the communities themselves should have been convinced and become participants in the planning and implementation of the resettlement program. There should have been an independent mechanism to resolve grievances and disputes. All these safeguards have been totally ignored and hundreds of thousands of indigenous people have been removed from their land and placed into villages against their will; more forced settlements are on the way.

The systematic violations of tribal rights in the Gamballa region and in the Omo valley and the scale of the oppression is so huge and will never be known as there is no freedom of the press. Donor governments like the UK and the US have been reluctant to act to ensure respect for the peoples basic rights. Foreign governments and agencies are funding the project of a government which has violated repeatedly the fundamental rights of its citizens and has continued to do so with impunity. The Ethiopian government has conspicuously failed to protect the land rights of the pastoralists supposedly guaranteed by the constitution, believing that these people are backward or primitive and will not challenge. UK's Department for International Development DFID, and Development Assistance Group DAG investigated the matter and found out that there were killings, involuntary disappearance, rape, harassment, beatings and arbitrary arrest to crush tribal opposition to the projects. But, even after all these findings and knowing the methods used by EPRDF to evict the tribes from their lands, twenty six foreign agencies have continued to fund the project. Western donor governments and their agencies whose help we appreciate have failed to exert their influence and protect the rights of these minorities; we can't appreciate that.

Food Shortage and Famine

Ethiopia came to be known for food shortage and famine during the last fifty years. Rain fall below average rain will have significant negative impact on crop production, pasture regeneration and replenishment of water resource. Ethiopia being the sources of so many mighty rivers that support life in neighboring countries from Somalia to Sudan and Egypt, this

314

shouldn't have happened if the governments encouraged and helped the local population to develop irrigation system. The main reason for the food shortage in Ethiopia is therefore government negligence, indifference and of course incompetence.

The chronic and massive food shortages in Ethiopia are the result of poor agricultural planning, incompetence of government officials and corruption. The last three governments led by Emperor Haile Selassie, Colonel Mengistu and Meles Zenawi, failed to train and educate the peasant, deprived him of land ownership and instead they have been trying to hide the magnitude of the recurring famine during the reign of each of them. If the peasant was given real ownership of his land he could have cared for it, but he is not sure if it will remain his next year. Because of the land policy and negligence, deforestation, soil erosion, overgrazing, environmental degradation and other ecological factors, crop production is all the time affected. Meles Zenawi's plan to end food shortage is by leasing out millions of acres of fertile land to the so called international investors, whose aim is to raise crops for export and for their own countries' people. So, other countries will use Ethiopia's fertile land to produce food crops to export and feed others while Ethiopians are dying of starvation. Ethiopia will be feeding the Middle East, India, Pakistan etc. while its own people are starving to death or living on food aid because the food crops so produced will be fully exported.

Zenawi had adamantly opposed private ownership of land which is the most important factor in ensuring food security. By owning all rural and urban land, the government seems to be using it as a political weapon to keep people hungry and dependent on government aid to generate support for the regime and to decimate the opposition parties. Those who oppose EPRDF or simply support the opposition parties are denied humanitarian food and relief aid by government cadres. They are also denied land or their plot size is reduced or moved to a drier land and denied access to fertilizers, improved seeds and loans or credit. These cases have been reported by Human Rights Watch and others repeatedly and all aid agencies know it fully well.

The government is not ashamed to use land and access to aid to routinely crush dissent. Zenawi has made it a weapon to decimate opposition and this practice has continued to this day to consolidate a repressive single-party system in Ethiopia. Humanitarian aid and food is being distributed in Ethiopia on the basis of political favoritism and everyone knows it. With all these atrocities, TPLF leaders are not ashamed to celebrate the anniversary of *Ginbot 20 (*May 29) the day they took power with big festivities. We would like to remind them what the American abolitionist leader Friedrich Douglas said about the celebrations of the United States Independence day July 4. *"What to the American slave is your Fourth of July? I answer; a day that reveals to him, more than all other days in the year, the gross injustice and cruelty to which he is the constant victim. To him your celebration is a sham; your boasted liberty and unholy license; ... your sounds of rejoicing are empty and heartless; ... your shouts of liberty and equality hallow mockery; ... all your religious parade and solemnity, are to him mere bombast, fraud, deception, impiety and hypocrisy- a thin veil to cover up crimes which disgrace a nation of savages".*

Many economists say that famine in Ethiopia is ninety percent man made; bad governance is at the core of famine here. If the government had a good agricultural plan to save rain water, dig wells, use irrigation systems, build small dams all around the country on the rivers that run wild, store reserve food grain, people would survive drought that is caused by rain shortages that occur once in a few years. The government has a policy to control the people and their land at all times, but not a workable food security policy. Here is what President Obama recommended for Africa in his speech in Accra, Ghana in 2009. *"Development depends on good governance. History offers a clear verdict: governments that respect the will of their own people and govern by consent and not coercion, are more prosperous, they are more stable, and more successful than governments that do not. No country is going to create wealth if its leaders exploit the economy to enrich themselves. No person wants to live in a society where the rule of law gives way to the rule of brutality and bribery. That is not democracy, it is tyranny....In the 21st century capable, reliable and transparent institutions are the key to success.... Strong parliaments, honest police forces, independent judges, an independent press, a vibrant private sector, a civil society are keys to success. . Those are the things that give life to democracy, because that is what matters in people's everyday lives"*. (Obama -2009, Ghana)

According to the United Nations report on regional cooperation, *"the root cause of hunger across the sub-region and the world today is not a lack of food. It is the economic and social distribution of that food which leaves population undernourished and hungry"*. People starve and die for lack of food while food is rotting in warehouses, served up to rats or destroyed by the corporations because it is cheaper to burn it than to distribute it to people in need; such is the inhumane attitude that underpins market fundamentalism. The Director-General of the Food and Agricultural Organization of the United Nations said on January 26, 2013, *"globally, a third of all food produced is wasted, and ... if one could avoid this waste, it could be possible to feed all the hungry people {in the world} and have food to spare"*.

Chapter Six

<u>Leadership Crisis</u>

*"Africa's woes have more to do with bad leadership and
the enabling role played by the Western governments and
institutions. The centralization of both economic and political
power turns the state into a pot of gold that all sorts of groups
compete to capture. Once captured power is then used to amass
huge personal fortunes, to enrich ones cronies and tribesmen, to
crush ones rivals, and to perpetuate ones rule in office. All
others are excluded (the politics of exclusion). The absence of
mechanisms for peaceful transfer of power leads to a struggle
over political power, which often degenerates into civil strife or
war. ...Thousands are dislocated and flee, becoming internal
refugees.*

(George Ayittey, Africa unchained P-48)

*'We shall do much in the years to come,
But, what have we done today?
We shall give our gold in a princely sum,
But, what did we give today?
We shall lift the heart and dry the tear,
We shall plant a hope in the place of fear,
We shall speak the words of love and cheer,
But, what did we speak today?'*
(Nixon Waterman)

I arrived in Salisbury, South Rhodesia, later named
Harare, Zimbabwe on April 17, 1980 accompanying the then
Derg Prime Minister of Ethiopia Fikre Selassie Wogderess. The
country was about to get its independence from white rule early
the next day. We boarded a van assigned for Ethiopian
journalists with a driver and a guide. The VIP reception afforded

318

to Ethiopian journalists was due in part to the significant logistical support given by Ethiopia to Zimbabwe's independence struggle. We arrived at our hotel, unpacked our stuff and drove to the city stadium for the independence ceremony. The celebration has already started all over the country, the festive mood in Harare was infectious, and the people of Zimbabwe were optimistic. Complemented by the wonderful weather of Zimbabwe the event seemed auspicious. The people of Zimbabwe are open, friendly, hospitable, and among the best educated in Africa.

So, I was in Harare, Zimbabwe that mid-night on April 18th, 1980 as a correspondent of Ethiopia's print and electronic media with a camera crew, to report on the lowering of the British flag (Union Jack) and the raising of another flag to represent the birth of Zimbabwe as an independent state. Since Ethiopia's Ministry of Information could not afford to send journalists from different media, I was ordered to get the events covered and recorded for all major government media, write a television script and report for radio and press about the event. This was not uncommon because of the austerity budget as a result of the civil war and the war we had with Somalia. I have been sent to different other countries to do the same, reporting to the different government media. I sent flash news about the highlights of the occasion that night to the Ethiopian News Agency ENA immediately. One of the highlights of the event that night was the speech made by the new leader Robert Mugabe which created a sense of hope and optimism. The hero of the *Chimurenga, (*the bush war for freedom from white rule*)* Mugabe, in his speech that evening called for a new vision and reconciliation.

"The wrongs of the past must now stand forgiven and forgotten. If ever we look to the past, let us do so for the lesson the past has taught us, namely that oppression and racism are

319

inequalities that must never find scope in our political and social system. It could never be a correct justification that because the whites oppressed us yesterday when they had power, the blacks must oppress them today because they have power. An evil remains an evil whether practiced by white against black or black against white". (Mugabe, April 18, 1980)

The following days I visited the capital city Salisbury, now Harare a clean and beautiful city much different from many African cities. The residential area within the city proper is so neat and beautiful I caught a glimpse of how the British colonizers lived. I also visited the shanty black townships outside the city and got a clearer picture about the degree of segregation, which ensured white supremacy by domination and by constructing the most elaborate racial edifice the world has ever seen.

Besides the joy and festivities of the people that week, a sense of hope and optimism followed as the new leader Robert Mugabe kept his promise of fair play and reconciliation and appointed two white ministers to his cabinet and also kept in place the former intelligence chief and the army chief. Mugabe reassured white businessmen and commercial farmers about the future on whom economic prosperity of the country largely depended.

Even though Mugabe accommodated the interests of the white community, he showed no tolerance towards his black opposition party ZAPU, led by Joshua Nkomo. After two years he created a pretext and split with ZAPU establishing a one party state run by his own party, ZANU-PF. The soldiers of ZAPU (Zipra), that were integrated into a new national army were picked out for reprisal and victimized. In Mugabe's drive to create a one party stat,e thousands of civilians were killed and many more were arrested and tortured. After demolishing his rivals, Mugabe was declared executive president by parliament at the end of 1987, in effect becoming head of state, head of government and commander in chief of all defense forces, with powers to dissolve parliament and declare martial law any time he wish, and to run for office for unlimited number of terms. He allowed his officials to engage in acquiring wealth illegally just to ensure their loyalty.

After ten years of independence, Mugabe implemented a chaotic land reform that was engulfed with scandal, international uproar and sank the country into an economic quagmire. There followed massive protest where even his most loyal supporters, war veterans, participated only to be arrested and tortured. While the politicians have enriched themselves, most Zimbabweans lived in abject poverty, and the once food exporting country has now to import a big portion of its food needs. When I went back to Zimbabwe after seven years to attend the annual African television film festival held in Harare, I found a polarized and demoralized society with fellow journalists I met at independence worried about the future of their country. Because of power hungry leaders, people have similar feelings in most other African countries with downward spiral from freedom to despair.

Unethical leadership

The grave problem and the root cause of all the problems including migration that are challenging Africa since independence from colonialism is the crisis of leadership. Africa is faced with immense and threatening problems like ignorance, drought, poverty, disease (AIDS, Malaria), desertification, and economic disaster. None of the problems that the continent has faced during the last fifty years are more critical or more relevant than failure of leadership. Even though Africans are anxious and willing to take the challenge and turn it around, they are often undermined and immobilized by divisive and deceiving leaders. Africa remained poor because her leadership is morally bankrupt. Most African leaders tend to prefer savagery acts and like to terrorize, torture, kill and mutilate their own people, than motivating them for greater achievement. They encourage their followers (cadres) to do evil things to silence the population. We have observed leaders of left wing and right wing extremists like Idi Amin Dada of Uganda, Emperor Bokassa of Central African Republic, Mobutu Sees Seiko of Zaire, Said Barre of Somalia, Colonel Mengistu and Meles Zenawi of Ethiopia to name a few who encouraged their secret service and army to commit acts of brutality on their own people just to stay in power.

After independence from colonialism, during the last 50 years, the major problem of the African people has been leadership crisis. Africa has suffered more in the hands of its own black leaders who are corrupt, power hungry, incompetent and brutal. As George Ayittey put it, because of the defective political system of Sultanism (personal rule) and the defective economic system of Statism (government control and ownership of the means of production) Africa is suffering badly. After independence the new African leaders followed the same colonial system which proved to be suicidal for the continents progress, and the newly independent nations started fighting each other to change the boundary lines. We blamed the Arabs, and Westerners for slave trade and colonialism, but five decades after the end of colonialism and more than a century after slave trade officially ended, Africa did not fully recover from the trauma.

In most African countries independence from colonial rule was only nominal. The only thing that changed was the skin color of the leaders and the flag they fly in front of public buildings. Political repression and exploitation of the resources continued unabated in the hands of black dictators. Five decades of independence brought nothing but political chaos, economic disaster, disintegration and cultural decay. Agricultural growth has declined, per capita income has gone down, famine and food shortages have become chronic, the new generation suffered from malnutrition and protein deficiency. If we are bold enough to talk about the truth that is the reality in most African countries today.

In 1981 I was in Khartoum, Sudan accompanying an Ethiopian delegation led by the then Derg Minister of Commerce, Wolle Chekol, (who happened to be my high school associate and roommate), to report on the Third African Trade Fair. The delegation was composed of Chamber of Commerce officials and a cultural musical troupe *"Wollo Kinet"* led by The General Manager of Ethiopian National Theatre, Getachew Abdi. The then leader of Sudan, Gaafar Numeiri, who took power in a military coup in 1969, was a secular left leaning politician trying to achieve a relatively balanced approach with South Sudan. At the trade fair Sudan had a big pavilion where they exhibited numerous agricultural and industrial products including Camel Beer. This was of course before the take of Sudan by the Islamists, who still rule Sudan presently.

After two years, in 1983 Numeiri abandoned the careful balance he tried as a policy to keep Sudan united and declared the country to be an Islamic Republic, governed by traditional Islamic law. In one of the highlights of his move Numeiri poured eleven million dollar worth of alcohol into the Nile River and banned western-style dancing. This move destroyed many of the benefits of liberal democracy – an independent judiciary, free press, parliamentary debate of secular politics and active professional associations and trade unions and placed Sudan in the hands of Islamic militants.

President Numeiri also arbitrarily dissolved the southern regional government, which drew in Sudan into civil war that cost millions of lives and a big sum of money. At the time Sudan was assisting anti-Gaddafi groups from Chad, and also supporting the Eritrean and Tigrayan rebels fighting for secession from Ethiopia; while Ethiopia's Military Derg and Libya's Gaddafi were supporting the South Sudan rebels. Numeiri was overthrown soon after and the real Islamists took power. Even though Numeiri was not as corrupt as his successors, the political mistake he committed cost Sudan dearly. Since the 1950's there have been a total of 206 coups attempts in Africa, out of which 100 were successful.

The new African leaders after liberation from colonialism and the coup leaders that followed were no better than the colonialists. Trying to participate in cold war politics and jumping from one western ideology to another they mismanaged the economy, looted the countries treasuries, destroyed indigenous African institutions, harassed and arrested opposition groups and severely abused human rights. The men and women of Africa who fought and struggled to liberate their countries got their independence but not their freedom.

"Much of post-colonial Africa came to be ruled by 'educated barbarians'. The elites and nationalists proved themselves to be no "noble savages." Recall that the illiterate peasants of Africa – the so called –savages- developed political institutions of participatory democracy based upon consensus. They also recognized the fact that consensus was impossible reach without a guarantee of freedom of expression. At village meetings, even non-tribesmen could express their opinion freely without harassment or arrest. After independence, however, the majority of African nationalists and the educated elites denied the people these rights. In fact, in most African countries criticisms of the government became illegal. The opposition was

gagged and its members, some of whom were the same nationalists who had fought for freedom alongside the new leaders, were thrown into jail or killed." (Ayittey, Africa Betrayed, P-102)

In Africa, political power is monopolized by the ruling tyrant individual and he entrench' himself in power by amassing wealth and controlling all key government institutions; he transforms the country into his personal property. The tyrant, his cronies, his tribesmen and party loyalists then proceed to plunder the treasury. All others are excluded from politics and a variety of tactics are used to weaken opposition; bribery, infiltration, intimidation, co-option and 'divide and rule'. If these tactics do not work, the tyrant will take ruthless action by arresting or killing opposition leaders. Most professional elites are bought by the dictator by being offered a high ranking post like ministerial post, diplomatic posting, or managerial post of a corporation etc. Many African intellectuals have betrayed their people and their principles for money. Out of frustration, many, especially skilled professionals leave the country for Europe or America. As such most African leaders have been a failure and a disgrace to their people.

Many African leaders have added to the toll of misery of their people instead of alleviating it. To bring about an African renaissance we must first learn how to govern ourselves; one party rule and power that emanates from the barrel of the gun should not be acceptable. African leaders must encourage the growth of the private sector and reduce government intervention. Party owned for profit companies should be illegal in practice and we should promote real democratic principles like free press, assembly, and organization of civic society, popular participation of the people, sound economic management, good governance and most of all freedom from fear of retribution by government cadres.

Because of bad governance, Ethiopia was weakened by 30 years of civil war in Eritrea and 16 years of insurgency in Tigray, the legacy of which is poverty, disintegration, and dispersion of the population to the neighboring countries and beyond. One major problem that the current leaders of Ethiopia have created is ethnic politics. They should learn how to balance ethnic loyalty with emphasis on national identity or nationhood. The leaders themselves have to believe that they are primarily Ethiopians and secondly their ethnic identity. Even though ethnicity is at the root of African political process, and a dominant element of life in the continent for a long time, nationhood is not new to Ethiopians as they have lived under central administration for many centuries; we don't want our leaders to turn back the clock to division and fragmentation.

Many politicians say that the hope that Ethiopia would serve as an example of unity in diversity and a stronghold of democracy came to an abrupt halt when Emperor Haile Selassie manipulated the Eritrean parliament to abolish the federation in favor of complete union with Ethiopia. Instead of expanding the federal system to the other major nationalities like the Amhara, Oromo, Afar, Ogaden etc. in 1962 the government abolished the very model of democratization. Shortly afterwards the Eritrean "Liberation" Front (ELF) was founded and later Eritrean People "Liberation" Front (EPLF) was organized, both with the help of the surrounding Arab countries, particularly the governments of Egypt, Sudan, Iraq and Syria.

With the coming to power of the military Derg and its 'Red Terror', Tigray "Liberation" Front (TLF) and Tigray People "Liberation" Front (TPLF) the Oromo "Liberation" Front (OLF) and others mushroomed. Ethiopia was soon engulfed by an intense civil war and tens of thousands of people were displaced and became refugees in neighboring countries, especially Sudan. There was another group of insurgents, TLF that was fighting for the "liberation" of Tigray, which was later destroyed by TPLF. Former members of TPLF Kahsay Berhe and Tesfay Atsbeha in their memoir of February22, 2008, described how the cheating and destroying of TLF was executed. *"In November 1976 TPLF led by Meles Zenawi and his confidants invited the members of the TLF for a meeting of reconciliation and unity in the rebel held area. At the end of the meeting that approved the merger of the two organizations, the TPLF leaders suggested that members of both fronts now united shall mix and sleep together. TPLF members were ordered by Meles and his confidants to kill all TLF members while they were asleep and thus TLF was destroyed. After eliminating TLF, then TPLF became the only organization leading the "liberation" struggle".* Many politicians say that TLF was destroyed because it was not in favor of Eritrean independence and TPLF's plan of secession of Tigray from Ethiopia. These two crucial issues were not brought to discussion with members of the front because the leaders of the TPLF including Meles knew that the Tigray people would not support the secession of Tigray and/or Eritrea.

The leaders of TPLF committed their army to fight alongside EPLF for the secession of Eritrea, thus for the disintegration of Ethiopia, making the second most populous black African nation a land locked country. Even though TPLF leaders suspended the 'liberation' (secession of Tigray) believing that three-fourth of bread is better than one-fourth, many people are still suspicious that they are only buying time and are working on it to implement it when they feel their power is threatened. The right to secede Article 39 of the Constitution, many think is crafted for this purpose and for further disintegration of other regions as they were already disappointed with TPLF brutal administration. There is no trust between the oppressor and the oppressed and the distrust is getting bigger every year.

The EPLF and TPLF with the help they got first from the Arabs and later from the West, because of Derg's pro-Soviet policy, were able to control wide areas in the northern part of Ethiopia. The Derg military government unable to propose a political solution was bombarding the area continuously with Soviet-made fighter jets and the situation got worse every year. As a result, tens of thousands of Ethiopians continued to migrate to the hinterland or neighboring Sudan. It is estimated that more than a million people have migrated to Sudan alone in a mass exile during Ethiopia's thirty years of civil war. Thus Derg created a recruitment bonanza for the so called "liberation" fronts.

It was September 1979, the 10th Anniversary of Libya's Revolution, which had brought Muammar Gaddafi to the helm. The place was the port city of Benghazi, which would later be the place that sparked his downfall. In the stands listening among a crowd of International Journalists was an Ethiopia News delegation including myself, brought in to hear a three hours speech by the late dictator. Libya's oil boom and its small population meant ordinary people receiving government handouts amounting to free housing and education. On the back of this, it was perhaps possible to rant for 3 hours on stage, as Gaddafi often did. The slogan of the event was "partners not workers", which was written on bill boards all over Benghazi and Tripoli. Gaddafi was pompous, and was clearly bolstered by the flow of petrodollars, which as he clearly stated in his speeches, would be used to support proxy wars in Africa and the Arab World. The people of Libya have already started to dislike him as he stayed too long in power and grew more corrupt. Gaddafi whose hobby seemed meddling in the affairs of other countries was killed at the end of a bloody civil war in 2011 after 42 years in power. In his book "The Fate of Africa", Historian Meredith wrote about Gaddafi, meddling in other countries.

"The army coup in Libya in 1969 brought to power a 27-year-old-signals officer driven by grand ambitions, fierce hatreds and a pathological penchant for meddling in the affairs of other countries, made possible by the huge flow of oil revenues at his disposal. ... Among the causes he supported were an array of Palestinian factions; the Irish Republican Army; Basque separatists; and Muslim insurgents in the Philippines and Thailand. In Africa he backed Eritrean guerrillas against Haile Selassie's regime; Polisario guerillas in the Western Sahara; Southern African liberation movements; and opposition factions in Niger and Mali. ...When Amin's army faced defeat in 1979, Gaddafi dispatched an expeditionary force to Uganda to try to prop him up, a venture that ended in humiliating failure". (Martin Meredith, P-352)

Most African leaders ruled with absolute power; some of these leaders and their loyalist's overseas bank accounts are stuffed with millions of dollars, and are concerned with their own self-interest and have little to do with the advancement of their people. Of every dollar that comes to their country in the form of foreign aid or loan, grant or business contract, they took a good percentage of it for their personal wealth, and it ended in foreign bank accounts. The hard working people of Africa know about the misdeeds of their leaders, but they only whisper about it among themselves, because the secret agents have penetrated every level of society. The Western and Eastern governments supporting these leaders know about it, but they are not concerned about the development of Africa to begin with; they are buying the loyalty of the leaders for their geopolitical interests. With no one trying to help Africans, shortage of food becomes critical as their leaders bank account soar to billions of dollars.

African tyrants rule with brute force and without law; whatever they utter is the law. Because of all these, people feel a sense of powerlessness and have lost the conviction that they can influence their leaders to do better. The consequences of these down feelings, is reflected in our society by drugs and alcohol abuse or exile to Europe and America. Our leaders keep on mumbling the slogans of yesterday while the problems of today go unsolved, it is frustrating!

Most of post-colonial African leaders became unethical and ignored the plight of their people. They failed to give respect to social values, and failed to motivate their people. They had no sense of service to the people; instead they chose to serve themselves and those around them. They betrayed the aspirations of the people, violated human rights and plundered the treasury and resources no less than the colonialists. They ignited unnecessary wars here and there that killed tens of thousands of people and spent millions of dollars.

"One of the major tragedies of post-colonial Africa is that the African peoples have trusted their leaders, but only a few of those leaders have honored that trust. What has held Africa back, and continues to do so have its origins in a lack of principled, ethical leadership. Leadership is an expression of a set of values; its presence, or the lack of it, determines the direction of a society, and affects not only the actions but the motivations and visions of the individuals and communities that make up the society". (Maathai, P-25)

African Union (AU) celebrated its 50th anniversary on May 25, 2013, but, there is a question surrounding the nature and value of the Union in meeting the needs and demands of ordinary African. Despite recent economic growth in Ethiopia and in few other African countries living conditions remain abysmal for many average African people, with the UN's report showing that 24 of the 25 countries at the bottom of the human development index are Africans. This fact describes the AU as a

330

talk shop, rudderless and crucially disconnected from African citizens. The predecessor, the Organization of African Unity, OAU established by 32 African countries on May 25, 1963 focused primarily on liberating countries of the continent from the grip of colonialism. The OAU soon earned the name of "dictators club" for failing to intervene and its inability to change the situation in member states during coups and/or government repression.

After the formation of the AU in 2002 with a renewed focus to solve conflicts, improve governance and engineer socio-economic development in different regions of Africa, the hard question remains over the political will of the AU to enforce freedom and good governance in member countries. During the Arab spring of 2011 the AU was a spectator and kept quiet during the armed struggle against Muammar Gaddafi in Libya, and the intervention of the French in Mali a year later. With so many Africans living in politically repressive regimes, with suppression of freedom of expression and restriction on opposition parties, the AU is not yet an honest broker of democracy or a representative of the African people. Since the AU charter starts with the sentence "we the Heads of States and Governments of Africa" unlike the UN charter which starts off with "we the people of the United Nations" it is still a club of heads of states and governments and not necessarily a body that truly represents the African people; as many believe the continental body is adrift from the aspirations of the African people.

Corruption and Massacre

The president of Zaire (Congo) Mobutu Sese Seko was a mere army sergeant before he took power. In a few years he became one of the wealthiest men in the world, with more than 5 billion dollar worth assets. He turned his relatives and friends from his Gbande tribe to millionaires. He built palaces and was only concerned about personal prestige. A big portion of the money coming in the form of aid or grant was taken by the big men on top and ended up in their foreign bank accounts.

Mobutu changed the countries name to Zaire, (meaning river) and expelled Asian merchants after expropriating 500 million dollars of their foreign enterprises. He kicked out most of the Belgians who had plantations in Congo and gave the business to his relatives and friends. With no knowledge how to run the business most of them simply sold the merchandise in stock and closed the shops. He even ordered all his countrymen to change their Christian names and have African names, and never wore European attire and neck ties, and designed a national uniform similar to Chinese communist leaders. While Mobutu was spending so much money, food shortage became critical in Zaire; patients were dying because of shortage of medicine, bandage and medical equipment. Even the government News Agency closed down for lack of paper.

The former president of Kenya, Arap Moi was a school teacher before he came to power. As soon as he became president he turned the country into a one party state, arrested journalists and critics. All those around him became millionaires in a short time through business deals and wide spread corruption. When Kenya's Air Force officers attempted a coup to overthrow him, he disbanded the countries Air Force and closed Nairobi University for nine months, whose students supported the coup. Whenever he feels insecure and needs acceptance and authenticity to his rule, he orders the people to come out for a mass demonstration in support of his policies. The people will do whatever they are ordered to do even though they have no love or respect for him.

The leader of Uganda, Idi Amin Dada was a military man with a second grade education. After he overthrew President Melton Obote who ruled the country since independence, he promised that the care-taker government will transfer power as soon as elections are held. But, instead strange things started to happen in the following days. Ugandan chief justice Benedicto Kuwanuka was taken by soldiers from his office and disappeared forever. The Army chief Brigadier General Suleiman Hussein disappeared. The vice chancellor of Mekerere University also disappeared. Hundreds of bodies were seen floating down the Nile along the Namanbe and Mabira forests. Tribes who supported the previous leader were wiped out. The prisons were full, so they were forced to stand in line and kill each other to death using sledge hammers; and knowing they were going to be killed, people lined up all day, day after day and fulfilled the orders. One might wonder why they didn't fight it out. By the end of his eight years rule 300, 000 Ugandans were murdered.

When Central African Republic got its independence in 1960 Army Sergeant Jean Bedel Bokassa became president and gave himself many titles, including President-for-life and Emperor. He used to idolize Napoleon Bonaparte of France, and one day he declared that his republic is now an Empire and that he is the Emperor. He spent more than 20 million dollars for the coronation robe and ceremony. In a crowded stadium he ascended the eagle shaped golden throne and just like Napoleon did he placed the crown on his balding head himself and took an oath. One could wonder about the shallowness of African leaders and the silent obedience of millions of Africans.

Bokassa converted from Christianity to Islam twice. When Gaddafi of Libya came to visit him Bokassa received two million dollars and converted to Islam. But, as soon as Gaddafi left in his airplane he declared he has again become the Christian Bokassa. After some time while he was on a visit to Libya to get more money, France flew its paratroopers to over throw Bokassa and restored David Dacko to power and arranged asylum for Bokassa in Cote de Ivoire with the agreement that he will stay away from political activity.

We can keep on talking about several other African dictators who were corrupt and power hungry; and we still have so many of them in office. In his book "The Fate of Africa" Martin Meredith wrote his observation.

"Africa by the end of the 1980's was renowned for its big men, dictators who strutted the stage, tolerating neither opposition or dissent, rigging elections, emasculating the courts, cowing the press, stifling the universities, demanding abject servility and making themselves exceedingly rich. Their faces appeared on currency notes; their photographs graced offices, and shops. They named highways, football stadiums and hospitals after themselves. Their speeches and daily activities dominate radio and television news and government newspapers. They packed the civil service with their own supporters and employed secret police to hunt down opponents, licensing them to detain torture and murder at will, if necessary". (Meredith, P-378)

African leaders and government officials have institutionalized looting and become the major exploiters of the continents wealth. They are responsible for the capital flight that has impoverished Africa. They embezzled the money that the country collected in the form of tax from poor peasants and also squandered, wasted and stolen foreign loan and aid funds that they received from lenders in the name of the poor people. Even worse they deposit the money they looted in overseas bank accounts. Every year more money flees Africa than the amount it received in the form of aid.

A privately published monthly paper from London, 'South', reported in 1989 that Kenyan government officials and their kinsmen have deposited more than five billion dollars abroad; which was more than the country's foreign debt at the time. Africa's government officials have pocketed billions of dollars in bribes and commissions on foreign contracts. No foreign company is given a permit to start business in Africa unless he gives a shareholder status for free or a big amount of money in bribes to the officials who have authority to issue them.

According to a French newspaper (Liberation), article written in January 1992, former head of state of Mali, Moussa Traore looted his country to amass a personal wealth of over two billion dollars. The article with a title "Le song des Pauvres" (The blood of the poor) was written by a Swiss member of parliament Jean Ziegler.

In 1988 Sierra Leone's three government ministers added the names of several ghost workers that never existed in government payroll and collected their salaries that were worth millions of dollars. It was reported by "West Africa", a privately owned weekly in London that the three ministers including Dr. Shamsu Mustapha the former minister of state were charged with such offences.

Mismanagement and corruption has continued to this day in Africa, more and more is looted and deposited overseas, eroding the continents economy; only a small percentage of the looted money is invested in the country in the names of their relatives, they know they will be ousted one day. Some African businessmen who have no faith in the country's future because of government corruption and political instability have also chosen to deposit their money in foreign banks.

It is difficult to find an African country and African leader or a government official who is clean from corruption. Given the economic state of African countries and standard of living of the people, being the poorest in the world, the degree of looting is a sellout. In Professor Ayittey's words, *"what modern Africa needs, perhaps more than anything else, is a common sense revolution"*. Astonishingly, even those highly educated intellectuals, lawyers, economists, political scientists, engineers etc. who ought to be the watchdogs have themselves joined the official gangsters who robe the countries' treasury.

"Divide and Rule"

African dictators are using 'divide and rule' to stay long in power and never allow pluralism to flourish. Whatever form of pluralism pops up among societies, the leaders keep on dismantling it before it gets strong, so that it will not be held together by mutual trust. They never tried to achieve a workable level of unity among the different nationalities; in real fact they preached fragmentation and division with no commitment at all to public interest or the common good of society. These leaders either preached oppressive unity or fragmentation and mistrust; they have a fatal ignorance of the psychology of their own people. Instead of trying to resolve conflicts, compromise and defuse disputes and look for the underlying sources of misunderstanding to build coalition, they foster conflict for their own self-interest.

No country can be built without the full participation of its people. The campaign of India's Mahatma Gandhi for non-violent resistance to the British rule and the civil rights movement in the United States led by Dr. Martin Luther King Jr. succeeded because millions of people, black and white, supported them and paid sacrifices. In the same manner for a sustainable and equitable development in Africa we need the full engagement of millions of citizens and an active civil society. But these concepts are merely theoretical and abstract in most African countries.

Likewise the leaders of Africa must stop preaching fragmentation and divisiveness and instead revitalize our shared values, a sense of community and mutual trust. We need leaders who truly understand the ingredients of community. They should preach unity and mobilize the resources by focusing on the real needs of the people; jobs, housing, health care, quality education and most of all freedom from fear.

Ethnic or religious differences inflamed by irresponsible leaders have been the pretext for violence in Africa. Tribalism when politicized can erupt into large scale bloodshed. Even though racial hatreds can create conflicts between tribes over pasture or water, their battles are brief and local, as they can tell their tribe chiefs to sit down and discuss a workable compromise. But when these tribal conflicts are politicized by leaders who want to exploit the situation, it becomes bigotry, treating individuals badly for the simple reason that they belong to a particular group.

In many African countries leaders stir up ethnic tensions instead of soothing them; they even make laws to discriminate between their own citizens on tribal or ethnic grounds. They introduce things like ethnic identity cards and carefully plan genocide on certain tribes to maintain their grip on power. One example is Rwanda where 800,000 Tutsis were killed in just six weeks. It was a government plan propagated over radio Mille Collins agitating Hutus to kill Tutsis.

In most African countries politicians play on tribal grievances and allow or even prefer political parties to be established on tribal lines, that way they can divide and rule like their former colonialists. Many African politicians prefer a political contest based on tribal horse trading than on principle, class interest or ideas. These leaders preach shamelessly as if politics is a struggle between ethnic groups, and people tend to vote along ethnic lines. This has to change if Africa has to progress. African leaders have done little to convince their people that nationhood offers more benefits than tribalism to improve their standard of living and security.

In African countries that are run by political tyranny, there is what one might call economic and political 'apartheid', the dirty politics of exclusion. In some of these countries the ruling party leaders hold all economic and political power, which ultimately leads to instability, civil strife and chaos. That is what happened in Zaire, Rwanda, Liberia, Burundi, Somalia, Ethiopia, etc. The leaders who took power in these countries entrenched themselves in office by rigged elections and by amassing wealth, power and controlling all key government institutions, thus transforming the country into their personal property. Their tribesmen and loyalists are allowed to plunder the treasury; all others, the oppositions and the masses are excluded from the countries politics. To weaken the opposition the ruling party uses bribery, infiltration, intimidation and 'divide and rule' methods. These will ultimately lead to strife or civil war which sends millions of refugees flowing in all directions.

The failure of leaders to motivate the people, to create social cohesion, to revitalize shared values, to heighten confidence and to renew cultural institutions has deprived Africans the capacity to mobilize their resources and focus their energies for a sustained commitment of development. The lack of visionary leaders who truly understand the ingredients of community, who instill confidence and morale, sense of community and mutual trust has created fragmentation and division among Africans. It has caused social disintegration and moral disorientation and in George Ayittey's words *'it has created deep and complex anxieties that is spinning the compass needle of our direction'.*

Collaborating with Ex-colonizers

One can say that colonialism and the cold war set the stage for leadership deficit in Africa. It is true that these two factors have contributed greatly to the failure of post-colonial Africa. But, Africans could have changed and chosen the right way to correct these ills, if they had good leaders. Instead they chose to continue with the inherited colonial system of governance, which was devised to exploit the natural resources and silence the people. In actual fact some of the newly independent African countries leaders collaborated with ex-colonizers and failed under their command; there followed the new era, neo-colonialism. The colonial masters made sure that the new leaders they help come to power will be obedient to them and continue to supply Europe with the necessary raw materials for their industries and cooperate politically; in return they get military and development aid. Those leaders who chose not to cooperate with USA and European powers were isolated, denied development assistance or were toppled by coups backed by foreign governments like in the case of Patrice Lumumba of Congo.

The cold war politics that divided West and East also affected Africa as the United States and Soviet Union struggled to create spheres of influence. Most independent African countries were forced to ally themselves with either one. Such direct and indirect meddling of the West and the East in the politics of the newly independent African countries paralyzed the free development of the continent; most of all our leaders lacked the courage to say no.

The Soviet Union and countries of North Atlantic Treaty Organization (NATO), sponsored proxy wars between countries they supported. Ethiopia and Somalia, Angola and Mozambique were engulfed in proxy wars in a struggle of the super powers to expand their spheres of influence. African dictators, who allied their countries to either of the super powers, were getting all the support from their ally even if they oppressed their people and violated human rights greatly. As long as these dictators helped USA to contain communism or in the case of USSR to kick out capitalism, they had all the right to silence their people with no tolerance for dissent.

Even though the condition of the continent has been made worse by incompetent and misguided leadership, corruption, mismanagement, violation of human rights, senseless civil wars, political tyranny and capital flight, it is clear that colonialism and cold war politics did not leave Africa in good shape. It is also true that African government officials often use the legacies of colonialism and the cold war as excuses to conceal their own failed policies and incompetence.

The colonial boundaries that were carved by European powers, Great Britain, France, Germany, Italy, Portugal, Belgium and others at the Berlin conference in 1884-5 is another great obstacle for peace and cooperation between neighboring African countries. European powers drew lines hurriedly across the map of Africa without any consideration of the nations and nationalities that are divided and separated among different neighboring states. Thus knowingly or unknowingly they set a time bomb of conflict. African leaders instead of trying to correct these mistakes by means of federal unity or confederation alliance they continued with these failed demarcations; and that became a reason for cross-border wars.

The colonial borders divided nationalities into three or four different countries. A good example is the Somalis that are found in millions in Ethiopia, Kenya and Djibouti. The Maasai were divided into two countries; Kenya and Tanzania; the Luo tribe in Kenya, Uganda and Tanzania; the Teso in Kenya and Uganda; and it is similar in other parts of Africa. Conflicts, coups, civil wars and corruption emanated from these colonial designs beyond imagination. The sad thing is that African leaders seem to be willing to fulfill the wishes and ill motives of their colonizers and the super powers that followed.

The capitalist West and the socialist East have not been helping Africans to get good leaders; instead they were protecting tyrants from being toppled as long as they serve their interest. It is also true that we should not keep on blaming others for our shortcoming; it is the responsibility of Africans to fix their problems themselves. Professor Ayittey emphasizes this truth in his book "Africa Betrayed", that, given the international political situation, Africans will have to fight their own battles to win their freedom, and expect little help from foreigners.

"It must be restated that it is not the responsibility of the West but that of Africans to clean up the mess in Africa. To be sure, the West has contributed to Africa's economic decline, not least by supporting brutal dictatorships. But so too did the East (the countries of Eastern Europe, the Soviet Union, and China)". (Ayittey, P-348)

The cold war ended with the fall of the Berlin Wall in 1989 and the collapse of the Soviet Union in 1991. Along with it multi-party system and free market economy found their way in Africa. Apartheid ended in South Africa and the decolonization of the entire continent was accomplished. Most of the first generation of leaders of Africa after independence were gone without achieving much; but the new second generation of leaders that came to power after the cold war did not do any better.

Second Generation of Leaders

At the end of the cold war Africans started to topple their dictators and engaged in opposition politics. The Western donor governments set up new rules to help African countries. Respect of human rights, establishing multi-party politics, curtailing corruption, focus on poverty reduction and improving governance became the criteria to get aid and loans from the West. With the new political change in the world at the end of the cold war it was assumed that free markets and free societies would reinforce each other and with globalization on the rise could end poverty in Africa; unfortunately that didn't happen.

The first generation leaders were gone, either toppled by coups or civil wars. The second generation of leaders, mostly young promised multi-party democracy, free press and free market economy supported by the Western governments. But some of the leaders that followed became more oppressive than the leaders they succeeded. Cross border and civil wars or both consumed many African countries; eg. Ethiopia, Eritrea, Congo, Rwanda, etc. Even though some of these countries set limited terms of office for the leaders and free elections every four or five years, some are still in power for over twenty years and elections are often rigged. Recent examples of elections that were not accepted as free and fair are in countries like Kenya, Zimbabwe, Ethiopia, Guinea, Nigeria, Togo, Cote de Ivoire etc.

Africans are not still empowered to be active participants of politics and development. Basic freedoms, human rights, individual rights are still a dream in most African countries. Yet, most leaders are being scrutinized by increasingly strong opposition movements, vocal civil society and a freer press. But, the second generation of leaders turned deaf ears to the plight of their people and continued to cling to power. Even though the leaders promised democracy at every election and they spelled it right in their constitutions, in practice most Africans are denied of it. There is no effective and truly representative government, independent judiciary, truly free press and strong opposition party in most African countries today. With no right to assemble, organize; advocate one's own view peacefully without fear of arbitrary arrest or reprisal and intimidation most African countries fall short of genuine democracy.

Africa is languishing again in the hands of second and third generation of dictators. Under such nominally multi-party but in practice a one party system political leaders are embezzling the resources of the continent among themselves and their cronies. The vast majority is excluded, dissenting voices arrested, most loans and donor's money the country gets goes for the benefit of few bureaucrats and their supporters. There is little accountability for government actions; citizens live in fear. Democracy is in jeopardy and conflict seems likely. The new leaders simply did not honor their promises for democracy; they lack the qualities of principled and ethical leadership. This makes us wonder why it has been so hard to get good leaders like Nelson Mandela of South Africa, Julius Nyerere of Tanzania, Ahmed Ben Bella of Algeria, Leopold Sedar Senghor of Senegal, Seretse Khama of Botswana and Kwame Nkrumah of Ghana in his early years.

So, one can dare say that the problems of Africa does not emanate as such from the legacies of European colonialism or the cold war politics, as some African leaders would like to put it to find a scapegoat. We cannot blame colonialism or the cold war for so long after it was over. We simply failed our people and instead of leading in a democratic fashion and developing our countries we preferred to engage in useless conflicts, civil wars, coups and corruption. Because of power hungry and corrupt leaders, Africa which has fertile lands, mineral resources and hardworking people is getting poorer. Africans are disappointed and ashamed to see so much waste, and negligence by their own leaders. A continent with so much abundance and potential can't feed its own people. Hunger stares at millions of Africans every day; even eating one meal a day has become a luxury; such a shame makes you sick.

When Kwame Nkrumah took office as the first president of Ghana, he proudly declared: "We shall achieve in a decade what it took others a century. ...and we shall not rest content until we demolish these miserable colonial structures and erect in their place a veritable paradise". (Nkrumah, 1957) But after independence genuine democracy and true freedom never came to most African countries. Instead things got worse; the continent was wrecked by continuous civil wars, coups, instability, poverty, malnutrition, and on top of that persecution, detention, arbitrary arrest and corruption plagued the continent. The democratization process has gone off track, insecurity is entrenched. The political environment created by these tyrant leaders is not conducive for citizens to engage in a creative and productive way for nation building. Citizens live in fear and can't hold their leaders accountable for their gross mismanagement and embezzlement.

In most of the countries in Africa today there is no openness, accountability, transparency, equity and fairness. Governments are not threatened by people's vote, as there are no free and fair elections. They are threatened by guns, coups and civil wars time and again; and those who come to power by the power of the gun turn to be tyrants who are no better than the men they replaced. Until they are driven out by the same method they plunder the countries' resources, they enrich the few, suppress democratic activities, harass civil rights movements, foment violence between political parties and mismanage development.

Often times I ask myself; how can we produce real good leaders? Leaders who respect their peoples common social values, who are humble enough to sacrifice for the common good of the people. What does it take to get good leaders who will not sell off Africa's fertile land and mineral resources for low price to foreign predators? How can we get leaders who can minimize corruption and allow their people to exercise their natural inalienable rights to freely speak their mind, organize, assemble, move and live anywhere in the country and access unfiltered information? I don't have the answers for these, but I am optimistic that a new generation of leaders will soon take office to empower the people and clean Africa from all these mess. I see some signs of hope in our children that we will soon get leaders who live for something greater than themselves, who have a vision for the continent, and forgo their own self- interests and work with honesty and integrity for the well-being of their peoples. Ghana's newspaper pointed for a need of common sense to this end in its editorial long time ago.

"Many a time we have wondered if the so-called African leaders sometimes lack the capacity to think and understand the ramifications of their actions. After all the bloodshed in Rwanda you would think we have learnt a lesson, but no! Idiocy of our power hungry leaders, seem to triumph over pragmatism and common sense. The rationale for the current fighting defies any logic. ...the world must be getting tired of us, given our self-inflicted tragedies galore. We seem to lack any sense of urgency to handle problems in an expedient manner devoid of bloodshed. Lord Have Mercy!" (Editorial, Ghana Drum, November 1996)

Africa has suffered a lot under its tyrant leaders; leadership crisis is the tragedy of most African countries. The continent has suffered in the hands of its misguided leaders more than anything else. Africa is in need of men with integrity, clear vision and a sense of service to their people. The first generation of leaders governed through the strength of their personality and their credit in liberating their countries. The second and third generation leaders are keen to master power politics, but are less nationalist. They have silenced all opposition and dissent, they have failed to groom successors; as a result you can see a leadership vacuum in many African countries.

Africa has fallen in the hands of unqualified and deceiving leaders with no popular support; multi-party democracy is only nominal, the leaders have consolidated power and it has become difficult to replace a president or prime minister. The great African novelist Chinua Achebe once said the following about his country, Nigeria.

"The trouble with Nigeria is simply and squarely a failure of leadership. There is nothing basically wrong with the Nigerian character. There is nothing wrong with the Nigerian land or climate or water or air or anything else. The Nigerian problem is the unwillingness or inability of its leaders to rise to the responsibility, to the challenge of personal example which is the hallmark of true leadership".

Of all the grave problems facing Africa today, from poverty to ill-health, environment degradation to unemployed/under employed troubled youth and unfair international competition, none is more critical than our crisis of leadership. Most of the continents' problems have practical solutions, but, it needs effective leadership to heighten motivation and confidence and mobilize the necessary resources and the people. We need leaders who could set a new standard for African renaissance by instilling confidence, morale and motivation in their people. Africans have been struggling in vain

346

to find political leaders who can restore democracy and trust to the political process; unite the people and encourage their full participation in development. In 2018 Ethiopia seems to have found that uniting visionary leader who started taking the country in a new democratic direction.

Ethiopia's new leader Dr. Abiy Ahmed traveled to the United States and Europe to formally meet and address Ethiopian diaspora. His new vision for a united Ethiopia, with the rule of law, democracy and justice for all attracted millions in all continents. He released political prisoners and invited all opposition political parties at home and abroad to participate freely in the country's political life. Almost all opposition parties leaders in exile including armed groups, went back home immediately and started organizing their supporters. Some established media headquarters in Addis Abeba. Vibrant democratic institutions and civic associations began to sprout; including an independent election commission chaired by Judge Birtukan Mideksa, a former famous opposition leader. Hope rises again in Ethiopia, and many intellectuals and investors in the diaspora are returning home for good.

Values and Public Policy

The dispersion of Africans is largely due to political tyranny and economic mismanagement, and the two are inseparable when it comes to African Diaspora. Between the fifteenth and the nineteenth centuries the pursuit of wealth and power by Americans and Europeans brought a forced dispersion of Africans due to slave trade. After the end of slave trade, before the continent recovered from the trauma of slavery it fell under the yoke of colonialism; and after independence from colonialism, neo-colonialism and the cold war combined with the dictatorial rule of African leaders, their poor economic policy and ethnic based conflicts and cross-border wars forced Africans to migrate as far as Europe and America for security and better life.

There could be many major reasons for African dispersion after independence; but, according to Professor Ayittey, one major factor for African Diaspora after the dance of freedom is because their leaders failed to base their national policy of the countries on the cultural values of Africans. They ignored the traditional or indigenous African way of life as backward and primitive, and preferred to copy foreign ideology. The so called 'modern' policy they try to impose on Africans is constantly clashing with the traditional values, causing spills, disruption and defective political and economic systems that has little or no relationship to Africans own indigenous system. Neglecting their own cultural heritage they failed to craft solutions based on what we have in our own backyard, and instead went abroad and copied all sorts of ideology (Socialism, Liberalism) for transplantation in Africa; and it did not work. Failure to return Africa to its roots and to establish a system based on its culture has greatly devastated the continent.

Indigenous African culture had free enterprise, participatory forms of democracy, customary law and accountability with an astonishing degree of functionality. African societies governed themselves in a very open and democratic system before the Europeans arrived. Their self-government structure had all necessary units like a chief, inner circle of confidants that advised the chief, a council of elders that solved conflicts, and a village assembly. The chief never imposed his decision on the council or the people, instead he assessed all ideas of the council and if unanimity was not reached on any issue he called a village assembly, thus making the people the final authority to decide on disputed issues.

Freedom of expression was an important element of village assembly.

The ancient empires or kingdoms were also a kind of confederation with a loose political association which gave the states a significant authority to run their own affairs and had a complex system of checks and balances. Africa's indigenous system was open, inclusive and participatory democracy. It is far better than the modern parliamentary system; no one was excluded in the decision making process. The other difference was the village assembly conducted its meetings under a big tree while modern parliament has an assembly building.

The chief in pre-colonial Africa usually encouraged alternative viewpoint or even dissent, and those who presented a different opinion did so without fear of arrest. The chiefs acted as guardian of their people because they strongly believed that they will get the blessing of their ancestral spirits by doing so. Even the chief's yelling at his people was considered as a violation of the code of conduct of the tribe. There were checks and balances such as the council of elders or the village assembly could advise the chief to administer properly or else he will be considered as insane and replaced or the people will abandon him. Thus, in ancient African states, accommodation, tolerance, autonomy, and peaceful co-existence was the norm to create harmony between different ethnic societies that came together under one kingdom.

The so called modern African leaders failed to establish a system based on indigenous African culture and persuade to remove or change some cultural obstacles to development. Professor Teshale laments how Ethiopian intellectuals ignored the countries' cultural heritage and jumped from one foreign ideology to another in vain.

"It is perplexing how a country like Ethiopia with its millennia-long history produced an intellectual class which finds nothing worth taking from her past but instead jumps from one Western episteme to another. It is as if Ethiopia in all its long history has produced nothing worth incorporating in the search for her modernity. The process of Eurocentric cultural deracination is so deep, so profound, and so formidable to make both Marxists and liberals agree: Ethiopia's salvation comes from without not from within. Ethiopia has become a TABULA RASA with nothing of her own to contribute to her renewal. As a blind beggar, she pleads with passersby to help her find her way. It is this aspect of Euro centrism that makes one shiver with anger and bewilderment. Where is our freedom if we are not going to stand on our two legs, but rather on someone else instead?" (Teshale, Modernity, Euro centrism, and radical politics in Ethiopia 1961-1991, P-368)

A country's economy is inextricably connected to the outlook, culture and life style of the people. Harvard University professor Samuel Huntington in the book "Culture Matters" which he co-edited with Lawrence Harrison explains to what extent cultural factors shape economic and cultural development, and how can cultural obstacles to development be changed or removed so as to facilitate progress. Another intellectual Daniel Patrick Mayniham has stated two truths. *"The central conservative truth is that it is culture, not politics that determines the success of a society. The central liberal truth is that politics can change a culture and save it from itself"*.

"The role of cultural values and attitudes as obstacles to or facilitators of progress has been largely ignored by governments and aid agencies. Integrating value and attitude change into development policies, planning and programming is, I believe, a promising way to assure that, in the next fifty years the world does not relive the poverty and injustice that most poor

350

countries, and under-achieving ethnic groups, have been mired in during the past half century". (Harrison, P-XXXIV)

Traditional explanations for the poverty and lack of democracy in Africa, was Colonialism, Imperialism etc. These explanations are no longer adequate even though the long term effects of these, is still felt. Increasingly many scholars are concluding that Africa's poverty lies in its cultural values and public policy that is not based on the people's culture. American journalist and author David Lamb in his book 'The Africans' describes what Africa needs to speed up progress.

"What Africa needs to develop is an African political system, imported from neither East nor West that combines elements of capitalism and socialism, both of which are inherent to the African character. It should include two concepts that Africans today mistakenly view as contradictory – economic incentive and social justice". (Lamb, P-58)

The political system that African elites established after independence is alien to the people's indigenous systems. Instead of figuring out a political system that has close resemblance to Africa's social democratic system, they simply continued with the colonial structure and kept on jumping from one foreign ideology to another. They should have dismantled the colonial authoritarian structure and returned Africa to its roots; administering by consensus. But, instead the new leaders strengthened the colonial apparatus and became even more dictatorial.

They began to introduce state of emergency and other draconian bills to silence opposition. They wanted to be seen as a messiah or a redeemer like Emperor Haile Selassie of Ethiopia, and any criticism was considered unpatriotic. They outlawed opposition parties; banned private media and arrested the editors. They declared that independent media and multi-party democracy is *"a luxury Africa can't afford"*. They failed either to adopt Western style democracy or to return Africa to its indigenous system. After independence, elections were held in most African countries which served only to confirm the incumbent leader and the ruling party in power. The so called modern African leaders used certain African social problems as a cover up to advance their own selfish political ambitions and established personal rule. They acted as if Africa has no culture, no history, and no indigenous institutions. They established a standing army including body guard divisions whose main responsibility is to protect those in power. Africa had only a militia unit before colonialism that is called upon to protect the country only at times of war. The result was economic decline; large segments of the middle class were impoverished and because of falling living standards migration of skilled professionals away from their motherland to Europe and America increased.

When Japan embraced the currents of modernity, it based the system on its people's culture and tradition and adopted the capitalist system while at the same time retaining its Japanese characters. Japan kept its culture and values and became modernized. They copied the ideas how the west industrialized, but rejected the western habits that were not helpful. The same way African countries need to learn from the developed world, but they do not have to abandon their culture and traditions in the process. The United States Secretary of State Henry Kissinger remarked the following about Japan.

"The amazing thing is that the Japanese respect for the past and sense of cultural uniqueness, have not produced stagnation. Other societies have paid for the commitment to tradition by growing irrelevance to the currents of modernity. Japan turned its feudal past into an asset by permeating its entire society with such a sense of shared respect that its internal

differences could never mar the essential unity with which it faced foreigners. ...Japan lost no face in adopting the methods of other societies; it could afford to adopt almost any system and still retain its Japanese character, which depend neither on forms of government nor on methods of economics but on a complicated, imbued, shared set of social relationships. Far from being an obstacle to progress, tradition in Japan provided the emotional security and indeed the impetus to try the novel".
(Henry Kissinger)

The crisis created in Ethiopia by the socialist-oriented military Derg and TPLF policies in defying tradition, culture, religion and morality is immense. Besides imposing foreign ideology, ethnic politics, ethics crisis, political corruption, insider trading, racial bigotry, selfishness, greed, loss of moral judgment, class struggle and state terrorism has forced out traditional and sacred Ethiopian values to fall from grace. Morality depends on religion, but, Derg and TPLF being socialist-oriented despised this moral vision of an extremely religious and traditional society to profound national embarrassment. The national self-image "Ethiopia stretches its hands unto God" morality cannot be maintained without religion in our deeply traditional society. The origin of morality and its justification being religion, these two pro-communist governments considered religion as opium, defying God and tried to kill moral truths. The fundamental shape of the Ethiopian experience and its traditional values cannot be understood without reference to the Judeo-Christian and Islam traditions which the country embraced for over a millennium. Even though some argue that we can take the moral truths that religion has given us (respect, tolerance, kindness, compassion, honesty, and fairness) and leave the religion behind, it is difficult to do so in a deeply religious and traditional society like ours. For such a society there cannot be binding moral rules without a supreme omnipotent being that can compel our obedience.

In our schools and colleges moral learning and character training should become the common sense of the time. This will help us to get back the new generation that has been confused by government materialistic and anti-religion propaganda, to be in line with morality. Having observed first-hand the most confusing decades of our society, I have witnessed that something has gone tragically wrong with the way of thinking and behaving of the new generation in recent decades, falling away from traditional Ethiopian values of; love for the country, respect for our common gallant history, social obligation (yulugneta), respect for others, honesty, integrity, thoughtfulness, et cetera.

The failure of our governments and institutions to educate and transmit the values contained in our cultural and religious heritage to the new generation has created various social ills costing us dearly. We need to respect and rejuvenate traditional Ethiopian values in our schools and colleges, training character as a remedy for the numerous public ills that assail us. By that I mean national identity (*Ethiopiyawinet/Africawinet)*, collective aspirations, communal virtues, decency, moral virtues, justice, political virtues, responsibility, intellectual virtues, courage, helpfulness, integrity, truthfulness etc. Along with these we need to fix our school curriculum and education system which is at present deeply flawed, in order to succeed nationally and to be able to compete globally. Leadership is about falling in love with the country and the people you want to serve; and the people falling in love with the person they vote for leadership.

Chapter Seven

Ethiopian Diaspora in USA

"Far better it is to dare mighty things, to win glorious triumphs, even though checkered by failure, than to take rank with those poor spirits who neither enjoy much nor suffer much, because they live in the gray twilight that knows neither victory nor defeat".

"Justice consists not in being neutral between right and wrong, but in finding out the right and upholding it wherever found, against the wrong".

(President Theodore Roosevelt)

'We must not hope to be mowers,
And to gather the ripe gold ears,
Unless we have first been sowers,
And watered the furrows with tears.
...It is not just we take it,
This mystical world of ours,
Life's field will yield as we make it,
A harvest of thorns or of flowers'.
(Johann Goethe)

Coming to America: Myths and Realities

How did we get here?

The dream of coming to America has been around for a very long time. In fact, since the first arrival of European settlers this has been more or less a continued phenomenon. Mainly this immigration was reinforced by a combination of economic inopportunity as well as political or religious persecution in the

355

home country. Although the initial arrivals seem to be motivated by venture of treasure hunting, financed by royalty, soon this gave way to the inflow of landless European peasants looking for livelihood and economic freedom denied to them for various reasons, mainly having to do with oppressive forms of governance. This may not hold true for all early settlers but it is the case for the majority. Thus we can look at examples all throughout the colonies to find evidence of this trend. The trend of people coming over from the old world, which provided them little economically, politically, and religiously is undeniable.

It is important to realize, that the social fabric of incoming settlers was not all of the downtrodden. There was also a small minority who held much power by way of landownership and laborers both slaves and indentured ones. This group would later be in power as the days of independence beckoned. The fate of many African slaves was even worse; though many efforts would later be made to mitigate this, the effect is still present today. In very general terms, for introductory purposes, this is the history of America briefly after the arrival of the first European settlers.

In our case we will focus on the issue of immigration to America, specifically as it pertains to people of Ethiopian descent in recent times. This introduction is meant to foster, in the reader the idea that the United States has always been a nation of immigrants. Although the details might differ, the underlying circumstances that force these people make the difficult choice of leaving their home countries are very much in line. They are primarily the search of economic, political, and religious freedoms, though the order of priority has differed in this list, given the fluctuation of history.

As for Ethiopians and their immigration to the United States, we can say this is a very recent phenomenon, bearing fringe isolated cases of early arrivals. For all practical purposes it is safe to state serious prospects for the immigration of Ethiopians to the United States began in the heydays of Emperor Haile Selassie. Among the earliest to arrive were those sent for purposes of higher education. This group, besides being very small, had no intention of a permanent stay, as a result most returned to Ethiopia where privileged positions awaited them. Their modern education, rarely found in a backward country was highly needed. However, it is obviously necessary to separate this group from the ones that followed subsequently. The older generation came looking for an education to take back home, where their status and prestige afforded them many privileges denied to their compatriots for various reasons. Many were also idealists who genuinely wanted to help build a strong and modern Ethiopia. The relative political peace and security, although under a monarchy, afforded them enough space to move back to Ethiopia.

Soon this relatively peaceful kingdom came to a predictable fate that had awaited it for long periods under the surface. For reasons having to do with bad governance and lack of genuine democracy, the inevitable revolution swept the old guard away. To make matters short the emperor was deposed and subsequently executed along with many of his confidants. Leaving the details for historians of higher caliber, this we can safely state was the genesis of the Ethiopian turmoil and the beginning of mass exodus. The economic, political, and social instability had become too much to bear that for many a life abroad was a path to be seriously contemplated.

Exodus to the United States was initially limited and was at most a trickle. As the repressiveness of the government increased, more and more Ethiopians sought refuge in neighboring countries before making their long and arduous journey to the more free western countries. The number of people that left Ethiopia is hard to estimate in this time because the exodus was mainly in secret and if reported it was rarely honestly. To add to this there is purposeful cover up perpetrated by the government. The egregious crimes of the military dictatorship were unlike what Ethiopians have known in the past. Given the country's historical rulers and the way they operated, communism coupled with military rule was a brutal awakening. It shocked the society to the core with effects still reverberating today.

The heavily traditional and religious society wasn't ready for this new sweeping changes brought forth by force. The people's grievances from the previous monarchy were never answered genuinely either. To add to this the now too familiar famine and drought was always on the brink. Omitting details to historians we can conclude in general, political repression playing part in in economic and social depravity was the beginning of Ethiopian mass exodus. In this regard the Ethiopian immigrants are very much similar to past and present immigrants to the United States. Simply put they came here for a better life. Through long and difficult journeys, sometimes via different countries taking different modes of transportation, like others before them from different nations.

Exodus from their ancestral land has become a far more familiar phenomenon for many Ethiopians. This trend has not subsided for obvious reasons, very similar as to the ones discussed. There are still those who make the tough and arduous journey in search of a better life abroad. Some attempt this trek in even more difficult circumstances still today. It is almost cliché to hear about people walking on foot to Kenya or Sudan, or crossing along the Gulf of Aden to the Arabian peninsula, often times with their kin from neighboring countries, packed in small vessels. There is no denying the fact that the search for economic opportunity is the driving force behind this exodus in our current times. The rising prices of goods and lack of sustaining income has once again left Ethiopians with no other choice. Real wages continually decrease while prices continually increase, especially for essential staple foods. Lack of quality education and massive unemployment, unfortunately tied to party affiliation will undoubtedly lead many to seek a better life abroad.

Wherever there is massive economic disparity, political repression is never too far away. The only way to sustain the hungry is to give them food or force them to accept it. This drift towards an unsustainable growth will continue and will more than likely cause many more to leave their homes and families in search of a better life abroad. Coupled with the ever growing population, often times resulting from bad education, this is a disastrous mix that has been going on for almost half a century. The state of turmoil, muted at times and more pronounced at other times continues. The search for better life abroad will undoubtedly follow this trend. This will mean more coming over to live in places such as the United States and Western Europe, not to mention the many who will make strides in the worst conditions of the Middle East and South Africa, just to mention a few.

Given the multitude of Ethiopians that began to arrive in the United States in the late 20th century, it is necessary to assume there were many differing views and imagination of what America would be like. Perhaps the best way to discern this is to look back at the time before their arrival; the views that were held by many and where these ideas came from. Early on before the minimal advent of media in Ethiopia, many people might have conjured up an image of the United States based on views they held about Europe. These went along the lines of viewing the country as being modern, technologically advanced, as well as being a strong nation state. Then of course, as relatives of émigrés began to relay information back to their home country, this began generate a more discernible image. For the most part this is how the American image was portrayed and transmitted. This limited picture was soon changed with the advent of popular American media that was beginning to take hold on Ethiopian society.

As time went on and world events began to shift once more, as in the fall of Soviet Union and Communism, the intensity with which Ethiopian people became consumers of American popular media increased. This process conjured up a whole new phase of cultural information flow. This flow was more or less a one way road. Entertainment material based on American culture was the main avenue by which Ethiopians became aware of America. In particular this has an overwhelming effect on younger people. The message being beamed constituted an image in their minds that what is America must be cool. In line with the younger folks, many of the older generation also took to this view in most instances. Many people, especially teenaged individuals grew up wanting to be American movie characters. They were mesmerized by pop stars and their life style. They began to dress and act like these people who they saw in the movies. This especially holds true for many living in urban areas. Tailored to these entertainment materials are also the reinforcing images held about American sophistication in technology and science. This highly entertaining material, presented in films, television, and print has gone a long way in shaping the image of America in Ethiopia, as well as many parts of the developing world.

The glorification of America, for all practical purposes, was the image conjured up in young people as well as older people in Ethiopia. As we have stated, this notion also holds true for many parts of the world. Having said this, it is important to admit the truth behind these images. Yes, the United States has made perhaps the greatest advancement in science and technology during the last century. The diversity in its culture and views are all to be admired. The shining cities and skyscrapers are real too. Nonetheless that does not entirely hold true for the whole American experience. In this way, many Ethiopians have a slight misconception about America, based on the information that was available to them. Not everything in America is Hollywood. Everyone doesn't look like they came off the set of Usher's latest music video either. For the sake of entertainment and cultural insight this is all great. Having a tangible image of America though, is perhaps a more useful characteristic for new immigrants. Absence of the accurate picture may lead to cultural shock or even worst disappointment, though this latter part is rarely the case for Ethiopian immigrants. The illusiveness of the real America is still evident today.

This lack of accurate information can lead new arrivals to disregard certain cultural sensitivities and subtleties. For instance, they might be insulted or insult others in their day-to-day affairs because they were not equipped with the right information at first. This could also cause people to be unhappy at their work place. Children and young adults may become disoriented and clash with parents and their values. There are many cases in which parents are unable to guide their children in this new environment for lack of information. Children therefore have to take more responsibility, while at the same time being subordinate to the parent due to Ethiopian cultural norms.

This may seem obvious in Ethiopia but balancing this issue in a culturally different society where children and parents continually being pulled apart are difficult. Another example related to the family unit is balancing work and family in this new environment. Many times parents are busy; this is especially true to those engaged in several jobs. In such cases overseeing children can be difficult and most new comer Ethiopians don't anticipate this for lack of information. They are unsure about how to accomplish this task. These are just a few examples of why accurate information is imperative. Anticipating the new life, its challenges and rewards alike will go a long way to easing ones transition to the new world.

Life is a balancing act. Therefore many of the cultural differences can be balanced to make life easier for new émigrés. If we are willing there is nothing that cannot be overcome. In fact that is exactly what many Ethiopians in the Diaspora all over the world have come to understand. Whether it is young children entering school in a foreign land, or adults trying to make ends meet, one of the keys to success is having a balanced life. The ability to function as a normal citizen of the new culture is important. This means speaking proper English as well as understanding the culture of the United States. Not faltering to false misconceptions we might have. Realizing the streets are not paved with gold, but with the right motivation and knowledge one can still make tremendous strides, yet to be guaranteed for all Ethiopians at home. Dreams can be turned to reality, as many can testify. Also dreams have turned into nightmares as some can also testify. In this way, America is no different from other places. For those with an appetite for knowledge and hard work, the sky is the limit, and the rewards are far greater than what we Ethiopians have known at home. This is why many have made great sacrifices to get here and continue to do so.

One of the greatest achievements of the United States immigration policy is the ability of the system to allow new immigrants equal protection under the law. Unlike what we see in other nations, who also have large immigrant populations; the United States is by far the only one that allows the most conducive environment for immigrants to succeed. This is partly a result of the history of the country, Immigration is nothing new here. Thus, you feel a sense of belongingness and achievement.

362

This undeniable fact is displayed in many success stories of the land for many first timers. This factor has also benefitted the domestic populations. New ideas are constantly infused into the society, making it a place of tremendous prosperity and insight. This freedom and fluidity has allowed it to recover quickly from crisis. It has also allowed it to have remarkable appeal to the world at large. Though it has flaws, it is an adaptable less rigid system, advantageous in many ways, able to conform to the needs of the many, aptly demonstrated by the election of President Barack Obama. This unlikely hero of African origin is perhaps the best example of the greatest of the American system; perhaps, an important lesson for many Ethiopian immigrants, as they consider their children's prospects, at home and abroad.

Hopes, Prospects and Anomalies:

The Ethiopian Diaspora's future is by no means bleak. On the contrary they are bright and promising. Despite the many shortcomings by a yet not so settled community, the future should hold many new burgeoning opportunities. The recent state of confusion on the role of the Diaspora can be equated with the infantile nature of this Diaspora at the current juncture. As we progress in time the life of the community should find its own solid ground on which to stand. Realizing this goal will necessarily mean understanding certain truths about the new society as well as the history of where we come from. Without history as a guiding compass, it is near impossible to succeed as a group in our new homes. For this reason, being cognizant of our historical journey as well as culture is an important tool to guide us to a brighter future.

History is our global positioning system. We must appreciate this fact; while simultaneously nurturing our understanding of the culture and language of the new society. Becoming the best of both worlds is very much possible, as aptly demonstrated by many immigrant communities. Life in the Diaspora presents us with an opportunity to experience a variety of circumstances. We must use and capitalize on these opportunities without hindering our historical and cultural dignity. This is especially true for those of us living in a democratic society such as the United States of America. Assimilation without compromising our identity should be the mantra of our community.

The hope is, as our community extends its stay beyond its historical borders, it will smarten up and take heed of the past as well as what the future holds. This process comes naturally to any group of people living in a tolerant democratic system, such as the United States. Nevertheless there are certain required elementary pressures we must apply to ourselves to achieve this goal. The first of this list is digesting and coming to terms with the new circumstance we find ourselves in. Thousands of miles away from the place we originally called home, the prospect of permanently repatriating in the near future is a dim light for most of us. There might be times when we visit our kin or take a vacation, but the chances of a wholesale repatriation on a large scale is very unlikely in the near future. Even for those hard-core homesick among us, returning permanently will be a difficult choice, undertaken by very few. Realties on the ground in Ethiopia dictate this fact.

The life style differences and the comforts offered to the lowest of wage earners in America, relatively speaking, make it difficult for most to abandon this and find something more suitable back in Ethiopia. As far as the evidence is concerned this trend will continue. To add to this many of us were yanked from our somewhat mundane circumstances, isolated from the world, and placed square in the heart of globalization. Given this fact assimilation is a gift we can ill-afford to miss. This is our new home for the foreseeable future. In fact we see more of our kin coming to join it. In this circumstance assimilation becomes necessary and beneficial. It can also be done in a manner that upholds our original identity and dignity. We should not remain an isolated fringe group despite our contrastingly low numbers. The benefits that come with assimilation, specifically in a place like the United States are very broad. They range from quality education, career, business opportunity, and a general betterment artistically and intellectually. All these things were very difficult to attain back home for a variety of reasons.

We Ethiopians have a tendency to become dogmatic in trying to achieve certain things. For the most part this cultural trait has been detrimental to our development historically speaking. We need to be pragmatic about the issues of assimilation therefore. A certain level of realism will not hurt our position either. The realities of assimilating to a society are a complicated undertaking. It means different things to different people. Comprehending all the nuances and subtleties of a new culture can be a daunting task; one that can take a life time to achieve.

There are for instance many among us who choose to live in the past to avoid this conflict; people who have been here decades without ever really assimilating. Always in a state of nostalgia about a home they had left beyond a world of oceans. Those of us who are of this group are always reminiscing about past mishaps that continue to anguish us. We know and like our new home but our hearts are not here. This is mostly true for many older émigrés, and to some extent we find in it those that came here when they were in their teens as well.

This group in general tries to seclude itself in its own protective social shell; rarely, if at all, interacting with the larger American society. The diaspora community is getting larger, and this trend is increasingly becoming possible. Folding inwards however is never a solution at all. It only serves as a temporary solution to shelter our fears and anxieties. More than likely this trend will be detrimental as well. Avoiding this trajectory is essential to becoming a well transitioned community to American life. Though the process of assimilation is painful and mentally confusing, it is necessary.

While assimilating is paramount and inevitable we must not let this turn into dogma. There is a lot worth saving in our cultures, languages, religions, history, and exodus. We can take note of the many episodes in our recent history where we tried to take apparent Eurocentric views and tried to implement them wholesale to our situation. We should by now be aware that this is the wrong pill to take. Marxism is a good example of this. The Ethiopian student movements of the 1960's and 70's tried in vain to implement, wholesale, the idea of Marxism to the Ethiopian situation. Assimilating of our community in the United States should not take the seemingly immovable and rigid approach as the Marxists student movement did. It should not just assimilate! Assimilate! Throwing away the past? It is possible to be the best of both worlds; let us not limit ourselves.

Yes, we need to be part of the new society, but denigrating our roots to achieve this goal is akin to loathing ourselves and what it means to be us. Besides, without a historical and cultural compass to guide us, not only do we hurt ourselves but become a burden to the new society in the long run. In addition there is a lot we can also contribute to the new society, even though we are a small bunch. Size is no issue to a sober minded people. To be prosperous and contribute positively to our new environment we must take this into account as well. Information and culture flow both ways as they should.

Perhaps the best opportunity to take advantage of in the new world is the high quality of education provided. To those who seek this as their goal, this is the best place to be. It has been proven above and beyond, throughout history, without any doubt, the most important factor to improving ones lot as an individual and as a community is to be educated. One of the reasons why we find ourselves in the current state of underdevelopment is lack of quality education. Given this fact, one should be expected to jump at the opportunity. Our own history of lack there should prompt us to do so. Learning is not attained by chance, but by hard work; nobody gets to the top without hard work. Only by learning can one increase marketability and confidence in life, and be a fit company for oneself. We could encounter failure, but we should not be defeated; instead, we should dare to take full responsibility and bounce back with a clear vision to follow our passion and succeed in life.

It is not secret that the better educated end up doing better in life overall. Statistic after statistic shows this to be true. It is one of the most heavily researched topics of our time. "A mind is a terrible thing to waste", that's true, and this is one of the things our community should desperately attempt to avoid. It is beneficial for us and our children, no one with a reasonable mind could deny this. What we need are ways of honoring the young members of our community who are in school and succeeding. Recognizing their efforts should be one of the ways to set a precedence of what our goals are.

There is no lackluster when it comes to Ethiopian American parents enticing their children to attend this or that university or in trying to influence them to concentrate on this field or that field. To be honest this can be a bit exhausting for the child as well. Ask any freshman diaspora and they will tell you what that is like. Still this is not to say that parents should not be actively involved in their children's education, nor their own for that matter. There are too many parents incessantly pushing their child to be a doctor or an engineer. There are also many more that don't care to even ask their kids about their school. Our community could perhaps do better without these two rigid extreme behaviors. Young people have minds of their own, though parents should share their relative experience with them, this should not be substituted by outright dictators on their future. Although it is understandable that parents should try to guide their child out of certain pitfalls, young people must be free enough to try things by their own and even make mistakes and learn from them as well.

The golden opportunity for quality education being of paramount importance, where does this leave those of us too worked up to take advantage of this. Well, luckily, there is no shortage of things to do to improve oneself. What is required is effort and dedication, there are many who have found financial success with minimal education as well; by doing business or by marketing their talents and their inventiveness. There is no better place for such minded people than the United States, as the history of this great country attests to this fact. We can pick generations of Americans from all backgrounds that have followed this path and found success. There is no shortage of Ethiopian immigrants in this bucket either; whether it is small business owners, who run restaurants and night clubs or innovative individuals, such as the inventors, artists and novelists are a few bright stars we can think of too. Minor but impressive given the size of the community; these hard working bunch has shown how it's done; it would be nice if more of us gave more attention. Coupled with academic accomplishment this spirit of entrepreneurship can be a driving force not only for our community but also the wider society in general. Undoubtedly, this would also have a positive impact on our ancestral home country. We should, as individuals and collectively, try to enhance and expand on these achievements.

"Press on. Nothing can take the place of persistence. Talent will not; the world is full of unsuccessful people with talent. Genius will not; unrewarded genius is almost a proverb. Education alone will not; the world is full of educated derelicts. Persistence and determination alone are omnipotent." (Calvin Coolidge)

No doubt many of the things mentioned are a bit too commonsensical; and they should be as well. It makes sense; however actually creating a thriving community will require us to be conscientious. We must raise our understanding of ourselves as individuals, a community, and as part of a much bigger society. With this awareness the next step should be to find a place in the setting for ourselves. Achieving this is by no means a simple task; it requires us to establish a medium for communication amongst ourselves. Fortunately with the modern technology there is no shortage of space in this platform. Social networking websites are a good example of this phenomenon. One can imagine the number of people on Facebook from the Ethiopian diaspora, and the limitless opportunities this medium offers for creatively linking with ourselves and others around the world. The medium is there and readily available for use in building bridges within our community and extending beyond.

What we need is to develop the will that is required. Erecting a media where we can democratically talk about issues faced by our community is another among the shortages we face. Our air waves are currently in use for political and personal score settling. This unconstructive trait we have carried with us should be dismembered in the new land, offering a fresh perspective. Again a pinch of effort is all that is required. Minimally speaking we should not allow this bad residue to leave its mark on our children; so they may not be tainted with blood from wounds we have inflicted on one another. Finger pointing is collective damnation; we can do much better.

Building consciousness of oneself therefore requires us to communicate with one another. For this we need gathering places, such as community centers, places of worship, or theatres. Tangible places to see each other face to face and teach and learn from one another. Places brewing with ideas and insight as well as culture. Assessing the Ethiopian American scene in different parts of this great country, there are no shortages of such locations. Perhaps the only disconcerting aspect being their current function; for instance we have witnessed the explosion of Ethiopian Orthodox Churches, with very little in the way of schools to supplant them. It is probably safe to assume mosques in our community follow similar trends.

Seemingly we are inherently quick at our feet to celebrate certain religious or national holidays, all attire in hand, flags waving. Yet our enthusiasm is less evident for more valuable things such as teaching our children our language, or languages to be exact. As if we are ashamed of ourselves we deny our children to take a part of us. May be we are afraid they will not learn English properly enough. This is unfounded claim as it has been proven that children can be competent in two or more languages. Young folks will surely damn us for this, if they haven't already; for not teaching them their ancestral language, depriving them their identity, and exposing them to a bigger problem; identity crisis. For all the parades and dancing we display with such youthfulness and vigor, unless we cap it off with sober actions, such as rooting the basics of language in our children, then all that festivity today is ephemeral at best. Being conscious of ourselves and the world we live in is paramount if we are to avoid such myopia. The first form of self-consciousness for any people, as linguists can testify, is, knowing one's language.

Mapping out what we want from our new lives in the new world is a starter. As alluded earlier, knowing ones

370

individual and collective history will save us from confusing ourselves. As many of us can testify, the new world does not come on a silver platter; we have to adapt to it. It is not going to conform to our comforts, tastes or distastes. When it comes to assimilation, there is no magic wand; it is a long and arduous journey. This road has been travelled by many people of different backgrounds throughout the history of the United States. As one of the latest extensions of that history, we have the fortune of learning from those that attempted this journey. If we are clever we would choose to assimilate without losing our dignity and identity; meaning while upholding our language, culture and history; something we must pass on to our children.

Sometimes we feel a break from the past is the ultimate salvation. Though a dream for a fresh start is what brought us here in the first place, we are always going to remain haunted by the past. We are all victims of our parent's generation; the past must not be thrown out. Avoiding the past doesn't prohibit it from depositing its residue on posterity.

Ethiopia is an ancient country with its traditions and culture stretching back more than three thousand years. We have many good things we can offer to our children and to the American civilization. Even at this early stage our contributions to American society are great and by and large they have been very positive. When considering the relative infancy of the Ethiopian American life span, these achievements should make us proud. The room for improvement, as always, is there. The more we discuss them openly the easier it will be to find solutions. This book will hopefully be one small step in the right direction to inspire those with more grasp on things. I believe this is the only way whereby incrementally we can correct the past mistakes and make whole generation.

The Dynamics of Migration

Ethiopia is pressed by population growth. The labor force is so big, but no jobs available for the great majority. Rapid urbanization and exodus to big cities is conjoint. Agricultural productivity is declining, wide spread unemployment and poverty is common. Political instability and ethno-religious conflict is high. The economies of the country being very fragile to absorb all these problems, it is weighed down by all these factors.

Cross border migration of nomads and seasonal workers is common in the outlaying lowlands. Ethiopia is experiencing challenges related to the migration of professional and skilled workers, particularly skilled health professionals, engineers, technicians, teachers, journalists, etc. who could have been the engine of development. Human trafficking to the Middle East countries has become a big business. Because of poverty, tyrannical unstable politics and ethnic conflict, most Ethiopians could not achieve basic needs like food, security, peace and sustainable development.

Ethiopian youth who are socially and economically dependent on their parents for too long, turn to the streets or prefer to migrate to neighboring countries or to Europe and America. Tens of thousands of young people become involved in daredevil ventures to the Middle East and the Western world. In the book entitled "International Migration" edited by Aderanti Adepoju an expert explains the migration of African professionals.

"About 2300 university graduates and 50,000 executives leave sub-Saharan Africa annually; about 40,000 of them with PHD now live outside Africa. For Nigerians and Zambians

highly skilled professionals constitute about half or more of
expatriates living in organization for economic cooperation and
development (OECD) countries. Twenty percent of the nationals
of Benin, Tanzania, Zimbabwe, Cameroon, Lesotho, Malawi and
South Africa in the Diaspora are highly-skilled professionals.

"Rich countries have contributed to the brain drain
crisis by creating a fatal flow of health professionals from the
region. More Ethiopian doctors are practicing in Chicago than
in Ethiopia; over half of Malawian nurses and doctors have
migrated and more Malawian doctors practice in Manchester,
U.K. than in Malawi; and 550 of the 600 Zambian doctors
trained in medical schools over the last decade have emigrated.
If statistics is to be trusted Ghana has lost 50 percent of its
doctors to Canada, Britain and the USA. Three quarters or more
of Zimbabwe's doctors have left the country since the early
1990's and half of its social health workers have relocated
abroad since 2001. In 2005 more than 16,000 nurses and about
12,500 doctors from the region were registered to work in
Britain (UK NMC 2005); a very similar scenario holds for the
education sector." (Adepoju, P-13)

The large exile of skilled professionals is hurting Africa
so much by depriving it to train the new generation of doctors
and to undertake research for development of the respective
countries. One driving force is the income and payment
differences they receive in their countries and abroad. A doctor
in Ethiopia earns about $70 dollars a month while the one with
similar qualification in USA gets $3000 dollars on an average.

Human Trafficking

The restrictions of Western countries to give visas to Africans have encouraged human trafficking. When the chances of legal entry to the rich countries become strict, human trafficking agents prop up and exploit would-be migrants by charging them so much money often in foreign currency. Some have to transit through several countries and cities, (as you can understand from the story of migrants in the next chapter), paying for agents at every entry point.

Trafficking women and children for cheap labor and prostitution is also becoming common in Africa. Many women from east Africa especially Ethiopia are taken to the Middle East and Europe to take the job of babysitting and waiting maid. Some are taken to Europe for commercial sex and pornography. Unemployment, broken homes and poverty has exposed Ethiopian women to traffickers. These agents promise good jobs and better life; but, most of the time these promises are false and the migrants find out too late.

In many cases the passports of these migrants remain in the hands of the traffickers or their employers and these victims are stranded and remain helpless in the hands of ruthless and bogus agents. Many end up being baby sitters or cooks and they are often exposed to sexual exploitation. Sometimes jealous wives beat or even kill these migrants at will. Most African governments don't follow up, keep track or data or not seem to care for their citizens who migrated hoping for a better life. Migrants often end up in the worst situation and there is no judicial framework to prosecute and punish trafficking crimes.

In the new millennia, Yemen, north east Sudan and Sinai Peninsula have become the axis of evil traffickers. These traffickers kidnap most of their victims from Shagarab refugee camps in north east Sudan and from Yemen by promising them good jobs and sell them to Sinai Peninsula criminals where they are abused and tortured. Traffickers torture their victims and relay their agony to family members or Diaspora groups to facilitate payment of ransom. Even if the ransom is paid the victims are transferred to other traffickers who repeat the process. If the ransom is not paid the victims are killed while their saleable organs (kidney, liver etc.) are extracted. Last year The New York Times interviewed some of the Eritrean refugees who managed to escape from their captors, and the newspaper estimated that about 7000 refugees have been abused this way in the past four years. Most of these refugees are originally from Eritrea, Ethiopia and Somalia.

South Africa has become both a recipient and sender of immigrants from sub-Sahara Africa and also a transit for them to cross the ocean to Europe and America. After the fall of apartheid and the establishment of majority rule, South Africa attracted many Africans and a new wave of immigrants from Zimbabwe, Lesotho, Mozambique, Zambia, Ethiopia and West Africa followed. Most of these are entering without paper documentation and working as street vendors or small traders. Even if they had visas to enter the country, most of them over stay their legal residency and at times some are deported by the South African government only to reenter illegally with the help of traffickers who know the clandestine routes.

Rich countries in Europe and America, like immigrant workers to do the dirty and dangerous jobs that their citizens don't like to do; like cleaning, trash collecting, mining, cotton picking, landscaping, construction etc. and they also need highly-skilled professionals like doctors, nurses and engineers who are in short supply. In periods of economic recession the nationals think that the immigrants took their jobs and politicians also use them as scapegoats to fan public discontent and get peoples vote. Migrants are blamed for the economic crisis and often expelled, beaten and even killed by locals as a scapegoat of a political problem. Because of these, all countries, (the origin, the transit or destination countries) are affected by international migration; which makes it difficult to come with a coherent migration policy.

Brain Drain / Brain Circulation

Recently skilled professionals obliged to leave their African homeland due to economic uncertainties have started heading to southern hemisphere countries like South Africa, India, China even Botswana and Taiwan instead of Europe and North America or the Middle East. These trends create a sort of brain circulation in Africa itself, and today one fourth of the teachers in Rwanda and Burundi are from the Democratic Republic of Congo. Many medical doctors who work in South Africa are from neighboring Zimbabwe, Congo and Cuba.

The changing trend of migration to the southern hemisphere countries we mentioned above is because of political stability, economic growth and good governance etc. in the destination countries. African governments should address abuse of human rights, job insecurity and the like to control brain drain. Particularly labor mobility within and between the countries of southern Africa can help for a sustained growth of the economy of the region. But, to facilitate these movement countries need to modify their laws and agree on some kind of sub-regional treaties.

African countries including Ethiopia need to place incentives to attract back their nationals in Diaspora and use their skills and money for the development of their country of origin. To encourage home coming African countries will have to offer a range of practical help like tax-free business services, expatriate affairs, Diaspora coordinating office, investment opportunities, residence permit, including dual citizenship. In the new globalized world, brain drain is changing to brain circulation while people in the Diaspora get the opportunity to return and help develop their country of origin. Some skilled Africans in the Diaspora are starting to shuttle and operate between the two countries simultaneously and are showing encouraging results. These days many Chinese, Indians and Brazilians in the Diaspora are returning to their countries of origin and assisting the development. Some operate between the two countries (the homeland and the motherland). Many Africans including some Ethiopians in the Diaspora are joining this effort by investing in real estate market and opening some kind of business that is assisting the growth in the motherland.

What experts call the new Argonauts – foreign born technically skilled entrepreneurs who travel back and forth between the West and their countries of origin are trying to create wealth in distant lands by launching companies in their motherland using the skills and the money they have acquired in developed countries. Their story illuminates profound transformations in the global economy. Economic geographer Anna Lee Saxenian has explained this fact in her research paper of 2010.

"...Scholars, policy makers and business leaders will benefit from these people first hand research into the investors and entrepreneurs who return home to start new companies while remaining tied to powerful economic and professional communities in the United States".

Economic geographers have followed these transformations exploring one of its paradoxes: how the brain drain has become brain circulation; a powerful economic force for development of formerly peripheral regions. The new

Argonauts – armed with the experience they acquired in Europe and America and using the relationships they have with successful companies are able to operate in two countries simultaneously. By quickly identifying market opportunities, locating foreign partners, and being able to manage cross border business operations, they are beginning to develop their countries of origin.

Some countries with totalitarian government are afraid of the Diaspora's demand for democracy and good governance and their support of the opposition. That is why some governments including EPRDF of Ethiopia do not want to give voting opportunity to the Diaspora abroad, afraid that they might be able to swing the vote in favor of the opposition, if at all it is not rigged. Many would agree that Diaspora is right to stand for their people's rights by condemning tyrant leaders and demanding democracy.

"And, of course, where there is poor leadership, Africans need to stand up for the leaders they want and not settle for the leaders they get. Too many African leaders have been the narrow heroes of their micro-nations rather than genuine statesmen for the whole macro-nation". (Maathai, P-285)

Even though African professionals migrate away from their motherland or countries of origin due to political or economic reasons, a great majority of them do not severe their ties with their home country, hoping to return some day and contribute to the development of their motherland. Globalization has helped to facilitate their wish by giving them a chance to be recruited by the destination country companies to work as their agent in their multi-national corporations in Africa. Just like Information Technology (IT) professionals in India and China are working for American companies. Such possibilities will help in the transfer of technology and information exchange. It is important to be able to engage the Diaspora in the development of their country of origin by creating a mechanism to attract them to return and use their skills, remittances, and fresh ideas to transform Africa. Migration is a factor of development, and the Diaspora with their energy, determination and dynamism can boost economic development and social organization by interchange of experience. In the book "International Migration" the editor professor Aderanti Adepoju emphasizes the challenge.

"As economic and political processes evolve, the major challenge is how to channel migration movements to benefit the three key actors: the migrants themselves, the origin and destination countries, and societies and families in places of origin. In that case we need to broaden our perspectives in dealing with migration and development issues with a focus on the three D's – demography, development and democracy". (Adepoju, P-38)

Governments who are trying to slam the door for fear of the demand for democracy and losing power should consider the growing economic importance of Diasporas, and the contribution they can make to their country of origin. According to The Economist magazine, in 2011 there were 215 million first-generation migrants around the world which is 3 percent of the world's population. These migrants with networks of kinship and language make it easier to do business across borders. As many of the emerging brightest minds are educated in Western universities, these Diasporas spread not only money but also ideas, and many go back home with money, skills and knowledge of democracy and reform to invest. A good example is China whose technology industry is dominated by "sea turtles" (Chinese who have been abroad and returned). Some 500, 000 Chinese have studied abroad and returned, mostly in the last decade. They dominate the think-tanks that advise the government, by moving up the ranks of the communist party.

According to an American think-tank Cheng Li of the Brookings Institution, they now make up 15 percent of its central committee, up from 6 percent in 2002. They also help the companies of their host countries in the west to set up enterprises in China without a joint venture with a local firm.

The same is true to Indian and African Diasporas; thus by linking the West with emerging markets around the world, hard-working and innovative Diasporas spur productivity and company formation by helping rich countries to plug into fast growing economies. It is a win-win situation where both origin and host, rich and poor countries are likely to benefit from migration. In a globalized world, as Adepoju elaborates, fears that poor countries will suffer as a result of "brain drain" is exaggerated; and rich countries claim of migrants on welfare as a drain on the public purse is overblown; the argument that competition from unskilled immigrants who work harder for less pay, depresses the wages of unskilled locals is also non-existent or the effect is small.

Remittances

The other benefits of the Diaspora are the remittances to their relatives and friends. The money these immigrants send back to their countries of origin have helped their families, the community and the countries by creating better housing, access to basic health services and schools. It has become a major source of foreign currency for the governments. The remittances serve as the platforms for improving health care, education and other infrastructural facilities like pipe water, electricity and feeder roads. Some governments have been promoting migrant remittances for domestic investment which helped the boom of real estate market.

The Diaspora community who were forced to leave their motherland due to government repression and lack of economic and educational opportunities has at least helped in sustaining their relatives and friends they left behind. If they are given the chance and incentive they could do more. But, for that to happen, governments will have to improve the democratic and investment environment; since the general causes of migration are corruption, military-like government and economic factors.

"Remittances form an important link that migrants maintain with their areas of origin at micro, mesa and macro levels – as life lines to poor family members. They are used to pay for basic services, to educate siblings and children, to set up small enterprises and to enhance agricultural production". (Adepoju, P- 39)

Unfortunately remittance has also negative effect, by prompting the youth to emigrate. When they see the money coming from relatives abroad and observe the home coming migrants spending spree young people are prompted to migrate.

African leaders must ask themselves why so many highly educated and even high school graduates are leaving their countries and migrating to Europe and America. The answer is simple and clear, because their governance is dictatorial and the political atmosphere is not hospitable. These young and educated citizens who do not want to risk their lives are attracted to go abroad where they can get basic freedoms and greater professional opportunities that they could not get in their own country. African leaders failed to make the continent more hospitable, as a result the most skilled men and women are being lured away to Europe and America for their security and greater opportunity to advance their professions. The only solution is to change the political atmosphere and follow the rules of good governance so that people can enjoy basic freedoms at home.

Chapter Eight
Migrants Long and Arduous
Journey :
In Their Own Words

"To a brave man, good luck and bad luck are like his right and left hands, he uses both."
(Catherine of Siena)

"I don't know anyone who has gotten to the top without hard work; ...it will not always get you to the top, but should get you pretty near".

(Margaret Thatcher)

When things go wrong, as they sometimes will,
When the road you are trudging seems all uphill,
When the funds are low and the debts are high,
And you want to smile, but you have to sigh,
When care is pressing you down a bit,
Rest! if you must, but never quit.
Success is failure turned inside out-
The silver tint of the clouds of doubt-
And you never can tell how close you are,
It may be near when it seems far;
So stick to the fight when you are hardest hit-
It's when things seem worst that you MUSTN'T QUIT.
(Mary Blaisdell)

Millions of Ethiopians have been migrating to neighboring countries and beyond for the last forty years, part of an ever increasing trek towards countries with more opportunities. Recently, the Middle East and South Africa have seen the largest influx of refugees from Ethiopia with main routes being via Yemen, Djibouti, Kenya, Sudan and Somalia. For most, this arduous journey does not usually end until they arrive on the shores of one of the developed countries. The migrant story from Ethiopia has political, economic, and personal dimension; underpinning it all is poverty, war and mal-governance.

Ethiopian migrants running away from tyranny, poverty and civil war had to cross, often on foot, dense forests, steep mountains, sunbaked deserts, and deep seas. They see hope beyond the mirage and desert dazzle; dreaming of a better future somewhere beyond these forbidding wastelands. Only the dreams and hopes they conceive in their minds give them the courage to endure, to cross these hostile wind-scoured and inhospitable lands. They traveled accompanied by omnipresent hunger and thirst only to embark across the shark-infested Red Sea crammed in a small boat prone to capsizing. Upon arrival many find their destinations just as unforgiving. What awaits them is below par intermittent jobs that are often dangerous with no sanctuary from extortionist dealers. In the Arabian Peninsula thousands of Ethiopian women and girls exist in virtual slavery as domestic laborers; striped of all rights, stranded with their passports confiscated by their employer or trafficker. More often than not their pay is withheld and they are beaten, even burned in a world seemingly oblivious to their plight. It's no surprise that so often many chose to kill or take their own lives. During all these testing times, the motherland is at the bottom of their hearts; attached with pride and pain.

Such horror stories have recently gotten some media attention but not nearly enough to dissuade more from gambling, lured by money, usually paid in the black-market in cash with no tax obligations. For the most part many are aware no treasure waits, yet they make the journey. Understanding the root cause requires a deeper perspective into individual motivations with common threads. Here are a few Ethiopians who had passed these hurdles, taking different routes, via Sudan, Kenya, South Africa, Mexico, etc. to set foot in the United States; and luckily survived to tell their story while many of their friends perished in the process. Through well-chosen details they are describing their journey in their own words (which I translated), making it ring through with a sense of place that transports the readers and gives the value and connectedness to the actions, whirling them off a magic ride to faraway places. The resulting experience being the next best thing to being there in person; the only thing lacking is the chance to register as refugees.

Lately, with the progress of the reform that started in 2018 mass migration seems to subside; and asylum applicants in the west have been denied residence permit with the assumption that Ethiopia is becoming democratic. Even though we are happy to see Ethiopia in a democratic path, it is sad that after going through all the trouble to arrive at the country of their choice, they are ordered to go back: bitter sweet.

It is also heartbreaking to see that during the progress of the new reform, millions of Ethiopians were evicted from their homeland, where they lived for generations, considered as settlers because of ethnic politics. Again, Ethiopia stood first in the world as the number one country of mass internal displacement because of ethnic politics and resources allocation, particularly land.

Running Away From "Red Terror"

(Eight years in Sudan Refugee camps)

Moges Tassew Bogale

It was 1977 and Ethiopia was in the midst of a convoluted civil war when I began to contemplate leaving the country. I embarked for the border with Sudan, nearest to my province of Gonder, which lays a little south of raging rebellions to the north in Tigray and farther north in Eritrea. The aggressively nationalistic regime of the Derg had inherited a quagmire of a conflict in Eritrea, now almost midway into its second decade. In addition to this turmoil, a border war had erupted in the east with Somalia. The ephemeral calm felt in the center would soon give way to the "Red Terror", a ruthless campaign of elimination conducted to cleanse so called insurrectionists, which in actuality included all opposed to the regime.

I was only sixteen, and like most of my peers sympathized with the opposition. Certainly this lent grave suspicion toward all youths at the time, and many would be victims of the "Red Terror". Those eighteen and older were forced to enlist for national service and join the army, which was increasingly keen on finding human fodder for its increasingly belligerent crusade. I knew that sooner or later I would be facing death. Urban Dwellers Associations (*Kebele*) in my locality, Gonder, were increasingly becoming dreaded. By limiting our movements within the small confinements of the village the local bosses had hardly won friends among the people. As part of an experiment on the merits of collectivization, administrators had thought it best that young folks rise early to plant the fields. Missing a day from this activity meant serious deviousness warranting interrogation by a local cadre. The program's goals seemed geared towards controlling activities and daily routines. These things had become tedious to the point where life felt like being in a forced labor camp. Increasingly dogmatic in their approach authorities had made life intolerable for many who had hope for the revolution.

My older brother who was a member of the opposition group Ethiopian People's Revolutionary Party, known by its acronym EPRP, returned from their base in Asimba, taking advantage of a short period of amnesty announced by the government. He had been away from home for close to two years. Asimba, which means Red in the local Saho language, is the highest peak among the unforgiving mountain ranges of northern Ethiopia's Irob district. For young radicals of the EPRP it had been their base. Its impregnable slopes offered a natural hiding place from roaming army units and rival rebel movements. EPRP's young idealists where quickly disillusioned by events on the ground which were quickly turning against them. In cities and towns they were being exterminated by a regime with impunity never before seen in Ethiopian history. Their short lived mountain hideaway became a common destination for surviving members still committed to the struggle. Their ranks having grown to a respectable number they sought to fight a Maoist style guerilla movement, but one that would soon come to clash with other leftist movements hiding

386

out in the bush. This proliferation of rivalries with seemingly identical goals is an irony of Ethiopian politics that was emerging in this period. My brother would learn the pitfalls of idealism here. His party desperately on the run and increasingly turning towards terrorist tactics, to stay alive, he had found it best to seek an opportunity and leave the front all together. However, the whims of village life were limited and unattractive to a young man who had had instilled in him a progressivism that was eccentric for the small hamlet. Nevertheless he came back home as it offered hiatus and a chance to think things through before leaving; in a few months he left for Sudan.

News was often coming from Sudan, mostly by word of mouth from traders and merchants that some of our friends and relatives had arrived in the refugee camps of Gedarif, Sudan, and some have even made it as far as the Port of Sudan, eminently awaiting to hop on a boat headed for the Arabian Peninsula from whence any other destination was supposedly reachable. Leaving our home and joining the growing number of expats was quickly becoming the discussion of choice among friends and family. Young folk having been exposed to politics and having grown more thoroughly conscious of the world would never settle for village life as their parents had once done. There was a palpable shift of cultural attitudes among my peers and increasingly among teenagers of the time. Undoubtedly the revolution had changed people, if not their circumstance. For people like my brother who had fought and endlessly discussed Mao and Lenin in their mountain sanctuary village life had nothing to offer them and leaving was a certainty.

One morning I left the town of Gonder along with three other friends, starting the long and difficult journey on a dilapidated and winding road towards the north-west. Initially hitching a ride from Ethiopian Highway Authority employees to our first destination Tikil Dengay 60 kilometers away, where some of my cousins live. We spent days in a relative's home until we found traders who often acted as guides to lead us to Sudan, along the same path embarked upon by my brother a few months earlier. Though my cousins had tried to convince me to go back home, I told them of how "revolutionary guards" were on the lookout for me. Going back would certainly mean arrest or even death. Failing to report to the local *kebele* for a day or two without permission or sufficient reason was an intolerable act bringing about grave punishment. Being the younger brother of a recently amnestied EPRP member who disappeared, lent further suspicion as to why I had stayed away. My cousin understood the situation right away and started looking for traders heading for Sudan. Shortly afterwards we found merchants one of whom happened to be a close associate of my cousins and arranged our journey with him. Fortunately these were traders and not traffickers, in fact one of them was a distant relative and therefore we did not have to pay anything.

We knew that the journey on foot was not going to be easy by any means. At the time heading northwest towards the town of Humera was a dangerous proposition. It would entail having to travel across a war zone and a no man's land of the northwestern plains. This area between the district of Welkayt and Humera had historically been a haven for outlaws and bandits called *shiftas*, who take advantage of this sparsely populated desolate region to rob passing traders and make a quick escape into their inaccessible interior camps, similar to the wild American west of the 19th century. The region's harshness and its equally hardened inhabitants meant it was never fully governed. This had attracted several of the burgeoning rebel movements of the seventies to set up camp here. It had once been a formidable hideout for Ethiopian patriots fighting Mussolini's invading army in the 1930s. Unable to cleanse this area from the patriots, the region was becoming a thorn in the flesh of Italian planners. Its proximity to the porous border with

Sudan to the west meant procuring items of war or anything else for that matter was relatively easy. This merger of circumstances did not bode well for our escape. Even if we could somehow avoid the roaming *shiftas*, we might get captured by government troops and forcefully enlisted, or we might be snatched by one of the rebels instead. Walking day and night across this semi brown bushy landscape meant inevitable encounter with poisonous snakes. With this in mind one could never sleep. Always you remained anxious. But first you would have to get through the steep Semien Mountains range which would entail several days of walking through rugged oxygen deprived slopes. If you were a guerilla movement trying to avoid roaring government jet bombers this was a perfect location. If you were a refugee passing by it was the worst of places to trek. But you had no choice.

All I had was five hundred Ethiopian Birr that my parents had given me, which was around fifty dollars at the time. We carried nothing extra except the cloth on our backs, and dried foods like mixed nuts (kolo), Dabokolo, Besso and Quanta, a kind of spiced dried beef jerky. As we started walking from Tikil Dingay heading north, the six merchants who have loaded their merchandise on three donkeys gave us a briefing of what to expect and the do's and don'ts of our journey. One of the rules was of how we would walk in two groups one a bit farther ahead and the other slightly behind, only coming together at designated meeting location to camp along our route. This was supposed to make us less attractive to anyone who wanted to follow along. In the worst case scenario it also meant at least half of us could escape capture or robbery, while the unfortunate bunch that were delayed would provide a signal that not all was well. In areas where the *shiftas* were destined to be we would travel by night veering off our regular path and making our own inconspicuous track. This however was a sure way to get lost, especially at

389

night, but our guides assured us it had been done before and we trusted them.

We set out for Sudan to face our fears and meet our hopes. Every few miles we met peasants who asked us who we were and where we were going. To which our merchant guides responded with certain casualness that proved their experience. They would calmly tell them that we were heading towards the boarder to sell our goods and that some of us were laborers heading to the sesame fields. This abated any suspension an informant among the locals might have and might be all too willing to report to a local *Kebele*, which would result in an army unit being sent out to tail us. The farther and higher we climbed the less people we encountered. Never have I been this far away from Gonder and if ever there was a moment to contemplate and change your mind this was it, whilst a safe return was still imaginable. That very first day we walked for fourteen hours with only a short break at the bank of a small river, right on the ten hour mark. Another four hours we would rest finding any soft ground to sleep only to wake very early in the morning and start all over again. The piercing cold of the mountain side, especially at night was unforgiving, making comfortable sleep a distant memory. Around mid-night the sound of a hyena roaring woke us. "Don't panic, it's ok", said our guide, with a slight smile, appearing to relish our frantic scramble. He turned on a flashlight and beamed it all around as if checking to see if his donkey was still there. The donkeys stood up with their ears pointed up like a horn. Out here this usually means that a hungry pack of hyena is closing in. After this event sleeping had become impossible and dawn was fast approaching. We awoke dreary eyed and with certain blandness to continue the same route, one day sleeping on a mountain top, another day in the valley; always cold and anxious.

At one point in our journey, may be three days later, we bumped into another group of young migrants from Addis and Gojam. For the most part they were fleeing the "Red Terror". Their hair style and the way they dressed had given away the Addis boys as outlandish city lads who probably thought we were familiar with these parts. Slightly displaying the bluster of young university students who had regularly visited one of the cafes in Addis, they were slightly more visible. After half a day of walking we were casually stopped by four bandits. Awkwardly slinging their AK 47 with hand on muzzle as if to demonstrate their willingness to shoot at the slightest of signals, they crept slowly at first and more freely down from their slightly hilly ambush. I reflexively thought about ducking down, in fact most of us did. Our assailants having sensed certain fragility within us grew more confident. This was all for the better. Having swiftly realized we offered no treasure-trove their expressions had grown less tense and their hostile demeanor had given way to disappointment. It was unnecessary to shake us down further. When one of them asked about what we were up to the teenager was already on his knees begging for their pardon by calling the names of several arch angels. Several of us were wearing jeans, a much coveted clothing item in this part of the world. At the time the only place to find jeans for sale was 600 miles away in Addis Ababa. One of them, a boyish looking lad of about twenty requested we take them off; which we dutifully obliged. In exchange we were given really short shorts of the kind regularly sported by local peasants busily tending their fields. This indicated our muggers were farm boys deciding to have a snoop around. It was common for peasants in the area to do this kind of thing just to bring in needed goods they themselves couldn't procure in the open market.

It had been our guess that these were members of the EDU armed militia who used such instances to raid those heading to Sudan. Originally the EDU had set up its base in this region. EDU, short for Ethiopian Democratic Unity was a euphemistically named amalgamation of former monarchists, and high ranking military officers deposed by mutineers in the revolution. Its rank however was largely composed of mediocre landlords opposed to the nationalization drive and the peasants they had managed to convince on religious and conservative grounds usually having to do with patriotism. Its conservative agenda lent a certain anachronism about it. In fact it was referred to by the more radical leftist parties as riffraff reactionaries of the old and despised landlord class. These latest farm boys turned highway robbers might have some lose connections with the organization. It was not out of the ordinary for illiterate peasants to bear arms in defense of their former lords; as a matter of fact this had been the way in which the empire was defended from invaders throughout its history. Epic battles and monumental victories such as the battle of Adwa in 1896 were won using such means of recruitment and organization. It wasn't until after World War II Ethiopia acquired a standing army, which quickly became one of the biggest on the continent. These EDU fighters were to be the last of a dying breed, a kind of last samurai.

After the incident we continued to the boarder under the cover of darkness to avoid more lurking bandits. Besides, walking during the day was becoming agonizingly tiresome. The lowlands adjacent the border seemed to bake in the sun. The weather here was hot, dry and always sunny, which made the body sluggish. You could hardly walk four miles of thorny plains and zigzag mountain trails without having to sit and rest. Finding water to drink was made even more difficult by the summer months which had dried up streams and lagoons. The water jugs we had originally loaded on the backs of the donkeys were running dry. The next village lay some 60 miles out; even then you might find the well empty, which was not uncommon for the season. We would need to use whatever resources we have left until we reached the small-scale industrial farms surrounding the town of Humera. But this would mean rationing out our dwindling resources now worth three days of ration. Walking at night provides safety from the shiftas, but it had its disadvantages. It means walking along paths infested with some of Africa's most venomous snakes and scorpions. One tragic step and you were sure to die an agonizing slow death. Our patched up and stitched sandals hardly provided protection. The advice from our trader friends turned park ranger was to walk quietly in a single line. Most if not all of us had a visceral fear of snakes as did most highlanders. I kept imagining a glossy black rope like creature glistening in the bright moon light. The yellowish dusty ground would make its feature even more apparent. Five nights of this was enough to drive you crazy. During days we would huddle around a sprawling acacia tree for shade and sleep as best we could, knowing all other creatures would also seek shade.

As we finally got closer to the border the land was noticeably getting flatter, sandier, and more arid. The surrounding thick patches of green had given way to drier boney shrubs that lent themselves perfectly suited for fire wood. Most of all you felt the heat and the wind that seemed to carry it from the Sahara. This was still tolerable earth for a highlander, yet it was paradise for Sudanese farmers willing to take advantage of a leaky border to farm the more fertile Ethiopian side, which regularly resulted in small skirmish over farm land and water. However this seemingly semi-desert would turn into lush green at the slightest of rains bringing forth unexpected abundance. In fact the rainy season transformed this section of land unrecognizably green, almost like a humid steamy forest with cushioning soggy short grass dotted by the occasional tree or shrub. Though Sahara desert was expanding south and even encroaching on the highlands through this terrain, it was still moist enough to attract the first of Ethiopia's rare modern farms.

Sesame was the crop of choice here and still is to this day, thought a few vineyards had by now slowly crept up here and there.

We shared a deep collective sigh of relief. We had made it that bit closer, still breathing and still alive. It was now safe enough to walk during the day. But there was one hazard to be warily avoided, the army, which had significant installation just south of Humera, the area we currently found ourselves in. Certainly a run-in with the army means definite enlistment, which almost surely resulted in death, almost as certain as dying from the snake bite. At the moment we would lay low before attempting to cross the border, preferably at night. About fifty kilometers from the border we came to a big farm. Its owner, a rather charming man of about seventy must have noticed us walking through his field when he let out a round from his antiquated rifle. The weapon was made even less threatening by the lengthy distance between us. Our guides waved their arms frantically, and began to whistle in particularly musical pattern. To our relief the man unexpectedly placed the rifle down and began walking towards us. His white cotton shroud perched intricately on his shoulder, and his dark face made magnificent by his noble white beard gave off a saintly appearance. Upon seeing us he smiled slightly at first before uttering the first words of greeting. Our merchant guides having ascertained the man's identity were happy too. After a swift stunned gaze at us he said, who are all these people? To which the merchant answered by telling the old man that we were his load. He'd carried us all the way up country and was going to unload us in Sudan. As if on cue the man invited us in to his residence in the middle of the farm and implored with us to eat in that emblematically Ethiopian of ways. Under normal circumstance such overwhelming hospitality should be greeted both with appreciation and refusal, but currently our empty stomachs did not allow for such folkdance to continue. At which point the man summoned someone to bring us spicy potato stew, an all season dish, one most of us were very familiar with.

We ate, drank, washed, and rested until we got back our strength. Our gracious host pleaded with us to return to our families. He couldn't comprehend why so many young people were abandoning their country. We understood his bemusement, but could not find the words to describe our motives. Conjuring up the words necessary to articulate the fast nature of events around the revolution was still difficult at the time, especially when you were living in it. Yet man's bewilderment was warranted. In his day it had been almost unfathomable to flee one's birth place. The most heinous criminal would not dare wander farther than the next province in avoidance of his plaintiffs before inevitably returning to face his judgment, which in all likelihood was settled amicably. By now those days had become a distant memory. Even that last bastion of refuge, the Ethiopian church which even the mighty emperors had stopped short of defiling was now powerless. Thoroughly coerced and intimidated by the state it had lost its ability to provide solace to the thousands fleeing for their lives. Out here so close to Sudan and so far away from the center of political life this must have indeed seemed vague. It was too far and too isolated to sense the colossal events reshaping a people forever. But that too would vanish, as a wave of land redistribution would sweep through the remotest parts of the country. Our kind host's beautiful plot would be nationalized. Perhaps he along with his family would pack up and leave. On this thought we said our goodbyes to this gentleman and readied ourselves to cross the border.

Surprisingly the bustling border town we had come to expect wasn't there. Most shops were either closed or had so little business it was hard to tell whether this was the border town from which most of Ethiopia's trade with Sudan occurs. Any conversation with locals inevitably led to the same topic, the dwindling nature of business. Humera had surely seen better days before. Most residents were headed for Sudan. The location of the town was too vital for rebels and army alike. Increasingly the town was becoming a hub for contraband and smuggling. Criminal gangs and rebels alike plotted to gain quick profits. This semi-chaotic situation was a haven for all kinds of scandalous characters. Prostitution was still one of the few thriving trades in town. Sesame export was eroding as bigger portions of trade now included weapons coming in and alcohol going out to satisfy the black markets in both countries. Within a year's time the town's bank had been robbed several times. There were frequent assassinations and revenge killings carried out by both government and rebel alike. Bribery and extortion were so widespread it seemed normal.

A few kilometers before the border we met Sudanese tradesmen traveling with their merchandise to Gonder. There were ominous warnings to avoid the town of Berekt Nuri and to head instead for Amra Koba refugee camp located northwest on the road to Khartoum. With this in mind we crossed the border with relative ease. It was the usual hot and dry day and besides the coming and going of trucks that blew dust on pedestrians the road was deserted for the most part. Camels outnumbered vehicles here ten to one. Walking along with them guaranteed you blended in as one of the herders. We were lucky not to have been stopped and questioned by police. On several occasions we came close but miraculously passed unnoticed.

As we came to the border everything changed; the landscape looked and felt different, as if the land itself knew to change with the man-made boundary. The wind brought the sand, hot stinging grains and it was like walking into an oven. The land was flat, the trees were short and looked half grown; the sand still swirling around in the wind filled the air. I could feel sand under my feet and it took some time to fully come in terms with it. Apart from the few hills doted across the land it was sun-baked sand rolling out endlessly in all directions. The scenery was incredible – vast and empty, a sand-filled nothingness, it was different from what I knew, and beautiful. The road was barely different from the rest of the scenery, other than the slight rise of the edge it was the same color and texture. Above all these, a sky so clear it looked as though it was melting under the hot sun; the heat was all but unbearable. Starting to feel home sick already, my mind began to race through what lay ahead, how many more miles we had to go, and not just in this country, but until we find a place comfortable to work, learn and live. Lord Have Mercy!

As we got farther away from the boarder and deeper into Sudan we veered off the main road and traveled through desert. The soft sinking sand made picking up one's feet stridently an exhausting task. Having picked up so much sand by now the sandals I had worn were perfectly blended in with ground. It might have been thirty or forty miles within Sudan when night fell and we finally rested. Before sleeping we put up a durable peace of signal indicating our route, making sure it never moved by harnessing it to our load. The one thing about sleeping in the desert was when you awoke the sandy landscape was rearranged by wind. Many migrants had died walking in circles for days because of it. We were not taking any chances. The thought of it haunted me still while I tried to sleep. Wandering in circles alone in the sun blasted desert for what seemed like an eternity must have been a gut reaching experience. The thought of it made your stomach churn and had to be consciously suppressed in order to stay sane. Laying there in the desert I imagined my destiny. The world awaiting me beyond these stretches of desolate sand dunes and distant buttes shimmering in the heat was a much more hopeful place, where children played in the afternoon shade while soft music played interrupted only by giggles. All we had was this hope and it was what kept us alive.

At dawn we continued to the next town of Amra Koba. Several hours of baking in the sun had passed before we could see the town from a distance. It looked more like a group of palm trees from this vantage point. If we hadn't been informed of its existence we would've simply passed by without noticing it. Most of the houses had a low laying structure almost flat to the ground. Upon arrival you could sense this was a center for refugees. In Amra Koba one met more foreigners than Sudanese and a good portion them had been Ethiopian. It was comforting to know you were among other like yourself. Everyone used this opportunity to meet and chat and exchange information. In the absence of formal structures we relied on each other to find food and shelter for the night, or even work. No one had money to pay for services rendered so you just gave your labor to someone who needed it. In a few days we had managed to build enough shelter out of branches and straw to house fifty to sixty people. We now had a small section within the town, which was now attracting many more police than when we arrived. Notorious for their corruption and ruthless in their method of extorting refugees, Sudanese police had a knack for shaking down a refuge and throwing him in jail for no apparent reason. To register ourselves officially lest we be captured and beaten by the police we headed up to Doka a few days later. Dodging the authorities constantly was an anxiety filled life. We just couldn't do it anymore. If we were going to stay in this country for an extended period of time then the running had to stop, at least for a short while, until we got things in order. It was upon this recognition we all began to feel more appreciative and homey. Sudan wasn't just going to be a short stop. By any estimate we were here for the long haul. Sometimes reality kicks in and challenging once preconceived notions.

In Sudan water is sacred, a communal resource shared by all. It had to be that way when you consider the aridness of the land. In that sense water was priceless. One can be greedy about everything else except water. People here had long discovered sharing it was far better than fighting over it. Everyone we encountered no matter how distant they seemed offered us tea. It was customary to invite strangers as guests in this land of big smiles and generosity. This image of Sudan has suffered a terrible blow over the years, as war and genocide began to replace it, but it had boomed on us so deeply, till this day I consider Sudan my other home. We spent the first night on rented ground in Doka. With the help of an interpreter we were allowed to sleep in a compound of seven small huts. Though the huts were not bedrooms, they were used as storage facility for beds, which seemed more like mats, and carpets which guests could rent to sleep on within the compound fence. Those who rent a bed pay five shillings a night, while some of us who used carpets made from elephant grass paid only two. Everyone had to pull his bed or carpet from one of the huts and sleep outside on the ground. Every few days, in the middle of the night, usually around midnight, the owner came waving a flashlight. He walked around the compound tapping each sleeping body on his torso in order to wake them so he could collect the rent before disappearing into the night once again. For those hard at sleep he beamed the flashlight directly on their closed eyelids. Every night the same routine applied. While most of us had meagerly managed to pay, there were times when few campers had to make do without a mat.

The precarious life of sleeping outside on a mattress you didn't own was far from what we had expected. By this standard village life in Gonder was far better, even without the personal freedoms we now enjoy all be it perilously. Some sense of security we had long nursed had never materialized during those few months. Yet, for obvious reasons Sudan wasn't to going be anyone's final destination. This sparsely populated giant could hardly meet the demands of its own population. The added pressure from people like us wasn't exactly welcome news. In those days the best way out of Sudan for refugees from Ethiopia or anywhere else for that matter was to have a full refugee status, which provided you with a link to some western organization that could possibly get you visas. Where we were there were plenty of refugees but none had been given a status as such. We were just part of the superfluous bunch. This meant we had no protection as some of us discovered the harsh way. The police or any civilian can do whatever they wanted to us. Though most Sudanese treated us fairly, there were episodes of harassment including beatings and extortion. To escape some of these excesses we sought recognition and the only way to do it was to head for the large camp of Gedarif, which lay 60 miles west.

International aid workers we met told us to register as refugees in Gedarif. This might just be our chance. We started looking for an Ethiopian who would tell us how to get there. After a few days of searching we learned of a way to reach Gedarif camp without being caught. He told us to hitch a ride on a freight truck and get off before the town, approximately 5 miles outside of town and walk to the Refugee Registration Center avoiding local authority. We made it to Gedarif and were able to register. On that day there were large crowds of refugees and aid workers were handing out clothes and food rations. Priority was given to registered refugees and since our names were nowhere in official records we were duly turned away. Hours after the rationing, we headed towards one of the open markets to look for some much needed supplies of food and shoes, and to our surprise we saw those same registered refugees selling the clothes and cooking oil they had just received. Local people had become accustomed to it and were buying from refugee sellers rather than pay a hefty sum. Because of this the sprawling camp had turned into a make shift markets of convenience during late afternoons when the sweltering sun had descended. Everything was sold and bought there, more than likely at prices well below the market average. The camp had become the preferred destination for customers looking to buy cooking oil because unlike many shops at the time the refugees turned merchants were rarely out of stock.

Be it Gedarif or Doka the area is full of insects, snakes and scorpions. In those first few months we could not afford to buy netting to protect us from insect bites as we slept. We simply used our bed sheets to wrap ourselves thoroughly. This caused discomfort of course and it made you extremely hot to the point making sleep agonizing. Often times you automatically unwrapped yourself in the middle of the night, grave error that resulted in a myriad of poke marks on your body mostly form insect bite. This left you tortured and itching everywhere for days. Even worse you contracted malaria. It had happened on a few occasions already. Most Ethiopians are not familiar with the disease. Malaria had been a peripheral issue around the highlands where we had come from. Protected by the thin cool air of the plateau we had come to ignore this most deadly parasite in Africa which was endemic nearly everywhere else on the continent. Overtime we adopted and got the items to make our stay livable. We earned enough money from odd jobs to by the three basic items one should have; a net (Musiya) to shield our body from the tormenting insects, a plastic water container (Kurtya), and flashlight.

One day while walking about the refugee registration center I saw a man dressed in jeans and a red shirt. He sported an overgrown afro caped with sunglasses, of the type I had always wanted. As he got closer the most awesome feeling of recognizing that he was my brother who had come months earlier rushed through my body. We were both speechless in disbelief. I had never spoken to him since the night he disappeared. Though I remained faithful of his wellbeing there was never any proof of it. This had left our mother heartbroken and to learn that her other son had also embarked on the same journey must have made things all the more devastating. At this moment I wished for her presence so she could feel the same sense of reassurance as I was feeling. After a big long hug he asked why I had come. I answered him with the same question. A few laughs later he asked us to join him for dinner drinks a little later. It would be the first real meal we've had in months. He'd managed to carve out a decent survival in Gedarif, enough so he could entertain guests. I never asked him how he'd adjusted so fast. Surely he must have had some people he'd known during his rebel days. My brother was always well versed in local customs. Wherever he went he seemed to blend in quickly. I remember him being studious and bookish even as a young boy. I wouldn't have been surprised if he had found a job at some aid agency or if he made his living less reputably either. These were all questions I pondered over our dinner, but never resumed to ask. In a sense I didn't need to. For the moment I was just happy.

I lived in Gedarif as a refugee for eight years. During that time I thought deeply about where I would end up. Of course the middle-east was a popular destination amongst refugees in the region, partly because of its closeness, but the process of getting there through official channels was lengthy and the unofficial route was dangerous. In any case it was all too common to end up in an abuse environment, and it was certain you would be treated badly by almost everyone you met. Many had made their way to Jeda in Saudi Arabia or Cairo in Egypt to work for families that abused them. You hear stories like that all the time in Gedarif, yet many would not be deterred. Anywhere else must be better was the unofficial mantra of refugees in Sudan. For those who aspired for more, Europe and North America were too distant and hence almost unattainable. For the most part many of us continued to live hesitantly, stuck between wanting to go back, staying put, or risking it all to go further.

Eight years would pass, working when there was work, receiving what little help refuges got from donors, and selling whatever you got your hands on. We survived in a small ghetto called Tiwawa, which was called "Ethiopian village" even by locals. Its isolation had served to make it a city within a city where local officials cared less about its inhabitants. That meant there was all kinds of criminality and children never went to school. This part of Gedarif was where Ethiopians of different ethnicity, religion, age, gender, party affiliation, and educational background lived, largely because it was the only place they could afford.

Almost on a daily bases a person was killed; essentially no law and order existed. Fights and stabbings were of everyday occurrence. Tens of thousands of refugees who had lost all hope and therefore didn't care much were living cramped in this small five block city square. By the time we arrived some had lived there for over a decade already. To see someone stabbed by a dagger right in front of you was not rare. These killings however were not meaningless. Usually it was over money and the black market trade involving alcohol which was banned by sharia law in Sudan. Racketeering was also a reason for the high death toll in Tiwawa. Sudanese police arrived late only to pick up the remaining corps and leave. No formal investigation was opened. There was no effort to fight the criminals who essentially ran these parts. As long as these quarters were cut-off from the rest of the city whatever happened here was none of their business. Children stole and so did parents and yet no one found this repulsive at any time. Put simply, eight year of my life were wasted in a real squalor. Retrospectively I think of it as time spent behind bars, incarcerated in an open prison where the stench of swaged followed you about everywhere.

If there is a quarrel for any reason, one has to kill the other; wounding him is not enough, he has to finish him;

otherwise sooner or later the other will kill him. There is no mercy or reconciliation for any wrong doing; nobody will let it go; one has to finish the other or the other will finish him next time. This was overwhelmingly true in Tiwawa. The ubiquitous sex trade had managed to flourish throughout town. Nearly everyone carried a knife. Finding a dead corpse lying about the dingy side street was so common it had aroused little if any controversy. This was Tiwawa in the 1980s.

We were drinking and chatting in a bar, with the music blaring loudly. The owner of this bar and another waitress are overtly flirtatious, teasing their customers for the bottom dollar. This was how the sex trade flourished around town, mostly in bars just like this one. Too many refugees, overwhelmingly men, stuck in static camps for years, almost on the verge of imprisonment had naturally led to this, or so it would seem. There was another group in the house already, and soon they started arguing with a group that just came into the bar. I saw everyone pulling out his dagger; I could see the reflection of the daggers against the kerosene light. Customers began to fling themselves across the bar. Tables and chair were smashed to pieces in the stampede. Luckily we escaped unharmed; I would later learn three people had been killed that day. I arrived at my shelter shivering in great shock and told the phenomenon to my room-mates. "It's ugly here; life has no value" said my brother, a while back. Those were indeed days of innocence. How shockingly those words had become true was deeply unsettling. I wanted to leave Sudan even more than I wanted to leave our little escarpment in Gonder.

Even though life was bad in the refugee camps, the first few years we were not very much interested to go to the United States. We thought there could be a government change in Ethiopia soon and we will go back to our parents. On the other hand the rumors we hear about refugees living in America were scary. They were telling us that if we go there the chances are that we will end up washing horses, dogs, dishes and we will not be allowed to go back to Ethiopia. Many of us declined the American s offer of visas for the first two years. The US consulate office in Gedarif started showing a photo exhibition of Ethiopians who left for America a year ago driving cars, dressing nice clothes and visiting museums. At the time we were tired of life in Gedarif and have lost hope that there will be government change in Ethiopia; and most of us started applying for refugee visas. Because of increasing interest of refugees to get visas the small American consulate office in Gedarif was getting crowded every day. In a few weeks they rented a bigger office and closed the old one for a few days until they moved all the equipment's to the new location. When the office got ready for operation, they put a notice for all to read about the new address and that it will open on a certain date.

The day the new office started accepting applications many Ethiopians wake up early morning and started flooding towards the new building from all directions. Some of them started running to be there before others; then every Ethiopian started running in the same direction to avoid long lines. Native Sudanese, who sow us running, joined the run, jumping out of their houses in sandals; some even jumping their fence and from their widows. It looked like a war scenario or an open Marathon. When we arrived at the consulate and stand in line the Sudanese started cursing us and returning. When we asked them why they are mad at us, they told us that they run because they thought we are running away from Gedarif getting news that Mengistu has dispatched jet fighters to bomb the city. There was a rumor that he will one day destroy the city, and the Sudanese conceived that fear for a long time.

I waited on line for several hours and when it was my turn to register and went into the office, the counselor told me that being under eighteen I can't register by myself. When I told them that my brother is next on line they told me to call him in and I registered under his name in his file. I found out late that it would have been faster if I told them to find me a sponsor in America, Canada, or Australia, as these were the major countries giving visas to refugees. After registering in my brother's file we were waiting with great hope that we shall land in America soon. Unfortunately there came the Gulf War (Operation Desert Storm) and the consulate put all its attention on it giving priority to war refugees. There were many Ethiopian refugees who were so eager to get visa and they not only go every day to the consulate office, but, there were also those who were living in tents and plastic shelters around the consulate. It took two more years for the consulate to start issuing visas again. I personally go every day to see the list of names called for Visa on the notice board.

One day I saw my brother's name on the list, I couldn't believe my eyes; I could feel my face glowing with happiness. I immediately went back and told him, and got the biggest hug of my life. The next day we went and stayed on line until he was called. When his name was called I followed him only to be blocked by the guard telling me to wait for my turn. I explained that I am registered in his file and insisted to enter with my brother. I succeeded in convincing the guard only to be told by the counselor that I am now over eighteen years old and will have to register anew independently and wait for my turn. I was devastated; I went crazy and acted violently, after four years as a refugee I have to register again as new and wait, God knows for how many more years. The counselor whom I tried to fight explained to me politely all the legal procedures and promised to get me a visa as soon as possible. I did not believe her; I thought she was just trying to console me and get me out of there. To my regret she told me that if I had registered as an under-age I could have got a sponsor and gone long ago. I started cursing myself, my brother, the counselor, and everyone and left the office.

It took another four years to get my refugee visa to the United States. During these years I have encountered so many problems, survived so many dangers, escaped a number of trials of deportation and led a miserable life. Some of my friends went back to Ethiopia, some died, committed suicide, some became insane, while others got refugee visas and left for Canada, USA, Australia and Scandinavian countries. During these years Ethiopian refugees were rounded up every now and then and taken to the border, in the process many died in the desert unable to reach a place where they can find drinking water. I survived the deportation by hiding in different houses and by avoiding public places.

Police will stop you any moment and ask you for your ID. If you don't have a Muslim name and you don't speak Arabic, they insult you, spit on you, and they sometimes tear it and throw it. Things got worse after President Nimerri declared Sharia Law. They tell us to go back to our country by saying "Smell the soil; (shim el wata) this is not your land". They lecture us that we came hungry and they fed us, we came nude they dressed us. I always wonder when I compare it to the Ethiopian hospitality and our slogan "Ager yegara, haymanot yegil new" (the country for all, religion for the individual).You will have to go through all the trouble of getting identity card again by bribing the officials; and for that you need money. Ethiopian women who work as house maid or are simply refugees, have suffered untold misery, often beaten, and some raped or even killed and thrown into the Nile River.

One of our friends Wondemu Alemu, who is now living in Canada, was a hard working young man. He got a job in a restaurant where his work was to sit outside and wash the dishes.

He uses a towel to fetch boiling water from the metal vessel that was sitting on a stove and with soap he washes the plates, rinse with cool water, dry with another towel, and pile them aside. It is astonishing how he can bear the hot sun and the heat from the stove. After he finished washing he went to the draining area, a few meters away from the restaurant to spill the water he used to wash the dishes. The police men who were rounding up to deport Ethiopian refugees stopped him. He showed them the vessel and the towel he used to clean the plate, to no avail. I was also stopped by police a little earlier and I am seating with the crowd. There were also other vendors carrying their merchandise with us.

Wondemu was still carrying the vessel and the dirty towel. We asked him why he doesn't throw it away for it is of no use now that we are going to get deported. He refused to throw it, for fear of not getting his job back in case he succeeded to come back. We sow big police trucks coming to take us to a desert area known as Basonda by the Ethiopian border. As we were moving to climb on the trucks one group started a fight and in the confusion some of us managed to run and escape as usual. Police fired shots to the air, but, no one was hurt. Wondimu was deported with his vessel and towel. While wondering in the wilderness with others, he came to a refugee camp run by Canadians by the border. Since he is fluent in English and Arabic they gave him a job, as a purchaser and after a few weeks came to Gedarif driving a Canadian aid agency truck. He was carrying a lot of money, and he invited us and told us that he will be heading to Canada soon.

In my later years in Sudan, I learned the language and took a Muslim name and got a temporary job here and there, and moved to Khartoum for a while. After leading a miserable life for eight years I got my refugee visa in 1985 and came to the United States. My useful youth years were squandered in Sudan

408

without achieving anything significant. To compensate for the lost years, I went back to school and started to work hard to acquire knowledge and make money. My journey to reach the United States, though long and strenuous ended; but, my life journey didn't stop there; I shall tell you that part of my story some other time. For now I am enjoying life with my wife Mahlet and our two children Meron and Samuel, here in the national capital area, Washington; the dreaming capital of America, stuffed with exiles who are always saying it is about time to go back home, but never go as the years turn into decades.

Crossing 15 Countries to Live the American Dream

Tadele Gebretsadik

Looking back at my long and arduous journey crisscrossing fifteen countries, risking my life at every move, I wonder what kept me going against all odds. I always believe that life is a journey, often difficult and sometimes incredibly cruel, but I knew if I have the force of will to live my dreams I will be the master of my destiny. I remember the old saying, "tough times don't last, tough people do"; and I developed a do or die attitude to realize my dream.

The most dangerous part of my journey was leaving Ethiopia and travelling across nine countries to reach South Africa. It was a long, risky and arduous journey where I had to walk the most part through the forests and the semi-arid desert land day and night. I left Ethiopia along with eight other friends, and we had to walk, ride on horses back or take a boat or a delivery truck by giving some money to the driver. We were arrested in Tanzania for four months, after which we had to return back to Kenya and take a different route via Uganda, Rwanda, Burundi, Zambia and Mozambique to South Africa. It took us several months, some died of accident and disease on route, others preferred to stay in one of the countries we crossed, and only two of us made it to South Africa.

After three years of hard work and saving money in South Africa for my next journey, I alone succeeded crossing the Atlantic. I had to cross six countries of Central America, (Cuba, Nicaragua, Honduras, El-Salvador, Guatemala and Mexico (where I was arrested for a few days), to set foot on US soil. I paid a lot of money for the traffickers and bribed law enforcement officers in each of these countries in Africa and Central America. I am glad that I made my dream come true, but, I also feel sad for my friends who died on route, and who became homeless and remained behind in other countries. I sometimes ask myself if it is worse the trouble. I would not have started this journey had I known the risks involved and that it would take so long. But, I made it; and here is the summary.

There were no opportunities in Ethiopia for a young man like me. Life was so boring and there was nothing to do except help my parents with the small business they had and remain dependent on them; but, for how long? I couldn't get admission to college, I couldn't get a job, I had no money to start my own business, and the want for independence was bugging me. Like many Ethiopian young men and women I had that American dream burning inside me, and I wanted to give it a try.

Incidentally, one young man I know in our neighborhood came back from South Africa and came to see my parents. He had been to South Africa for five years and he looked great. He told me and my other siblings how he first left, about life down south and the opportunities in that part of Africa. The way he described it was so exciting that I wanted to go with

411

him, and my family agreed. My parents gave me eight thousand Ethiopian Birr, which was equivalent to one thousand dollars at the time, and I started to pack things I need for the journey, including dried food like *Kolo*, *Beso*, and *Kuanta*.

Along with eight other youngsters in my neighborhood we started our journey with him, with the hope that we will be in South Africa in a matter of days. Our journey started from Addis Ababa south bound by way of Awash Valley in between the rift valley lakes to Agere Mariam and the border town of Moyale. Our journey through southern Ethiopia was spectacular. I used to hear when people say that a trip to southern Ethiopia is like a 'pilgrimage' to the naturalists as a journey to the north is to historians. We found out about it to be true when we looked at the beautiful scenery, the chain of sparkling lakes, abundant wildlife and birds, and a kaleidoscope of colorful cultures.

The topography of the remarkable Great Rift Valley adds much to the appeal of this region. According to geologists the rift valley represents the last great massive movement of planet earth. The valley has a marvelous string of lakes that stretch from Ethiopia into Kenya, Tanzania and beyond. Ethiopia has a chain of national parks along this route. This part of the country is also home to many diverse peoples and cultures; the Dorze famous for their weaving of cotton clothes; the Konso who practiced terracing and intensive agriculture for centuries in their steep slopes, and others living pastoral life with some hunting and fishing. We were mesmerized by the natural beauty of our country at the same time asking ourselves why we remained poor.

After a day in Moyale, we walked to the border of Kenya and got visa by bribing the officials in charge. Looking for the cheapest means of transportation to the capital city, Nairobi, we had to ride a truck carrying cattle. While riding on

412

the truck I was dreaming of how my life will change once I arrive in South Africa. On our way to Nairobi Kenyan police stopped our truck at every village and knowing that we are foreigners they asked us to give them some money by threatening to arrest us. For fear of arrest we paid every police man who stopped us and checked our ID.

As soon as we arrived in Nairobi we asked for the neighborhood where many Ethiopians live and went there. We stayed in Kenya for several days gathering information from fellow Ethiopians how to proceed to South Africa and by calling our friends in South Africa who used the same route. Nairobi is a beautiful city. It was founded in 1899 as a stores depot, shunting yard (place where trains are shifted from one track to another) and a camping ground for thousands of Indian laborers employed by the British to work on the railway line. The railway line was constructed by the British colonial officials to transport raw materials and goods from Uganda to the Kenyan port of Mombasa in the Indian Ocean. Nairobi means "stream of cold water" and was derived from the native Masai tribe word *enairobe*. Due to its cool climate and fertile soil, the British decided to make it the capital of Kenya, which they colonized until 1963.

Our lead person who brought us from Addis Ababa was disappearing every evening to the town center. Since we have given him most of our money to hold it for us, we felt suspicious. One mid-night he came back drunk and we got mad, and felt that he was spending our money. We received our money by threatening to harm him. Later we got information that this guy was a lazy, unproductive drunkard, whose only talent is to crack jokes; and depended on some friends in South Africa who liked his humor. We also found out that when he came to Addis to see his parents he had no penny and lied to them that he forgot his wallet and bag in the taxi cup that he rode from the airport. We lost hope in his ability to lead the group and started gathering helpful information as to how to continue to our destination.

During our stay in Kenya the major problem was the police; every time they see a black foreigner they stop and ask for a visa. Even after showing the visa we had, they insist that we give them some money or they are going to arrest us with any false pretext. They show us the handcuff they are holding and threaten us that they will lock us in a police station nearby. Since the police officers are corrupt and this is one of the ways they make money; the best advice was to bribe them and go away. We decided to leave Kenya as soon as possible.

We had two different routes to choose from to proceed to South Africa; one was via Tanzania without visa, the other through Uganda with visa. We preferred to try the short cut through Tanzania illegally. We set on foot in a south east direction, through the forest in the area of the Masai tribe, who we were told are merciless to foreigners. We were crossing a wildlife park, an open savannah land covered in green thorn bushes and elephant grass. After we succeeded to cross Kenyan territory without incident in two days we took a bus toward the port city of Tanzania, Dar es Salaam.

Tanzania is home to some of Africa's most spectacular sights, including the continent highest peak Mount Kilimanjaro and Ngorongoro Crater which is 12 miles wide, and the famous Serengeti National Park. Unfortunately we did not have the luxury to enjoy the natural beauty, for now we are looking for a place of opportunities where we can work and make a decent living. Before we arrived at the port city we had to cross a big lake by boat. We decided to cross separately, two at a time so that the police at the check point will not be suspicious. The bus itself had to be transported to the other side on a boat. After all

414

of us crossed we sat together under a tree and discussed about our next journey.

We started walking southbound towards Mozambique a little before sun set. While walking in Tanzania savanna land we did not see an elephant or giraffe. But we could sense their presence by looking at the tamped-down patch of grass, the sandy imprints of migration and an infinite variety of animal droppings with semi-digested nuts and grass, and dead animal skull and bones. As we see these things we got more scared of walking in the wilderness. This flat land Acacia savanna support one of the world's most spectacular migration of large animals, moving north to south and vice versa in search of food as the season changes.

Walking under a bright moon light for six hours in the Tanzanian savannah, we all felt tired around mid-night and decided to rest. Before sleeping under a tree, we put a mark on the next trees so that we will continue southbound the next day. After a few hours of sleep a loud noise of a hyena nearby woke us up; we got scared and preferred to continue walking. Holding a long rope and following one another like blind men, so that we shall not disperse, continued walking through the forest. At dawn it started raining, and as we were thirsty we felt so happy, and opened our mouths towards the sky trying to quench our thirst. Being tired and sleepy we decided to rest for some hours under the trees.

Our guide who was supposed to lead us to South Africa asked permission to go to the village we see nearby and rent a van for the group. We rightly guessed that he wants to buy food and drinks for himself and told him to be back as soon as possible. He left us at ten in the morning and came back at six in the evening. While he was away we sent two of our friends to get us water and some fruits. They brought enough water for the day and ten Mangos. Some others wanted to go and get some more; we told them that it could make the people suspicious and call police. Just like we suspected, the police arrested one of them and the other run away. The police fired to the air to stop him; he run and disappeared, and we never sow him again.

Since we were tired of walking, the rest of us decided to go to the highway nearby and stop a bus for a cross country ride to the border town with Mozambique. We stopped a big bus that came along with enough empty seats to accommodate us and sat separately between natives. When we arrived at the next village we sow our friend arrested by police in a handcuff. The police stopped the bus and coming inside asked for any foreigners without visa to step down. The other passengers pointed at us and we were arrested. We tried to bribe them, and found out that they are not like others where we managed to get our way with a few Shillings.

Tanzania's prison is very dirty. We were thrown into a small prison cell with fifty others. The prisoners urinate in a big container (barrel) placed at the corner of the room, and smells so bad. After a few weeks we started hunger strike; they told us either we eat whatever is available or die of hunger, the choice is ours. They abused us so bad, they even bit us with a stick on our knees, elbows and ankles; it hurt so much. One prison guard told us that a few months ago some Ethiopian prisoners escaped while they were given permission to go to the bushes and pass urine. Because of that the guards were reprimanded and their pay was cut; as a result we have become an object of retaliation. After they punished us enough they transferred us to UNHCR refugee prison.

The new prison is cleaner and the food is also better. When we asked when they will let us go, we were told that will happen after two years. We were so eager to arrive in South

Africa and make money; but now we are going to stay in prison for two more years. We started hunger strike again, asking to be sent back to Kenya, which didn't work. They told us that after two years we will be sent back to Ethiopia. There was a Nigerian prisoner who was about to be set free soon. We wrote a letter to the Ethiopian Airlines office in Tanzania and asked him to mail it or give it to them.

The following week Ethiopian Airlines employees, four of them ladies, came to see us and brought us some food. They felt so sad, some even shade tears when they heard our story and see that some of us are in our teenage years. They promised to help us out of prison as soon as possible and left. As they were trying to find the pertinent authorities for our release, they kept on coming once in a while with delicious Ethiopian food. After four months we were set free; first four of us and after a few days the rest of them. They told us that they got this result by bribing higher officials. They gave us pocket money and paid our bus fare to Kenya.

Near the border with Kenya we got off the bus, since we have no visa to enter. We found two Somalia traffickers and with fifty dollars they led us through the woods to Kenya. After four months of suffering in prison we came back to Kenya and called our parents. My mother was crying on the phone; she thought I was dead. At this point our parents who gave us the blessing for the journey wanted us to get back home. Some in our group wanted to go back, others wanted to stay in Kenya; two of us decided to continue the journey via Uganda. We told our decision to our parents and asked them to send us some money. They send us the money which they said saved for our burial and "cry fest" (*teskar*).

Since the short cut via Tanzania didn't work, we started gathering information how to go through Uganda, Rwanda,

Burundi, Zambia and Mozambique to South Africa. We called our friends who arrived in South Africa using the same route. They told us who to contact at each border crossing and gave us their address. These traffickers are either from Somalia, Ethiopia or Eritrea. Since we cannot afford to eat beef, we became vegetarians eating Tomatoes and lettuce to save money.

Using the directions and procedures our friends in South Africa gave us we proceeded to Uganda. We rented bicycles to cross to Uganda as per their instructions so that the police will not be suspicious. Uganda is very green with rolling hills, grassy verges and trees. This part of Africa (Uganda, Rwanda, Burundi and Congo) is one of the most beautiful regions. But politics aside, I thought of the countries children who were the first victims during the civil war. Over a twenty year period tens of thousands of children were snatched from their homes to fight for Lord's Resistance Army (LRA) led by Joseph Kony who was later indicted by the International Criminal Court (ICC). We managed to get visa for Uganda by paying twenty dollars each. In the evening we asked where many Ethiopians live and went there to get additional information. According to the directions they gave us we travelled from one town to the next. At the border we paid sixty dollars each to get visa for Rwanda, and twenty dollars each for Burundi.

Before we get to the border of Rwanda I thought of the civil war that took place a few years back. One million people were massacred in one hundred days, because of bad politics, bad leaders and extreme tribalism. As we crossed the border check point I felt scared and quite emotional passing through a country with such a terrible history of unbelievable violence, and still so beautiful. I wondered how on earth it managed to heal itself and where in Africa will the next tribal massacre occur. Along the way I smell wood smoke and eucalyptus; it reminded me of Ethiopia and felt home sick for a minute.

All around we could see the rain forest and the mountains shrouded in a blue mist. The land was very green, the soil looked virgin and fertile, and the air thin and damp, even when it is not raining. We followed a narrow path through the sea of green forest and when we came to a clearing every now and then we see the gorgeous mountains. At one point we sow movement in the trees; a couple of young Gorillas are playing high in the branches, they were about twenty meters away. As we came out of the trees we sow a female lying on the side of the road with her three youngsters. Again, a few meters away we sow a huge Gorilla striding up the slop slowly, looking sideways at us like a king surveying his domain; we were a little scared.

During our stay in Rwanda for a few days we talked to a number of residents how the country is doing after the civil war between Hutus and Tutsis. They told us there is unity after the genocide, people would say they were no longer Hutu or Tutsi, they were simply Rwandan. We found out that at the end of every month there was a day of public works where the people would do something for their country. In such a historically divided nation, at last there is an overwhelming feeling of unity. We only hoped that other African leaders who are fond of ethnic politics to divide and rule would learn something from Rwanda. Genocide is part of their history, but it is not going to decide the future, because they are so determined to make sure it never happens again.

We crossed Rwanda in a day, but, had to stay in Burundi for two weeks waiting for a ship that would take us across Lake Tanganyika to Zambia. The natural beauty of Burundi is just as beautiful as Rwanda. Riding on a boat to Zambia was even more entertaining and we were so relaxed and got a chance to enjoy the natural beauty of the region without being scared. Travelling on foot, on wheels, and on water we got an intimate look at east and southern Africa where there is plentiful wildlife, stylish bush camps and river lodges, hoping that one day we might return with enough money as tourists to enjoy this under-the-radar safari destination.

Summer days around Lake Tanganyika can reach over 100 degrees F. But that day we took our boat, with the breath off the water and the sun slightly at our back it felt unusually cool. As we glided by the edge of the lake the grass looked emerald-green and we could see hippos, water buffalos, elephants and crocodiles in the shallow part of the lake along the way. From our boat, the buffalo on shore looked so big and the elephant as tall as the baobab trees. White-headed eagles skate the surface of the water for fish. All of them are far on land and posed us no threat on the water.

Further down at a point where a river flows into the lake, we sow the water in front of us crowded with 15-feet-long crocodiles. They look at us with their milky green marble eyes and as we approached they would slither silently into the stream, vanishing beneath our boat. Once in a while hippos pull their heads to the surface of the water staring at us with their bulging and unblinking eyes, then, they too disappear below the surface. The boat captain told us that hippos can hold their breath for up to six minutes. Seating upfront and scanning the water we were a bit scared that we might pass over one of these beasts and an angry hippo or crocodile could topple our boat. Along the bank of the river and the lake we could see tourists with cameras outside their river lodges and bush camps. Once in a while we see tour boats with few white people and their guides. I kept on thinking of the day that I might join them at this post-card perfect resort. It was the most relaxing journey we experienced in our trip down south, and before we know it we were in Zambia. We took a bus to the capital Lusaka.

Somalia traffickers in Lusaka rented us their bedroom for a reasonable price and gave us their best advice about the best route to South Africa being through Mozambique instead of Zimbabwe. As per their advice we went to Mozambique embassy in Lusaka the next day and requested for a visa. At first they refused us saying that 'you Ethiopians do not return'. We begged the official promising to return and kneeling down on our knees asking for his kind consideration. He gave us a visa for forty dollars each; God knows if the money is going for the government or the individual as we never received a receipt at any consulate.

The cheapest means for us to travel to Maputo, Mozambique was a truck that transports wood or fruits. Instead of paying forty dollars for a bus we paid only ten to ride a truck that has loaded fruits. Seating on top of the fruits and eating the sugar cane, banana and mango we are seating on, we continued to Maputo. Even though the dust that come from the road as the truck moves covered our body and clothes, we felt very happy for the first time since we left our beloved country. Because we have been told that once we come into Mozambique it is easy to enter South Africa. It is just like arriving in Mexico to cross to the United States.

The truck driver stopped for a snack at a small village in the middle of the forest. As we have been eating fruits from the truck load, we did not want to spent money in buying food. Instead we lay down under the trees and waited for the driver, admiring the natural beauty of the area. At the top of the giant tree a few feet away a black and white spider monkey is swinging, and butterflies are gliding through the still darkness of the forest. Beneath the giant trees spreads a second layer of smaller trees whose wide crowns interlock to form a forest canopy, and the wet branches below them turn into hanging gardens. Frogs, insects, chimpanzees and apes live here making their own trails and hideouts. The rain forest contains an enormous variety of plants and animals along with millions of poor Africans like us; what a paradox.

Upon arrival in Maputo, the capital of Mozambique, we had only forty dollars left. We started looking for Ethiopians or Somali people who could give us information as to how we shall continue our journey. We met Somalia nationals who took us to Ethiopians neighborhood, walking with us for half an hour. Our brothers from Somalia help Ethiopians so much in such situations; they are the best people we came across in our difficult journey. God Bless their heart!

Earlier we have been told that there are three Ethiopian traffickers in Maputo who help people going to South Africa. We were warned that one of the traffickers named Tesfu is a ruthless criminal who lock up and arrest travelers in his house insisting that they call their parents and get him money. We were told to avoid this guy and look for the Good Samaritan called Eneyew who has a Rasta hair do. As usual our brothers from Somalia gave us all the necessary information we need and took us to the good guy. When we met Enyew we felt as if we met our brother.

He took us to his house, allowed us to take shower and rinse the dust all over us, gave us clothes and even fed us. He had information that we have been arrested in Tanzania and he felt very sympathetic. He entertained us like a VIP for one week until we received money from our parents. Even though we had no money to spend, we truly enjoyed our stay in the beautiful city of Maputo with a psychological satisfaction that we have only one more border to cross.

Maputo was known as Lourenco Marques before independence, after the name of the 1544 Portuguese navigator who was sent on a voyage of exploration. After Mozambique got its independence from Portugal in June 1975, the city was given the name of the river and the bay that glorify its beauty. The city is located on the east side of Maputo Bay where four rivers, Tembe, Motalo, Infulene and Umbeluzi drain. The bay is 95 kilometers long and 30 kilometers wide. It is known as the city of Acacia in reference to acacia trees along its avenues, also referred to as the Pearl of the Indian Ocean. The central area of Maputo corresponds to a planned city with square blocks and wide avenues with the colonial master's Portuguese traces and their typical architecture. On the eastern side of the bay and the city is the island of Inhaca. The city of Maputo with a population of over 1.7 million is only 120 kilometers from the South African border.

Eneyew charged us only fifty dollars each for the room and food he provided us for the whole week. Besides, before taking us to the mini bus that took us to South Africa, he hid two hundred South African Rand in an audio cassette and gave us to hold it. So that if they take our money at the check points we shall be left with something. It is amazing that there are such good people here and there; with his help, we felt our hope rising again and our dream lives on.

We were around fifty people in that mini bus. But, we did not feel the suffocation; all we wanted was to enter South Africa. At every check point we had to take off our shoes. I had hidden paper money in my socks; luckily they did not find it. We were instructed to get off the bus before arriving in Johannesburg. We got off the bus in a small town just before Johannesburg. Since we did not have enough money and resident ID to rent a hotel room, we looked around for a place to sleep. We found a small hidden place between a high rise building and storage. We slept in between the walls on packing boxes; and as we were so tired and sleepy, we didn't wake up until sun rise.

We got scared that the sun is up and we are sleeping on some once property.

The next morning while looking for a means of transport to Johannesburg, we found another Somalia shop owner who ordered one of his employees to take us to the Ethiopians neighborhood. There we met Ethiopians we knew in Addis Ababa, and we felt at home. They told us that it has been a long time that Ethiopians have come using this route via Maputo. All Ethiopians we met here are businessmen; small or big. They invited us to stay as their guest for one week and they will send us to Johannesburg. As we were so eager to go, we asked them to allow us to go in three days. They gave us four hundred Rand and also paid for our train ticket. During my stay in South Africa I observed that Ethiopians help one another so much like no place else.

We arrived in Johannesburg and we could not believe our eyes. We got off the train at the business center of the city. We sow the big electronic messaging sign that we were told about as a landmark. We were advised to walk to the tenth street from here and continue until we come to a place where we shall see many Ethiopians. We started asking for the tenth street; we are used to asking directions while crossing nine countries; and we are not ashamed to do so. We ask more than one person for confirmation. We came to the now famous tenth street and walked in the direction we were told until we met many Ethiopians. Out of nine friends who left Ethiopia together, only two of us made it to South Africa. Even the guy who was supposed to lead us the way couldn't make it. Later we got news that some returned to Ethiopia, some died, and some others are homeless working temporary physical labor in Nairobi.

When we arrived at mostly Ethiopian open air market; it looks like our *Merkato* in Addis Ababa. To our surprise we found friends from back home who were our neighbors. Some, about whom we were told that they have crossed to Europe and America were still there selling goads at the open air market. When some of these old friends start calling me in my nick name I felt at home. Everyone we knew invited us to stay in his apartment and be his guest. We did not want to be a burden on one individual, and we decided to stay at different places. When they acquainted us to others they don't say meet my friend, they say my brother. They gave us enough pocket money, the very first day for any personal need. Ethiopians living in South Africa are very friendly and cooperative. They help each other and are selfless, not self-centered like those you meet in the United States. If someone can't find a job to support himself, they cover his expenses until he find one. I have not seen our community in such a cohesive manner anywhere I have travelled; I don't know how it happened in South Africa.

The next day we did not want to idle and spend time; with the advice from friends we set out to the refugee office to get a residence permit (*Oumhafer*). We came back with a residence permit the same day. We made a photo copy of our permit; kept the original at home and carry the copy in our wallet in case law enforcement officers ask for it. The authorities are so good that they gave us the permit the same day we applied and we started work the next day. The work available right away was buying goads from a whole sale store and retail selling it at the Open air market. The following day we bought items from a whole sale store with the money we borrowed from our friends, and made reasonable profits after selling them at the open air market. I found out what items sell fast, and I continued doing this job every single day with no rest, making nearly one hundred percent profit.

Johannesburg is the largest city in South Africa. Formally established in 1886 with the discovery of gold by white colonizers it is now the center of learning and entertainment for all of Africa. With Europeans competing to control the resources (fertile land and mines), tensions developed between foreigners and blacks. The British colonizers displaced blacks by burning their villages and killing livestock. They instituted Land Alienation Acts, and Group Areas Acts, forcibly displacing blacks from the fertile lands and inner city Johannesburg areas. They forced them to settle in black townships they established in the outer suburbs, legalizing Apartheid. Today, Apartheid gone, the city's suburbs seem integrated and multi-racial. But, there is de facto segregation and high crime in the city as most blacks cannot afford to buy house and land in certain areas.

My friend, who came with me all the way to South Africa, started to enjoy every day and spend money on drinks and women. I preferred to go out for entertainment only in the weekends; the other evenings I go to the Gymnasium and go to my room after workout. I was determined to save as much as I could and cross to the United States as soon as possible. I have learned a lot from our difficult journey. I am hungry to work and make money; the profit is so sweet; my dream for America so great; nothing is going to stop me. Since I set a goal, I came to know how to handle money; with good money management and using my time wisely, my bank account balance kept rising. I have seen many extravagant Ethiopians who work hard only to spend their money on drinks, women, and night clubs. Those guys are still doing the same work; they couldn't even open their own shop. What matters is not how much you make; it is how much of it you save. The money you spend negligibly will punish you some day when you need it most.

In a few months I saved enough money to buy a spot for myself in the open air market. I got my own permanent space to spread my goods and sell; no more roaming around with items on my shoulder and my hand. Later, I found a share-holder; and when we need more items, one of us will go and get more from the whole sale store. We even started hiring temporary workers to help us when it gets busy. In two years I saved 35,000 dollars. If I continue for one more year, I knew I would open my own permanent store. But, I did not want to continue this same work; and my American dream is bugging me. When I think of it now, I feel that it was a mistake I didn't continue there. When my savings reached 40,000 dollars, I sent 15,000 dollars to my parents and decided to use the rest for my journey to the United States, where migration comes to a dead end.

I started looking for traffickers to America, and at least one other Ethiopian who share my dream. I met an Ethiopian called Henock, and together we set out to look for an agent to help us out. We found an Eritrean trafficker and tried to make a deal. He demanded 30,000 Rand each for the flight to Cuba, and told us that from there we can continue to Nicaragua and northbound to Mexico. Even though we agreed, we did not want to give the money straight to him. We wanted a dependable, well to do person we all know, who will do the money transfer and guarantee that the promise will be fulfilled. In the mean time we started to spread rumors and gossip that we have hit men to hire, if the agent fails to fulfill his promise after taking our money. We made sure that he got the message, and in actual fact we started looking for dare devil individuals in case he breaks his promise.

At last we found a good and dependable individual who has respect from the community who brokered the deal. We went to Cape Town and stayed there for one month until the agent made a deal with the South African Airline authorities to take our flight to Cuba. During our stay visiting the Mansions of Michael Jackson, Will Smith, and other African American stars in the beautiful city of Cape Town, we found another Ethiopian to join our journey.

Cape Town has unusual contrasts; affluent and yet bearing the scars of the country's disease, Apartheid and intense poverty. It is at once African and European. It is a historic city, a destination for the rich and famous. Perched on a peninsula that protrude into the Atlantic Ocean at the southern tip of Africa, with dazzling beaches, sheer cliffs and the distinct image of Table Mountain, its breath taking scenery will force a visitor to fall in love with Cape Town. A visit to Nelson Mandela's prison at Robin Island off the coast of Cape Town reminds the country's history, Apartheid, which is not a distant memory. The island which is only seven miles from Cape Town housed prisoners and freedom fighters for nearly 400 years. It is now a museum and one of the best places to learn about South Africa's troubled past.

After one month in Cape Town, we got a six month visa for Cuba and took our flight by way of Argentina. The first night in Havana we had to pay fifty dollars for a hotel room. The next day we asked where Ethiopians are living and went to their neighborhood. It is amazing that there are Ethiopians in almost every country; and they rent us a room for seven dollars a day. During our stay we called our friends in the US who used the same route, and gathered information how to continue from here. They gave us the names and telephone numbers of all the agents in each country in Central America we had to cross.

Havana is a beautiful city. Even though the communist party's dictatorial policies have induced wide-scale suffering in Cuba, the 1959 Revolution has made significant strides in many arenas. The greatest thing Cuba has achieved under Fide Castro I would say is probably racial harmony. Race relations in Cuba is so good that it seems light years ahead of other nations in the Americas. There is a respect for African people, their heritage and culture that even African American journalists say that they feel more comfortable in their skin color when they come to Cuba.

Afraid to take a ship, which would have been cheaper, we decided to fly to Nicaragua. We went to Nicaragua embassy in Havana and got a visa for thirty dollars each. In the capital Managua using the information we were given, we met one Ethiopian and another Eritrean who work together as traffickers. We paid three hundred dollars each, for them to arrange our trip through Nicaragua, Honduras, El Salvador, and Guatemala. Our trip was in a big trucker trailer, where they packed three of us in a small room with a mattress behind the driver's compartment for the whole day. We crossed all these small countries in one day and arrived at the border with Mexico. Our agreement with the traffickers was up to this point.

While we were gathering information earlier as to how to enter Mexico, we were told by our friends in the US, to go to the border and give ourselves up to the Mexican police. We took a taxi to the border town of Capitola where Mexican police arrested us. On the third day they took us to Mexico City and handed us over to the United Nations refugee camp. In this camp there were about sixty Ethiopian refugees.

After a few days in the camp we met a Mexican lady, who works for a Christian charity organization. The other refugees told us that she comes often with food and clothes for the refugees. They also told us that she has an Ethiopian boyfriend and sometimes helps Ethiopians to get residence permit in Mexico and even to get them to the US border. According to our informants she used to tell the migrants to give little money to the driver who takes them to the US border. But, nowadays they said she has started demanding some money for herself. We approached the Mexican lady and asked her frankly; and with one hundred dollars each she helped fifteen of us out of the camp and got us a residence permit. Before we left the camp, a TPLF agent from the embassy came and tried to convince us to go back home, by lecturing how peaceful it is in Ethiopia. We yelled at him and threatening to smack him, and chased him out.

Even though we got a residence permit, we were ordered to go to the refugee camp every Friday and sign once a week to show that we are around. We started asking for the last trafficker to get us to the US border. With the help of other refugees we found a man from Ghana whose wife is Mexican and good to do the job. He asked us to pay 1,200 dollars each, which was very expensive; but, we had no other choice. Nine of us were able to pay; and having signed at the refugee camp on Friday, we started our last adventure the next day to the border of the United States.

The trip was in a car relay; we had to change to different vehicles several times. At first they took us in small trucks; then they transferred us to a big bus luggage compartment. The driver was acting as if he is cleaning the body of the bus, arranging the luggage and closing the compartment doors when we arrived. Our trucks stopped abruptly and they pushed us to the luggage compartment. They gave us a container in which to pee and nine of us were squeezed inside; some seating, others lay on their back. The good thing is that they had made holes on the compartment doors so we could get fresh air. After several hours ride the bus stopped and the driver opened the luggage compartment; they transferred us to vans. During the transfer they yell at us to make it quick, rapido! rapido! Amigo! We had to jump and run to the next vehicle. After a few hours ride again they transferred us to trucks waiting in line. The trucks pulled up immediately like an emergency vehicle in a critical mission. After hours of drive they stopped at a single house dropped us and left immediately. We were told to take shower and get ready for the last ride. The journey was rough and uncomfortable, with no food and water for fifteen hours; still it was better than what we experienced in Africa.

It seems that some police officers have a role with the traffickers. Our traffickers know what time the police officers exchange for their shift, when they will be on patrol, and when it is safe for their movement. All of a sudden there came that shout again; rapido! Rapido! Amigo! And we jumped into the trucks that just arrived. This time our journey was through the woods. Sometimes they ask us to sit down on the floor or hide our head below the windows. They dropped us near a lake by the US border and left immediately. We were confused; we thought they left us to die in a desert.

While we were looking all around us in confusion, there came two Mexicans in a swim short walking towards us. They have two big inflated plastic tires like balloons tied to a rope. They asked us to sit on the inflated rubber, two at a time on either side of the balloons, so it will balance, and started pulling them as they swim across the lake. After eight of us were transported to the other side of the lake, and the swimmers were on their way to bring the last member of the group, we sow two police men coming towards the lake. We could see our friend shaking in fear, and about to dive into the lake. The policemen took out their hand guns and ordered him, hands up! Soon the swimmers arrived and talked to the police and gave them some money; and they left. It looked like they are used to getting money at this location. Our friend came across shivering in fear. The swimmers walked us for about half an hour to the US border and said, Adios Amigos!! When we see the wire mesh fence and the US flag on the other side, we gave them some money, extra clothes and shoes and said goodbye.

We approached the fence carefully at where it is leaning and mounted over it to set foot in the US soil, after several years of a difficult journey. It was the state of Texas, the lone star state; we walked to the nearest town. We have been told to give ourselves up to the border patrol or police. When we entered the town we started walking in line of two. We have assigned one person among us who is the best in English, to speak to the police, and decided that the rest of us keep quite; so we shall not contradict one another. We have agreed what to say to the police. The time was right after the uprising and protest in Ethiopia, following the 2005 rigged elections, where hundreds of peaceful demonstrators were killed by government forces.

The border patrols came towards us in jeeps and rounded us up, blocking the walk-way from the front and behind. Their first question was where are you from? At first we all kept quiet, and even tried to continue walking. They shouted and ordered us to stop. Our leader Henock told them that we are from Ethiopia and that we need to go to the immigration office to apply for political asylum. In the meantime other patrols came in their jeep and surrounded us. They took us to the police station and gave us drinking water.

The officers ordered us to take off our clothes and they checked our skin if for tattoo. When they found out that none of us have one, they asked us if we have relatives in the United States to take care of us. We told them that we all have close relatives, and gave them the addresses we have for them to prove. We have been told by our informants in the US that if we assure them that we have relatives who will take care of us, they will let us go. We had names, addresses and telephone numbers ready to prove to them. They told us that we are free to go to join our relatives. We expressed our thanks by shaking hands with them, and hugged each other. We were so happy and thought for a moment, what if it was the Ethiopian police?

In the detailed information that we have gathered for this journey, we had the address of the cheapest hotel in this town. Our Ethiopian friends who used the same route have given us all the necessary information. We could afford to rent only one bedroom; so exhausted, most of us slept on the floor like a baby. The next day, we contributed money for those who don't have enough for a bus fare, and bought our ticket for 125 dollars each to Washington DC. A Gray hound bus transferring us from one bus to the other at different cities like our traffickers, we continued to the nation's capital. Eating sandwiches at every lunch break, we thank God for making our dream come true. Seating in the bus, I sometimes think of my friends who died in the journey, got lost, become homeless in foreign cities and left behind.

We arrived in Washington and met our friends; I could not believe my eyes. It was one of the happiest moments of my life. When I called my parents and told them that I am in Washington, they couldn't believe it. They came to believe only after I passed the phone to our cousins who have been here for several years and talked to them. After I received my residence and work permit, I got a job, and admitted to a community college I found out first hand that America is still a land of opportunities worth the trouble to pursue. My journey of migration came to a dead end; but, my life journey continues with the hustle and bustle of Washington. Working two jobs day and night, going to bed after midnight, waking up before dawn, not having enough sleep, paying bills, sitting in a traffic jam, feeling stressed out in the fast pace of life; welcome to America!!!

For Better Opportunities

(Seven and half years in Kenya Refugee Camps)

Daniel W. Baharue

I don't want to categorize or classify my case as a political asylum or an economic refugee; to me they are one and the same. I just left for better opportunities, hoping to end up somewhere in western industrialized countries using Kenya as a stepping stone. In fact I would say I was an exile in my own country; not having a job, or not admitted to college, remaining dependent on my parents at young adult age and sharing the food of my younger siblings. At the time there were only few universities and colleges that were not able to admit even ten percent of high school graduates. After completing high school I used to spend the day at a street corner with other friends exposed to the same misfortune; out of school, out of work, out of money, and out of hope.

No one would leave his motherland without a compelling reason. I didn't even have the luxury to leave with a visa and air ticket. I used ground public transportation along with my twelve other friends southbound up to the border town of Moyale near Kenya. On the way we passed forests, savanna grassland, gently rolling hills and slopes. The view of southern Ethiopia was staggering; mountains that stretched for mile after mile, valleys between them green with trees, but the roads were pretty terrifying with zigzags and hairpin turns. We met hundreds of people walking or driving cattle, sheep and goats, donkeys laden with goods, all sharing the road. Sometimes we had to stop for them to cross the road. We saw many kids all the way on the road side with light clothes, some bare feet, others with sandals. We passed stands of eucalyptus and acacia trees, coffee plantations and obviously rich moist soil, but poor inhabitants, yet proud and hospitable; what a paradox. We stealthily sneaked into Kenya on foot using the information we got from other refugees. We walked across a semi-desert area to the nearest refugee camp, Oda.

I left my original country Ethiopia in June 1991 at the peak of government change, while EPRDF was taking government power and the military rulers were running for their life. At the time, members of law enforcement and armed forces were themselves fleeing away from the little known TPLF led insurgency. The government structure was in a state of collapse, the border was open, and nobody stopped us until we arrived in Kenya.

After staying a few days at Oda refugee camp near the border we continued down south 120 kilometers towards the capital city, Nairobi and reached a better refugee camp known as Walda. This trip we made south bound, some of it on foot, some on a delivery truck was dangerous. The area is known for clan warfare, poaching and general banditry who like to target foreigners. The road was red gravel that blended into the landscape of what they call the African prairie, which was low with lots of bushes and few trees. As we went down south the land was not any different from the drier region we had just passed through.

Walda refugee camp was run by the United Nations Higher Commission for Refugees (UNHCR), and as such better organized and more comfortable. But, we did not feel secure in Walda because there were many Ethiopian refugees who were found dead in the bushes, killed by unknown armed men; some suspected they could be TPLF assassins as most of those killed were political activists and military officers from the Derg regime. The site was in the middle of a very hot semi-desert area full of wild animals; from poisonous snakes to Scorpion, Hyenas and Lions. All of us registered formally as refugees and started building our shelter with plastic and wood which was supplied by the refugee administration. The refugee camp office used to give us our food ration every fortnight per head. But, the amount we receive was only enough for twelve days; we had to starve the last few days until the next supply. Besides, they give us only wheat flour and edible oil, and without salt the food was not tasty. It was a kind of communal life; we eat together, sleep together, wear any cloth available as long as it fits, no private property.

Every day we walk to the refugee camp administration office to ask for more help and how we can get a visa to Europe or America or Australia. Sometimes we organize peaceful protest on the way we are treated and our case is handled. The camp administration office did not have enough food supply to the ever increasing number of refugees. Most of the refugees were from Ethiopia, and there were some from Somalia and other east African countries. Out of the foreigners, refugees from Somalia were best friends to Ethiopians. Most Ethiopian

436

refugees were members of the military and high school graduates like us who couldn't get an opportunity for higher education or a job.

The refugee camp administration had difficulty to give food ration and medicine to all who need them. Things got worse and nothing seemed to improve. After two years of miserable life in a refugee camp we lost hope and some of us wanted to return to Ethiopia. I returned to Ethiopia with five of my friends only to find out that everything is the same and nothing has changed except the leaders. We could not find any kind of job, or we could not get admission to a college or a higher education institution. We started the same old boring life again, doing nothing. Some people who know that we have been away started bothering us by asking all kinds of questions and ridiculing. After several months in Ethiopia I returned to Kenya with other friends.

The journey was not difficult, and we did not need visa or air ticket; we sneaked in bribing border patrols and other police officers who stopped us to get pocket money. This time we went to a refugee camp called Tika near the capital, Nairobi. We were back again to the same cycle of impoverished life, living on a ration of food. During our stay here for several months we tried hard to get refugee visa to any country in the western world; but, the chances got dimmer and gloomy. After a while we moved to another refugee camp known as Marafa near the port city of Mombasa, hoping that we might get lucky here. There was nothing better, and after some months we went back to Tika.

When we were at Tika there came a rumor that UNHCR is negotiating with the Ethiopian government for a possible repatriation of refugees. Some refugees who were afraid of repatriation left for Nairobi and became homeless street boys. I myself and a few friends were scared and decided to move further away from the capital city, and went to a refugee camp known as Kakuma in the north west of Kenya. In a few weeks both refugee camps Tika and Marafa were closed with the refugees repatriated or evacuated.

Kakuma is located in Turkana district in the north western region of Kenya. Kakuna is a Swahili word meaning nowhere, epitomizing the seclusion of the area. The area has a challenging semi-arid desert environment. The climate is ill-suited to agriculture with average day time temperature being 40 degree Celsius or 104 degree Fahrenheit. Kakuma refugee camp is big and at one time had over 90,000 refugees who fled wars and turmoil from neighboring countries, Sudan, Ethiopia, Somalia, Eritrea, Congo, Uganda and Burundi. The camp is a city of tents, thatched roof huts, mud abodes and shacks in the desert of Kenya. Once you register as a refugee and admitted to the camp you cannot leave without the permission of Kenyan government. It is equally a sanctuary and a prison at the same time where children age to adulthood. It is administered by UNHCR with aid from several NGOs and international relief agencies.

Situated in the middle of a semi-desert, in summer the early rays of the sun rising from the east disperse the chill of the night. In a few hours there comes the blinding heat of noon, like a furnace sucking the moisture from our bodies. Each one of us sitting quite in our little shelter with our own thoughts about the future and none spoke. As we sit in the rays of the summer sun, fear hit me time and again that we might die here in the burning wilderness. Every now and then I had to struggle against a panicky impulse urging a return to Ethiopia, and I fight it down. I believe my other friends did the same struggle every day.

There are tens of thousands of Ethiopian refugees here. They built market places filled with shops with almost all kinds of items that refugees want to buy. There are coffee houses and restaurants with television sets that show CNN, BBC and the latest football match in Europe. The shops were started with a loan from NGOs or with money from a relative abroad. When a visitor or a new comer observe' Ethiopian refugees enjoying coffee together and watching English Premier League soccer match, he would think they are content and calm, but the truth is different. While their bodies in Kakuma, but every ones souls are travelling in the world of day dreams, resettling in America, completing college studies, making enough money somewhere et cetera. Sometimes conflicts arise between Ethiopians, but solved without becoming too serious, except domestic problems between married couples.

The longer you stay in the refugee camps you become absent minded. Some don't remember what day, month or year it is, and are more affected than they realize. Many show strange behavior, have anxiety and are unable to make decisions, some left absent-mindedly and disappeared. We report to the police and conduct a search with them for a day or two in the surrounding bushes and hills and give up; the person is forgotten without ever confirming dead or alive. Sometimes locals report finding the remains of the disappeared ravaged by wild animals; we bury it and feel we buried something of ourselves.

Sometimes some good rumors pop up and spread around the camp, everyone harbor's hope. When the rumor created by a mind starved of hope and information to feed on doesn't come to reality, then emptiness returns until someone comes with another rumor, and so on it goes. With good rumors hope rises again and the dream lives on; if there is a negative rumor heads are down, faces are pale and gloomy, signboards of unspeakable sorrow. Some start crying for very little thing or sickness; they are weeping for themselves not only for fear of death, but of dying unfulfilled of their dreams.

I was unprepared for what I encountered in the different refugee camps. I was totally unprepared for the sense of panic that arises once in a while and the nothingness that surround the camp. If you are in a shelter at the edge of the unfenced camp, or not yet admitted and have to stay further away with your children in the wilderness, you will panic every night when Hyenas circle the area looking for the weakest; you dare not step out to pass urine. I always wondered how single mothers at the far corner of the camp with little children feel and handle the situation. I talked to these strong women from Somalia at Oda refugee camp and found out that they are not only taking care of their own children, but also other unaccompanied minors who are probably orphans whom they found along their perilous journey to Kenya. These kind women who have been repeatedly raped and robbed of their possession along the way are extending their warm embrace to orphans in addition to their children. The faces of these women haunt me, their kindness and determination inspire me, when they tell me their stories I am filled with wonder how they are finding their strength.

There were thousands of Ethiopians in almost all refugee camps I lived in Kenya. There were many soldiers, officers, high ranking officers, including Generals. There were hundreds of college graduates, thousands of high school graduates and students. There were women of all ages. There were separate camps for women, soldiers and civil males for a good reason. Most of the soldiers were from Blaten military training camp in southern Ethiopia. Some refugees started making money, selling salt and onions that they bring from the farmers in the area. I have seen an army General selling onions. These were loyal citizens who volunteered to sacrifice their life for the unity and territorial integrity of Ethiopia; and this is what they got for their service.

Being a refugee is one of the worst and a difficult experience for any human being. Living in a refugee camp is worse than being a prisoner. Usually a prisoner knows how long he is going to be in jail, and when he will be released. A prisoner have been to court, testified in his case and has been given some kind of judgment. But, if you are a refugee tomorrow is out of hand and don't know what will happen to you; it is in the hands of politicians, agencies or the governments involved. The food you eat, the place you sleep, the sickness, the weather and the hardships you face is depressing, killing you physically, mentally, psychologically and morally.

The refugee problem in Africa can only be solved if we Africans try to find solutions to our differences in a democratic manner. If we stop trying to solve every conflict with arms and war, and instead use our brain and solve our problems and differences in a round table discussion with a genuine sense of democracy, compromise, and power sharing, we can come out of this chronic problem.

Life in Kakuma became even worse as time goes by; the weather was terribly hot, snakes and Scorpions are in abundance as it is situated in the middle of a sandy desert. Some of my friends died, and I got seriously sick after being infected with Malaria, lost 20 pounds in three weeks, and somehow survived. I have seen refugees die of common sickness due to malnutrition. Some were eaten by a hyena or a lion, some died of snake or scorpion bite. To bury the dead it takes us half a day; because as you dig out the sand, it goes back down and you have to shovel it out time and again. Besides, we are under fed, and we have little energy to do the job in a sun-seared desert. We had to make the coffin ourselves by chopping wood and rap the body with UNHCR blanket.

I got so scared of the whole situation after I was infected with Malaria. I traveled to Nairobi and called my elder brother to send me money so that I can get back to Ethiopia before I die. I received the money from home, and took a bus back to Addis Ababa for the second time after five and a half years of another try. All together I spent seven and half years of untold suffering in Kenya refugee camps dreaming of a better future. Sometimes I ask myself, what if I have tried something else. The one good thing I did while in the different refugee camps was that I had the time to read the bible thoroughly with fellow refugees and I became an ardent Christian. The very fact that Jesus himself was a refugee at young age with his mother Mary and Josef was a great consolation for many refugees.

A few years after I got back to Ethiopia I won a Diversity Visa Lottery that the United States gives to under-represented third world communities. It was one of the happiest moments of my life. I immediately came to the US and tried to take advantage of the chance I was given. I did not find America as I expected; what I imagined based on their smart public relations work and the Hollywood film projection is far from the reality. But, still America is a land of opportunities, and I am trying to do my best to live the American dream.

I am here having survived all those hardships in the refugee camps. Until recently I used to ask myself, was it worse the trouble? I was burdened by what I did, but, by analyzing that under the circumstances it was the right thing to try at the time, I forced out the crippling sadness, burdensome memories and emotions. I put them in a perspective that is positive rather than negative with the rich experience I got from my actions, thereby cutting off their painful roots in my subconscious. I succeeded to get better, not bitter.

My advice to all Ethiopians is that life is more meaningful when you are always looking to do better, following your passion and working towards a goal to pursue and live your dreams. Like President Theodore Roosevelt said; we shall seek opportunity and take a calculated risk to dream and build, to fail and succeed. We shall refuse to live from hand to mouth, and remain a common man. We shall say no to injustice anywhere. It is our heritage to stand up for our rights and freedom and face the world boldly.

Bibliography

Amharic

Tamerat Semegn -Yedimocracy Meseretoch BeEthiopia – Signature Book Printing, USA 2008

Dr. Tadesse Woldegiorgis- Ethiopiyawyan Beamerica Maheberawina Senelebonawi Tentena – Addis Ababa University Press 2009

Zenebe Feleke- Neber –Universal Book Addis Ababa 2010

Fantahun Engida- Beqedamawi Haile Selassie Astedader Goltew Yeweqtu Yepoletica Chigroch- Addis Ababa, Berhanena Selam Matemiya Bet 2005

Wosenseged Gebrekidan- Yeqaliti Mestiroch – Litman General Trading, Addis Ababa- 2011

Professor Mesfin Wolde-Mariam, Addis Ababa,

        1) Seltan- Poleticana Mercha - 2011

        2) Mekshef Ende Ethiopia Tarik - 2012

        3) Yekehedet Kulkulet - 2011

        4) Adega Yanzabebebet Yeafrica Kend - 2012

Mehammed Selman – Piyassa - Litman General Trading, Addis Ababa- 2011

Mehaba Jemal- Sedetegnaw Beawropa –Mega Publishing, Addis Ababa, 2005

Tesfaye Gebreab - Yegazetegnaw Mastawesha –Cape Town, South Africa, 2009

Captain Tesfaye Erestu- Mesekernet –Addis Ababa Printing, 2008

Major Getachew Yerom - Seem Kemeqaber Belay –Self-Published, USA 2008

Tekle Tsadiqe Mekuriya -Atse Tewodrosena Yeethiopia Andenet –Kuraz Publishing Agency, Addis Abab, 1968

Sisay Agena – Yekalitew Mengest – NPA books, 2012

English

Abebe Shimeles, Dilip Ratha, Sanket Mohapatra, Caglar Ozden, Sonia Plaza, William Shaw – Leveraging Migration for Africa – New York, The World Bank Group Writers, 2011

Adepoju, Aderanti – Intrnational Migration within to and from Africa in a Globalized World – New York, Sub-Sahara Publishers 2010

Auletta, Ken – Backstory, USA The Penguin Press- 2003

Ayittey, George – Africa Unchained, New York, Palgrave Macmillan -2005

                -Africa in Chaos - New York, St. Martins Paper-back edition- 1999

                -Africa Betrayed - New York, Transnational Publishers Inc. 1991

Bahru Zewde – A History of Modern Ethiopia 1855-1974, (London, 1991)

Bassey, Nnimmo – To Cook a Continent, Cape Town, Pumbazuka Press - 2012

Bennett, Lance – The Politics of Illusion – New York, Longman 1988

Bennett, William (editor) – The Book of Virtues, New York, Simon & Schuster 1993

Benson, Kathleen and James Haskins – African Beginnings, Lothrop, Lee & Shepard Books 1998

Brim, Gilbert – Ambition, USA, 1992

Boahem, Adu – African Perspectives on Colonialism, John Hopkins University Press 1989

Bowersock, G W – The Throne of Adulis, Oxford University Press - 2013

Brown, Les – Live your Dreams, New York, Avon Books Inc.1992

Burns, Jennifer – Career opportunities in Journalism, New York, Infobase Publishing, 2007

Burns, Eric – All the News Unfit to Print, New Jersey, John Wiley & Sons Inc. 2009

        -Infamous Scribblers, Cambridge, Perseus Books Group – 2006

Cary, John – The Social Fabric, New York, Harper Collins Publishers, 1991

Central Statistical Authority, Ethiopia: The 1994 and 2007 population and housing census of Ethiopia.

Chomsky, Noam – Hegemony or Survival, New York, Henry Holt and Company, LLC. 2004

- Failed States, New York, Metropolitan Books, 2006

- Media Control, Canada, Seven Stories Press, 2002

- Chomsky on Americanism, Canada, AK Press, West Virginia, 2005

Chomsky, Noam and Herman Edward – Manufacturing Consent, New York, Pantheon Books, 2002

Cole, David – No Equal Justice, New York, The New Press, 1999

Daley, James – Great Speeches by African Americans, New York, Dover Publications Inc. 2006

Dambissa Moyo – Dead Aid,

Davidson, Jeff – Breathing Space, USA, Master Media Limited, 1991

Davidson, Basil – Modern Africa, New York, Longman Inc. 1983

Dowden, Richard – Africa- Altered States, Ordinary Miracles – UK, Portobello Books 2009

DuBrin, Andrew – Personal Magnetism, New York, AMACOM, 1997

Ellison, Sarah – War-The Wall Street Journal, New York, Houghton M Harcourt, 2010

Ethiopian Human Rights Council (EHRCO) – Democracy, Rule of Law and Human Rights in Ethiopia, Addis Ababa, 1995

Fergeson, Donald and Patten, Jim – Opportunities in Journalism Careers, McGraw-Hill, April 2000

447

Fuller, Edmund – Anecdotes, for all occasions, New York, Avenel Books, 1990

Galeano, Eduardo – Open Veins of Latin America, New York, Monthly Review Press, 1997

Gardner, John – On Leadership, New York, Macmillan Inc. 1990

Gay, Martin – The New Information Revolution, ABC-CLIO Inc. Santa Barbara, California, 1996.

Guest, Robert – The Shackled Continent – Power, Corruption, and African Lives, Smithsonian Books, 2004

Harris, Joseph – Africans and their History, New York, Penguin Books 1987

Harrison, Lawrence and Huntington, Samuel – Culture Matters, New York, Basic Books, 2000

Heinrichs, Ann – Ethiopia- Enchantment of the World, USA, Canada, Children's Press, 2005

Huffington, Arianna – How to Overthrow the Government, New York, Harper Collins Publishers, 2000

Jencks, Christopher – Rethinking Social Policy, USA, Harvard University Press, 1992

Jenson, Carl – Stories that Changed America, New York, Seven Stories Press - 2000

Kaplan, Steven – The Beta Israel (Felasha), New York University Press, 1992

Kidder, Rushworth – How Good People make Tough Choices, New York, Fireside, 1996

Kindred, Dave – Morning Miracle, New York, Random House, 2010

Kissinger, Henry – The White House Years, Boston, Little Brown & Company, 1979

Klibanoff, Hank & Roberts Gene – The Race Beat, New York, Random House 2006

Klein Shelly – The Most Evil Dictators in History, New York, Barnes & Noble, 2004

Lamb, David – The Africans, New York, Vintage Books, 1987

- The Arabs, New York, Vintage Books, 2002

Lang, Susan & Lang, Paul – Censorship, USA, 1993

Lyons, Len – The Ethiopian Jews of Israel, Woodstock, Vermont, Jewish Lights Publishing, 2000

Maathai, Wangari – The Challenge for Africa, New York, Random House Inc., 2009

McChesney, Robert and Nichols, John, The Death and Life of American Journalism, Nation Books, Philadelphia- 2010

Meredith, Martin – The Fate of Africa, New York, Public Affairs, 2011

Middleton, John (editor) – Africa- an encyclopedia for Students, Volume 1, Princeton NJ. Visual

Education Corporation, 2002

Mills, Claudia – Values and Public Policy, Orlando, Florida – Harcourt Brace Jovanovich Inc. 1992

Moyers, Bill – A World of Ideas, New York, Double Day Publishing, 1989

Pankhurst, Richard – The Ethiopians, USA, UK, Australia, Blackwell Publishing, 1998

Reader, John – Africa, USA, National Geographic Society, 2001

Reich B. Robert – Beyond outrage, Vintage Books USA 2012

-    Aftershock, Vintage Books 2010

Sheehan, Sean – Ancient African Kingdoms, New York, Gareth Stevens Publishing 2011

Stiglitz E Joseph – The Price of Inequality, USA Norton & Company Inc.

Tibebu, Teshale – The Making of Modern Ethiopia 1896-1974, Lawrenceville, NJ – The Red Sea Press Inc. 1995

Thompson, Vincent – African Diaspora, New York, Longman Inc. 1987

Untermeyer, Luis – Makers of the Modern World, New York, Simon & Schuster, 1955

Warburton, Nigel – Free Speech, UK, Oxford University Press, 2009

Wattenberg, Ben – Value Matters Most, New York, The Free Press, 1995

Wrong, Michela – In the Footsteps of Mr. Kurtz –Mobutu's Congo, New York, Harper Collins Publishers, 2001

-It's Our Turn to Eat, Great Britain, Fourth Estate, 2009

Zinn, Howard – A Peoples History of the United States, New York, HarperCollins Publishers, 1999

Periodicals

1) Addis Zemen newspaper
2) Amnesty International
3) Blumberg Media
4) Ethiomedia
5) Ethiopian Human Rights Council Reports
6) Freedom House
7) Heritage Foundation
8) Human Rights Watch
9) News Week
10) New York Times
11) New Africa, A Privately owned monthly, London
12) South – Private monthly, London (leftist)
13) Times
14) The Economist
15) The Guardian
16) The Washington Post
17) Wall Street Journal
18) West Africa – private, weekly, London

Research Papers

Berhanu Abegaz – The Case for a New Development

Berhanu Nega – Identity Politics and the Struggle for Liberty and Democracy in Ethiopia

Daniel Fyassu (Meraf) – TPLF and "Revolutionary Democracy"

Fekadu Bekele – From Structural Adjustment to WTO Membership – Squaring Poverty!

Gebre Medhin Araya - Yetigray Betelat eji Mewdekina Beethiopia Yasketelew Mezez

Kahsay Berhe & Tesfay Atsbeha – 33 Years of TPLF and 32 Years of Meles Zenawi – Suppression in the name of Liberation

Manaye Sewasew – Yeethiopia economina Yaltechebete Edget

Teshale Tibebu – Modernity, Euro-centrism and Radical Politics in Ethiopia

- Ethiopia – The "Anomaly" and "Paradox" of Africa

The World Bank Group and International Monetary Fund (IMF)